Forensic Communication

Application of Communication Research to Courtroom Litigation

Emmet —

   It finally came out! Hope parts will be interesting to you.

      Best wishes,
      Michael

COMMUNICATION AND LAW
Susan J. Drucker, *series editor*

Free Expression in Five Democratic Publics: Support for Individual and
Media Rights
Julie L. Ansager, Robert O. Wyatt, and Ernest L. Martin

Freedom, Democracy, and Responsibility: The Selected Works of
Franklyn S. Haiman
Franklyn S. Haiman

The First Amendment: Theoretical Perspectives
Joseph J. Hemmer

Forensic Communication: Application of Communication Research
to Courtroom Litigation
Michael T. Motley (ed.)

Outsiders Looking In: A Communication Perspective on the
Hill/Thomas Hearings
Paul Siegel (ed.)

Real Law@Virtual Space: Communication Regulation in Cyberspace 2/e
Susan J. Drucker and Gary Gumpert (eds.)

Forensic Communication

Application of Communication Research to Courtroom Litigation

Edited by

Michael T. Motley

HAMPTON PRESS, INC.
NEW YORK, NEW YORK

Library of Congress Cataloging-in-Publication Data

Forensic communication : application of communication research to courtroom litigation / edited by Michael T. Motley.
    p. cm. — (Communication and law)
  Includes bibliographical references and index.
  ISBN 978-1-61289-080-7 (hardbound) — ISBN 978-1-61289-081-4 (paperbound)
 1. Evidence, Expert—United States.   2. Forensic psychology—United States.
3. Communication in law—United States.   4. Communication—Research—
United States.   I. Motley, Michael T.
  KF8961.F66 2012
  614'.150973—dc23   2012000168

Hampton Press, Inc.
307 Seventh Ave.
New York, NY 10001

Contents

List of Illustrations

TABLES

FIGURES

Introduction

Sometimes we can remember how we got the idea for one of our endeavors and sometimes we can't. In the case of this book, I remember very clearly. I was watching a TV talk show interview featuring a forensic pathologist as the guest. The talk show host remarked on the recent flurry of public interest in forensics as demonstrated by the popularity of TV shows such as *CSI, Forensic Files,* and *Investigators.* The guest replied that indeed the field of forensics, although relatively young, was growing very rapidly as evidenced by the fact that new schools and departments of forensic science were opening in colleges and universities across the country.

He pointed out also that virtually every discipline now has a recognized subarea in forensics—forensics being the *application of expertise to matters of courtroom litigation.* We have forensic pathology, forensic entomology, forensic psychology, forensic anthropology, forensic dentistry, forensic linguistics, forensic engineering, and on and on.

You probably can see where this is going. It struck me that on the one hand there is no recognized subarea of forensic communication. Yet on the other hand, I knew that I, as well as a few others in our discipline, serve frequently as consultants or expert witnesses in legal cases. Moreover, I could easily think of several colleagues whose scholarship certainly could be applied to litigation issues if they were to be so inclined. I happen to enjoy my own expert-witness and consultation work tremendously, and I speculated that there may be many other communication scholars—new students and seasoned veterans alike—who might likewise enjoy working with attorneys on legal cases if made aware of their potential to do so.

This book evolved as an effort to share the idea that certain kinds of research in communication may be applied in the courtroom and other legal contexts. It has three goals. The primary goal is to introduce communication scholars to the various ways that their own and/or others' communication scholarship

1

may be applied to courtroom litigation. A related goal is to provide a bit of direction to those who might be interested in assisting litigation as a consultant or expert witness. A third goal is to introduce attorneys to the availability of communication scholars as consultants and expert witnesses for some of the issues they argue from time to time.

Essentially, there are the two ways of applying communication scholarship to court cases. Sometimes one's expertise is applied such that he or she actually testifies in court as an "expert witness." Expert-witness testimony is intended to present and support an opinion regarding one or more specific issues in a court case. An expert witness might give an opinion as to whether a warning label communicated its intended message adequately, or whether the presumed author of a will was indeed the actual author, for example. The other application is to offer one's expertise as a consultant. As a consultant, one typically does not testify, but rather advises an attorney or the court on various strategies or procedures before and/or during the trial. A consultant might advise an attorney regarding the selection of a jury or advise the court regarding the relevance of pretrial publicity to a change of venue, for example.

The authors who have contributed to this volume include academicians, professional legal consultants, and an attorney. Most have already applied their expertise as a consultant or expert witness and the others are certainly able to. In all cases the expertise has been acquired by intensive study, of course, and the same will be necessary for readers who might wish to apply their own or others' research to litigation contexts. The chapters were written as examples of how serious study may be applied, not as a handbook by which an untrained reader may claim competence merely by reading them.

Some will probably balk at my use of the term *forensic communication*. Although *forensic* technically implies application of expertise to any courtroom issue, its use by the popular media promotes the connotation of application in criminal cases only. Some of the chapters that follow do indeed have more to do with criminal cases, but others have more to do with civil cases and a few may be applied to either.

Moreover, there will be a few readers old enough to remember when the communication discipline used the term *forensics* as a label for contest oratory—tournament debate, competitive oral interpretation of literature, and so forth. I trust that the book's subtitle, along with today's lay familiarity with forensic science in the courtroom, precludes that meaning here.

Likewise, the focus here is different than the most common (thus far) application of communication expertise to work by attorneys. Specifically, we are not concerned here with what often has been termed *communication and lawyering*, that is, the application of pedagogy or scholarship to the improvement of attorneys' communication skills in the courtroom. There are many sources already available to coach attorneys on basic or advanced communication skills. We are instead concerned here with using communication research to help solve *legal issues* that arise in court.

Because communication expertise usually is applied to courtroom cases either as an expert witness who is expected to testify, or as a consultant who typically does not, the book is organized into two main sections accordingly. It begins with nine chapters on attorney/court *consultation*, with these organized according to consulting regarding matters that arise primarily *before* trial and those arise mostly *during* the trial. Seven chapters on *expert-witness* roles follow. These are organized according to expertise and opinion regarding the *content* of examined material, and expertise regarding the *presentation* of information to juries.

CONSULTATION: BEFORE THE TRIAL

Chapters 1 and 2 discuss what is probably the most well-known application of communication research to legal consulting, namely, advising on the matter of *jury selection*. These two chapters take quite different approaches and together present a very comprehensive treatment of the science (and art) of jury selection. Chapter 3 discusses the effects of *pretrial publicity* on jurors' predispositions, and includes potential solutions to the associated problems. Chapter 4 first summarizes a large body of work on *deception*, including the motives for deception, the ostensible cues of deception, and the (in)accuracy of judgments about others' deception. Courtroom applications include suggestions for behaviors to make attorneys and witnesses more believable, ways by which attorneys can make jurors less likely to believe testimony, and others.

CONSULTATION: DURING THE TRIAL

Chapter 5 discusses *jury decision making*, specifically, the variables that do and do not affect the process and outcomes of jurors' deliberations and decisions. Chapter 6 focuses on *hindsight bias* as a specific variable in jury decision making. Hindsight bias is the psychological tendency to form a biased opinion of what *others* should have assumed *before* an event—the bias coming from what *we* have learned about that event's outcome *after the fact*. If not tamed, the bias can lead to unfair jury decisions. Chapter 7 discusses the paradox whereby on the one hand defendants' rights must be protected in our legal system, whereas on the other hand there is an important need for the *victim's voice and rights* to be heard and respected, as well. Chapter 8 discusses *unwanted pursuit*, or *stalking*, as a case of communication (in both directions), and describes how it is dealt with by the legal system. Its discussion of legal consulting applications includes, among other things, helping prosecuting attorneys to paint a representative picture of the stalking phenomenon for juries. Chapter 9 discusses both technology and cognitive psychology affecting choices that attorneys and consultants should consider when preparing *graphics and visual aids* of various kinds for presentation in the courtroom.

EXPERT-WITNESS TESTIMONY: CONTENT

Chapter 10 describes research and experience behind the author's expert testimony on the *effects of pornography on communities*, including the determination of community standards regarding obscenity, the effect of strip clubs and adult bookstores on communities, and more. Chapter 11 describes expert-witness work on cases where one of the issues is *the likely interpretation of messages*—warning labels, advertising claims, safety instructions, contracts, and so forth—by their target audience. Chapter 12 provides an introduction to the field of *forensic linguistics* generally, and focuses especially on linguistic analyses used in identifying the true author of contested wills, threatening letters, crime-scene notes, and the like. Chapter 13 introduces *computer forensics* and discusses the legal issues and forensic approaches to cybercrimes such as fraud, cyberstalking, pornography, and others.

EXPERT-WITNESS TESTIMONY: PRESENTATION

Chapter 14 discusses research that challenges the veracity of both *confessions and eyewitness testimony*. Because jurors tend to assume that confessions and eyewitness reports are highly credible, research and expert-witness testimony to the contrary can be valuable in court. Chapter 15 introduces the viability of *testing expert-witness opinions empirically*. Sometimes expert opinions represent hypotheses that can be tested via typical quantitative research methods, and it can be very persuasive in court when they are empirically supported. Chapter 16 assumes that many readers have not yet had experience as a legal consultant or expert witness, and that some might like to give it a try. The chapter is a sort of *primer for the novice expert witness or consultant*. It also serves as a reminder to attorneys of the areas in which new consultants and experts may need advice.

These chapters represent issues facing communication-oriented legal consultants today. Tomorrow may be different, of course. As is always the case, the volume does not purport to be the "final word" on the matter—partly because findings from scholarship constantly evolve, and perhaps especially because the society within which the courts operate is constantly evolving. It is certainly possible, for example, that a single high-profile stalking case in the near or distant future could affect the kinds of jury sensitivities addressed in Chapter 8 on stalking, or that "hindsight bias" could become sufficiently familiar within our everyday language and consciousness as to affect the sensitivities addressed in Chapter 6 on jurors' hindsight bias naïveté. Similarly, new ways in which entertainment and news media represent the courtroom experience—almost always fictionalized before but now presented via "reality" versions, as well—might impact the issues discussed in Chapter 5 on jury decision making and Chapter 7 on consideration of victims. Moreover, despite decades of research showing that we, including jurors of course, cannot detect others' deception, the several new TV shows implying otherwise might contaminate jurors beyond the ways discussed in Chapter 4 on deception. And the various approaches to electronic social networking certainly might add to the kind of work described in Chapter 13 on computer forensics, or might exacerbate the problems discussed in Chapter 8 on stalking. Similarly, today's increase in available sources of news—news alert software on our computers, news applications on smart phones and iPads, radio and highway-sign Amber alerts, and so forth—might complicate the problems discussed in Chapter 3 on pretrial publicity. In short, in addition to progress via new research, the dynamic changes in the society's media, technology, and communication will almost certainly affect the nature of the crimes and cases that go to court, as well as the expectations and biases of jurors who deliberate and the opinions of the consultants and expert witnesses who advise.

Certainly there are legal applications of communication research that could not be represented in this volume for one reason or another. I am aware of some of these and imagine that there are others of which I am not yet aware. In any case, there should be enough variety among these chapters both to satisfy the reader who simply is curious about applying communication research to the courtroom, to alert attorneys to some of the ways that communication scholars may be able to assist on cases, and to provide encouragement to those who might be inclined to apply their own expertise to the pursuit of truth in the courtroom.

I

Communication Applications

Attorney/Court Consultation

Before the Trial

1

Musical Chairs in the Jury Box

Trial Consulting and Jury Selection

Mark A. deTurck

There is a great deal of mystery and misunderstanding surrounding the role of trial consultants in selecting a jury. Perhaps the most significant misconception is that trial consultants evaluate prospective jurors to determine who would render a favorable verdict for their client. In fact, jury selection is really a process of *deselection*—identifying jurors predisposed to find against a given party. The public's perception of the role of a trial consultant in jury selection has been molded almost exclusively by novels, Hollywood film, and television programs, and as often is the case, that portrayal is inaccurate.

Attorneys focus on how the law can be used to protect the interests of their clients, believing that if jurors simply follow the law then they should find in favor of their clients. By focusing on the legal parameters to shape their message to jurors, attorneys fail to consider a key factor in the classic model of communication (Berlo, 1960)—the receiver of a message, jurors, and how their psychological evaluation of the case will affect their verdicts. Attorneys often are shocked to learn that jurors do not always follow the path established by the law, but instead rely on their own psychological compass (Johnson & Haney, 1994).

Trial consultants' knowledge and experience in social science research methodology, as well as the literature on human information processing, persuasion, and decision making makes them uniquely qualified to take the lead on who will be seated in the jury box as the triers of fact at trial. The goal of this chapter is to provide a review of issues and literature regarding jury selection. More specifically, I discuss the following:

- How and why trial consulting has emerged as a major force in the courts,

- The process of voir dire,

- An overview of scientific jury selection and its criticisms, and

- Anecdotal evidence from working with attorneys to exemplify the difference between attorney-based decision making and that of a trial consultant.

VANISHING TRIALS

The *"vanishing trial"* phenomenon refers to the fact that in 1962 a jury decided 11.5% of civil cases in the federal courts, whereas by 2002 the percentage of civil cases that were resolved in the federal courts by a jury dropped to 1.8% (Galanter, 2004). Over the same period of time, the number of dispositions in federal court increased from approximately 50,000 in 1962 to more than 250,000 in 2002—a fivefold increase.

Although the available evidence for state civil courts is not as extensive as for the federal courts, a similar decrease in state courts' cases disposed of by juries has been observed. Across 21 states and the District of Columbia, the percentage of cases decided by a jury dropped from 36.1% in 1976 to 15.8% in 2002 (Ostrom, Strickland, & Hannaford, 2004). There is an even greater decline in state civil trials (52%) if the time frame is shortened from 1992 to 2005 (Langton & Cohen, 2008). Although the number of trials has fallen off dramatically, there seems to be no shortage of new civil cases being filed.

A snapshot analysis of state court civil cases in 2005 showed that, although the courts disposed of 29,950 cases, approximately 7.4 million new cases were filed (LaFountain, Schauffler, Strickland, Raftery, & Bromage, 2007). The dramatic decrease in the number of jury trials from 1992 to 2005 varies greatly depending on the type of case. Although the number of products liability cases dropped by 66% from 1992 to 2005, the number of medical malpractice cases decreased only 9.5%.

Two key implications emerge from these trends. First, jurors might reasonably conclude that civil cases that see the light of the courtroom possess greater merit than those resolved by an alternative method (e.g., arbitration or mediation). Stated differently, it is not unreasonable for jurors in civil cases to conclude that a plaintiff's claim against a defendant is likely to be legitimate, otherwise the court would have dismissed the case, or pushed the parties to settle. Indeed, the fact that plaintiffs prevailed in almost 60% of the civil cases disposed in 2005 indicates that jurors perceived the complaintants' cases had more merit than the defendants' (Langton & Cohen, 2008). Additionally, the longevity of a case also enhances its economic value in jurors' perceptions. In medical malpractice cases, for example, damages paid to a person allegedly injured by a physician's negligence more than doubled from the time before a lawsuit was filed (no jury: $131,000) through discovery until cases were disposed by a jury ($322,000; Cohen & Hughes, 2007).

Second, the dramatic decrease in trials since 1962 is especially significant in light of the more dramatic surge in the number of attorneys over the same general time period. From 1960 to 2000, the number of lawyers increased more than 250%, from 286,000 in 1960 to 1,066,328 in 2000 (Carson, 2000; Galanter, 1983). The exponential growth of attorneys suggests that there are more attorneys vying for the same diminishing resource—trial experience, which includes selecting a jury.

Taken together, these implications suggest that attorneys are navigating increasingly complex and difficult litigation waters, with less trial experience. This is the historical backdrop against which trial consultants emerged as significant players in the courtroom theater.

VOIR DIRE

Voir dire is a French term, which roughly translated means "to speak the truth." Voir dire refers to the pretrial phase in which the court and/or counsel representing the parties ask prospective jurors (the venire) questions to determine their suitability to hear a case and deliberate to a verdict. The court's primary purpose for asking the venire questions is to ensure that members of the jury pool are jury eligible. Attorney-led voir dire is designed to expose jurors who have attitudes or experiences that might prevent them from being fair and impartial in terms of how they evaluate evidence, witnesses, attorney arguments, and jury instructions.

Some attorneys believe that the goal of voir dire is to establish rapport with jurors. Although ingratiation might nurture jurors' positive affect toward an attorney, the increase in positive feelings for an attorney is not reflected in jurors' verdicts (Brodsky, 2006; LeVan, 1984). However, when defense attorneys' strategic purpose during voir dire is to activate jurors' sense of fairness, they were more successful in obtaining a favorable verdict for their clients (Reinard & Arsenault, 2000).

In federal court, the voir dire most likely is conducted by the judge and not the attorneys. Judge-led voir dire in federal court is typically very limited in terms of the information solicited from jurors, and is generally focused on demographic information (e.g., employment, marital status, children, etc.). In a quasi-experimental design, Jones (1987) found that an attorney-led voir dire, as compared to a judge-directed voir dire, provided more probative information for determining which members of the venire posed a threat to the parties.

Research by Moran, Cutler, and Loftus (1990) indicated that a more extensive voir dire increases the likelihood of accurately predicting jurors' verdict orientations. Over the course of two trials, a limited voir dire predicted jurors' verdicts at the same level as expected by the flip of a coin (50%) compared with an extended voir dire, which revealed useful juror information so as to increase the predictability of individual juror's verdicts to 78%. An extended voir dire is particularly likely to reveal juror biases if attorneys employ open-ended questions (Middendorf & Luginbuhl, 1995) because they allow jurors to state their positions and expound on the rationale for their attitudes, whereas close-ended questions restrict responses (e.g., "yes" or "no"). In addition to the format of voir dire questions, whether the questions are asked publicly or privately can influence whether jurors even respond to them.

The Honorable Gregory Mize (1999, 2003) conducted research in his capacity as a judge and found that jurors often fail to disclose case-relevant biases during a group voir dire (members of the venire present) in both criminal and civil trials. In a more systematic study across state courts in California, Hannaford-Agor and Waters (2004) found that almost 15% of jurors failed to respond to any voir dire questions across 20 different categories of questioning, and that 75% of the jurors responded affirmatively to only one or two categories of questions. A tacit assumption by attorneys and the court is that jurors' silence following a question is a negative response. Although jurors' silence can be frustrating in deciding which members of the venire to strike, the explanation for jurors withholding information during voir dire should not be surprising.

Voir dire requires jurors to answer questions, which at times, can probe into personally private events in jurors' lives. Despite the Supreme Court's decision to uphold the right for public voir dire (*Presley v. Georgia*, 2010), jurors might be too embarrassed to reveal personally private information in a public forum. Even though jurors are typically offered an opportunity to answer personal questions in camera (in judge's chambers), this more private context still requires jurors to reveal potentially compromising information to a number of total strangers.

A number of years ago, for example, when I was selecting a jury on a case involving a contract dispute, a juror took up counsel's offer to the venire to discuss in private any issue that might prohibit them from serving on the jury. When she was called to chambers to discuss her personal situation, she stopped at the door in shock: There were more than 15 people in the room including the judge, clerk, both trial teams, and consultants. She was clearly embarrassed and had difficulty telling us that she was incontinent. Although this is not a bias that might impact her verdict decision, clearly it underscores the difficulty jurors encounter when confronted with revealing personally sensitive information in a public context.

A more private method for obtaining jurors' case-relevant attitudes and experiences is a supplemental juror questionnaire (SJQ). These are questionnaires the court distributes to a jury pool to be completed prior to voir dire. A scoring sheet is generated to rate jurors' responses on the key questions and an overall score for each juror is created. Because members of the venire can complete their questionnaires without members of the venire listening in, it can provide a relatively nonthreatening method for obtaining a rich source of information regarding potential jurors' case-relevant experiences and biases. Nonetheless, attorneys at times are willing to substitute their superstitions for valuable data representing jurors' personal take on the case issues.

When selecting a jury for an employment case in San Francisco, the court allowed the use of SJQ. I had reviewed and scored the SJQ for the venire. A woman from the jury pool was returning to the jury box from a break during voir dire and momentarily stopped by the opposing counsel's table to say something. The client grabbed my arm and insisted we use a peremptory challenge to strike her immediately, despite the fact she hadn't been called on to answer any questions in voir dire. I reassured the client not to judge her in haste and that her SJQ indicated she was likely to be extremely supportive of our story. When she was asked questions during voir dire, she essentially did our closing argument; counsel opposite moved to have her dismissed for cause.

There are three reasons that jurors may be struck from a jury: hardship, challenge for cause, or peremptory challenge. Although decisions regarding a juror's hardship (e.g., family care obligation, self-employment, scheduled medical procedure) are up to the discretion of the court, a judge might seek input from attorneys regarding whether they are willing to excuse the juror. Keeping a juror despite his or her hardship can be a very risky strategic decision for attorneys. Compelling jurors to serve in the face of a difficult hardship is likely to activate strong resentment or anger; and, it is all but impossible to know which, if any, party jurors would target their negative affect toward.

Judges know that jurors bring a wealth of personal experience with them to the courtroom, and do not expect them to check their biases at the courtroom door. The purpose of voir dire is to determine whether or not a juror's experience and attitudes prevent him or her from being fair and impartial to all the parties. If a juror expresses doubt regarding his or her ability to be fair to an attorney's client, the attorney can move to strike the juror for cause. However, the opposing attorney has an opportunity to retain the juror using the litmus test for determining if a juror's bias exceeds the court's tolerance. To have a chance to retain a biased juror, counsel must elicit a concession from the juror that he or she will follow the court's instruction (law), even if it conflicts with his or her personal beliefs. In the end, it is up to the court to decide whether the juror has been rehabilitated and can serve.

Peremptory challenges are strikes an attorney can exercise to eliminate jurors from the venire because the attorney is concerned that the juror's biased attitude or life experiences will prevent him or her from being fair to his or her client. Attorneys can use their peremptory challenges to strike a juror without stating a rationale (see section on Batson challenges for an exception). The number of peremptory challenges depends on the venue and court (state vs. federal court). Because peremptory strikes are limited, they are a precious commodity to be used by attorneys when selecting a jury. Yet, research indicates that attorneys "burn" more peremptory challenges than necessary because they first fail to move to have biased jurors dismissed based on challenges for cause (Hannaford-Agor & Waters, 2004).

Understanding the psychological impact of jurors' life experiences is vital when deciding how to prioritize peremptory challenges. For example, a few years ago when selecting a jury for the defense in a medical malpractice case (failure to diagnose cancer), the client wanted to strike a young woman from the venire because she felt her father died from undiagnosed stomach cancer. The key to my decision to keep the juror was the fact she and her mother did *not* file a lawsuit against her father's physician. Following a defense verdict, post-trial juror interviews revealed that she was a very strong leader for the defense during deliberations.

Assessing a juror's potential leadership during deliberations is also a key consideration during voir dire. A juror's prior jury experience is a useful index for predicting the extent to which a juror participates in deliberations and attempts to influence the verdict. Hastie, Penrod, and Pennington (1983) found that jurors with previous jury service were more talkative during deliberations compared with "rookie" jurors. Kassin and Juhnke (1983) obtained results that indicated jurors with prior jury experience were not only more loquacious, but their remarks were also more persuasive, and they were less likely to acquiesce to a majority opinion during their jury's deliberations. Moreover, research reported by Hannaford-Agor and Waters (2004) indicated that the state courts in California favored recycling jurors with previous jury experience, presumably because they have been deemed suitable to sit in other cases.

To be sure, more information does not always enhance the predictability of jurors' verdict orientations. An underlying assumption in voir dire is that jurors are completely truthful and forthcoming. Research by Johnson and Haney (1994) revealed that jurors were unable or unwilling to follow the court's instructions despite their oath as a juror. This is consistent with our research over the years with tens of thousands of surrogate jurors in mostly civil cases: Approximately half of the surrogate jurors in our studies indicated that they would follow their personal beliefs as opposed to the court's instructions.

BATSON CHALLENGES

In 1986, James Kirkland Batson, a Black man charged with burglary, brought an action against the State of Kentucky based on the fact that the prosecutor used peremptory challenges to strike the four Blacks on the venire, creating an all-White jury (*Batson v. Kentucky*, 1986). Counsel for Batson moved to have the jury discharged because prosecutor's conduct violated Mr. Batson's rights under the Sixth (jury drawn from a cross-section of the community) and 14th (equal protection of the laws) Amendments. The court never ruled on the motion and Mr. Batson was convicted.

Mr. Batson's attorney fought the case all the way to the Supreme Court, which decided 7–2 in favor of Mr. Batson, and overturned the lower courts' decisions. As a result, if an attorney suspects that counsel opposite is striking jurors from the venire due to race, he or she can challenge opposing counsel's peremptory strikes and the court might rule that he or she must provide race-neutral reason(s) for striking a juror. More recently, this protection has been extended to race-neutral peremptory strikes in civil cases (*Edmonson v. Leesville Concrete Company*, 1991), and the demographic scope has been broadened to include gender-neutral peremptory strikes (*J.E.B. v Alabama ex rel. T.B.*, 1994).

STEALTH JURORS

A particularly difficult task confronting attorneys during jury selection is identifying *stealth jurors*. These are jurors, who upon learning the nature of the case, seek to enforce a verdict so as to fulfill their personal agendas—making a statement for or against a given party due to their own bias. They perceive their jury duty as an opportunity to correct a personal loss (e.g., layoff at work, bad surgical outcome) or social injury (e.g., recent bank failures, product recalls) they experienced. During voir dire, these members of the venire might deceive attorneys (deliberately withhold information or answer a question inaccurately) with the hope of concealing their bias and being seated on the jury so they can realize their plan. These jurors are referred to as stealth jurors because they attempt to evade attorneys' radar for detecting their bias.

Popular media portrayals imply that it is easy to identify stealth jurors based on their behaviors during voir dire (Dimitrius & Mazzarella, 1999). However, the impression that jury selection is a matter of knowing how to "read" jurors is grossly misguided. A key finding in the scientific literature on observers' ability to judge communicators' veracity from their behavioral cues indicates observers' subjective ratings of their success far exceeds their objective abilities. Indeed, the discrepancy between an observer's subjective accuracy and actual accuracy can exceed 30% (deTurck, 1991). In other words, an observer judging the veracity of a relative stranger could believe he or she is accurate 75% of the time (subjective accuracy), but only be able to evaluate another's truthfulness accurately 45% of the time.

A substantial line of research indicates that observers' ability to detect deception from relative strangers is about what would be expected from random guessing—a 50% success rate (Zuckerman, DePaulo, & Rosenthal, 1981). Evidence indicates that the difficulty in detecting deception from behavioral cues is compounded by a number of factors, including personality (self-monitoring) and contextual (opportunity to rehearse) factors. Individuals high in self-monitoring are like "social chameleons" adept at tailoring their communicative behavior to the demands of the context so as to conceal their true underlying attitudes and emotions. Detecting deception from individuals high in self-monitoring is particularly difficult if they have had an opportunity to rehearse their fabricated answers to questions (Miller, deTurck, & Kalbfleisch, 1983). Personality aside, unless a juror is the first called on during voir dire, he or she has an opportunity to hear the questions and practice a response so as to portray a truthful facade.

Granted, there is research that links deception to certain nonverbal cues, but these tend invariably to be cues that cannot be detected without laboratory equipment or concentrated training, so that overreliance on any one behavioral cue, or set of cues in evaluating a potential juror's veracity is a very risky decision-making strategy for a trial consultant (deTurck, 1991; deTurck, Feeley, & Roman, 1997; deTurck, Harszlak, Bodhorn, & Texter, 1990; deTurck & Miller, 1985, 1990).

SCIENTIFIC JURY SELECTION

Scientific jury selection (SJS) refers to the application of social science research methodologies to identify the profiles of pro-prosecution or pro-defense (criminal case) jurors or pro-plaintiff or pro-defense (civil case). Prior to SJS attorneys, to a large extent, would rely on traditional approaches—hunches and stereotypes—to determine which members of the venire to strike and which to keep. Traditional approaches to jury selection have relied on outdated stereotypes (e.g., gender, ethnicity, race), and invalid information (e.g., bumper stickers). Attorneys' reliance on these traditional strategies have proven to be no more efficacious in identifying jurors' verdict tendencies than randomly selecting jurors based on the flip of a coin (e.g., Kerr, Kramer, Caroll, & Alfini, 1991; Olczak, Kaplan, & Penrod, 1991). The advent of SJS can be traced to the trial of the Harrisburg Seven. In 1972, U.S. Attorney General John Mitchell prosecuted well-known anti-war activist Phillip Berrigan and six others in the central Pennsylvania community of Harrisburg (Herbsleb, Sales, & Berman, 1979).

The prosecution took 5 weeks to present its case to jurors, including a plot by the defendants to kidnap Henry Kissinger, then national security advisor to President Nixon. Ramsey Clark, former attorney general under President Lyndon Johnson, when asked to call his first witness for the defendants addressed the court: "Your Honor, the defendants shall always seek peace. They continue to proclaim their innocence. The defense rests." Clark's bold strategic ploy was empowered, in part, by a scientific analysis of the jurisdiction to identify factors associated with pro-prosecution jurors so the defense could use the pretrial intelligence of the community as a basis for striking potential jurors.

All too frequently clients ask us to recite the demographics of the ideal juror. They want to know if the ideal juror we're looking for is younger or older, female or male, engineers or teachers, and so on. The demographic profile of jurors is a readily available set of cues in any courtroom. Although relying on demographic indices of jurors is extremely tempting for attorneys, the simplistic appeal of using demographic factors to identify jurors' verdict orientation has not been supported in the research literature (e.g., Moran & Comfort 1982; Wissler, Hart, & Saks, 1999). Jurors' demographic characteristics proved to be equally impotent indices of their damage awards in civil cases (Goodman, Loftus, & Greene, 1990).

There are several reasons that jurors' demographic backgrounds have not emerged as strong predictors of verdict orientations. First, the types (criminal vs. civil) and idiosyncrasies of a case (e.g., products liability, toxic tort) influence jurors' decision making. In a criminal trial, a demographic factor may predict jurors' verdict preferences if that factor is crucial to case-relevant attitudes (e.g., juror gender in child sexual abuse cases). However, in civil cases, the link between a juror's demographic background and case-relevant attitudes is rarely self-evident or robust across the unique dynamics of various cases (e.g., products liability, employment, medical malpractice, toxic tort, contract).

In researching the effects of case dynamics in state civil trials, Langton and Cohen (2008) obtained results indicating that plaintiffs clearly enjoy an advantage over defendants; and, that plaintiffs' advantage is greater in contract (66%) as opposed to tort claims (56%). Specifically, for trials involving contracts, plaintiffs' prevailed over defendants 89% of the time in mortgage foreclosure cases, 75% of the cases in selling a product or service, and about 61% of the time in an employment discrimination and fraud claims. Plaintiffs' winning in tort claims ranged from a high of 75% in cases involving animal attacks to 64% in motor vehicle accidents and about 22% in medical malpractice cases and non-asbestos product liability cases.

At first blush, the evidence suggests that plaintiffs in medical malpractice and non-asbestos product liability trials have a relatively dismal winning record compared with plaintiffs in other civil disputes. However, jury damage awards in medical malpractice and non-asbestos product liability cases have increased more than monetary awards in other tort or contract cases from 1992 to 2005. Despite the public's outcry over the impact of litigation on the costs of health care and manufactured goods, the evidence indicates that juries are willing to award increasingly higher damages to plaintiffs in medical malpractice and non-asbestos product liability cases.

Second, the venue of a case is likely to play a role in jurors' verdict orientation. The prevailing community attitudes regarding a specific issue and industry vary from venue to venue. A key attitudinal issue for trial consultants to consider is jurors' willingness to award damages. Approximately $6 billion in compensatory and punitive damages was awarded to plaintiffs who prevailed in civil trials in 2005, with a median damage award of $28,000. Jurors' damage awards varied greatly depending on the venue. The median jury awards (compensatory and punitive damages) ranged from lows of $6,000 in DuPage, Illinois, to $245,000 in Los Angeles, for example (Langton & Cohen, 2008). Similarly, although only 4% of juries awarded punitive damage to plaintiffs seeking to punish and deter defendants' conduct in 2001, ranging from juries in DuPage awarding punitive damages in 1.2% of the cases in which plaintiffs prevailed to jurors in Honolulu awarding punitive damages in almost 22% of decisions favoring the plaintiffs.

Trial consultants come to a jury selection armed with varying levels of information regarding how jurors might react to thematic arguments, witnesses, exhibits, and so on. Prior to selecting a jury, a trial consultant often has conducted one or more jury research exercise (e.g., focus group, mock trial) and is well informed of jurors' reactions to the case fact pattern. Although focus group or mock trial studies are very informative research tools, they are not designed to generate juror profiles. The number of surrogate jurors participating in a mock trial or focus group study is generally too low to provide adequate statistical power, unless the anticipated effect sizes are very large. In some situations, multiple mock trials are conducted on a given case enabling the trial consultant to collapse the data across the research exercises so as to boost the statistical power of the analysis.

A juror profiling study is designed to identify the characteristics of jury-eligible residents in the trial venue who are statistically significant predictors of actual jurors' decisions for a given case. The number of surrogate jurors required for a jury-profiling study can vary, but generally between 200 and 300 jury-eligible citizens from the trial venue are randomly selected to participate as surrogate jurors. The demographic profile of the venue is matched in the sample selected for the profiling study.

Participants listen to a party-neutral synopsis of the case (key facts are stated without any advocacy) and provide feedback to case-relevant attitudinal and experiential questions, as well as demographic information. Although some broad attitudinal questions are important to obtain insight into jurors' general opinions regarding a particular industry or issues (e.g., pharmaceutical companies, automobile manufacturers healthcare, intellectual property), the more specific questions have greater predictive value regarding jurors' ultimate disposition at trial (Kraus, 1995). Using statistical techniques, a mathematical model is created that identifies the best predictors of jurors' verdict orientations.

Most juror-profiling studies have been conducted via telephone surveys, and to a lesser extent, filling out questionnaires in person. However, online computer technology makes it feasible to collect large amounts of data from surrogate jurors without the intrusiveness of inconvenient telephone calls, or the high costs of in-person data collection (see, e.g., LookinGlass at www.lg-juries.com). Surrogate jurors can easily participate in jury research from their home computer.

CRITICISMS OF SCIENTIFIC JURY SELECTION

Attacks of SJS concentrate on two general fronts: effectiveness and legal (Stolle, Robbenolt, & Wiener, 1996; Strier, 1999). There is a dearth of research testing the effectiveness of trial consultants in the jury selection process. Nietzel and Dillehay (1986) found that when a jury consultant was retained for the defense in capital offense trials, the jury sentenced defendants to death in 33% of the cases as opposed to 61% of the cases in which a jury consultant was not retained. In a replication of this ground-breaking research, Nietzel, Dillehay, and Himelein (1987) confirmed the effectiveness of challenges made by trial consultants in death penalty cases. There is no systematic scientific evidence bearing on the efficacy of trial consultant's decision making in other kinds of trials, however.

Although there is little scientific evidence one way or the other about the effectiveness of trial consultants, there are other tentative indicators. One currency for evaluating the effectiveness of trial consulting is the financial success of the industry. The fact that trial consulting has grown into a $400 million industry with an estimated 700 consultants in more than 400 firms (Strier, 1999) suggests that more than attorneys' fancy is driving their decisions to retain trial consultants. By the time this book is published, it will have been almost 40 years since trial consultants were first retained to assist trial teams in striking a jury. Surely by now attorneys would have had ample opportunity to determine if a trial consultant's judgments during jury selection has contributed to the persuasive impact of their case among jurors.

One of the central arguments against the effectiveness of SJS is that demographic factors are weak predictors of jurors' verdict orienta-tions and are not robust across cases (e.g., Kressel & Kressel, 2002). Trial consultants have long known that jurors' demographic profiles are notoriously inaccurate predictors of verdict orientations across a broad spectrum of cases. That is why trial consultants channel their empirical energy toward identifying the case-relevant attitudes and experiences that differentiate jurors' verdict orientations. Research indicates that jurors' general attitudes toward tort reform affected their verdict decisions across criminal and civil cases (e.g., Hans & Lofquist, 1994). Not surprisingly, jurors with pro-tort reform attitudes hearing a civil case were less willing to award damages than jurors who did not share their belief that an overhaul in tort reform was necessary.

In jury-profiling research, trial consultants assess jurors' general attitudes regarding case issues, and also hone in on very specific case-relevant attitudes. Additionally, consultants assess the life experiences that form the basis for jurors' attitudes. Critics of SJS do not address the role of jurors' case-relevant experiences (e.g., jurors' good/bad experiences with doctors in a medical malpractice case). To the extent scholarly research continues to focus on the predictive value of mere demographic variables in criminal cases, we can anticipate more null results with little relevance to the actual research in the SJS of most trial consultants.

Critics argue that to the extent that trial consultants do impact the attitudinal composition of a jury, then the use of SJS violates citizens' rights under the Sixth Amendment to a trial by an impartial jury. However, SJS was first implemented in the Harrisburg Seven case to help defendants whose rights were being violated as being unfairly targeted in the federal government's sweep of anti-war protesters. Rulings by the Supreme Court have disallowed litigants from exercising systematic bias in striking jurors (e.g., the Batson case). Moreover, research has shown that jurors are far from forthcoming during voir dire. Seltzer, Venuti, and Lopes (1991) obtained results indicating that approximately half of the jurors failed to reveal a significant bias in their beliefs regarding the burden of proof. Jurors mistakenly believed that a defendant must prove his or her innocence, as opposed to the government (state or federal) bearing the burden of proof.

To the extent that the purpose of a jury trial is to reach an accurate verdict based on the evidence, recent research suggests that juries do not do a particularly good job of getting it right (Spencer, 2007). There are a number of reasons why jurors would reach a verdict that is not commensurate with the evidence in a case. First, it is apparent from the research reviewed earlier that jurors often fail to reveal biases that could prevent them from being fair and impartial. Second, even if jurors do disclose a strong bias that would warrant striking them, attorneys do not maximize the strategy of their peremptory strikes so as to eliminate jurors who are particularly dangerous for their clients. Whether deliberate or unintentional, biased jurors often fly under the radar of many attorneys during voir dire and land unchallenged in the jury box.

A third reason jurors' verdicts are inconsistent with the evidence at trial is because they often do not understand the instructions read to them by the court prior to deliberating. In fact, research results obtained by (Kramer & Koenig, 1989; Reifman, Gusick, & Elsworth, 1992) indicated that jurors' comprehension of the law in criminal cases is disappointing at best and often an outright failure. Similar results can be found in the literature studying jurors' comprehension of the law in civil cases (e.g., Greene, Johns, & Smith, 2001). Jurors incorrectly base their decisions of defendants' liability on an apportionment of responsibility, rather than first deciding "yes" or "no" as to whether a defendant is liable. Greene and Johns (2006) found that poor comprehension of the law by jurors was not improved by providing them with a written copy of the instructions to review after hearing them read by the court. However, jurors did display better comprehension of the law after deliberations. This clearly underscores the persuasive influence from jurors who assume strong leadership roles during deliberations and are able to educate/persuade other jurors of the legal parameters in reaching a verdict, and the need to accurately assess leadership potential among members of the venire.

In our jury research at R&D Strategic Solutions, we routinely observe jurors mistakenly applying the more stringent beyond-a-reasonable-doubt burden of proof appropriate to criminal cases across a broad spectrum of civil cases (medical malpractice, products liability, contract, intellectual property), when the more lenient burden of proof, preponderance of evidence, should be applied. We also frequently observe jurors shifting the burden of proof from the plaintiff (where it belongs) to the defense, for example, jurors believe a doctor has to prove he or she did not breach the standard of care (negligence) in a medical malpractice case. More importantly, critics of SJS miss the point of the role of retaining a trial consultant for jury selection: The goal of SJS is to *minimize* unfair bias from invading a jury's verdict. Judges respect that jurors have attitudes and life experiences they bring with them to the courthouse and do not expect jurors to suddenly erase their cognitive and emotional experiences once they are impaneled.

Failure by jurors to use the law for guidance also is observed in their decisions for damages in liability cases. Hastie, Schkade, and Payne (1998) found that jurors award punitive damages without ever considering the legal parameters for whether punitive damages are warranted. Hastie et al. (1998) reported that 100% of the juries that never discussed the legal elements for awarding punitive damages awarded punitive damages, compared with only 45% of the juries that did discuss the legal aspects of awarding punitive damages. In a follow-up report, Hastie, Schkade, and Payne (1999) discussed how jurors' punitive damage awards are tainted by a reliance on sympathy, a strong bias against wealthy defendants, and a willingness to make outrageous monetary awards.

Unfortunately, some jurors come to the courtroom with a goal to fulfill more than their civic duty. Lucrative book deals await jurors savvy enough to navigate voir dire and be impaneled in high-profile cases. Even jurors dismissed from high-profile cases (e.g., Michael Jackson's molestation trial) are able to sell their stories; it seems that the public has an insatiable appetite for the harrowing details of what it was like to be questioned by Jackson's legal team. As if these reports are not disturbing enough, reports have suggested that jurors in Paul Little's obscenity trial in Tampa, Florida, were accused of auctioning their verdicts to the highest bidder in a dual for a book deal (Richards & Calvert, 2009). Apparently, the profit margins are greater with a guilty verdict than with a not guilty one. Juror profit notwithstanding, there is evidence that some jurors foist their own political agendas on the courts (Hammerstein, 2002).

APPLYING SCIENCE AND RESEARCH

Trial consultants are not always afforded an opportunity to conduct a jury-profiling study, focus group, or mock trial prior to being retained to assist an attorney in selecting a jury. In these situations, a trial consultant must be able to call on a vast knowledge of social science research and experience in juror' information processing and decision making for determining when to use peremptory challenges to strike jurors. Although jury selection is informed by a broad spectrum of social science disciplines, the literature on attribution theory, heuristics, and biases in human judgment are particularly useful in predicting how jurors will evaluate a specific set of facts (Kahneman, Slovic, & Tversky, 1982; Shaver, 1985).

Attribution Theory

Attribution theory is concerned with how people assign or apportion responsibility for the outcome of an individual's or some entity's behavior. Jurors apportion more responsibility to a corporation than an individual for the same behavioral transgression (Bornstein, 1994; Hans & Ermann, 1989). MacCoun (1996) tested the commonly held "deep-pocket" bias ascribed to jurors—jurors find against corporations because of their actual or perceived financial status. His results indicated that jurors attributed more responsibility to a corporation than an individual defendant, even when the defendant was an affluent individual. Moreover, MacCoun also found that jurors awarded higher monetary damages to a plaintiff when the defendant was a corporation as opposed to a wealthy defendant who was an individual person. Thus, jurors' bias against corporations is more than a simple matter of deep pockets.

The code of conduct jurors expect from corporations is predicated on an unreasonably high standard (Hans, 1994). To the extent jurors hold corporations to a higher standard of conduct than an individual, it can be extremely difficult for corporations to meet their obligations to the seemingly incompatible financial and legal marketplaces. Whereas jurors expect good products and services from corporate entities, they are not very forgiving of the inherent risk–cost analysis in corporate decision making (Viscusi, 2000).

One specific type of attribution jurors make is a defensive attribution. Individuals form a defensive attribution primarily because they want to distance themselves psychologically from the behavioral outcome caused by someone else (Walster, 1966). Jurors are likely to develop defensive attributions when they can easily perceive themselves to be in the same situation, and to be personally similar with a litigant, and therefore likely to make the same mistakes (Shaver, 1970). In other words, jurors are more likely to blame a seemingly innocent victim for serious outcomes of an accident because a defensive attribution "psychologically protects" them.

In some cases, attorneys' decisions to strike jurors are based on erroneous assumptions. Years ago I was retained to assist an attorney for an automobile manufacturer that had been sued by a young mother in Pennsylvania who had a one-car accident that caused serious injuries to her children and blamed it on problems with the car. The defense claim was that she caused the accident by looking over her shoulder at her children in the back seat instead of at the road. The client wanted to avoid female drivers, especially young mothers, because he was concerned that they would identify with the plaintiff and be more sympathetic toward her fight against the automobile manufacturer. Although research indicates that demographics are poor predictors of jurors' verdict orientations across a broad spectrum of cases, the facts of this particular case suggested that gender would be a useful basis for striking jurors. So long as females/young mothers had no salient biases toward the manufacturer, I chose to use our peremptory strikes on male jurors rather than females because of the likelihood that young mothers would make a defensive attribution: "I would not make the same mistake (watching the back seat instead of the road) when driving with my own children."

We went with striking male jurors in an effort to seat more females on the panel. The panel of 10 women and 2 men returned with a defense verdict. To be sure, there is no way to verify that the jury's verdict was due to the decision to strike men from the venire. However, experiences like this challenge attorneys' stereotyped notions about jury selection and prompt them to consider that jurors might base their verdicts on alternative psychological parameters.

Heuristics and Biases

Heuristics are simple decision rules that jurors employ to evaluate a person or issue or persuasive message (Chaiken, 1986; Kahneman et al., 1982). People, including jurors, are cognitive misers; we prefer to use heuristics or mental shortcuts so as to minimize the amount of cognitive effort we invest in processing information. The use of heuristics abounds in litigation from voir dire to verdict (e.g., Saks & Kidd, 1980). Understanding when and why certain jurors' judgments will be influenced by a particular heuristic or bias can be very helpful during voir dire. When seating a jury, one consideration is how jurors are likely to process information over the course of the trial. Rather than selecting a message "off the rack" and hoping it "fits" jurors' processing style, it is to a trial team's advantage to tailor its messages to impaneled jurors' information-processing profiles.

Availability Heuristic. The availability heuristic refers to individuals' tendency to base their judgments on information that is most easily recalled. People tend to overestimate the likelihood that an event will occur when they can easily recall information related to the event, regardless of its actual probability (Slovic, Fischoff, & Lichtenstein, 1982). For example, when people estimate the causes of death, they overestimate events like accidents, fires, drownings, shootings, and so on because they are widely covered in the media and the outcomes are typically devastating. By contrast, people tend to underestimate the occurrence of common causes, such as stroke or heart disease because they did not receive the same emotionally charged coverage in the media.

The vividness of information is a key determinant of the ease with which jurors can recall (Shedler & Manis, 1986). Information is vivid to the extent that it triggers an affective reaction, activates an image, or is temporally or spatially salient to a juror. The vividness of trial information influences a wide variety of jurors' judgments including, but not limited to, evaluations of witnesses (deTurck, Texter, & Harszlak, 1989) and damage awards (Bornstein, 1998; Greene & Bornstein, 2003). For example, we still hear jurors in our research cite *Liebeck v. McDonald's Restaurants* (1995) during deliberations because the media were saturated with reports of the case and the damage award ($2.86 million later reduced to $684,000).

Representativeness Heuristic. The representativeness heuristic refers to people basing judgments on the extent to which information seems to identify an event or person with a specific characterization. For example, to what extent does a plaintiff's injury seem to be indicative of an innocent accident versus deliberate negligence; or, to what extent does a witness' behavior suggest he or she is a credible source or a liar (Feeley & deTurck, 1995). Jurors' judgments arising from the representative heuristic are based on their ability to use probabilities, but unfortunately, the literature is replete with examples of individuals' failures to accurately use probabilities or base-rate information in evaluating events (see, e.g., deTurck & Steele, 1988).

Jurors' damage awards are easily influenced by their misunderstanding of information as being representative of what is appropriate. For example, although only 4% of juries awarded punitive damages in state courts in 2005 (Cohen, 2001), Greene and Bornstein (2003) reported that potential jurors believed that almost 50% of jury verdicts included a punitive damage award. Similarly, Rachlinski (2002) found that jurors' damage awards were strongly influenced by plaintiffs' suggested damage awards. Plaintiffs' suggested award to jurors serves as a potent anchor that jurors perceive as being representative of a reasonable award, despite there being no statistical basis for their judgments.

Hindsight Bias. We've all heard the axiom that "hindsight is 20-20." As it implies, the hindsight bias refers to people overestimating the predictability of past events (Fischoff, 1982). Although the hindsight bias is observed in juror decision making across criminal and civil cases it is particularly relevant to jurors' judgments in professional malpractice cases (e.g., medical malpractice). Jurors judging whether a physician was negligent start with the knowledge that there was already a bad outcome for the plaintiff. Working backward from a patient's bad outcome, jurors can easily find something to criticize about a physician's conduct. Despite instructions from the court that jurors are not permitted to judge a doctor's care and treatment in hindsight, research indicates that this remedial step in the courts is not sufficient to neutralize the effects of the hindsight bias (Harley, Carlsen, & Loftus, 2004).

Expectations. The knowledge and life experiences that jurors bring with them shapes their expectations regarding what they will hear and see during a trial. Jurors' expectations also are determined, to a large extent, by their exposure to the media (Greene, 1990). A review of the research (Lieberman & Arndt, 2000) indicates that it is extremely difficult to overcome the biasing effects of pretrial publicity on jurors' verdicts. The effects of the media on jurors' expectations are not limited to pretrial publicity.

The very popular television program *CSI* has been blamed for elevating jurors' expectations regarding the value of evidential currency (Shelton, Kim, & Barak, 2007). Although it has become known as the "CSI effect," jurors' expectations for increasingly technological evidentiary proof can be traced to the emergence of all forensic science programs like *CSI* (e.g., *Bones, Cold Case, Numb3rs*). Technology not only influences jurors expectations for sophisticated evidence in courtrooms, jurors also rely on it (e.g., iPhone, Blackberrys) to conduct their own research prompting a number of mistrials (Schwartz, 2009).

SUMMARY

Contrary to the popular notion that trial consultants select which jurors would be predisposed to favor a litigant's case, trial consultants are focused on which jurors would harbor a bias against a particular party. Over the past four decades, there has been a dramatic decrease in the number of cases that go to trial, while there has been an even more dramatic increase in the number of attorneys. As a result, many attorneys lack experience in deciding which jurors to strike from a jury pool. Moreover, research indicates that attorneys' accuracy in identifying jurors with a bias against a litigant is not better than if they based their decisions on the flip of a coin—50/50.

Voir dire is an opportunity for the court and attorneys to ask jurors questions designed to determine if they are unfairly biased against a litigant. SJS is a research methodology employed by trial consultants to identify the attitudes and experiences of jurors that might prevent them from being fair and impartial triers of fact. Critics of SJS have leveled the lion's share of their arguments against research evidence that jurors' demographic factors are not reliable and robust predictors of their verdict preferences. Trial consultants have long known that jurors' demographic profiles are unreliable indices of their verdict preferences, and focus their empirical efforts toward revealing jurors' attitudinal and experiential profiles for determining which jurors to strike from a venire.

Although there is a dearth of research testing the effectiveness of trial consultants in striking a jury, there is evidence that trial consultants' decisions regarding which jurors to strike results in fewer death sentences in capital cases. Trial consultants bring a wealth of knowledge in social science, including research methodology, as well as the research literature regarding human information processing, persuasion, and small-group decision making. Their rich history of being in the litigation trenches in the courtroom is an invaluable resource for attorneys who lack insight into identifying jurors who are likely to be unfairly biased against a litigant's position.

REFERENCES

Batson v. Kentucky, 476 U.S. 79. (1986).

Berlo, D. (1960). *The process of communication.* New York: Holt, Rinehart, & Winston.

Bornstein, B. H. (1994). David, Goliath, and Reverend Bayes: Prior beliefs about defendants' status in personal injury cases. *Applied Cognitive Psychology, 8,* 233–258.

Bornstein, B.H. (1998). From compassion to compensation: The effect of injury severity on mock jurors' liability judgments. *Journal of Applied Social Psychology, 28,* 1477–1502.

Brodsky, S.L. (2006). Ingratiation in the courtroom and in the voir dire process: When more is not better. *Law & Psychology Review, 30,* 103–117.

Carson, C.N. (2000). *The U.S. legal profession in 2000. The lawyer statistical report.* Chicago: American Bar Foundation.

Chaiken, S. (1986). The heuristic model of persuasion. In M.P. Zanna, J.M. Olson, & C.P. Herman (Eds.), *Social influence: The Ontario symposium* (Vol. 5, pp. 3–39). Hillsdale, NJ: Erlbaum.

Cohen, T.H. (2005). *Punitive damage awards in large counties, 2001. Bureau of Justice Statistics: Selected findings. Bureau of statistics: Special report.* Washington, DC: U.S. Department of Justice.

Cohen, T.H., & Hughes, K.A. (2007). *Medical malpractice insurance claims in seven states, 2000–2004. Bureau of statistics: Special report.* Washington, DC: U.S. Department of Justice.

deTurck, M.A. (1991). Training observers to detect deception: Effects of gender. *Communication Reports, 4,* 79–89.

deTurck, M.A., Feeley, T.H., & Roman, L.A. (1997). Vocal and visual cue training in behavioral lie detection. *Communication Research Reports, 14,* 249–259.

deTurck, M.A., Texter, L.A., & Harszlak, J.J. (1989). Effects of information processing objectives on judgments of deception following perjury. *Communication Research, 16,* 434–452.

deTurck, M.A., Harszlak, J.J., Bodhorn, D.J., & Texter, L.A. (1990). The effects of training social perceivers to detect deception from behavioral cues. *Communication Quarterly, 38,* 1–11.

deTurck, M.A., & Miller, G.R. (1985). Deception and arousal: The behavioral correlates of deception. *Human Communication Research, 12,* 181–201.

deTurck, M.A., & Miller, G.R. (1990). Training observers to detect deception: Effects of self-monitoring and rehearsal. *Human Communication Research, 16,* 603–620.

deTurck, M.A., & Steele, M.E. (1988). Once a liar, always a liar: Effects if individuating information on the utilization of base-rates in deceptive attributions. *Communication Reports, 1*, 59–67.

Dimitrius, J., & Mazzarella, M.C. (1999). *Reading people: How to understand people and predict their behavior anytime anyplace.* New York: Ballantine.

Edmonson v. Leesville Concrete Company. 500 U.S. 614. (1991).

Feeley, T.H., & deTurck, M.A. (1995). Global cue usage in behavioral lie detection. *Communication Quarterly, 43*, 420–430.

Fischoff, B. (1982). For those condemned to study the past: Heuristics and biases in hindsight. In D. Kahneman, P. Slovic, & A. Tversky (Eds.), *Judgment under uncertainty: Heuristics and biases* (pp. 335–354). Cambridge: Cambridge University Press.

Galanter, M. (1983). Reading the landscape of disputes: What we know and don't know (and think we know) about our allegedly contentious and litigious society. *UCLA Law Review, 31*, 4–71.

Galanter, M. (2004). The vanishing trial: An examination of trials and related matters in federal court. *Journal of Empirical Legal Studies, 1*, 459–570.

Goodman, J., Loftus, E. F., & Greene, E. L. (1990). Matters of money: Voir dire in civil cases. *Forensic Reports, 3*, 303–329.

Greene, E. (1990). Media effects on jurors. *Law and Human Behavior, 14*, 439–450.

Greene, E., & Bornstein, B. (2000) Precious little guidance: Jury instruction on damage awards *Public Policy and Law, 6*, 743–768.

Greene, E., & Bornstein, B. H. (2003). *Determining damages: The psychology of jury awards.* Washington, DC: American Psychological Association.

Greene, E., Johns, M., & Smith, A. (2001). The effects of defendant conduct on jury damage awards. In R.P. Ogloff (Ed.), *Journal of applied psychology of the field* (pp. 225–284). New York: Kluwer Academic Press.

Hammerstein, T. (2002). *Stealth juror: The ultimate defense against bad laws and government tyranny.* Boulder, CO: Paladin Press.

Hannaford-Agor, P.L., & Waters, N.L. (2004). *Examining voir dire in California.* Final report presented to Judicial Council of California, San Francisco.

Hans, V. P., & Ermann, M. D. (1989). Responses to corporate versus individual wrongdoing. *Law and Human Behavior, 13*, 151–166.

Hans, V.P., & Lofquist, W.S. (1994). Perceptions of civil justice: The litigation crisis attitudes of jurors. *Behavioral Sciences & The Law 12*, 181–196.

Harley, E.M., Carlsen, K.A., & Loftus, G.R. (2004). The "Saw-It-All-Along" effect: Demonstrations of visual hindsight bias. *Journal of Experimental Psychology: Learning, Memory, and Cognition, 30*, 960–968.

Hastie, R., Penrod, S., & Pennington, N. (1983). *Inside the jury.* Cambridge, MA: Harvard University Press

Hastie, R., Schkade, D., & Payne, J. (1998). A study of juror and jury judgments in civil cases: Deciding liability for punitive damages. *Law and Human Behavior, 22*, 287–314.

Hastie, R., Schkade, D.A., & Payne, J.W. (1999). Juror judgments in civil cases: Hindsight effects in judgments of liability. *Law and Human Behavior, 22*, 597–614.

Herbsleb, J.D., Sales, B.D., & Berman, J.J. (1979). When psychologists aid in voir dire: Legal and ethical considerations. In L.E. Abt & I.R. Stuart (Eds.), *Social psychology and discretionary law* (pp. 197–217). New York: Van Nostrand Reinhold.

J.E.B. v. Alabama ex rel. T.B., 114 S. Ct. 1419, 62 U.S.L.W. 4219. (1994).

Johnson, C., & Haney, C. (1994). Felony voir dire: An exploratory study of its content and effect. *Law and Human Behavior, 18,* 487–506.

Jones, S.E. (1987). Judge- versus attorney-conducted voir dire: An empirical investigation in juror candor. *Law and Human Behavior, 11,* 131–146.

Kahneman, D., Slovic, P., & Tversky, A. (Eds.). (1982). *Judgment under uncertainty: Heuristics and biases.* Cambridge: Cambridge University Press.

Kassin, S.M., & Juhnke, R. (1983). Juror experience and decision making. *Journal of Personality and Social Psychology, 44,* 1182–1191.

Kerr, N.L., Kramer, G.P., Carroll, J.S., & Alfini, J.J. (1991). On the effectiveness of voir dire in criminal cases with prejudicial and pretrial publicity: An empirical study. *American University Law, 40,* 665–701.

Kramer, G.P., & Koenig, D.M. (1989). Do jurors understand criminal jury instructions? Analyzing the results of the Michigan juror comprehension project. *University of Michigan Journal of Law Reform, 23,* 401–437.

Kraus, S.J. (1995). Attitudes and the prediction of behavior: A meta-analysis of the empirical literature. *Personality and Social Psychology Bulletin, 21,* 58–75.

Kressel, N.J., & Kressel, D.F. (2002). *Stack and sway: The new science of jury consulting.* Boulder, CO: Westview Press.

LaFountain, R., Schauffler, R., Strickland, S., Raftery, W., & Bromage, C. (2007). *Examining the work of state courts, 2006. A national perspective from the court statistics project.* National Center for State Courts, Williamsburg, VA.

Langton, L., & Cohen, T.H. (2008). *Civil bench and jury trials in state courts, 2005. Bureau of statistics: Special report.* Washington, DC: U.S. Department of Justice.

LeVan, E.A. (1984). Nonverbal communication in the courtroom: Attorney beware. *Law and Psychology Review, 8,* 83–104.

Liebeck v. McDonald's Restaurants, P.T.S, Inc. No. D–202 CV-93-02419, 1995 WL 360309.

Lieberman, J., & Arndt, J. (2000). Understanding the limits of limiting instructions: Social psychological explanations for the failures of instructions to disregard pretrial publicity and other inadmissible evidence. *Psychology, Public Policy, and the Law, 6,* 677–711.

MacCoun, R. (1996). Differential treatment of corporate defendants by juries: An examination of the "deep-pockets" hypothesis. *Law & Society Review, 30,* 121–162.

Middendorf, K., & Luginbuhl, J. (1995). The value of a nondirective voir dire style in jury selection. *Criminal Justice and Behavior, 22,* 129–151.

Miller, G.R., deTurck M.A., & Kalbfleisch, P.J. (1983). Self-monitoring, rehearsal, and deceptive communication. *Human Communication Research, 10*(1), 97–117.

Mize, G.E. (1999). On better jury selection—Spotting the UFO jurors before they enter the courtroom. *Court Review Magazine, 31,* 10–15.

Mize, G.E. (2003). Be cautious of the quiet ones. *Voir Dire, 10,* 1–4.

Moran, G., & Comfort, J.C. (1982). Scientific jury selection: Sex as a moderator of demographic and personality predictors of impaneled felony jury behavior. *Journal of Personality and Social Psychology, 43,* 1052–1063.

Moran, G., Cutler, B.L., & Loftus, E.F. (1990). Jury selection in major controlled substance trials: The need for extended voir dire. *Forensic Reports, 3,* 331–348.

Nietzel, M.T., & Dillehay, R.C. (1986). *Psychological consultation in the courtrooms.* New York: Pergamon.

Nietzel, M.T., Dillehay, R.C., & Himelein, M.J. (1987). Effects of voir dire variations in capital trials: A replication and extension. *Behavioral Sciences & the Law, 5,* 467–477.

Olczak, P.V., Kaplan, M.F., & Penrod, S. (1991). Attorney's lay psychology and its effectiveness in selecting jurors: Three empirical studies. *Journal of Social Behavior and Personality, 6,* 431–452.

Ostrom, B.J., Strickland, S., & Hannaford, P. (2004). Examining trial court trends in state courts: 1976–2002. *Journal of Empirical Legal Studies, 1,* 755–782.

Presley v. Georgia. (2010). U.S. 558: 09-5270

Reifman, A., Gusick, S.M., & Elsworth, P.C. (1992). Real jurors understanding of the law in "real cases." *Law and Human Behavior, 16,* 539–554.

Reinard, J.C., & Arsenault, D.J. (2000). The impact of forms of strategic and non-strategic voir dire questions on jury verdicts. *Communication Monographs, 67,* 159–177.

Richards, R.D., & Calvert, C. (2008). The 2008 federal obscenity conviction of Paul Little and what it reveals about obscenity law and prosecutions. *Vanderbilt Journal of Entertainment & Technology, 11,* 543–595.

Saks, M.J., & Kidd, R.F. (1980). Human information processing and adjudication: Trial by heuristics. *Law and Society Review, 15, 123–160.*

Schwartz, J. (2009, March 17). As jurors turn to web, mistrials are popping up. *New York Times,* p. A1.

Seltzer R., Venuti, M.A., & Lopes, G.M. (1991). Juror honesty during the voir dire. *Journal of Criminal Justice, 19,* 451–462.

Shaver, K.G. (1970). Defensive attribution: Effects of severity and relevance on the responsibility assigned for an accident. *Journal of Personality and Social Psychology, 14,* 101–113.

Shaver, K.G. (1985). *The attribution of blame: Causality, responsibility, and blameworthiness.* New York: Springer-Verlag.

Shedler, J., & Manis, M. (1986). Can the availability heuristic explain the vividness effect? *Journal of Personality and Social Psychology, 51,* 26–36.

Shelton, D.E., Kim, Y.S., & Barak, G. (2007). The study of juror expectations and demands concerning scientific evidence: Does the "CSI Effect" exist? *Vanderbilt Journal of Entertainment & Technology, 9,* 331–368.

Slovic, P., Fischoff, B., & Lichtenstein, S. (1982). Facts versus fears: Understanding perceived risk. In D. Kahneman, P. Slovic, & A. Tversky (Eds.), *Judg-*

ment under uncertainty: Heuristics and biases (pp. 463–489). Cambridge: Cambridge University Press.

Spencer, B.D. (2007). Estimating the accuracy of jury verdicts. *Journal of Empirical Legal Studies, 4,* 305–329.

Stolle, D.P., Robbenolt, J.K., & Weiner, R.L. (1996). The perceived fairness of the psychologist trial consultant: An empirical investigation. *Law and Psychology Review, 20,* 139–177.

Strier, F. (1999). Whither trial consulting? Issues and projections. *Law and Human Behavior, 23,* 93–115.

Viscusi, W.K. (2000). *Jurors, judges, and the mistreatment of risk by the courts.* Harvard Law School John M. Olin Center for Law, Economics and Business Discussion Paper Series.

Walster, E. (1966). Assignment of responsibility for an accident. *Journal of Personality and Social Psychology, 3,* 73–79.

Wissler, R.L., Hart, A.J., & Saks, M.J. (1999). Decision making about general damages: A comparison of jurors, judges, and lawyers. *Michigan Law Review, 98,* 1751–1826.

Zuckerman, M., DePaulo, B.M., & Rosenthal, R. (1981). Verbal and nonverbal communication of deception. In L. Berkowitz (Ed.), *Advances in experimental social psychology* (Vol. 14, pp. 1–59). New York: Academic Press.

2

Factors Influencing
Jury Decision Making
Before the Trial Starts

Ann Burnett

Consider the following case: A Lutheran pastor (we'll call him Pastor John) engaged in several illicit affairs with women parishioners over a period of 7 years. After one of the women reported her affair with him, Pastor John resigned. Shortly thereafter, a second woman (we'll call her Frances) reported an affair with the pastor, and filed a lawsuit against him for sexual exploitation. She also sued the local church and the synod (an organization comprised of many churches) of which he was a part, claiming they should have known about the incident and stopped him. All attempts to settle this lawsuit failed, and the case went to trial before a jury.

If you were Frances, what type of jury would you prefer? Do you think women would be more sympathetic to your case? And what about Pastor John, who argued that the affair was mutual and that no sexual exploitation had taken place? Do juror attitudes about marriage make a difference in terms of which jurors to select? Should the church and synod be concerned about juror attitudes about organized religion? The answer to these questions is, yes, that many factors play a role in jury decision making. I had the opportunity to work with the attorneys for the pastor, church, and synod in this case (they worked together, creating a unified front). Throughout this chapter, I refer to this case and other cases to illustrate how important a variety of factors are in determining a jury verdict. I begin by discussing methods of traditional jury selection and scientific jury selection (SJS; the process in which juries are selected is a French term, *voir dire*). Then, I examine literature about jury characteristics in the areas of demographics, persuasibility, and nonverbal cues, which will provide insight into how attorneys and social scientists can use this information to select effective juries.

TRADITIONAL JURY SELECTION

For some attorneys, jury selection is based on hunches, stereotypes, and intuition (Kovera, Dickinson, & Cutler, 2003; Matlon, 1988). According to Fulero and Penrod (1990), folklore on how to select a jury comes from anecdotes published in legal literature, workshops, and word of mouth. Here are some of the more interesting stereotypes that attorneys have relied on. Clarence Darrow (a famous lawyer in the early 20th century, best known for his work in the Scopes trial and for defending Leopold and Loeb) contended that the Irish are emotional and sympathetic, Presbyterians are cold as ice, wealthy men tend to convict, and female jurors should put any attorney on edge (Matlon, 1988). I worked with one attorney who tended to select "happy jurors" because he felt he could be more persuasive with people who had good attitudes. Naturally, some attorneys desire a more scientific way to analyze their jury pools because they realize that decisions based on hunch are not always very accurate; some have even turned to SJS.

SCIENTIFIC JURY SELECTION

In 1972, a group called the Harrisburg Seven was indicted on a number of charges involving anti-war activities. The government selected Harrisburg, Pennsylvania for the trial because it was known to be a conservative area, and there had been raids on draft boards in Pennsylvania. The defense attorneys hired social scientists to assist with jury selection, and for the first recorded time in U.S. history, led by Jay Schulman, volunteers collected demographic data from nearly 1,000 individuals via telephone survey (Kovera et al., 2003; Schulman, Shaver, Colman, Emrich, & Christie, 1973). After additional in-depth, face-to-face interviews, the team of scientists developed a profile of the ideal juror for their case. They wanted young, Black jurors, and they sought people who were opposed to authority (Schulman et al., 1973). Eventually, the case ended in a mistrial, and the government did not pursue another trial. Although there is no clear-cut way to prove that the social scientists' surveys and assistance with jury selection made a difference in the verdict, it stands to reason that jurors who were young and liberal and who were not happy with the war in Vietnam would be more open to listening to the defense issues in this case. In specific cases such as the Harrisburg Seven, demographic information, personality studies, and attitude assessments *could* make a difference in a trial, despite mixed results regarding the utility of these measures (Kovera et al., 2003).

Since 1972, social scientists have been increasingly involved in jury selection, especially in important trials. Although science may or may not play an effective role in jury selection, scientists might be helpful in determining what types of arguments jurors find convincing or not convincing (Diamond, 1990). In my trial consulting business, I often run focus groups prior to jury trials to see how lay citizens respond to a variety of trial issues. More often than not, the attorneys and I gain an inkling as to the type of juror we want, but we learn a great deal more about argument choices. In fact, often in jury focus groups, the lay citizens give us ideas for case themes that we use at trial.

Scientists also use surveys to assist attorneys with change of venue motions (requesting the trial be moved to another place due to pretrial publicity or other prejudicial factors). I had the opportunity to work on a change of venue motion in a case involving a university hockey team and difficulties with the ice in its arena. The people who live in the town and who are affiliated in any way with this university are extremely devoted hockey and university fans. Our fear was that the strong emotion about hockey, the team, and the university would bias individuals against the contractor who designed the arena, especially because the contractor was not from the same city or state. A random survey of potential jurors in the community confirmed our suspicions, revealing that the fervor for hockey and the university was prevalent in about 80% of the survey respondents who expressed the sentiment that any problems associated with the hockey rink must be the fault of the outside contractor. Although the change of venue motion never came before a judge, the strength of the argument made as a result of these surveys persuaded both sides to settle the case before it went to trial.

These examples, in which focus groups and surveys were used prior to trial, demonstrate the value of SJS. However, most cases do not warrant SJS either because of financial or logistical constraints. Even if attorneys do not choose to hire experts to assist with *voir dire*, it behooves them to be aware of the literature about various juror characteristics so that if they use more traditional methods of jury selection, they make decisions based on more than intuition.

DEMOGRAPHIC DATA

In traditional jury selection, we have learned that attorneys sometimes use demographic information as folklore to choose juries, and in SJS, attorneys and trial consultants use demographic information as a guide to making their decisions. It is not clear whether or not reliance on demographic information is helpful; some scholars say it is not (Mills & Bohannon, 1980; Simon, 1980), whereas others say it could be helpful, especially in particular cases (Frederick, 1978). In this section of the chapter, I describe different demographics on which attorneys have relied in *voir dire* and that social scientists have analyzed in preparation for jury selection. In summary, after reading this section, it will be apparent that reliance on piecemeal information or stereotype is not helpful, but demographic data can be useful in specific cases, especially when examined with other factors.

Age

Folklore varies on the optimum juror age. One version suggests that younger people are more likely to favor the plaintiff, and another version suggests the opposite (Matlon, 1988; Simon, 1980). Do older people relate more to defendants in civil cases because they can relate to the pain, or do they not sympathize as well because subjectively they feel the plaintiff has not experienced real pain? There is more agreement among researchers that guilty verdicts increase with age (Mills & Bohannon, 1980), and older people award lower civil settlements (Matlon, 1988). As a trial consultant for defendants, I am less likely to select older people (who I arbitrarily define as over 65 years of age) because in criminal cases they may be more rule-bound and more likely to find the defendant guilty, and in civil cases they may be less likely to award large damages. However, if I am working for the prosecution in a criminal case or the plaintiff in a civil case, I am more likely to recommend selecting older individuals.

Sex

As with age, folklore about male and female jurors abounds. For example, are female jurors more sympathetic? Are male jurors more likely to favor an attractive female defendant and vice versa (Simon, 1980)? In fact, it appears that female jurors are more likely to initially believe in a defendant's guilt, although there are no significant differences in verdict based on gender, except that females are more conviction-prone in rape cases (Matlon, 1988). In general, if there are differences in verdict between male and female jurors, those differences are not clear (Frederickson, 1978; Simon, 1980).

Race

Race may make a difference in a trial. For example, a juror is more likely to judge individuals of his or her race more favorably (Matlon, 1988). Juror race also might affect deliberations. According to a recent study (Sommers, 2006), heterogeneous groups (those with White and Black jurors) deliberate longer. Additionally, in those heterogeneous juries, White jurors raised more facts, made fewer errors, and were more open to discussion than they were in homogeneous groups (all-White). Therefore, Sommers (2006) argued, racial diversity contributes to the deliberation process.

Education

Results regarding the effect of education on a jury also are mixed. Some researchers say that as the level of education increases, acquittals increase as well (Mills & Bohannon, 1978), whereas others say the opposite (Matlon, 1988). I tend to select more educated jurors as the complexity of the case increases, and I select less educated jurors if the emotional impact of the case is more salient.

A few years ago, I assisted attorneys with a case in which a farmer had been accused of setting up sham farms in order to collect Farm Service Agency benefits. The case was extremely complex, with testimony about various agencies, land purchases, and crop insurance payments. In a mock trial, we found that higher educated jurors were better able to follow the defense's arguments and to put more emphasis on instructions and the law.

Back to Pastor John's case. There are some clear laws about the role of pastors regarding personal relationships with congregants, and a more educated person could be more likely than a less educated person to analyze and appropriately apply the letter of the law. However, in Pastor

John's case, because Frances apparently had been a willing partner in the affair over several years, there was evidence to support the view that the sexual relationship was a mutually consensual one. Another consideration was the fact that Frances' husband also was a well-known professor at the local university. In light of these circumstances, the team of attorneys and I concluded that individuals with less education might be less likely to recognize the complications inherent in this relationship than individuals with more education and also would be less likely to sympathize with the husband as professor. Thus, we attempted to select jurors with a high school education or less.

Religion

Clarence Darrow, mentioned earlier, relied on Catholics and Presbyterians rather than Baptists and Methodists, supposedly because they were more likely to prosecute. He felt that Jews were more lenient (Simon, 1980). How accurate was Darrow? Most social scientists put little stock in his recommendations (Matlon, 1988; Simon, 1980). However, in some cases, religion or religious belief can be pivotal. Religion was a key factor in the Pastor John case. We were most comfortable with those who practiced no religion at all because they would be less likely to perceive a mutual affair as breaking the sanctity of the pastor–parishioner bond, and we attempted to remove the jurors who appeared passionate about their religious faith for the same reasons.

Socioeconomic Status

Social scientists have found that individuals relate more to those with similar socioeconomic status (SES; Matlon, 1988). Therefore, it might prove difficult for a person of lower SES to award large damages in a civil case. Correspondingly, jurors with a higher SES might be more willing to award large damages, but also might be less sympathetic to the plaintiff (Matlon, 1988). Perhaps more interesting are some recent findings that those of higher SES appear to be the most influential in jury deliberations (York & Cornwell, 2006). Jurors perceive those with higher SES to be more competent and to possess greater skill at deliberation than other jurors. Therefore, when attorneys are selecting jurors, they must consider who might emerge as leaders, and select those with higher socioeconomic backgrounds who also possess other favorable demographic traits. In other words, if an attorney seeks young, female jurors, then one who also has higher SES would be an excellent selection, whereas an older male individual with higher SES might be a poor choice.

Occupation

Perhaps most predictive of all demographic characteristics is a juror's occupation (Matlon, 1988), a factor that often is used as a means of selecting juries (Simon, 1980). Generally, occupations involving detail and precision tend to go with jurors who are more likely to be pro-prosecution in criminal trials and pro-defense in civil trials. For example, engineers, military personnel, computer programmers, bankers, accountants, and farmers tend to fall into this group. Individuals in professions such as these follow rules and guidelines, so would more likely respond to prosecutors who desire to invoke the law against a defendant, and would support individuals who are being sued, particularly if they view the lawsuit as frivolous. These jurors are more likely to support harsh punishment for individuals who have been convicted and to award minimal damages in a lawsuit.

On the other hand, occupations involving opportunities for flexibility and interpretation tend to produce jurors who are more likely to be pro-defense in criminal trials and pro-plaintiff in civil trials. For example, artists, waiters and waitresses, blue collar workers, and entertainers tend to fall into this group. These jurors are more likely to understand what it is like to be oppressed, and they may view the law as grey versus black and white. As a result, they may sympathize with the defendant in a criminal case, and be more likely in a civil case to support the plaintiff's lawsuit.

Knowing a juror's occupation assists me and the attorneys for whom I work in a number of ways. First, combined with spouse/partner's occupation, it can reveal information about how the juror feels about finances, politics, religion, or authority. Second, combined with other demographic data, such as age or education, occupation can help create a composite picture of a prospective juror.

PERSUASIBILITY

In addition to demographic variables involved in understanding jurors prior to deliberation are several factors related to persuasibility, that is to say, factors that contribute to an attorney's success in attempting to convince a juror. Note that in many cases, demographic characteristics may work in conjunction with some of the persuasion variables, again demonstrating the importance of examining a variety of factors when selecting jurors.

Attitudes

All jurors bring attitudes, beliefs, and values into deliberation with them. These attitudes can prove helpful if they bolster an attorney's case, but they can be extremely harmful, sometimes to both sides of the case. To begin with, most potential jurors have attitudes about our judicial system. On the one hand, some individuals are proud of our judicial system and are confident that it does its best to promote just verdicts. On the other hand, others are skeptical of the law and the institutions that uphold it, believing that the system is inherently unfair. There are those who feel strongly that some people have criminal tendencies that deserve only punishment, whereas others believe in the possibility of rehabilitation. It is, therefore, essential for both attorneys to gain knowledge about potential jurors' attitudes, particularly regarding a tendency to convict, confidence in the judicial system, cynicism about criminal defense work, racial bias, beliefs about criminal behavior, and beliefs about social justice (Lecci & Myers, 2008). No matter the attitude, jurors can be predisposed toward certain verdicts because of the attitudes they bring into deliberation.

Attorneys can delve into these issues in several ways. First, if the attorney so chooses, a trial consultant/social scientist can create a pretrial questionnaire to tap into various attitudes. In most jurisdictions, potential jurors routinely fill out brief questionnaires, but only regarding basic demographic information, ability to understand English, and any constraints that might prevent them from being effective jurors. Although these questionnaires provide some fundamental information, they do not ask jurors about their attitudes regarding legal- or case-relevant material. Typically, however, judges are willing to send out supplemental questionnaires, as long as both sides have access to the information. In my experience, these questionnaires are invaluable sources of information about jurors' case-specific attitudes that can form a basis for further questions in *voir dire* and for informed decisions about which jurors to select.

The second way to learn about juror attitudes is to ask them in *voir dire*. In most circumstances, judges ask a series of closed-ended demographic and legal system-related questions, and then allow attorneys to ask their own questions. These opportunities offer attorneys an excellent way to ask open-ended questions that delve into juror attitudes. Several targeted, well-phrased questions can reveal useful information. However, socially unacceptable attitudes are hard to detect, as potential jurors, under the pressure of the courtroom and judge and wishing to appear socially acceptable, are reluctant to admit prejudice or dissatisfaction with the legal system, for example. Attorneys would be wise to ask questions about issues regarding sensitive attitudinal issues in an indirect manner so as to garner more honest responses.

Research into specific attitudes has not been extensive, but some areas have received a great deal of focus. First, as mentioned earlier, racial prejudice on the part of jurors can affect not only a juror's perspective, but can taint deliberation as well. Certainly attorneys have a right to ask potential jurors about racial prejudice they might have (Wyckoff, 1986). Yet, jurors may be reluctant to disclose such prejudice. In that case, indirect questions that relate to racial prejudice could be helpful, such as asking the jurors' opinions of the O.J. Simpson or Kobe Bryant cases.

In my trial consulting business, racial attitudes matter more than the demographic characteristic of race. I live in a homogeneous community of predominately White Scandinavians, and I have found it difficult for some defendants to have a jury of peers in terms of race. Not only is this a problem of not having a representative sample of potential jurors, but my surveys suggest that prejudice against individuals who are not White is alive and well. For example, in an appeal for a new trial in my community, a young Latino male argued that the jurors were not representative of his race. In fact, my analysis of the *voir dire* transcript revealed that a potential female juror described her hatred toward the Latino population because a Latino man had raped her sister. The entire jury pool heard her story, and even though that juror was not selected, I believe the prejudice voiced against the Latino population may have affected the remainder of the jury pool. In the end, my client was denied his appeal.

The second area of research focus has been on juror attitude about insanity. In fact, attitudes about the insanity defense are strongly held and may actually prevent jurors from following the judge's instructions (Eno Louden & Skeem, 2007; Skeem, Eno Louden, & Evans, 2004). Attorneys who are using this defense should assess these attitudes carefully, again through careful questioning so that jurors will be open about their reluctance to consider the insanity defense.

Another area of specific research on juror attitudes is in regard to the death penalty. In an analysis of 14 studies on juror attitudes about the death penalty, Allen, Mabry, and McKelton (1998) found that a favorable attitude toward the death penalty is related to an increased willingness to convict. As with other strong and potentially harmful attitudes, attorneys must be extremely careful when screening for jurors' attitudes toward the death penalty.

Personality

Juror personality may have an impact on deliberation. Some personality types can be particularly persuasive, whereas other personality types may be easily influenced by others. Research on juror personality has been most extensive in relation to the characteristic of authoritarianism (Frederick, 1978; Mitchell & Byrne, 1973; Narby, Cutler, & Moran, 1993). Authoritarian individuals tend to be conviction-prone; they may display hostility to "out-groups" such as persons of color, sex offenders, or non-Christians. They also tend only to respect authority of those with similar beliefs, and they are exceptionally rule-bound (Narby et al., 1993). As a result, such jurors may be attractive to prosecutors in criminal matters and defense attorneys in civil court. Criminal defense and plaintiff attorneys should be alert to assessing authoritarian personality types in jury selection so that these individuals can be deselected.

In a child sexual abuse trial that I studied, one of the jurors displayed some authoritarian personality traits during jury selection. He was outspoken about his beliefs in the legal system; his occupation was in bookkeeping, and he had strong Christian beliefs. He also was able to disguise his more strident beliefs and came across as a reasonable person; to discover his authoritarianism, the defense attorney should have spent more time questioning jurors in *voir dire*. According to the other jurors I interviewed post-trial, he was so insistent on finding the defendant guilty (and the jury did vote to convict) that even after the trial was finished, he researched the sentencing date and appeared in court to make sure the defendant received a harsh sentence. Had the defense attorney been more aware of the dangers of an authoritarian personality, he or she might have removed this juror.

Researchers have scrutinized several other personality factors. The locus of control may have an effect on jury verdicts; individuals with an internal locus of control (meaning they feel they have some control over what happens to them) tend to attribute more responsibility to the defendant in a criminal trial; in other words, internals might be better jurors for the prosecution (Frederick, 1978).

Extraversion also has been studied as a personality factor. It has been associated with being elected foreperson; in juries in which the foreperson is an extravert, deliberation lasts longer (than deliberation with non-extravert forepersons), and jurors perceive the foreperson as having a great deal of influence (Clark, Boccaccini, Caillouet, & Chaplin, 2007). If an extravert has other demographic or personality characteristics the attorney desires, then an extravert would be a wise juror choice as that person could be highly persuasive in deliberations. Additionally, extraversion, coupled with the personality trait of neuroticism, contributes to both male and female pro-death penalty jurors. Conscientiousness and openness to new experiences are more related to anti-death penalty dispositions (Robbers, 2006).

Participation Styles

The final factor potentially affecting persuasibility is juror participation style. Scholars have investigated juror participation style in two main areas: gender and education. Traditionally, research has suggested that men participate in juries more than women (Hastie, Penrod, & Pennington, 1983; Strodtbeck & Mann, 1956). More recent studies have revealed that jurors in male-dominated juries tend to focus on the positions held by men, and jurors in female-dominated juries tend to focus on the women's positions (Hyme, Foley, & Pigott, 1999). Additionally, jurors in female-dominated panels appear to be more confident of their decisions than jurors in male-dominated panels. Further research indicates that gender differences occur because male jurors tend to sit at the head of the table during deliberations and jurors often select a male more often than a female foreperson. These differences also occur because men are perceived as having higher status than women and therefore tend to participate more in discussions, are perceived as being more persuasive with the minority, and are more liable to establish power relations in the jury room (Grossman, 1994).

Another area of participation style that has garnered attention is the notion that level of education and social status are related to participation in deliberation (Mills & Bohannon, 1980). A recent study suggested that jurors who display knowledge, self-confidence, and civic engagement tend to speak the loudest and with the most force in deliberation (Gastil, Burkhalter, & Black, 2007). As with the extraversion personality style, if a juror has a level of education that would befit the case, as well as other favorable characteristics, an attorney should keep this person in mind as a possible jury foreperson who could help persuade the jury on his or her behalf.

NONVERBAL CUES

During the *voir dire* process, attorneys have a chance to observe the nonverbal behaviors of the potential jurors. Some attorneys heavily rely on their observations of facial expressions, eye contact, and body movement, whereas others believe that there is no direct link between the nonverbal behavior and its meaning (Matlon, 1988). Certainly caution is in order; attorneys should avoid analyzing nonverbal cues in isolation. For example, some jurors dress up when called to jury duty. In a child sexual abuse case I worked on, the juror who ended up being the foreperson dressed up every day of the trial so that he would stand out to the other jurors as being a leader. In post-trial interviews, the others jurors noted that they elected him because of his appearance. Other jurors use jury duty as a good reason to not dress up. I do not use this as a reason to *not* take the juror seriously, but rather look at other nonverbal cues such as eye contact and facial expressions to get a more complete perception of the juror. In other words, clothing could indicate a juror's predisposition, but it should be analyzed with other information (Suggs & Sales, 1978; Tate, Hawrish, & Clark, 1974).

I have used a variety of nonverbal behaviors to assist my decision making during jury selection. For example, during jury selection in a different child sexual abuse case one of the jurors looked nervous and upset during *voir dire*. When it came time to question her, she asked to be questioned alone in the judge's chambers. As it turned out, she had experienced abuse, and the subject matter of this trial had upset her; she was released from service. Although this is an obvious example, and she ultimately got to verbalize her concerns, an observant attorney or trial consultant should be able to observe nonverbal cues such as hers to make wise selections during *voir dire*. Other factors, such as nervousness and a lack of eye contact, what the juror brings to read, jewelry, and bumper stickers they report being on their cars can provide bits of information, coupled with their jury survey and what they say during *voir dire*.

SUMMARY

This chapter has reviewed a variety of factors that may be important in influencing jury decision making. Traditional forms of jury selection involve making hunches or guesses about what type of juror might be effective, whereas SJS might be helpful but is not practical for all cases, either financially or logistically. However, attorneys can make informed decisions about potential jurors by evaluating demographics, persuasibility, and nonverbal behaviors. Demographic characteristics, when not examined in isolation, might be helpful, especially in particular cases. Persuasibility factors, including attitudes, personality, and participation style can provide strong clues as to the "fit" of an individual on a jury. And nonverbal behaviors, when coupled with demographics and persuasibility, can alert attorneys to acceptable and unacceptable jurors.

Let us visit the Pastor John case once more. Ultimately, we searched for young, female jurors who were not actively involved in organized religion. We deselected jurors with strong, traditional attitudes about marriage and religion, tried to avoid any jurors with strong personalities, and hoped the female-dominated jury would reflect the viewpoint of the women on the jury, while allowing everyone to participate. In the end, the jury found the church and synod without responsibility, Pastor John 60% responsible for the sexual relations, and Frances bearing 40% of the responsibility. The attorneys for whom I worked were pleased they used a social scientist to conduct a pretrial focus group, administer pretrial jury surveys, and assist with *voir dire*. Chapter 5 discusses how combinations of individuals with these varied characteristics, personalities, and attitudes, can come together to make decisions such as this.

REFERENCES

Allen, M., Mabry, E., & McKelton, D. (1998). Impact of juror attitudes about the death penalty on juror evaluation of guilt and punishment: A meta-analysis. *Law and Human Behavior, 22,* 715–731.

Clark, J., Boccaccini, M.T., Caillouet, B., & Chaplin, W.F. (2007). Five-factor model personality traits, jury selection, and case outcomes in criminal and civil cases. *Criminal Justice and Behavior, 34,* 641–660.

Diamond, S.S. (1990). Scientific jury selection: What social scientists know and do not know. *Judicature, 73,* 178–183.

Eno Louden, J., & Skeem, J.L. (2007). Constructing insanity: Jurors' prototypes, attitudes, and legal decision-making. *Behavioral Sciences and the Law, 25,* 449–470.

Frederick, J.T. (1978). Jury behavior: A psychologist examines jury selection. *Ohio Northern University Law Review, 5,* 571–585.

Fulero, S.M., & Penrod, S.D. (1990). The myths and realities of attorney jury selection folklore and scientific jury selection: What works? *Ohio Northern University Law Review, 17,* 229–253.

Gastil, J., Burkhalter, S., & Black, L.W. (2007). Do juries deliberate? A study of deliberation, individual difference, and group member satisfaction at a municipal courthouse. *Small Group Research, 38,* 337–359.

Grossman, J. L. (1994). Women's jury service: Right of citizenship or privilege of difference? *Stanford Law Review, 46,* 1115–1160.

Hastie, R., Penrod, S.D., & Pennington, N. (1983). *Inside the jury.* Cambridge, MA: Harvard University Press.

Hyme, H.S., Foley, L.A., & Pigott, M.A. (1999). A comparison of male and female dominated juries in a case of coerced sex with a male plaintiff. *American Journal of Forensic Psychology, 17,* 67–80.

Kovera, M.B., Dickinson, J.J., & Cutler, B.L. (2003). Voir dire and jury selection. In A.M. Goldstein & I.B. Weiner (Eds.), *Handbook of psychology, vol. 11: Forensic psychology* (pp. 161–175). Hoboken, NJ: Wiley.

Lecci, L., & Myers, B. (2008). Individual differences in attitudes relevant to juror decision making: Development and validation of the pretrial juror attitudes questionnaire (PJAQ). *Journal of Applied Social Psychology, 38,* 2010–2038.

Matlon, R.J. (1988). *Communication in the legal process.* New York: Holt, Rinehart & Winston.

Mills, C.J., & Bohannon, W.E. (1980). Juror characteristics: To what extent are they related to jury verdicts? *Judicature, 64,* 22–31.

Mitchell, H.E., & Byrne, D. (1973). Effects of jurors' attitudes and authoritarianism on judicial decisions. *Journal of Personality and Social Psychology, 43,* 123–129.

Narby, D.J., Cutler, B.L., & Moran, G. (1993). A meta-analysis of the association between authoritarianism and jurors' perceptions of defendant culpability. *Journal of Applied Psychology, 78,* 34–42.

Robbers, M. (2006). Tough-mindedness and fair play: Personality traits as predictors of attitudes toward the death penalty—an exploratory study. *Punishment and Society, 8,* 203–222.

Schulman, J., Shaver, P., Colman, R., Emrich, B., & Christie, R. (1973, May). Recipe for a jury. *Psychology Today,* pp. 37–44.

Simon, R.J. (1980). *The jury: Its role in American society.* New York: Lexington Books.

Skeem, J., Eno Louden, J., & Evans, J. (2004). Venirepersons's attitudes toward the insanity defense: Developing, refining, and validating a scale. *Law and Human Behavior, 286,* 623–648.

Sommers, S.R. (2006). On racial diversity and group decision making: Identifying multiple effects of racial composition on jury deliberations. *Journal of Personality and Social Psychology, 90,* 597–612.

Strodtbeck, F.L., & Mann, R.D. (1956). Sex role differentiation in jury deliberations. *Sociometry, 19,* 3–11.

Suggs, D., & Sales, B.D. (1978). Using communication cues to evaluate prospective jurors during the voir dire. *Arizona Law Review, 20,* 629–642.

Tate, E., Hawrish, E., & Clark, S. (1974). Communication variables in jury selection. *Journal of Communication, 24,* 130–139.

Wyckoff, M. (1986). Sixth amendment—Right to inquire into jurors' racial prejudices. *The Journal of Criminal Law and Criminology, 77,* 713–742.

York, E., & Cornwell, B. (2006). Status on trial: Social characteristics and influence in the jury room. *Social Forces, 85,* 455–477.

3

Pretrial Publicity Research

Influences of Media Content and Stylistic Characteristics

Nadia Lepastourel
Benoît Testé

Law and the media are inevitably intertwined. Crime is definitely a central theme running though many forms of communication in society (Potter & Kappeler, 1998) and media play a role in the formation of public attitudes toward crimes and criminals. As relatively few people have direct experience with the justice system, public knowledge of the legal system (Hans, 1990) and public opinion about sentencing (Roberts & Doob, 1990) are largely drawn from the way they are presented by the media (Surette, 1998). Thus, an important body of research has been set up to investigate the media coverage of legal issues and the impact of the media on social attitudes and judgments. Studies on the impact of pretrial publicity (PTP) recognize the collision of two guarantees: the right of freedom for the press (in the United States, the First Constitutional Amendment; in Europe, Article 10 of the Convention on Human Rights) and the right to a fair trial for a defendant (in the United States, the Sixth Amendment; in Europe, Article 6 of the European Convention on Human Rights. See

Brandwood, 2000; Leclerc & Théolleyre, 1996, for discussions on tensions between these two rights in Western democratic countries). This conflict of media effects is crucial both to the defense and the prosecution. Several studies have been conducted to check the prejudicial effects of media coverage, often at the request of judge and/or lawyers. Two questions in this research area are whether the PTP will affect the opinion of a potential juror in a case and whether the PTP will affect his or her ultimate decision. Thus, guidelines for courts have been developed so as to determine whether publicity is too extensive. Research (see Daftary-Kapur, Dumas, & Penrod, 2010, for a recent review) also has examined some potential remedies to improve the problem. Thus, for example, voir dire usually attempts to find jurors with no knowledge of the case or its litigators. Changes of venue attempt to determine in what place the potential jurors will not be overly prejudicial. Classically, PTP research has focused on media's prejudicial information (i.e., informative content of media) independent of media form. Considering the distinction between information (i.e., semantic content) and writing style (e.g., syntactic form of newspaper articles), we assume that both should be considered when studying media influences (Gans, 2004). Therefore, this chapter proposes a review of research—press analyses and empirical studies—of the influence of media content and writing style on both the general perception of criminality and the specific judgments about the defendant. The chapter outlines various aspects of semantic and stylistic pretrial publicity that can affect the litigation process, and discusses how press analysis and experimental research in social psychology can inform attorneys' strategies.

IMPACT OF THE MEDIA'S INFORMATIONAL CONTENT

First, let us consider some classic PTP research on the effects of informational content on receivers' general perceptions of crime and more specific judgments about the defendant.

Perception of Delinquency and Criminality

Analyses of the media's coverage of crime and justice show that media content does not accurately reflect reality. First, journalists can be the victims of biased representations of reality and they can select to report certain social events and to ignore others. Thus, crime and law news are reported with more frequency than other social issues, such as health, education, and poverty (Simon, Fico, & Lacy, 1989). Massively, coverage of serious crime dominates news reports (e.g., Antunes & Huerley, 1978; Humphries, 1981). In a content analysis of news reports (Graber, 1980), murder accounted for 25% of crime stories, although it constituted less than 1% of all reported crimes. Several press analyses have shown that media significantly over-report crimes involving violence and sex (e.g., Ditton & Duffy, 1983; Potter & Kappeler, 1998). Finally, ethnic minorities are more often presented as perpetrators of crimes (Beaudoin & Thorson, 2005; Romer, Jamieson, & De Coteau, 1998; Surette, 1998). The findings of Dixon and Linz (2000) indicated that Blacks and Latinos (vs. Whites) were less likely to be portrayed as victims of crime on television news, and also that Blacks and Latinos were generally more likely to be portrayed as lawbreakers than as victims on television news, whereas the reverse is true for Whites.

Implicit in the research is the assumption that media coverage affects the public. As presented by Roberts and Doob (1990), the Canadian Sentencing Commission, in 1986, concluded that "the public . . . is forced to build its view of sentencing on a data-base which does not reflect reality" (pp. 95–96). Media effects on reality construction have been described in agenda-setting research (Edelstein, 1993; McCombs & Shaw, 1972). Agenda setting has grown out of the metaphor that the mass media do not tell you "what to think" but "what to think *about*" (Cohen, 1963, p. 13). In other words, "readers learn not only about a given issue, but learn also how much importance to attach to that issue from the amount of information and its position" (McCombs & Shaw, 1972, p. 176). Thus, the media select certain pieces of information and define the themes that are "worth" collective attention (Neveu, 2001).

Beyond this agenda component, an important body of evidence indicates that people's growing anxiety about crime is not commensurate with increases in crime itself. As Sheley and Ashkins (1981) point out, media crime reporting bears little resemblance to the presumed reality represented by police statistics. Among the first, Gerbner and Gross (1976) showed that heavy TV viewers inhabited a scarier world (i.e., perceived more crime) than light viewers. This pattern of results has been replicated many times in many areas, confirming a positive link between media overexposure of crimes and people's perception of crime (Valkenburg & Patiwael, 1998), fear of crime (Heath, 1984; Heath, Kavanaugh, & Thompson, 2001), and confidence in the police (Holland Baker, Nienstedt, Everett, & McCleary, 1983). In a broader perspective, studies report a positive correlation between media representations and public attitudes. Exposure to the media increases (a) the general perception of risk, (b) the perceived seriousness and pervasiveness of the exposed problem (e.g., weapons possession), and (c) the perceived need for government intervention (Tyler & Lomax Cook, 1984). Exposure to the mass media definitely affects one's perception of crime's dangers and one's personal fear of crime (for more general reviews, see Heath & Gilbert, 1996; Wood & Gannon, 2009). Moreover, recent developments in mass media such as crime reenactment TV programs, violence via cable TV, 24-hour news programs, and the Internet expose the public to more and more information about crime and law (e.g., Goodman-Delahunty & Tait, 2006; Heath & Gilbert, 1996). In this age of information technology, potential jurors are increasingly exposed to pretrial publicity, especially in the case of high-profile trials.

Influence of PTP on Attitudes Toward Defendants

An important aspect of media coverage is the way the accused is described. Among several major decisions in the 1960s, the Judicial Conference of the United States recommended that a lawyer involved in criminal litigation should not release information or opinions about the litigation if there is a likelihood that such a release will interfere with the equity of the trial ("Report of the Judicial Conference Committee," 1968, see Francke, 2001; Studebaker & Penrod, 1997). The American Bar Association (ABA, 2007) identified eight types of information that lawyers should not disseminate "by means of public communication" because of their potentially prejudicial impact:

1. The prior criminal record of the accused;

2. The character or reputation of the accused;

3. The existence of any confession, admission, or statement given by the accused (or the refusal to make a statement);

4. The performance of any examinations or tests (or the refusal to submit to an examination or test);

5. The possibility of a plea of guilty to the offense charged or to a lesser offense;

6. Any opinion as to guilt or innocence of the accused or as to the merits of the evidence in the case;

7. The possibility of a plea of guilty to the offense charged, or other disposition;

8. Information that the lawyer knows or has reason to believe would be inadmissible as evidence in a trial.

This list is largely composed of dispositional and/or categorical informations concerning the accused (first six categories). Therefore, studies examining the nature or content of PTP have typically focused on the prejudicial (i.e., anti-defendant) content. In a content analysis of 14 American newspapers, Imrich, Mullin, and Linz (1995) noted that 27% of the suspects described in crime stories are associated with at least one of the ABA categories. Tankard, Middleton, and Rimmer (1979) brought to light that 67.7% of pretrial articles contained at least one violation of ABA guidelines. The most frequently violated ABA categories were statements about the character, guilt or innocence of the accused (35% of the stories); opinions concerning evidence or arguments in the case (25%); and statements concerning the credibility or testimony of possible witnesses (24%). A similar finding has been reported in French newspapers (Testé, Dumas, Lepastourel, & Fernagut-Samson, 2007). Studies show no content difference between newspapers in states that had adopted voluntary press-bar guidelines and newspapers of states without guidelines.

The Fundamental Attribution Error (FAE; Ross, 1977) is another way to consider the defendant's description. The FAE describes the tendency to overvalue dispositional or personality-based explanations for the observed behaviors of others while undervaluing extenuating situations and circumstances. Some studies show that journalists use such dispositional explanations for crimes, and particularly if the accused is a member of an out-group (Menon, Morris, Chiu, & Hong, 1999). In a content analysis of press articles reporting a crime, Morris and Peng (1994) predicted that American reporters would make more attributions to personal dispositions of the murderer (i.e., a trait or characteristic the murderer possesses generally as an ingrained personality trait, value, or attitude; such as bad character or psychological problems) and Chinese reporters make more attributions to situational pressures (i.e., particular extenuating circumstances such as an emotional crisis, stress at the workplace, having been fired, etc.). Results confirmed this prediction. Authors also observed that American journalists made even more dispositional explanations when the accused was Chinese (i.e., a member of the out-group). This bias corresponds to the ultimate attribution error (Pettigrew, 1979)—people view negative acts committed by out-group members as a stable trait of the out-group, and view positive acts committed by out-group members as exceptional.

Empirical research on the influence of media coverage can be separated into two types—surveys of real cases and experimental studies.

Surveys have led to several conclusions concerning the influence of PTP on potential juror's attitudes toward a defendant. For one, a link has been established between level of exposure to media, recall of information on the case, and prejudicial prejudgment (e.g., Arbuthnot, Myers, & Leach, 2002; Costantini & King, 1980–1981). Conducting a phone survey on 130 potential jurors a week before the beginning of a heavily publicized murder trial, Simon and Eimermann (1971) reported that 79% of those surveyed had heard or read about the case, and that those who remembered details about the crime favored prosecution more than those who could not supply details. Moran and Cutler (1991) obtained similar results when comparing two separate criminal cases, one highly publicized and one poorly publicized. Once again, pretrial knowledge of the case (detailed vs. general awareness) was related to perceived guilt of the defendant. However, the correlation was weaker when people only had a general awareness of the case. This study showed also that the participants' knowledge of the case was not correlated with their reported ability to be impartial. Respondents seemed unconscious of the bias risk. Those who claimed they could ignore PTP influence did not judge the accused less guilty than people who had admitted they could not be impartial (Studebaker & Penrod, 1997). Nietzel and Dillehay (1983) provided some results on local news. In five murder trials, 90% of respondents in the venues' counties had heard or read about the crime compared with only 40% in other counties. The former were more likely to know details about the case, including inadmissible information. These surveys clearly suggest that pretrial publicity does influence the potential juror and that prejudicial attitude partly depends on learning of prejudicial content.

Another methodological approach to studying the link between pretrial publicity and jury decisions is based on jury simulations. Experimental studies have confirmed the prejudicial effect of some media information, in particular those of the ABA list (Fulero, 2002). Mention of a confession is the most prejudicial, but other information that influences judgments includes negative content about the defendant's character, inadmissible statements by a neighbor of the defendant, and a prior police record for the defendant, possibly among others (Otto, Penrod, & Dexter, 1994). Therefore, jurors' judgments are based on factual information (e.g., confession by the defendant, or mention of his prior record) but also on the jurors' personal attributions regarding the defendant's behavior or character. Both incline attributions to the defendant's dispositional characteristics rather than to situation or circumstances. Among the prejudicial information, Ogloff and Vidmar (1994) also made a distinction between factual information (e.g., prior record, legal rules) and emotional information (e.g., a weak childhood, a poor family). Emotional information on victims is highly prejudicial to the defendant (Kramer, Kerr, & Carroll, 1990; Voss & Van Dyke, 2001; Wilson & Bornstein, 1998). A meta-analysis by

Steblay, Besirevic, Fulero, and Jimenez-Lorente (1999), brought together 44 studies published between 1966 and 1997 (n = 5,755). It confirmed a link between media coverage and culpability judgments. Although the data indicated a small average effect size (r = .16), an important heterogeneity of effect sizes demanded that PTP effects be considered in the context of several moderators. Authors observed that PTP influence was more important when the subject pool is drawn from potential jurors (r = .30) rather than students (r = .08), when judgment on the accused was delayed (after more than 1 week, r = .36), when stimulus material was made of real pretrial publicity (r = .29) rather than fictitious (r = .12). Influence was also moderated by the type of crime (murder, r = .26; sexual abuse, r = .28, disorderly conduct, r = .08). Meta-analysis also confirmed that exposure to the trial reduced but did not eliminate PTP influence (pretrial, r = .28 vs. post-trial before deliberation, r = .10 and post-trial after deliberation r = .15). Finally, television impact (r = .16) was not much more important than newspapers (r = .15) but exposure to both media had an additive effect (r = .23). Two additional results were provided by this meta-analysis. First, PTP influence also appeared in civil cases (Bornstein, Whisehunt, Nemeth, & Dunaway, 2002). Second, media coverage of a specific case can influence verdicts of other cases, therefore becoming generalized (Greene & Loftus, 1984). According to Greene and Wade (1988), the consequences of "general" PTP are difficult to predict and can be more problematic than "specific" PTP (for more on general vs. specific PTP, see Mullin, Imrich, & Linz, 1996).

As concluded by Studebaker and Penrod (2005), "even though the presentation of PTP may not consist of explicit attempts to persuade the public to think in particular ways about a case or the parties in a case" (p. 21), it certainly seems to influence perception of crime and attitudes toward the defendant. Thus, two conclusions can be drawn. First, media information is massively predispositional and leads to more judgments of blame on the defendant than on the situation. Second, research confirms the existence of prejudicial content and its influence on culpability judgments. These studies generally have very practical aims. For instance, surveys determine if a change of venue would be necessary. Thus, lawyers must know if a prejudice against the defendant exists in the district where the prosecution is pending. Also, lawyers may use experiences in voir dire to educate jurors about the perils of PTP (Kovera & Greathouse, 2008). Thus, focusing explicitly on the informational content of media messages may have the consequence of neglecting the form of the discourse, which may also have had an influence on jurors, albeit more subtle. PTP must be considered more globally and the link between media content and form (Gans, 2004) is evident in the social psychology of communication.

Certainly, "form" can matter within a variety of media types (e.g., photos, videos, typography, etc.). Form characteristics in part depend on the channel or mode of delivery (TV, Internet, press). They also depend on the journalist's constraints (see Brooks, Kennedy, Moen, & Ranly, 2001). For example, time constraints might force a journalist to replace a detailed verbal description with a photo or video clip. Within the various aspects of form, certainly discourse style (written or oral) has been the most studied, presumably because it occurs in all media. The second part of this chapter discusses how forms of discourse, more specifically media "style" can have prejudicial effects on general perceptions of crime and on attitudes toward a defendant.

IMPACT OF MEDIA'S LANGUAGE STYLE

One issue addressed in this chapter is whether the style of a pretrial press article affects its prejudicial impact. Surprisingly, this important issue rarely has been investigated in a global manner. According to Higgins (1978), the lack of research could be due to "the extreme difficulty of defining and operationalizing style" (p. 665; see also Scherer, 1979, for a discussion on the complexity of definition of style). Sandell (1977) defines *style* as "a characteristic way of making non semantic linguistic choices" (p. 6) and most researchers have agreed on a distinction between semantic versus nonsemantic features (Blanchet & Mirabel-Sarron, 1997; van Dijk, 1988). In this chapter, we propose a review of some significant research focusing on the influence of stylistic characteristics. The approach often used in these studies combines sociolinguistic field observation (to identify linguistic forms that actually occur in a given context) with experimental manipulation and assessment (to determine the effects). As argued by Semin (2000), "language is a device by which aspects of reality or an idea are presented strategically in communication with a view to influencing or shaping the social cognitive processes of the recipient of a message" (p. 76). Semin (1995) considers language as a tool and considers linguistic devices (e.g., verbs and adjectives in his studies) as cognitive tools. Stapel and Semin (2007) argued that linguistic categories constitute features having general effects beyond the specific and descriptive meaning of each clue. They call this kind of stylistic effect a "meta-semantic" effect (Semin, 2000; Stapel & Semin, 2007). Such an idea also is emphasized by Erickson, Lind, Johnson, and O'Barr (1978). These authors considered that "the meaning of an utterance is more than its literal meaning" (p. 270). In other words, style does not have an explicit meaning per se but has an implicit meaning for the receivers.

Linguistic Clues and Perception of Delinquency and Criminality

The Linguistic Category Model (LCM; Semin & Fiedler, 1988) provides a useful starting point for research on language and cognitive process. The LCM distinguishes four different linguistic categories, organized on a concrete–abstract continuum. Toward most concrete are descriptive action verbs (DAVs; i.e., verbs that imply a physically invariant component; as in *to kick* implying a foot as the instrument), interpretative action verbs (IAVs; i.e., verbs that do not share a physically invariant instrument, and that also carry an evaluative component; as in *to aid* or *to destroy*), and state verbs (SVs; i.e., verbs that refer to either a cognitive state— e.g., *to remember, to comprehend*—or to an emotional state—e.g., *to love, to dislike*). Most abstract are adjectives (e.g., She is *kind*). At one end of the continuum, actions or events can be described in a relatively concrete, objective, nonevaluative and situation-specific manner by using DAVs. IAVs incorporate more of an evaluative/interpretive component but remain contextually bound. SVs represent actions in terms of relatively stable conditions not situationaly bound. SVs also tend to be more evaluative/interpretative in nature than the other categories. Finally, adjectives tend to be highly abstract, evaluative and situationaly free descriptions of the event. The first studies conducted on the LCM (Semin & Fiedler, 1988) showed that as sentences contain more abstract categories, readers evaluate the syntactic subject of the sentence as more informative and consider the external situation as less explanatory. Implicit causality in interpersonal verbs is a systematic finding in language and social cognition research (e.g., Burguet & Girard, 2008; De Poot & Semin, 1995; Platow & Brodie, 1999; Semin & De Poot, 1997; Semin, Rubini, & Fiedler, 1995).

Based on the LCM, the Linguistic Intergroup Bias (LIB) predicts that desirable in-group and undesirable out-group behaviors will be described in more abstract terms than undesirable in-group and desirable out-group behaviors (Maass, Salvi, Arcuri, & Semin, 1989). Maass, Corvino, and Arcuri (1994) showed that this trend can be found in naturally occurring mass communication. In a first study, they analyzed newspaper reports of an anti-Semitic episode that had occurred in Italy (during a basketball game between an Italian and an Israeli team, right-wing groups had exposed anti-Semitic banners). They observed that both Jewish and non-Jewish journalists described the neo-fascist attacks in clearly negative terms. However, they differed greatly in language abstraction. Non-Jewish journalists described the behavior of the aggressors in a more concrete way (96% vs. 75%), whereas Jewish journalists used more abstract formulations (25% vs. 4%). The authors specified that this difference was not attributable to a general difference of writing style, as the trend toward more abstract formulations did not appear in comments concerning the in-group. In another analysis of Italian TV news broadcasts, Maass et al. (1994) found that during the first Gulf War, the more negative the statements were about Iraq, the more abstract they tended to be. This correlation between abstraction and negativity did not appear in the descriptions of behavior of the in-group. The authors concluded that the way journalists used language in intergroup contexts was a powerful source of bias. Moreover, two elements indicated that the journalists were unconscious of this linguistic distortion: First, although they explicitly condemned the anti-Semitic act, their speeches were biased. Second a pro-Jewish communist newspaper used as much linguistic bias as a democratic Christian newspaper. Thus, these subtle variations of language would escape consciousness and control. Other research exploring the link between group identity, social cognition, and language, found that speakers shift from verb phrases to noun phrases (nominalization) when describing negative behavior of out-group members (Cole & Leets, 1998). The LCM and the LIB are well-known models that offer an integrative frame for analysis of discourse effects.

Other research has focused on the use and the implication of active versus passive voice in media's discourse. Bostian (1983) approaches two subjects. First, passive voice either eliminates the actor or places the actor at the end of the sentence, whereas active voice emphasizes the actor. Therefore, the use of passive or active sentences can influence attributions to the agent or the situation. Second, journalists use more verbs in the active voice. In an analysis of newspaper headlines referring to ethnic minorities in the Netherlands, Van Dijk (1988) found that minority groups had agency in only about 7% of the stories in which they appeared. Moreover, they tended to be presented as agents of negative acts. This finding is similar to those concerning the overrepresentation of ethnic minorities as responsible for crimes.

Linguistic Clues and Influence of PTP on Attitudes Toward Defendants

Studies have shown that linguistic clues may influence judgments toward a defendant. Schmid and Fiedler (1998) observed effects of implicit causality in a simulated courtroom setting. They studied attorneys' closing speeches based on the same evidence, comparing those for the defense with those for the prosecution. First, the language style of closing speeches was analyzed. It was observed that discourse during trials is, in general, less abstract than other discourse, because of the court's procedural norm of describing events. It was noted also that prosecution lawyers make more negative assertions about the defendant using more negative IAVs to induce negative dispositions about the accused, whereas defense attorneys supported negative intentional attributions to the victim using more negative IAVs and adjectives. In a second study, they investigated the judgments and guilt attributions of independent judges who were presented with the speeches. Severity of punishment is positively related to, among other things, two linguistic strategies. Considered within the LCM framework—use of the abstractness dimension to emphasize disposition or circumstances, and use of interpersonal SVs (vs. action verbs) to attribute lack of control or responsibility for the behavior. The conclusion was that subtle language strategies did have a noticeable effect on attributions of blame and guilt in a legal setting.

The impact of active versus passive voice has been investigated by Henley, Miller, and Beazley (1995) by examining this syntactic variable (verb voice) with reference to a semantic variable (verb topic) within the context of mass media and the phenomenon of violence against women (VAW). They supposed that the way people interpret a message depends, in part, on the verb voice used to phrase the message—active voice (e.g., "In the U.S. a man rapes a woman every 6 minutes") or passive voice (e.g., "In the U.S. a woman is raped by a man every 6 minutes"). First, a content analysis of newspaper items for verb characteristics was conducted. The data showed that the passive voice was the predominant construction for describing male sexual and nonsexual violence, whereas the active voice predominated for positive and neutral acts. Among 1,501 verbs coded for voice in news stories, sexual violence was written significantly more frequently in the passive rather than the active voice. A second study exploring the differences in frequency of usage of these 1,501 verbs revealed that the use of the passive voice increased with the extremism of the act. Finally, in a third study, they tested the effects of passive voice on reader perceptions. College students read mock news reports of violence directed specifically toward women (e.g., rape, spousal abuse) or more general violence toward men and women (e.g., battery, murder). They rated victim harm and perpetrator responsibility after each, and completed scales of attitudes toward sexual violence. Results revealed that both women and men showed more acceptance of VAW with passive voice. Moreover, men reading passive-voice passages attributed less victim harm and less perpetrator responsibility for VAW than when reading active voice passages. (For a general explication of the effect of voice on obscuring agency see Lamb & Keon, 1995). Finally, Henley et al. (1995) noted that selection of passive voice is not necessarily conscious.

Research by Lepastourel and Testé (2004, 2008, 2011) has been conducted with the explicit aim of extending the research on pretrial publicity (Studebaker & Penrod, 1997) by studying the influence of media style on reader judgments. A first study (Lepastourel & Testé, 2004) found that a pretrial article written in typical style (vs. atypical, typicality being determined by a discourse analysis of pretrial articles in the French press) leads to better recall of information and to more severe culpability judgments about the defendant. Style typicality also affected the credibility granted to the articles (Lepastourel & Testé, 2011). In another experimental study, Lepastourel and Testé (2008) investigated the effects of narrative syntactic characteristics of media communication. Narrative writing style has two main characteristics (e.g., Fayol, 1985; Kintsch & Van Dijk, 1975). It situates action in the past (e.g., tense of verbs) and insists on causal and temporal links (e.g., tense modalizations, relative pronouns, cause connectives). Forthcoming court cases are particularly favorable to a narrative writing style. In fact, temporality is essential to the understanding of facts, motivations of actions, and relationships between characters. Participants read a press article on a pending inquiry, either in a narrative or non-narrative syntactic style. Results indicated that the narrative style is perceived as easier to read and leads to more severe judgments of culpability.

In all these studies, authors assessed two things: the language tools that are spontaneously used by communicators from different perspectives and their impact on the receivers' attributions and judgments. Furthermore, although the cues via vocabulary or lexical choices can be consciously eliminated by a communicator, stylistic clues, being more "subtle," would not be as controllable (Bromberg & Trognon, 2005; Laver & Trudgill, 1979). Thus, these clues must be further considered by journalists on the one hand, and by legal professional on the other.

> The more knowledge we can accumulate about the effects that certain forms have on readers, the more empowered we will be as writers and readers ourselves to control these effects. (Henley et al., 1995, p. 82)

CONCLUSION

Three conclusions can be drawn from this review, leading to new paths of research.

If content and form certainly both influence judgment, further studies will have to shed light on their interaction. As we have already said, Erickson et al. (1978) suggested that content would provide an explicit meaning, whereas syntax would provide an implicit one. Thus, it would be the interaction between syntax (structure) and semantics (meaning) that would contribute to the general comprehension of discourse by receivers (Henley et al., 1995). Syntax partially determines sentence meaning, and participants do show recall for syntactic features that determine meaning (Sachs, 1967). For instance, verb voice does affect comprehension of and memory for language. Although, it is only a surface syntactic feature of a sentence, the effect may result from the generation of additional information, such as causal attributions, during encoding of sentence meaning (Henley et al., 1995). Future research will need to work further on the relation between content and form.

From our point of view, PTP research needs to be completed by research on psychological mechanisms behind pretrial effects, which as yet have been largely ignored (Kovera & Greathouse, 2008). A few studies have focused on explaining the effects of PTP (Hope, Memon, & McGeorge, 2004; Kovera, 2002; Lepastourel, 2007; Otto et al., 1994). They suggest two general mediating mechanisms. The first has to do with retention and encoding. According to Otto et al. (1994), jurors first encode PTP content into their long-term memory, and then trial information follows. Therefore, jurors may be making memory-based judgments (Hastie & Park, 1986) in which they are drawing on not just the evidence actually presented in the trial but also their PTP information. Close to this idea, Kovera (2002) considers that cognitive accessibility of information has a mediating role on judgments (Shrum & O'Guinn, 1993). The second explanation has to do with the influence of a coherent impression of the target (Otto et al., 1994). PTP may lead potential jurors to spontaneously form a coherent impression of the defendant, which may influence their subsequent judgments. This hypothesis is based on the "story model" (Pennington & Hastie, 1986, 1988) whereby jurors rebuild information in their minds in order to get a coherent story explaining the crime. So PTP does not simply give isolated and independent information to the receivers (i.e., prospective jurors) but rather provides a belief frame regarding the defendant's culpability (Steblay et al., 1999; Studebaker & Penrod, 1997). Knowledge is considered as stored in narrative format (Hastie & Dawes, 2001; Hastie & Pennington, 1995). PTP effects can be explained by the quantity of retained and accessible information or by the construction of a coherent global representation of the information, most likely, a combination of both. This field of study, still young, certainly needs to be further pursued. But, in parallel, research on the effects of form has clearly shown how syntax determines recall of pretrial information. From this point of view, it is clear that style must be taken into account to protect a defendant's right to a fair trial.

To illustrate this idea, we give two very practical examples of applications that should be adopted. First, during the voir dire, when lawyers educate jurors about the perils of PTP, they should certainly include some of the research on discourse style influences (e.g., discourse analysis of an article's title, checking active and passive voice concerning the accused or the victim, and checking the kinds of verbs used in the messages). Also, whereas potential jurors tend not to believe the prejudicial effects of pretrial information and claim they can remain unbiased, they might be more likely to believe in the unconscious effects of style, as it appears to be a very subtle influence. It could therefore be a way, for lawyers, to counterbalance jurors' belief of impartiality. Second, whereas a change of venue traditionally has been based only on content analysis of media information, those analyses should be made complete by adding an analysis of discourse style. Indeed, analysis of content could show no difference in amount of pretrial information against or in favor of the defendant, whereas the two types of information could differ on form. Therefore, potential jurors could be more influenced than experts would have initially thought. These two potential improvements certainly could be applied if experts considered both media content and form. More broadly, the understanding of the social psychology of the law would benefit from a consideration of both factors—both in deciding on prospective jurors during voir dire or in deciding whether PTP has been so biasing as to require a change of venue.

A final conclusion that can be drawn from this review is that both informational content and style of discourse take part in a tendency to individualize crime (Bittle, 2001).

> [Thus,] a lot of news consists of moral-character portraits of demon criminals, of responsible authorities. . . . The emphasis on individual morality is not only a dramatic technique for presenting news stories as serial narratives involving leading actors but also a political means of allocating responsibility for actions and attributing accountability. (Ericson, Baranek, & Chan, 1999, p. 8)

More widely, "By individualizing problems on a case-by-case basis, the news and law rule out systemic and structural accounts that might question the authority of cultural values, the state, and the news and legal institutions themselves" (Ericson et al., 1999, p. 9). It is about an evolution of thought by the journalists, and more generally of the society. The professionals of justice will have to take it into account.

More broadly, the struggle to reconcile freedom of the press with the right to a fair trial for the accused remains a problem. Particularly, research on style effects still needs to be developed, as well as studies on mechanisms. Within this chapter, we hope to have drawn the attention of psycholegal scholars (e.g., consultants and expert witnesses) to issues in this research area.

REFERENCES

ABA. (2007). *Criminal Justice Section Standards*, 2007. Retrieved from www.abanet.org/crimjust/standards/fairtrial_blk.html.

Antunes, G.E., & Hurley, P.A. (1978). The representation of criminal events in Houston's two daily papers. *Journalism Quarterly, 55*, 756–760.

Arbuthnot, J., Myers, B., & Leach, J. (2002). Linking juror prejudgment and pretrial publicity knowledge: Some methodological considerations. *American Journal of Forensic Psychology, 20*(3), 53–71.

Beaudoin, C.E., & Thorson, E. (2005). Credibility perceptions of news coverage of ethnic groups: The predictive roles of race and news use. *The Howard Journal of Communications, 16*, 33–48.

Bittle, S. (2001). *Le traitement médiatique, dans la presse écrite, de la haine en tant que circonstance aggravante en matière de détermination de la peine: Une étude de cas* [Press coverage: Hate as an aggravating circumstance to determine sentences: A case study]. Report for the Department of Justice of Canada.

Blanchet, A., & Mirabel-Sarron, C. (1997). Négation et psychopathologie [Negation and psychopathology]. In A. Blanchet (Ed.), *Recherches sur le langage en psychologie clinique* (pp. 11–37). Paris: Dunod.

Bornstein, B.H., Whisehunt, B.L., Nemeth, R.J., & Dunaway, D.L. (2002). Pretrial publicity and civil cases: A two way street? *Law and Human Behavior, 26*(1), 3–18.

Bostian, L.R. (1983). How active, passive and nominal styles affect readability of science writing. *Journalism Quarterly, 60*, 635–640.

Brandwood, J.A. (2000). You say "fair trial" and I say "free press": British and American approaches to protecting defendant's rights in high profile trials. *New York University Law Review, 75*, 1412–1451.

Bromberg, M., & Trognon, A. (2005). Communication et contrat de communication [Communication and communication contract]. In N. Dubois (Ed.), *Psychologie sociale de la cognition* (pp. 209–252). Paris: Dunod.

Brooks, B.S., Kennedy, G., Moen, D.R., & Ranly, D. (2001). *Telling the story: Writing for print, broadcast and online media*. New York: St. Martins.

Burguet, A., & Girard, F. (2008). La Coupe du Monde de Football 2006 : Analyse de la production des biais linguistiques intergroupes [The FIFA Worldcup 2006: An analysis of intergroup linguistic biases]. *Cahiers Internationaux de Psychologie Sociale, 79*, 85–103.

Cohen, B.C. (1963). *The press and foreign policy*. Princeton, NJ: Princeton University Press.

Cole, T., & Leets, L. (1998). Linguistic masking devices and intergroup behavior: Further evidence of an intergroup linguistic bias. *Journal of Language & Social Psychology, 17*(3), 348–371.

Costantini, E., & King, J. (1980–1981). The partial juror: Correlates and causes of prejudgment. *Law and Society Review, 50*(1), 9–39.

Daftary-Kapur, T., Dumas, R., & Penrod, S. D. (2010). Jury decision-making biases and methods to counter them. *Legal and Criminological Psychology, 15*(1), 133–154.

De Poot, C. J., & Semin, G. R. (1995). Pick your verbs with care when you formulate a question! *Journal of Language and Social Psychology, 14*(4), 351–369.

Ditton, J., & Duffy, J. (1983). Bias in the newspaper reporting of crime news. *British Journal of Criminology, Delinquency and Deviant Social Behaviour, 23*(2), 159–165.

Dixon, T.L., & Linz, D. (2000). Race and the misrepresentation of victimization on local television news. *Communication Research, 27*(5), 547–573.

Edelstein, A.S. (1993). Thinking about the criterion variable in agenda-setting research. *Journal of Communication, 43*(2), 85–99.

Ericson, R.V., Baranek, P.M., & Chan, J.B.L. (1999). *Representing order: Crime, law and justice in the news media.* Toronto: University of Toronto.

Erickson, B., Lind, E.A., Johnson, B.C., & O'Barr, W.M. (1978). Speech style and impression formation in a court setting: The effects of "powerful" and "powerless" speech. *Journal of Experimental Social Psychology, 14*(3), 266–279.

Fayol, M. (1985). *Le récit et sa construction. Une approche de psychologie cognitive* [Narrative construction: A cognitive psychology approach]. Paris: Delachaux & Niestlé.

Francke, T. (2001). Press rights, human rights, and cryptocracy. *Human Rights, 28*(4), 11–16.

Fulero, S.M. (2002). Afterword: The past, present, and future of applied pretrial publicity research. *Law and Human Behavior, 26*(1), 127–133.

Gans, H.J. (2004). *Deciding what's news? A study of CBS Evening News, NBC Nightly News, Newsweek, and Time.* Evanston, IL: Northwestern University Press.

Gerbner, G., & Gross, L. (1976). Living with television: The violence profile. *Journal of Communication, 26*(2), 172–199.

Goodman-Delahunty, J., & Tait, D. (2006). Lay participation in legal decision-making in Australia and New Zealand: Trials and administrative tribunals. In M.E. Kaplan & A.M. Martin (Eds.), *Understanding world jury systems: Through social psychology research* (pp. 47–70). New York: Psychology Press.

Graber, D.A. (1980). *Crime news and the public.* New York: Praeger.

Greene, E., & Loftus, E.F. (1984). What's new in the news? The influence of well-publicized news events on psychological research and courtroom trials. *Basic and Applied Social Psychology, 5*(3), 211–221.

Greene, E., & Wade, R. (1988). Of private talk and public print: General pretrial publicity and juror decision-making. *Applied Cognitive Psychology, 2*(2), 123–135.

Hans, V.P. (1990). Law and the media: An overview and introduction. *Law and Human Behavior, 14*(5), 399–407.

Hastie, R., & Dawes, R.M. (2001). *Rational choice in an uncertain world: The psychology of judgment and decision making.* Thousand Oaks, CA: Sage.

Hastie, R., & Park, B. (1986). The relationship between memory and judgment depends on whether the judgment task is memory-based or on-line. *Psychological Review, 93*(3), 258–268.

Hastie, R., & Pennington, N. (1995). The big story: Is it a story? In R.S.J. Wyer (Ed.), *Knowledge and memory: The real story* (pp. 133–138). Hillsdale, NJ: Erlbaum.

Heath, L. (1984). Impact of newspaper crime reports on fear of crime: Multi-methodological investigation. *Journal of Personality and Social Psychology, 47*(2), 263–276.

Heath, L., & Gilbert, K. (1996). Mass media and fear of crime. *American Behavioral Scientist, 39*(4), 379–386.

Heath, L., Kavanaugh, J., & Thompson, S.R. (2001). Perceived vulnerability and fear of crime: Why fear stays high when crime rates drop. *Journal of Offender Rehabilitation, 33*, 1–14.

Henley, N.M., Miller, M.D., & Beazley, J.A. (1995). Syntax, semantics and sexual violence: Agency and the passive voice. *Journal of Language and Social Psychology, 14*(1–2), 60–84.

Higgins, E.T. (1978). Does persuasive style have a "boomerang" effect? *Contemporary Psychology, 23*(9), 655–657.

Holland Baker, M., Nienstedt, B.C., Everett, R.S., & McCleary, R. (1983). The impact of a crime wave: Perceptions, fear and confidence in the police. *Law and Society Review, 17*(2), 319–335.

Hope, L., Memon, A., & McGeorge, P. (2004). Understanding pretrial publicity: Predecisional distortion of evidence by mock jurors. *Journal of Experimental Psychology: Applied, 10*(2), 111–119.

Humphries, D. (1981). Serious crime news coverage and ideology: A content analysis of crime coverage in a metropolitan paper. *Crime and Delinquency, 27*, 191–205.

Imrich, D.J., Mullin, C., & Linz, D. (1995). Measuring the extent of prejudicial publicity in major American newspapers: A content analysis. *Journal of Communication, 45*(3), 94–117.

Kintsch, W., & Van Dijk, T.A. (1975). Comment on se rappelle et on résume des histoires [How we remind and summarize stories]. *Langages, 40*(9), 98–116.

Kovera, M.B. (2002). The effects of general pretrial publicity on juror decisions: An examination of moderators and mediating mechanisms. *Law and Human Behavior, 26*(1), 43–72.

Kovera, M.B., & Greathouse, S.M. (2008). Pretrial publicity: Effects, remedies, and judicial knowledge. In E. Borgida & S.T. Fiske (Eds.), *Beyond common sense: Psychological science in the courtroom.* Malden, MA: Blackwell.

Kramer, G.P., Kerr, N.L., & Carroll, J.S. (1990). Pretrial remedies, judicial remedies, and jury bias. *Law and Human Behavior, 14*(5), 409–438.

Lamb, S., & Keon, S. (1995). Blaming the perpetrator, language that distorts reality in newspaper articles on men battering women. *Psychology of Women Quarterly, 19*, 209–220.

Laver, J., & Trudgill, P. (1979). Phonetic and linguistic markers in speech. In K. R. Scherer & H. Giles (Eds.), *Social markers in speech* (pp. 109–146). Cambridge: Cambridge University Press.

Leclerc, H., & Théolleyre, J.-M. (1996). *Les médias et la justice* [Media and justice]. Paris: CFPJ éditions.

Lepastourel, N. (2007). *La communication médiatique judiciaire: Les effets du style d'écriture sur la reception d'articles de presse et les jugements* [Media communication: The effects of writing style on the reception of press articles and judgments]. Unpublished doctoral thesis, Rennes 2, Rennes.

Lepastourel, N., & Testé, B. (2004). L'influence médiatique sur les jugements judiciaires: Rôle du style d'écriture dans la formation des jugements [Media's influence on judiciary judgments: Impact of writing style on judgments elaboration]. *Psychologie Française, 49*(4), 473–488.

Lepastourel, N., & Testé, B. (2008, July). *The pretrial effects of narrative and argumentative writing style of press articles.* Paper presented at the XXIX International Congress of Psychology, Berlin, Germany.

Lepastourel, N., & Testé, B. (2011). Attentes langagières et réception de l'information médiatique [Language expectancy and reception of judicial news]. *Année Psychologique, 111*(1), 41–68.

Maass, A., Corvino, G., & Arcuri, L. (1994). Linguistic intergroup bias and the mass media. *Revue Internationale de Psychologie Sociale, 7*(1), 31–43.

Maass, A., Salvi, D., Arcuri, L., & Semin, G.R. (1989). Language use in intergroup contexts: The linguistic intergroup bias. *Journal of Personality and Social Psychology, 57*(6), 981–993.

McCombs, M.E., & Shaw, D.L. (1972). The agenda-setting function of mass media. *Public Opinion Quarterly, 36*, 176–187.

Menon, T., Morris, M.W., Chiu, C.-Y., & Hong, Y. (1999). Culture and the construal of agency: Attribution to individual versus group dispositions. *Journal of Personality and Social Psychology, 76*(5), 701–717.

Moran, G., & Cutler, B. L. (1991). The prejudicial impact of pretrial publicity. *Journal of Applied Social Psychology, 21*, 345–367.

Morris, M.W., & Peng, K. (1994). Culture and cause: American and Chinese attributions for social and physical events. *Journal of Personality and Social Psychology, 67*(6), 949–971.

Mullin, C., Imrich, D.J., & Linz, D. (1996). The impact of acquaintance rape stories and case-specific pretrial publicity on juror decision making. *Communication Research, 23*(1), 100–135.

Neveu, E. (2001). *Sociologie du journalisme* [Sociology of journalism]. Paris: La découvertes, Repères.

Nietzel, M.T., & Dillehay, R. C. (1983). Psychologists as consultants for changes of venue. *Law and Human Behavior, 7*(4), 309–355.

Ogloff, J.R.P., & Vidmar, N. (1994). The impact of pretrial publicity on jurors. A study to compare the relative effects of television and print media in a child sex abuse case. *Law and Human Behavior, 18*(5), 507–525.

Otto, A.L., Penrod, S.D., & Dexter, H.R. (1994). The biasing impact of pretrial publicity on juror judgments. *Law and Human Behavior, 18*(4), 453–469.

Pennington, N., & Hastie, R. (1986). Evidence evaluation in complex decision making. *Journal of Personality and Social Psychology, 51*(2), 242–258.

Pennington, N., & Hastie, R. (1988). Explanation-based decision making: Effects of memory structure on judgment. *Journal of Experimental Psychology: Learning, Memory, & Cognition, 14*(3), 521–533.

Pettigrew, T.F. (1979). The ultimate attribution error: Extending Allport's cognitive analysis of prejudice. *Personality and Social Psychology Bulletin, 5*(4), 461–476.

Platow, M.J., & Brodie, M. (1999). The effects of linguistic voice on evaluations and attributions of ingroup and outgroup members. *Asian Journal of Social Psychology, 2*(2), 187–200.

Potter, G.W., & Kappeler, V.E. (1998). *Constructing crime. Perspectives on making news and social problems.* Prospect Heights, IL: Waveland Press.

Roberts, J.V., & Doob, A.N. (1990). News media influences on public views of sentencing. *Law and Human Behavior, 14*(5), 451–468.

Romer, D., Jamieson, K.H., & De Coteau, N.J. (1998). The treatment of persons of color in local television news. *Communication Research, 25*(3), 286–305.

Ross, L. (1977). The intuitive psychologist and his shortcoming: Distortions in the attribution process. In L. Berkowitz (Ed.), *Advances in experimental social psychology* (Vol. 10, pp. 173–220). New York: Academic Press.

Sachs, J.S. (1967). Recognition memory for syntactic and semantic aspects of connected discourse. *Perception and Psychophysics, 2*, 437–442.

Sandell, R. (1977). *Linguistic style and persuasion.* London: Academic Press.

Scherer, K.R. (1979). Personality markers in speech. In K.R. Scherer & H. Giles (Eds.), *Social markers in speech* (pp. 147–210). Cambridge: Cambridge University Press/Editions de la Maison des Sciences de l'Homme.

Schmid, J., & Fiedler, K. (1998). The backbone of closing speeches: The impact of prosecution versus defense language on judicial attributions. *Journal of Applied Social Psychology, 28*(13), 1140–1172.

Shrum, L. J., & O'Guinn, T.C. (1993), Processes and effects in the construction of social reality: Construct accessibility as an explanatory variable. *Communication Research, 20*(3), 436–471.

Semin, G.R. (1995). Interfacing language and social cognition. *Journal of Language and Social Psychology, 14*(1/2), 182–195.

Semin, G.R. (2000). Language as a cognitive and behavioral structuring resource: Question-answer exchanges. In W. Stroebe & M. Hewstone (Eds.), *European review of social psychology* (pp. 75–104). Chichester: Wiley.

Semin, G.R., & De Poot, C.J. (1997). The question-answer paradigm: You might regret not noticing how a question is worded. *Journal of Personality and Social Psychology, 73*(3), 472–480.

Semin, G.R., & Fiedler, K. (1988). The cognitive functions of linguistic categories in describing persons: Social cognition and language. *Journal of Personality and Social Psychology, 54*(4), 558–568.

Semin, G.R., Rubini, M., & Fiedler, K. (1995). The answer is in the question: The effect of verb causality on locus of explanation. *Personality and Social Psychology Bulletin*, 21(8), 834–841.

Sheley, J.F., & Ashkins, C.D. (1981). Crime, crime news, and crime views. *Public Opinion Quarterly*, 45(4), 492–506.

Simon, R.J., & Eimermann, T. (1971). The jury finds not guilty: Another look at the media influence on the jury. *Journalism Quarterly*, 48, 343–344.

Simon, T.F., Fico, F., & Lacy, S. (1989). Covering conflict and controversy: Measuring balance, fairness, defamation. *Journalism Quarterly*, 66, 427–434.

Stapel, D.A., & Semin, G.R. (2007). The magic spell of language: Linguistic categories and their perceptual consequences. *Journal of Personality and Social Psychology*, 93(1), 23–33.

Steblay, N.M., Besirevic, J., Fulero, S.M., & Jimenez-Lorente, B. (1999). The effects of pretrial publicity on juror verdicts: A meta-analytic review. *Law and Human Behavior*, 23(2), 219–236.

Studebaker, C.A., & Penrod, S.D. (1997). Pretrial publicity: The media, the law and common sense. *Psychology, Public Policy and Law*, 3(2/3), 428–460.

Studebaker, C.A., & Penrod, S.D. (2005). Pretrial publicity and its influence on juror decision making. In N. Brewer & K.D. Williams (Eds.), *Psychology and law: An empirical perspective* (pp. 254–276). New York: Guilford.

Surette, R. (1998). *Media, crime and criminal justice: Images and realities*. Belmont, CA: Wadsworth.

Tankard, J.W., Middleton, K., & Rimmer, T. (1979). Compliance with American Bar Association for fair trial-free press guidelines. *Journalism Quarterly*, 56, 464–468.

Testé, B., Dumas, R., Lepastourel, N., & Fernagut-Samson, M. (2007). L'impact du mode de restitution des procès criminels dans la presse sur la formation d'une conviction de culpabilité chez les lecteurs [Impact of criminal trials press reports on reader's culpability judgments]. 8ème Congrès International de Psychologie Sociale Appliquée, Besançon.

Tyler, T.R., & Lomax Cook, F. (1984). The mass media and judgments of risk: Distinguishing impact on personal and societal level judgments. *Journal of Personality and Social Psychology*, 47(4), 693–708.

Van Dijk, T.A. (1988). *News as discourse*. Hillsdale, NJ: Erlbaum.

Valkenburg, P.M., & Patiwael, M. (1998). Does watching court TV "cultivate" people's perceptions of crime? *Gazette*, 60(3), 227–238.

Voss, J.F., & Van Dyke, J.A. (2001). Narrative structure, information certainty, emotional content, and gender as factors in a pseudo jury decision-making task. *Discourse Processes*, 32(2–3), 215–243.

Wilson, J.R., & Bornstein, B.H. (1998). Methodological considerations in pretrial publicity research: Is the medium the message? *Law and Human Behavior*, 22(5), 585–597.

Wood, J., & Gannon, T. (2009). *Public opinion and criminal justice*. Portland, OR: Willan.

4

Deception and Deception Detection

Timothy R. Levine

The Clarence Thomas Supreme Court nomination hearings took place not long after I published my first two papers on deception in 1990. Much attention and speculation focused on Anita Hill's claims of sexual harassment by Thomas, which Thomas categorically denied. It appeared to most observers that either Hill or Thomas must have been lying.

At the time of the confirmation hearings, I was a new acting assistant professor at Indiana University. Some of my colleagues who were aware of my research interests in deception asked my opinion, thinking that I could simply read Thomas' and Hill's body language and render an authoritative opinion on the veracity of Hill's allegations. The absence of empirical connections between deception and nonverbal cues made this impossible, however.

There is much more research on deception now than there was then. Still, however, in the absence of independent corroborating or disconfirming evidence, people's ability to judge others' honesty is highly fallible. Nonverbal presentation is important because it strongly impacts *perceptions* of honesty, but it is not often an accurate gauge of honesty or deceit. That is, nonverbal behaviors are a strong determinant of whether someone *will* be believed but not whether they *should* be believed.

This chapter summarizes what is currently known about deception, with a focus on legal applications. The content is based on 40 years of social scientific research on deception and has clear and important implications for legal policy, the practice of law, and law enforcement.

DEFINING LYING AND DECEPTION

Let us begin by defining *deception* as knowingly or intentionally misleading another person or persons. A *lie* is deception that involves knowingly providing false information with the intent of misleading others. Not all false information counts as deception or as a lie. An honest mistake is not a lie, nor is an obviously false statement, because they lack deceptive intent.

The easiest and most common way to mislead another person, however, is not by lying but by passive omission (Levine et al., 2002). Often, simply not volunteering information can achieve the same ends as a lie without the risk for being caught in a lie, per se. Whether people see this as deception depends on the situation. For example, omission of pertinent information is seen as more deceptive when it can hurt the receiver than when it cannot (Levine, Asada, & Massi, 2003). Other more active forms of deception that fall short of outright falsification include evasion, which involves actively diverting talk away from hidden information, and equivocation, which involves strategic ambiguity (McCornack, 1992). The skilled communicator, when faced with information he or she does not wish to disclose, will simply not bring up the topic. Only if necessary will the conversation be subtly diverted away from the hidden information, or information will be provided in such a way that although it is literally true, the real meaning will not be grasped by the listener. It is only when confronted with a direct and unambiguous question that precludes effective evasion or equivocation, that an outright lie is necessary.

THE WHY, WHEN, AND HOW OFTEN OF LYING

People lie when the truth is problematic for them (Levine, Kim, & Hamel, 2010). People generally do not lie when the truth will work just fine. Typically, lying is a tactical decision to achieve some desired outcome when the truth gets in the way of that desired outcome.

Lying and deception are usually tactics, not motives. That is, the ultimate goal of deception is not to mislead, per se, but rather to achieve an objective when the truth gets in the way. Understanding when people are likely to lie, therefore, depends on understanding situations in which the truth is problematic.

My research finds that when the truth is sufficient, people are honest nearly 100% of the time (Levine et al., 2010). For example, when innocent people are asked if they committed a crime or misdeed, most will answer honestly and deny the misconduct. However, when the truth thwarts a person's goals or desires, then sometimes, but not always, that person will lie. In my research, I asked people who had just cheated for financial gain in an experiment if they cheated. I had set up the cheaters in a stinglike operation. I asked other people to imagine that they got a gift they did not like. These people were asked what they would say to the gift-giver. Other people were asked what they would say if they had a female friend who was gaining weight and asked if she looked fat. Across situations such as these and others, I find that about two-thirds of people lie. In the cheating situation, for example, about one-third confessed even though they might have gotten in trouble. Nevertheless, some people were honest even when they have a reason to lie. Without a reason to lie, however, virtually everyone is honest. My research team has questioned nearly 300 noncheaters so far and we have not yet gotten a single spontaneous false confession in my cheating studies. Although the lack of false confessions may not be surprising to many readers, psychology research (e.g., Kassin & Kiechel, 1996) and examination of actual legal case studies (e.g., Blair, 2005) show that false confessions can be made to happen.

To understand the situations that are likely to prompt lying, my research team (Levine et al., 2010) asked people to describe situations in which they lied to someone else or in which they were lied to. Sometimes we used the word lie, other times we said deceive. We asked both students and older working adults. We collected data in Egypt, Guatemala, Pakistan, Saudi Arabia, and the United States. We found that the vast majority of lies were motivated by one or more of the 10 reasons listed in Table 4.1. The most common motivations, together accounting for about two-thirds of the deceptions, were to hide a personal transgression, to obtain some kind of advantage for the self (economic or otherwise), and to avoid people. Lying to make a good impression also was reasonably common. What all these situations have in common is that they are situations where the truth is problematic. Others' research suggests that most people tell about two such lies per day, with a few telling many more than that (Serota, Levine, & Boster, 2010).

It is not entirely clear why, in situations where the truth is problematic, some people choose honesty, although most people do not. The decision to lie or not likely rests on some combination of (a) the extent to which the truth is problematic, (b) the strength of the individual's moral acceptance or

Table 4.1. Common Deception Motives from Levine et al. (2010)

1. *Hide Personal Transgression.* A lie to cover up a misdeed (e.g., lying to hide relational infidelity, making false excuse why one was late to work).

2. *Economic Advantage.* A lie motivated by monetary gain (e.g., knowingly selling defective products, seeking loans under false pretenses, and con artist schemes).

3. *Nonmonetary Personal Advantage.* A lie to seek some desirable outcome for the self other than economic advantage (e.g., a bogus excuse to get class notes for a missed class or to get a co-worker to do a disliked task).

4. *Social-Polite.* Lies told to conform to social rules or avoid rudeness (e.g., saying that one liked a gift that was not liked).

5. *Altruistic Lies* (other than social-polite). A lie told to protect another person, or another person's advantage (e.g., a father hiding a health problem from a child to avoid upsetting her).

6. *Self-impression management.* Lies motivated by the desire to appear more favorable to others (e.g., exaggerating one's accomplishments to impress a romantic interest).

7. *Malicious.* Lies to cause harm to others (e.g., spreading false rumors about another person to harm their reputation, or sabotage a relationship).

8. *Humor-Joke.* Deception to be funny or prank another.

9. *Pathological Lies.* Lies without apparent motive or purpose out of delusion or with blatant disregard for reality.

10. *Avoidance.* Lies told to avoid another person (e.g., fabricating an excuse to avoid attending an event with a friend).

rejection of deceit as a communication tactic, and (c) the perceived likelihood that an attempt to deceive will succeed and avoid detection.

Fear of detection is a factor with interesting implications. If a lie is detected, it means not only that the goal motivating the lie probably will not be achieved, but also that there may be negative consequences associated with being seen as a liar. This deterrence provided by possible detection has two important implications. First, a person in an awkward situation in which the truth is problematic often can be prompted to honesty by the belief that the listener already knows the truth. So, for example, police may try to bluff a suspect by suggesting that they already have evidence of guilt. Second, people who believe themselves to be poor liars probably lie much less than those who believe themselves to be good liars. Not everyone is equally likely to lie, and large individual differences exist in the proclivity to lie (Serota et al., 2010). There are large individual differences also in how believable people are. The two individual differences are likely related.

NONVERBAL DECEPTION CUES

The idea that clues to deception leak out via nonverbal behavior dates back to the seminal and very influential work of Paul Ekman (Ekman & Friesen, 1969). The idea was that liars can control what they say better than they can control what they do. So, although people can easily manipulate their words to fool others, they are less conscious of their body language and consequently clues to deception slip out in their nonverbal performance. This, at least, is how the theory goes.

Research aimed at verifying nonverbal leakage has been, on the whole, pretty much a failure. There have been literally hundreds of experiments investigating nonverbal deception cues over the past 40 years, and most individual studies find some differences between truths and lies. The problem is, findings just don't replicate from study to study.

In recent years, a new research strategy called *meta-analysis* has been gaining popularity in the social sciences. Meta-analysis allows researchers to average research findings across studies to get the big picture of the research findings and to try to make sense of mixed and contradictory results. According to three recent meta-analyses on deception cues (DePaulo et al., 2003; Sporer & Schwandt, 2006, 2007), some behaviors that laypersons assume to be significantly correlated with deception simply are not (e.g., gaze and eye contact, fidgeting, and posture shifting). Some other behaviors do correlate significantly with deception, but only when detected by laboratory equipment; that is, they are so microscopic that they are not detectable by everyday communicators (e.g., vocal pitch increase, vocal response latency, and increased speech errors).

Let us take a closer look at the "sting-operation" research mentioned earlier. My research team recruits students to take part in what they believe is a study of teamwork. They are paired with another student as a teammate, and together they play a trivia game for $5 each per correct answer. During the game, the researcher gets called out of the room on an emergency, and the answers and money are left within easy reach. The subject's partner is actually working for me and always suggests cheating. Subjects decide for themselves whether to cheat or not. Some subjects cheat, but most (about two-thirds) do not. The experimenter returns and the game continues. After the game, subjects are taken to a different room where they are interviewed on camera about teamwork, and ultimately about cheating. Those subjects who cheated are then put in a position to lie. As mentioned previously, about two-thirds lie and about one-third confesses under questioning (although the confession rate depends on how they are questioned; more on that later).

This procedure has produced a collection of several hundred truthful and deceptive interviews. We, of course, know exactly who cheated and who didn't, so we know which denials are genuine and which are lies. We do not tell our subjects to cheat or lie. They decide that for themselves. If they do cheat, however, technically they have violated the university code of conduct and are potentially subject to expulsion. Also, they were attempting to defraud federal funds. So this is a situation of some consequence and realism. The subjects, of course, are not in any real trouble, but they do not know that until the end of the experiment when they are debriefed.

I have now watched these tapes many, many times. When I know up front who the liars are, it is easy to spot nonverbal tells. There are, however, two catches. First, different liars have different tells. So, what will work to catch one liar might not work for the next. Second, there are many truth-tellers who do the same things as the liars. So, what one notices with hindsight is of little use when one does not know beforehand if the person is honest or not. Some of the liars, for example, act nervous. But, so do some of the honest people. In fact, accusing an honest person of cheating can be very disruptive and arousing.

The experience of watching these tapes combined with the knowledge of the results of the recent meta-analyses has convinced me that nonverbal behaviors are not very useful in distinguishing truths from lies. Deception-based leakage happens. I can see it in my own data. But, the signals are sometimes weak and very inconsistent from person to person. And, all the behaviors that sometimes signal deceit also are sometimes present in honest people. Honest people are sometimes nervous for reasons other than deception, and some people just act more nervous than others regardless of honesty.

Some strong but somewhat indirect evidence against the nonverbal leakage view comes from research looking at communication modality and detection accuracy. If useful clues to deception were leaked nonverbally, then it should make a difference if lies were watched, heard, or read, and judges should be better able to spot lies under audiovisual observation than under conditions in which nonverbal cues are absent or limited. Meta-analysis suggests that although the communication medium makes a statistically significance difference, the differences are small. For example, according to Bond and DePaulo (2006), accuracy is 50.5% with video and no audio, 53% with audio and no visual, and 54% in studies involving audiovisual presentation of lies. Therefore, the slightly-better-than-chance accuracy finding seems general across communication media. More recent research has been looking into lie detection in the context of various new electronic media, but there is little reason to expect that new media will yield different findings than before because it seems to matter little whether the lies are watched, heard, or read.

Although nonverbal performance is not very useful in distinguishing truth from lie, it is very much the case that nonverbal presentation affects who is and who is not believed. On this, the research is clear and convincing, and the findings are strong and consistent. Nonverbal behaviors matter a great deal for *perceptions* of honesty and deceit.

People were surveyed and asked, "How can you tell if someone is lying?" Can you guess what most people answered? I'm guessing that the reader knows the answer. Almost everyone answers the same way. By far, the No. 1 answer is eye contact. It is very widely believed that a liar will not look you in the eye. Although this finding is obvious, there are at least two very interesting facets to the finding that are not so obvious. First, despite it being a very widely held belief, it appears to be objectively false. Eye gaze has been found to be completely unrelated to actual deception. The liars-won't-look-you-in-the-eye belief has absolutely no validity. Second, the reader may be surprised to learn just how wide spread the liars-won't-look-you-in-the-eye myth really is. Bond and the Global Deception Research team (2006) surveyed people in 75 different countries and found the belief is held literally around the world. People everywhere hold this false belief.

Eye contact, however, isn't the only behavior associated with perceptions of honesty and deceit. For the past 4 years, I have been showing my collection of cheating interviews to different research subjects and I ask them to guess, based on watching the interviews, who cheated. I have found many interesting findings, but one observation is especially important here. Judges tend to see some of the tapes the same way. Some of the interviewees are almost always believed by everyone. Other interviewees are almost always judged to be cheaters. Some of those who are always believed were in fact cheaters and some of those who are most often judged as cheaters did not in fact cheat.

Once I noticed this pattern in the data, the first thing I did was to test the consistency of perceptions across judges. I had one set of judges rate a large set of interviews. From those, I picked out the interviews on which judges tend to agree. Then I showed those tapes to a different set of judges, and another, and another. The findings were amazingly consistent. Some people are more believable than others. I call this characteristic "demeanor" and I define demeanor as the tendency to be believed independent of honesty.

Next, I set out to ascertain what it is that gives some people an honest demeanor and others a dishonest demeanor. So, I had my judges watch the tapes again. This time I asked them why a person was believable or not. I distilled the answers down to a list of 11 behaviors or impressions. Then, I had yet another group of judges watch the tapes and rate each interviewee on each of the 11 demeanor cues. The ratings on each of the 11 demeanor cues distinguished those who were initially judged uniformly honest from those judged dishonest. But most interesting, I found that the 11 ratings tended to converge and could be scored as an index of believability. These 11 demeanor-linked behaviors and impressions are listed in Table 4.2. People who follow the four do's and avoid the seven don'ts tend to be seen as honest by virtually everyone. The more people deviate from these, the more likely they are to be doubted.

Table 4.2. The 10 Keys to an Honest Demeanor

The Four Do's
1. Confidence and Composure
2. Pleasant and Friendly Interaction Style
3. Engaged and Involved Interaction Style
4. Given Plausible Explanations

The Seven Don'ts
1. Avoid Eye Contact
2. Appear Hesitant and Slow in Proving Answers
3. Vocal Uncertainty
4. Fidget with Hands or Happy Feet
5. Appear Tense, Nervous, Anxious
6. Portray an Inconsistent Demeanor Over Course of Interaction
7. Verbal Uncertainty

DECEPTION DETECTION ACCURACY

After nonverbal deception cues, the second major focus of deception research is on people's ability (or lack thereof) to detect other's lies. There have been literally hundreds of deception detection studies over the past 40 years, and, for the most part, like the nonverbal cues literature, the findings are pretty consistently meager.

In deception detection experiments, subjects serve as judges who are asked to assess the truth or deceptiveness of some set of messages. Most often, judges watch videotapes, but some detection studies involve text, e-mail, voice only, or face-to-face interaction. The medium of communication does not seem to make much difference. What makes a bigger difference is that judges are almost always shown an equal number of truths and lies, with accuracy being calculated as the percentage correct averaged across truths and lies (more on this later). So, for example, in my detection experiments, I show subjects selected video clips from my cheating experiments and see how well they can distinguish the cheating liars from the honest noncheaters. Sometimes I find what most other studies find, but I also find results that differ in both directions from what is typical of the research literature as a whole.

There have been four recent meta-analyses looking at deception detection accuracy and together they provide a very consistent picture. In fact, deception detection experiments may replicate more consistently than just about any other set of findings in the social sciences. What is most often found is that people are only slightly better than chance at distinguishing truths from lies in deception detection experiments (Bond & DePaulo, 2006). People are, on average, just under 54% accurate where 50% is chance, and the vast majority of individual studies report accuracy near this level regardless of the variables investigated. Furthermore, nonverbal training improves accuracy only slightly (about 4%; Frank & Feeley, 2003; Levine, Feeley, McCornack, Harms, & Hughes, 2005, found gains this large with "bogus training") and it does not seem to matter who the subjects are (e.g., Bond & DePaulo, 2008). Age and professional experience are unrelated to accuracy, and there is little difference in ability across judges (Bond & Depaulo, 2008). There appear to be some exceptions, which are noted later, but most studies, and all the meta-analyses, converge on these conclusions.

My current thinking is that there are four major reasons why most deception detection experiments find slightly better than chance accuracy, and that these reasons have important implications for lie detection outside the lab, including legal settings. The key to understanding why studies are done the way they are and why they find what they do is to remember that the idea of nonverbal leakage and deception have dominated thinking about the topic of deception. Most studies (and people) presume that leakage is how people detect lies so this is what the research has been designed to test. And this is why, I think, accuracy is almost always a little better than chance. There is just enough of a grain of truth in nonverbal deception cues that they help just a little bit. I call this idea "a few transparent liars" (Levine, 2010). I think that there is a small percentage of people who are really bad liars and who reliably get caught by just about everyone. Deception detection experiments usually randomly assign senders to be honest or not, and a few people just cannot pull off very credible lies. Thus, judges succeed only at chance-level accuracy in most cases, but get the few bad liars right. The net result is slightly above chance accuracy.

Judges, however, seldom do much better than chance. I think there are four reasons for this low accuracy ceiling. First, as mentioned earlier, there are only a *few* transparent liars. Most people can lie pretty well. So, although some people are leaky, most are not. Second, people vary much more in demeanor than they do in transparency (Bond & DePaulo, 2008), and these differences in demeanor lead to predictable errors. The existence of really smooth liars and creepy, deceptive-looking honest people keeps accuracy from being very high. Third, all that people have to go on in most deception detection experiments is demeanor. Content (i.e., what is said) and projecting motive are usually of little use because motive is usually the same for everyone and because judges lack the outside evidence and context to make effect effective use of content. Finally, deception detection experiments require an immediate judgment. Judges are not allowed to go do a fact check, although this is what is often done outside the lab (Park, Levine, McCornack, Morrison, & Ferrara, 2002).

All this said, the conclusion that people are slightly better than chance at detecting deception is not quite right. It is true that accuracy hovers around 54% in most experiments, but this value is obtained by (a) averaging across truths and lies where (b) there is an equal number of each. This is misleading because judges are more often than not truth-biased (Levine, Park, & McCornack, 1999). Truth-bias refers to the tendency to believe others independent of their actual honesty. What makes it a bias is that people miss lies more often than they miss truths. And, this truth-bias is a very common finding. It shows up in meta-analysis (e.g., Bond & DePaulo, 2006) and literally every deception detection experiment I have ever done. Truth-bias is always greater than 50%! What's more, these are deception detection experiments. If being in a deception detection experiment would not make people skeptical and suspicious, what would?

Truth-bias leads to what I call the *veracity effect*. The veracity effect is the finding that the actual veracity of the message strongly predicts the accuracy of judgments about it. People are much more likely to be right about truths than lies. Accuracy for truths is always above 54% (usually between 65% and 82%). Accuracy for lies, in contrast, is consistently below the 50% point (usually between 30% and 40%). So, one should not interpret the "better-than-chance" finding to mean that people are getting lies right more often than not. This is not what happens. People do well on the truths, poorly on the lies, and the average of the two tends to be a little above 50%. This average hides the fact that direction of errors depends on the veracity of the message being judged and that it applies only to situations where half the messages are lies. The greater the likelihood of truth, the higher the accuracy, the more lies there are in the mix, the lower the accuracy (Levine, Kim, Park, & Hughes, 2006).

An interesting implication of the veracity effect accounts for some of the more interesting and counterintuitive findings in the deception detection literature. It follows from the veracity effect that any factor that influences the probability of someone being believed also will affect accuracy. Anything that increases the likelihood that a person will be believed increases truth accuracy but lowers lie accuracy, with the net result being little change when the two are averaged. The same applies, but in the exact opposite manner, to anything that increases skepticism. Lie accuracy goes up, truth accuracy goes down, and net accuracy is largely unaffected. In short, things that affect believability, like demeanor, affect the direction of errors but not the frequency of errors. Three other things that function this way are closeness of relationship between sender and judge, face-to-face interaction, and suspicion. Researchers used to think that if people knew each other, or if the judge could interact with the source, or if judges were made suspicious enough to lower truth-bias, then they might be more accurate. Each of these proved not to be the case. Knowing the other person and interacting face-to-face enhances the probability that someone will be believed, but not that they will be correctly believed. Suspicion works the opposite way. In the language of the veracity effect, relational closeness and face-to-face interaction increase the veracity effect (i.e., make the difference between truth accuracy and lie accuracy larger) while suspicion reduces the strength of the veracity effect. None of these, however, meaningfully affects accuracy because the gains and reductions in truth and lie accuracy cancel out.

There are, however, at least three things that can have substantial effects on accuracy and that are relevant to legal settings. These are question effects, projecting motives, and content in context. This discussion of detection accuracy will conclude with an examination of each of these.

My interest in question effects dates back to before the Thomas hearings. There was a brief interest in something I called the "probing effect," which I now think was a huge red herring. It was originally presumed that if people could interact with senders and ask questions, then they should be more accurate about the other's veracity. That is, asking, or even watching someone else ask probing questions should be useful in getting at the truth. This logic underlies interviews, interrogations, depositions, cross-examinations, and so on. The thing is, all the early studies found that compared with people who were not questioned, questioning enhanced believability, not accuracy (see Levine & McCornack, 1996b, 2001, for reviews). This is the probing effect. Questioning enhances believability, not accuracy. It was a very counterintuitive finding, and explaining it theoretically proved to be controversial (see Buller, Stiff, & Burgoon, 1996; Levine & McCornack, 1996a, 1996b). The impact of the probing-effect finding was to throw researchers off the trail of what now looks likes a very important consideration.

What changed my mind about question effects is the accuracy findings that have been coming out of work using the cheating tapes. The old probing-effect research looked at the presence or absence of probing and whether or not the questioning was confrontational or supportive. Those aspects of questioning do not seem to make much difference. But in my cheating tapes, it seems that certain questions do make a consistently big difference. Once I started realizing this, I began trying to write better and better questions. To date, I have tried out seven different question sets on more than 300 potential cheaters. My findings are departing from the 54%, slightly-better-than-chance status quo in both directions.

In our initial set of tapes, the questioning ended with asking subjects if they cheated and why they should be believed. Studies using this question set with student judges yield accuracy rates that are very much consistent with the literature as a whole, 52.8% to be exact. No surprise there. But, in a couple of studies that showed these tapes to experts (experienced police detectives in one case, and federal polygraphers in the other), accuracy dropped to significantly below chance, a dismal 36.3%. This should not be, because the evidence is clear that police and other professionals do better, not worse, than students in judging high stakes lies (O'Sullivan, Frank, Hurley, & Tiwana, 2009). Something important is going on here.

Here is what I think. The last question, "Why should I believe you?" is key. In watching the tapes, that question often is disruptive to honest folk. Honest people believe that if they just tell the truth, they will be believed. The last question comes as a shock and they cannot think of a good answer. How could they prove their innocence on the spot? The professional observers pay more attention to demeanor so they tend to pick up on the change in the honest senders' presentation and incorrectly infer deceit. Remember, demeanor can be misleading.

The second time we did the cheating experiments, we changed the last question from "Why should I believe you?" to "When we interview your partner, what will they say?" Accuracy for students jumped almost 10% to 62.3% and accuracy for experts goes up more than 30% to 67%. One little question, it seems, can make a huge difference. The reason, I think, is because honest people do not know why they should be believed but they do know that their partner will clear them. The reverse is true for cheaters. Given that they did not have a chance to get their stories straight with their partners, they don't know what their partner will say. So, want to know the truth? Think of a question an honest person but not a liar will be able to answer with confidence. The way to be fooled is to unwittingly make an honest person defensive.

Armed with these findings, we wanted to see if we could do better still. In the third version, we asked the question four different ways. Nonaccusatory questioning asked *if there was any reason the person did well that had not been disclosed.* Accusatory questioning *asserted that to do so well the person must have cheated, so they should just admit it.* The bogus evidence was that *their partner had said that they had cheated, so they should just admit it.* The bait question asked *if there was anything their partner might have said that would have contradicted their story.* All four question sets worked well yielding accuracy rates around 70%. Where they differed (although not significantly) was in the confession rates. Only 20% of cheaters confessed under nonaccusatory questioning, whereas 80% of cheaters confessed with false evidence. The other two question sets were half way in between and yielded 50% confessions. No noncheater false confessed.

In the most recent iteration, we added some additional questions asking subjects which questions they got right and to explain how it was they knew the answer. Accuracy on these tapes is above 70% in both of two studies. So, it appears that asking the right questions can lead to improved accuracy but asking the wrong questions can hurt accuracy. Furthermore, knowing the right questions requires knowing something about the context. For example, if the subjects had coordinated answers with their partners, then answers to the "what will your partner say?" question would likely be misleading.

A second useful finding coming out of our lab relates to motive. So far, all the accuracy results discussed have been limited to denials. What if we had included confessions? Because no one ever spontaneously false confesses in our cheating studies, we believed confessions would yield perfect accuracy. We have included confessions in some of our accuracy studies and, not surprisingly, they are almost always believed. People who deny wrong-doing may or may not have a motive to lie, but those who admit wrong-doing do not appear to have a motive for deception. Since people tend to lie for a reason and do not lie when they lack a motive to so, projecting a motive makes sense as a strategy of inferring honesty.

We recently tested this reasoning in a series of three studies (Levine, Kim, & Blair, 2010). We had judges watch confessions, denials, or both. Once I noticed that confessions were occurring in the cheating experiment, I asked a few noncheaters if they might go on tape and say that they cheated when they did not. This gave us tapes of both true and false confessions and denials. What we found was that confessions were almost always believed regardless of their truth or falsity. When the confessions were valid, subjects were right between 86% and 95% of the time, but when confessions were false, accuracy plummeted to between 12% and 26%. Because people do not false confess in my experiment, using the projected motive strategy has considerable validity. There are, however, situations where false confessions become likely (see Kassin & Kiechel, 1996). Under such circumstances, the believability of confessions is notably dysfunctional.

Finally, the truths and lies in most deception detection studies are decontexualized, making message content of little use. Outside the lab, however, people have background knowledge and can compare what is said to what they already know. Police and attorneys in criminal cases, for example, may have knowledge of the crime scene or statements from other witnesses and the like. This can make content (what is actually said) useful in a way it is not in most experiments. Most experiments, after all, are interested in the idea of nonverbal leakage, and useful content would be considered contamination to be avoided. But, if the goal is not testing a favored theory, but instead actually getting at the truth, then content looks to be very useful.

Two recent lines of research point to the utility of content in deception detection; Hatwig, Granhag, and Stromwal's work on strategic use of evidence (Granhag, Stromwal, & Hartwig, 2007; Hartwig, Granhag, Stromwall, & Kronkvist, 2006) and my work with Pete Blair on content in context (Blair, Levine, & Shaw, 2010). Strategic use of evidence is where the investigator initially withholds evidence during an interview to see if the interviewee says something that contradicts that evidence. Later, interviewees can be confronted with the contradictions. This technique appears very promising and yields accuracy rates more than 80%. In our content in context research, we find average accuracy of 75% just by providing judges with a little useful background knowledge (e.g., that the trivia questions were very difficult and few people know more than one or two without cheating).

In conclusion, research shows that people are only a little better than chance at deception detection and actually worse than 50% at detecting lies per se when all they have to go on is sender demeanor. The idea that people can ferret out lies by reading body language, facial expressions, or vocal stress is inconsistent with the vast majority of research to date. But, consideration of motive, listening to what is said for plausibility given some relevant prior knowledge, and listening to the answers of well-designed questions leads to accuracy well above chance. Perfect accuracy does not appear possible, but both our lab and research teams from Europe are now producing accuracy rates in the 70% and 80% range.

CONCLUSION

I love doing deception research. The big criticism of social science is so often that it only documents the obvious. Well, this is not the case in deception research. Some findings may seem obvious with hindsight, but again and again deception research shows that common sense can be very misleading when it comes to understanding deception and deception detection. I began this chapter with a discussion of some memorable Supreme Court confirmation hearings. My message then and now is that nonverbal demeanor can be very misleading. The distinction between what is seen as believable testimony and if testimony should be believed is key.

The social scientific study of deception has numerous implications for the legal professions and the practice of law. But the implications of deception research go so far beyond what is admissible as evidence in the courtroom. The research discussed here on demeanor, for example, suggests ways for attorneys and witnesses to be seen as more believable. The research on truth-bias suggests most juries will be at least somewhat gullible, but it also suggests ways in which juries can be made less likely to believe testimony. The research on deception detection suggests that juries may not be very good at distinguishing truths from lies, and they likely overestimate the utility of demeanor in making those judgments. There is a wealth of good research findings on deception that are just waiting to be applied, and the practitioners who are aware of these findings will have advantage over those who do not.

REFERENCES

Blair, J.P. (2005). A test of the unusual false confession perspective using cases of proven false confessions. *Criminal Law Bulletin, 41*, 127–144.

Blair, J.P., Levine, T.R., & Shaw, A.J. (2010). Content in context improves deception detection accuracy. *Human Communication Research, 36*, 423–442.

Bond, C.F., & The Global Deception Research Team. (2006). A world of lies. *Journal of Cross-Cultural Psychology, 37*, 60–74.

Bond, C.F., Jr., & DePaulo, B.M. (2006). Accuracy of deception judgments. *Review of Personality and Social Psychology, 10*, 214–234.

Bond, C.F., Jr., & DePaulo, B.M. (2008). Individual differences in judging deception: Accuracy and bias. *Psychological Bulletin, 134*, 477–492.

Buller, D.B., Stiff, J.B., & Burgoon, J.K. (1996). Behavioral adaptation in deceptive transactions fact or fiction: Reply to Levine and McCornack. *Human Communication Research, 22*, 589–603.

DePaulo, B.M., Lindsay, J.J., Malone, B.E., Muhlenbrick, L., Charlton, K., & Cooper, H. (2003). Cues to deception. *Psychological Bulletin, 129*, 74–118.

Ekman, P., & Friesen, W.V. (1969). Nonverbal leakage and clues to deception. *Psychiatry, 32*, 88–106.

Frank, M.G., & Feeley, T.H. (2003). To catch a liar: Challenges for research in lie detection training. *Journal of Applied Communication Research, 31*, 58–75.

Granhag, P.A., Stromwal, L.A., & Hartwig, M. (2007). The SUE technique: The way to interview to detect deception. *Forensic Update, 88*, 25–29.

Hartwig, M., Granhag, P.A., Stromwall, L.A., & Kronkvist, O. (2006). Strategic use of evidence during police interviews: When training to detect deception works. *Law and Human Behavior, 30*, 603–619.

Kassin, S.M., & Kiechel, K.L. (1996). The social psychology of false confessions: Compliance, internalization, and confabulation. *Psychological Science, 7*, 125–128.

Levine, T.R. (2010). A few transparent liars: Explaining 54% accuracy in deception detection experiments. *Communication Yearbook, 34*, 41–62.

Levine, T.R., Asada, K.J., & Massi, L.L. (2003). The relative impact of violation type and lie severity on judgments of message deceptiveness. *Communication Research Reports, 20*, 208–218.

Levine, T.R., Feeley, T., McCornack, S.A., Harms, C., & Hughes, M. (2005). Testing the effects of nonverbal training on deception detection accuracy with the inclusion of a bogus train control group. *Western Journal of Communication, 69*, 203–218.

Levine, T.R., Kim, R.K., & Blair, J.P. (2010). (In)accuracy at detecting true and false confessions and denials: An initial test of a projected motive model of veracity judgments. *Human Communication Research, 36*, 81–101.

Levine, T.R., Kim, R.K., & Hamel, L.M. (2010). People lie for a reason: Three experiments documenting the principle of veracity. *Communication Research Reports, 27*, 271–285.

Levine, T.R., Kim, R.K., Park, H.S., & Hughes, M. (2006). Deception detection accuracy is a predictable linear function of message veracity base-rate: A formal test of Park and Levine's probability model. *Communication Monographs, 73*, 243–260.

Levine, T.R., Lapinski, M.K., Banas, J., Wong, N., Hu, A.D.S., Endo, K., Baum, K.L., & Anders, L.N. (2002). Self-construal and self-other benefit. as determinants of deceptive message generation. *Journal of Intercultural Communication Research, 31*, 29–48.

Levine, T.R., & McCornack, S.A. (1996ba). A critical analysis of the behavioral adaptation explanation of the probing effect. *Human Communication Research, 22*, 575–589.

Levine, T.R., & McCornack, S.A. (1996ab). Can behavioral adaption explain the probing effect? *Human Communication Research, 22*, 603–612.

Levine, T.R., & McCornack, S.A. (2001). Behavioral adaption, confidence, and heuristic-based explanations of the probing effect. *Human Communication Research, 27*, 471–502.

Levine, T.R., Park, H.S., & McCornack, S.A. (1999). Accuracy in detecting truths and lies: Documenting the "veracity effect." *Communication Monographs, 66*, 125–144.

McCornack, S.A. (1992). Information manipulation theory. *Communication Monographs, 59*, 1–16.

Park, H.S., Levine, T.R., McCornack, S.A., Morrison, K., & Ferrara, M. (2002). How people really detect lies. *Communication Monographs, 69*, 144–157.

O'Sullivan, M., Frank, M.G., Hurley, C.M., & Tiwana, J. (2009). Police lie detection accuracy: The effects of lie scenario. *Law and Human Behavior, 33*, 530–538.

Serota, K.B., Levine, T.R., & Boster, F.J. (2010). The prevalence of lying in America: Three studies of reported deception. *Human Communication Research, 36*, 1–24.

Sporer, S.L., & Schwandt, B. (2006). Paraverbal indicators of deception: A meta-analytic synthesis. *Applied Cognitive Psychology, 20*, 421–446.

Sporer, S.L., & Schwandt, B. (2007). Moderators of nonverbal indicators of deception: A meta-analytic synthesis. *Psychology, Public Policy, and Law, 13*, 1–34.

During the Trial

5

Factors Influencing Jury Decision Making

Prior to and During Deliberation

Ann Burnett

Scholars who study the law are fascinated about how juries function. Unfortunately (or maybe fortunately) the courts rarely provide direct access to actual juries due to the fear of jury tampering. Because researchers cannot study actual jury behavior, they resort to interviewing jurors after the completion of the trial (Pettus, 1990), using shadow juries (Kerr & Bray, 2005), or conducting mock trials (Miller, Fontes, Boster, & Sunnafrank, 1983). Think of all the problems that can occur with these research protocols. Interviews rely on reflection that can be tainted by the passage of time; shadow juries might not have the same characteristics as actual juries; and mock trials and simulations typically are greatly condensed portions of trials, sometimes with no deliberation; and these studies are usually conducted with college students as jurors. Now, there is nothing wrong with college students, except they tend to be more educated, more liberal, and have a higher socioeconomic status than the typical juror (Bornstein, 1999). Therefore, it is difficult to learn how juries make decisions.

So, how can we know about juries? Except for one occasion in 2004 in which a judge allowed ABC to film six jury deliberations for the program, *Inside the Jury*, there are few alternatives to the ones presented here. Luckily, researchers have found that, despite the seemingly awkward methods we have for studying juries, mock trial results compare with actual trials (Bornstein 1999). Moreover, researchers can make wise choices to ensure validity (such as allowing mock juries to fully deliberate; Miller et al., 1983), and social scientists can make better methodological decisions if they know the law (Kerr & Bray, 2005). Additionally, even if post-trial interviews are not ideal, by talking with many jurors and hearing multiple perspectives that often overlap, interviews provide a unique way to learn about jury behavior. In the remainder of this chapter, I discuss how juries behave based on findings using the social scientific methods just described. It may be surprising to see how much knowledge we have about this secretive, sacrosanct aspect of our judicial system.

JURY DECISION MAKING: A GROUP PERSPECTIVE

One way to understand how juries function is to examine the group as a whole. This is more difficult than studying individual behavior in groups (groups are complicated!), but group behavior is essential to understanding juries nonetheless. When juries convene for deliberation, it is important to remember that until this point in time, assuming they have followed the judge's instructions, the jurors have not discussed the case with one another. (However, they might have cheated. Some jurors I have interviewed have said they could not keep their thoughts to themselves, so they visited with one another at lunch, away from the courtroom.)

Nearly all of the jurors whom I have interviewed reported being uneasy as to how to begin deliberating. Usually, after a period of helping themselves to coffee and engaging in some small talk, they proceed to select a foreperson. Generally, that process is casual—someone recommends that the person at the head of the table be foreperson, or the juror who initiates the conversation about foreperson selection is nominated. In one jury I studied, the sole male on the panel became the foreperson (Pettus, 1990). After the foreperson is selected, the jury begins its work.

Decision Procedure

Typically, juries are either verdict- or evidence-driven (Hastie, Penrod, & Pennington, 1983). Verdict-driven juries take a preliminary straw vote almost immediately upon convening and periodically take votes throughout the process to gauge progress toward a final verdict. Evidence-driven juries elect to discuss and evaluate the evidence before taking a vote on the verdict. As can be suspected, deliberation in evidence-driven juries is longer and more thorough than deliberation in verdict-driven juries (Hastie et al., 1983). In fact, one of the juries I studied in a murder trial was impressive in that they began by discussing whether or not the defendant was guilty. After determining he had some degree of culpability, they discussed the lesser charge, criminally negligent homicide. They decided as a group that he was at least guilty of that charge, then moved on to manslaughter, then second-degree murder, each time carefully discussing evidence related to that particular charge before taking a vote. A verdict-driven jury might have started with the most serious charge and not had as full and complete a discussion.

Regardless of decision procedure, the group tends to move as a unit toward a verdict. There are two explanations for this phenomenon. First, group polarization theory posits that if several group members express the same feelings or attitudes about a subject, the group will tend to move in that same direction (Isenberg, 1986; Moscovici & Zavalloni, 1969). Therefore, if a few jurors express their belief that a plaintiff in a civil case should be awarded damages, the group may all begin to be persuaded by their reasoning and may even believe more strongly in the plaintiff than before deliberation (Boster, Hunter, & Hale, 1991). Second, social comparison theory explains that people are motivated to be socially desirable (Isenberg, 1986). In jury deliberations, then, individuals might tend to agree with others, even if their opinions are different, in order to present themselves in a positive light. Depending on the case and how dominant the majority is, jury behavior could be explained by either polarization or social comparison (Kaplan & Miller, 1987).

In the movie, *Twelve Angry Men*, both polarization and social comparison appear to operate. Henry Fonda (in the original version of the movie), a lone juror arguing for acquittal, successfully persuades 11 other jurors to change their minds. As he presents his arguments, the group tends to be increasingly passionate about the defendant's acquittal (group polarization), and some of the jurors appear to change their minds in order to fit in (social comparison). Regardless of which decision procedure one would prefer, it is most important to appreciate the phenomenon of the group acting in concert.

Rarely do lone jurors successfully persuade all the others to change their minds in such dramatic fashion as in *Twelve Angry Men*. In fact, early jury researchers Kalven and Zeisel (1966) found that the final verdict usually matches the initial vote taken in deliberation, suggesting that the group majority appears to prevail most of the time. In fact, sometimes even after a verdict has been reached (in a non-unanimous decision), the majority still may continue to try to convince the minority to change their minds. However, if the minority consists of only one person, the majority will tend to ignore that person and direct discussion toward the majority position (Kessler, 1975). A unanimous jury verdict makes it seem as though the jury has a solid front, but the verdict masks disagreement that may have occurred as the result of a strong majority presence (Davis, Holt, Spitzer, & Stasser, 1981). In fact, the jurors I have interviewed who were in the minority position in deliberations reported that after extensive disagreement, they "gave in" due to the pressure placed on them by others, time constraints, and feeling hopeless about convincing the other jurors.

Size, Decision Rule, and Gender

Three additional factors appear to have an impact on the group perspective of jury decision making. Considerable debate has been waged over 12- versus 6-person juries. The Supreme Court has argued that 12 is an arbitrary number, and that justice can be served with juries of six people (*Williams v. Florida*, 1970). Some scholars argue that 12-person juries represent a greater cross section of the community and have longer, more robust discussions (Gelfland & Solomon, 1977; Grofman, 1976). Other experts argue that introverts might be more willing to contribute to the discussion in 6-person juries, and smaller juries cost less (Arnold, 1976). In a meta-analysis of 17 studies on jury size, Saks and Marti (1997) found that 12-person juries are more likely than 6-person juries to contain at least one person of color; smaller juries do not necessarily save time; and larger juries have greater evidence recall. Suppose you were accused of committing a felony. What would you prefer? A 12-person jury in which there is a greater chance of a fair representation of the community but in which several quiet individuals do not speak, or a 6-person jury in which everyone feels comfortable in voicing their opinion?

Another issue related to jury size is whether or not verdicts should be unanimous. In *Apodaca v. Oregon* (1972), the Supreme Court ruled that defendants do not have a constitutional right to a unanimous verdict. The justices, assuming the fair-minded nature of jurors, contended that non-unanimity allows for the stray juror (the random bullet) and prevents some of the majority pressure on the minority. On the other hand, unanimity has been shown to give jurors greater confidence in their verdict, provide an avenue for full consensus, create a more open venue for conflict, and allow for more opinion change as opposed to non-unanimous verdicts (Nemeth, 1977). The above issues are still debated. In some jurisdictions, civil trials are comprised of six to eight jurors and in other jurisdictions only a two-thirds majority is needed for decision. Even some criminal trials consist of as few as eight jurors, but rarely is non-unanimity a decision rule. Let us return to your felony conviction. Would you rather have a unanimous verdict in which some jurors are pressured to agree, or a non-unanimous verdict in which clearly some individuals do not buy your case?

The final factor that has an impact on the group of deliberating jurors is gender. In general, male jurors are more likely than female jurors to participate actively and to be elected foreperson (Marder, 1987). Furthermore, male jurors are perceived to be of higher socioeconomic and educational status than are female jurors, which grants them more power in deliberations (Marder, 1987). Female jurors may encourage contributions from quiet members of the panel, and may be more prone to promoting the evidence-driven form of deliberation. Gender-oriented perspectives provide unique standpoints from which to view evidence, especially in rape and sexual harassment cases. Therefore, in order for all the facts and evidence to be fully covered in deliberations, Marder recommends that women talk more and men listen more.

JURY DECISION MAKING: AN INDIVIDUAL PERSPECTIVE

When studying how juries make decisions, it often is easier to examine what each individual juror thinks and how each behaves. A great deal of research has been done on the juror in an attempt to better learn how juries as a whole make decisions. In this section of the chapter, I discuss mathematical and cognitive models that attempt to predict jury behavior, then I delve into communication research that examines jury decision making. Although each of these approaches focuses on jurors from different perspectives, all of them provide insight into how juries make decisions.

Mathematical Models

Probability models are based on the idea that jurors have mental yardsticks that adjust as they evaluate evidence in a trial (Levett, Danielson, Kovera, & Cutler, 2005; Penrod & Hastie, 1979). According to these models, sometimes called Bayesian models, the yardstick represents the probability that an event has occurred, with jurors assigning each piece of evidence a probability that is then matched against the yardstick.

Implicit decision rules models claim that jurors operate on a set of explicit and implicit rules (Penrod & Hastie, 1979). These rules result in a wide variety of potential decision schemes based on the number of jurors in the majority. Through mathematical equations, it is possible to determine a jury's verdict based on the initial vote. Extending the notion of decision schemes, Stasser and Davis (1981) proposed a social interaction sequence model in which each juror's choice is related to the probability of others preferring that choice and the certainty that the choice is correct. Similar to these models, communication scholars Boster et al. (1991) argue that after jurors hear an argument in deliberation, they shift their opinion toward that message; they also have mathematically mapped out that decision scheme.

Mathematical models have been critiqued as not being complex enough to reflect jury behavior (Ellsworth & Mauro, 1998; Levett et al., 2005; Winter & Greene, 2007). The argument is that models measure one unit—a mental yardstick or a decision scheme, for example—and that jurors are complex human beings who make decisions about multifaceted cases that models simply cannot emulate.

Cognitive Models

Psychologists have a keen interest in juror behavior because trials require high order thought processes (Hastie, 1993) that play a role in jury decision making (Winter & Greene, 2007). Unlike mathematical models that portray jurors as weighing each piece of evidence separately, explanation-based cognitive models view jurors as active decision makers.

Perhaps the best-known cognitive model is the story model (Hastie & Pennington, 1996; Pennington & Hastie, 1981, 1986, 1991). The model consists of three stages: Jurors evaluate evidence through constructing a story, they learn about the verdict options, and they reach a decision based on how their story fits the most pertinent verdict. Story construction obviously is the critical component in this model. Jurors first determine the central action in the story, then they interpret what the central action means, then, finally, they evaluate their interpretation of the story (Bennett & Feldman, 1981). To be considered believable, stories must have coherence, in that facts must unite (Hong, 1997), and fidelity, in that the story must be believable (Fisher, 1984).

Let us consider an example from a criminal trial, one I alluded to earlier. A fight breaks out in a bar between two men. A third man, George, pulls a gun out of his boot, planning to aim it toward the ceiling and shoot. In the process of raising the gun, it discharges. Cal is shot in the head and dies. George is charged with second-degree murder. George's story is that he became concerned when the fight started, and he tried to get the other men's attention by shooting his gun. It was an accident that

Cal was shot. Cal's attorney argues that George should not have gone to the bar armed with a loaded gun and that there were other ways to stop the fight. Which story has more coherence and fidelity to you? In constructing the story, the jurors might have determined the central action to be *George shoots Cal*. In interpreting the central action, the jury in this case thought George's actions were reckless—one does not normally pull a gun out of one's boot in a crowded bar and commence shooting. In their evaluation of this interpretation, they determined the story of George's recklessness to be compelling. Then, as per Pennington and Hastie's (1991) model, they decided that negligent homicide and manslaughter did not match the story, but that the charge of second-degree murder did, in fact, cohere with the story.

The main challenge with the cognitive model is that there is no way to determine how jurors will construct their stories in deliberation, and the model focuses on the individual and not the jury as a whole. On the other hand, the story model provides rich ground for communication experts in terms of crafting cases that tell a "good" story.

JURY DECISION MAKING: A COMMUNICATION PERSPECTIVE

Until this point, we have learned a great deal from psychologists and social psychologists about jury behavior, and the body of research from these disciplines is immense. However, there also is a critical role for the communication field to play in understanding jury behavior, as juries are, after all, groups in which people communicate. In this section, I introduce some of the recent work in which researchers have linked communication principles to jury decision making.

Jurors' Rules

Unlike other small groups, juries are different in that they are isolated from others during deliberation, bailiffs guard and protect them, they have no access to food or drink until provided by the court, they are required to serve when asked, they are selected sometimes due to their inexperience, and they are passive recipients of the information (Sunwolf & Seibold, 1998). As a result of the structures placed on them, jurors face a number of communication challenges, including selecting a foreperson, agreeing on a decision procedure, deciding when to ask the court for assistance, reporting member misconduct, and determining whether or not to continue deliberating. In examining a variety of potential communication challenges in these areas, citizens not selected for actual juries were asked to list rules they would follow in each of those situations. They reported, for example, that they would select a volunteer to be foreperson, vote with a secret ballot, send a note to the trial judge if a question arose, ignore information that a juror previously withheld, and keep trying to talk about the case to try to reach agreement. This study demonstrates the value of understanding implicit rules about jury deliberation.

The most striking example I have of jurors dealing with misconduct occurred in a trial in which one of the jurors was dating the cellmate of the defendant on trial (not disclosed in jury selection and unbeknownst to court personnel). Through the cellmate, she learned more about the defendant and his perspective on the case than was presented in the trial. When she brought up this extra information in deliberations, the other jurors attempted to ignore her and tell her that she was being inappropriate. In the end, the jury voted to find the defendant guilty, but according to her and the other jurors, she held out as the sole minority before relenting and voting with the majority. In this case, the implicit rule the jury followed served well. But there are other cases in which juries have decided to follow a verdict-driven decision rule and did not discuss all the possible case scenarios, and when juries ended their deliberations despite the opportunity and need for additional discussion. Structures, or implicit communication rules, can affect jury outcomes, as these communication scholars demonstrated.

Decisional Regret Theory

Do you ever think about what might have been? What if you had chosen that other college? What if you had roomed with this person instead of that person? What if I had broken up with him or her sooner? This is decisional regret, or counterfactual thinking (Sunwolf, 2006, 2007). Groups, such as juries, engage in counterfactual thinking as they create stories in deliberation. What if George (who pulled the gun from his boot) was trying to stop the fight? What if George was extremely drunk and thought he looked pretty cool and threatening at the same time he wielded a pistol? What if he had not been in the bar in the first place? Imaginary narratives constructed from these "what if's" encourage others to reproduce, alter, disconfirm, or create a new story (Sunwolf, 2006). Jurors whom I have interviewed say they go through many iterations of questioning to create a story, sometimes even after they reach a verdict in order to be sure of their decision. Jury decisions often can be serious and life-altering, and decisional regret weighs heavily on jurors. By using counterfactual reasoning, jurors can attempt to allay some of their fears when asked to reach a verdict.

Juror Argument

In discussions of jury behavior, the term *argument* is used in two ways. Two or more people can have an argument (i.e., argue among themselves), or one person can present an argument (i.e., make or support a claim). In the latter sense, a colleague and I attempted to study the types of arguments made by individual jurors during jury deliberations so that we could learn more about types of jury communication (Burnett & Badzinski, 2000). We conducted a study of 80 mock jury deliberations, coding each argument made by each juror. Our conclusion was that jurors' arguments are not complex. Rather, they typically consist of assertions with little support ("I just think that guy is guilty") and agreement with other jurors ("Yeah, you're right"). Initially, it bothered us to think that jurors' arguments are not sophisticated, but we concluded that because juries are so unique (they are isolated, guarded by bailiffs, have little choice in when they eat/drink, are required to serve, and most importantly, are not allowed to ask questions or pursue lines of reasoning during the trial), they face distinct levels of argument—one in the courtroom where attorneys tell them what their arguments are and the second in the jury room where they must repeat and re-tell what they heard in court. As a result, it is no wonder when a juror's argument is simple, as jurors must base their decisions on testimony that they recall in deliberation. Additionally, we believe jurors might construct arguments as a team in which one juror makes an assertion, another juror supports that assertion, and another juror agrees. We will continue to study that possibility (Burnett & Badzinski, 2000).

JURY DECISION-MAKING FACTORS

Let us now examine factors that jurors consider when making their decisions. All of these factors are used within the models and theories presented here. In other words, the mathematical models rely on the idea that jurors discuss evidence, whereas the cognitive models assume that jurors use evidence and the law to construct stories, and these stories might emerge from counterfactual reasoning about the evidence provided. Although some factors of jury decision making may be obvious (e.g., the evidence), others are perhaps less so.

Time of Decision

As might be apparent by now, some of my research has involved observing criminal trials and interviewing jurors afterward (Pettus, 1990). I was younger then and full of confidence that jurors would do as they are told, including deliberating before making a decision. To make sure they were doing just that, I asked the jurors to talk about the trial with me, indicating what they thought after each stage in the proceedings (*voir dire*, instructions, opening statements, witnesses for the prosecution, witnesses for the defense, closing arguments, and deliberation). In all three of the trials I studied, many of the jurors had made up their minds after the prosecution had closed its case, and in a few circumstances, jurors indicated they knew the defendant was guilty at first sight (during *voir dire*). In fact, in another study, 67% of the jurors reported they would have reached the same decision that the jury reached had there not been a deliberation (Simon, 1980; see also Kalven & Zeisel, 1966; Leigh, 1984).

Some research suggests that decisions are made after opening statements (Linz & Penrod, 1984), and although contrary evidence indicates the impact of opening statements is not that powerful, they can certainly create a favorable framework for a story creation (Diamond, 2006; Pennington & Hastie, 1991). If jurors do, in fact, make their decisions prior to deliberation, it is incumbent for attorneys to do all they can to create ways for jurors to view the case from their perspective at the start. Some of that work involves the following decision-making factors.

Evidence

When I interviewed trial jurors, they talked a great deal about the evidence in the trial (Pettus, 1990). They evaluated its effectiveness and used it extensively to create coherent and valid stories about "what really happened." Jurors appeared to examine the evidence through the lens of the law, comparing evidence with the elements of the charge or the reasonable doubt standard (Wright & Hall, 2007).

Evidence is offered most commonly through witness testimony and through physical objects, documents and the like. However, in a technological age, more options are becoming available. For example, video recreations of the crime or civil action have been used and found to not affect the verdict (Fishfader, Howells, Katz, & Teresi, 1996). In addition to video re-creations, judges increasingly are being asked to decide matters of new technology and evidence admissibility in regard to computer animations and simulations, video settlement brochures, and virtual environments (Feigenson & Dunn, 2003).

The role of expert evidence is a particular area of scholarly focus because frequently experts are asked to testify due to the belief that they have more credibility than nonexperts. In fact, expert evidence can affect jury verdicts (Levett et al., 2005); specifically, the quality of the expert evidence, the expert's credibility, and the plaintiff's credibility positively relate to a jury's decision (McAuliff, Kovera, & Nunez, 2009). But not all experts are created equally. I discussed the Pastor John case in Chapter 2. Frances, who accused Pastor John of sexual exploitation, called a supposed expert in pastoral sexual abuse. The so-called expert was eccentric, had a lack of knowledge, and swore (used the "F" word!) during her testimony. Frances' team had brought her to our jurisdiction at great expense, but any attempts to demonstrate the gravity of the pastor's offense were completely undermined by the expert's testimony.

A recent development in the area of expert testimony is videotaping in which experts are examined about a particular, complex issue, such as how DNA evidence is collected and tested. Once a videotape has been created, that tape conceivably could be played in any case in which DNA evidence is used (McAuliff, Nemeth, Bornstein, & Penrod, 2003). Courts are still undecided as to whether "generic" expert witness tapes are admissible.

Expert witnesses increasingly are asked to present complicated evidence, statistical and probabilistic findings, and intricate scientific processes. Complex DNA evidence, convoluted accounting practices, accident probabilities under varying road conditions, and so forth, can be difficult to follow. It is still unclear if jurors can process this complex information (McAuliff et al., 2003). Additionally, if jurors are confused, they might decide that if it is scientific, it must be true, creating more challenges regarding the use of scientific evidence.

Attorneys

Whereas most of the time jurors make their decisions based on the attorneys' arguments, there are times in which extra-legal factors, such as the attorneys' attributes and performance appear to carry some weight. In the trials I studied, the jurors' verdicts mirrored the more positive comments in the trials; in other words, when the jurors positively described the attorneys and found their performance noteworthy, they also sided with those attorneys (Pettus, 1990).

Nonverbal communication influences juror's perceptions of the attorneys. For example, attorneys with disfluencies (hesitations in speaking style, use of fillers) are not as impressive as attorneys who are fluent, and verdicts tend to favor those attorneys who are fluent (Barge, Schlueter, &

Pritchard, 1989). Other nonverbal cues such as body movements, gestures, and proximity to the jury appear to affect the decision, as jurors prefer greater nonverbal immediacy (Stockwell & Schrader, 1995). Additionally, physical attractiveness and style of dress can impact juror perception (LeVan, 1984).

In my experience, jurors have a heightened awareness of court personnel, especially the attorneys. In one trial in which I assisted, a juror was terribly bothered that one of the attorneys was missing a button on the cuff of his suit jacket. Of another attorney, a juror remarked, "she has a few nervous habits that are distracting" (Pettus, 1990). Jurors are exposed to a variety of crime and law programs via the entertainment media, and they tend to compare the attorneys they see in court with those on television. Regarding all the attorneys in one case, a juror stated: "They were young. I was surprised at how young they seemed to be" (Pettus, 1990). In fact, if the attorneys are not quick on their feet, are plodding through multiple legal pages of minutia, or are speaking in a monotone, that is not what jurors expect from trial attorneys because lawyers on television are dramatic and exciting, and toned-down behaviors can turn jurors against them.

Even the use of time can be a factor in evaluating the attorneys. In a trial in which the defense attorney was to deliver his closing argument before lunch, he promised the judge he would be finished in 30 minutes. An hour later, well past the lunch hour, he finally brought his speech to an end. The jurors were so angry that he broke his promise, they looked poorly on him and voted to convict his client. It would be difficult to prove that the attorney's use of time led to the guilty verdict, but it surely did not help.

Witnesses

Although jurors have a great deal to say about the attorneys, they have even more to say about the witnesses (Pettus, 1990). Jurors reflected on positive attributes ("truthful," "believable") and negative attributes of witnesses ("he looked kinda burned out"). They also discussed witnesses' positive and negative performances ("he stuck with his same story," and "he did everything *but* answer the question"). A landmark study on witness character attractiveness revealed that the more attractive the victim is, the harsher the sentence, and the more unattractive the defendant is, the greater the sentence (Landy & Aronson, 1969).

Nonverbal cues play a role in evaluating witness credibility. For example, attorneys should work with their witnesses on behaviors that might signal that the witness is lying (nervous, anxious behavior, as jurors may conclude, justifiably or not, that a nervous witness is not a truthful witness; LeVan, 1984). Similarly, witnesses who do not sound confident or powerful tend to lack credibility, so powerless speech styles can hamper both witnesses and attorneys (Erickson, Lind, Johnson, & O'Barr, 1978).

In my experience, attorneys do not spend enough time working with their witnesses prior to trial. Imagine how frightened most people are to take the stand, yet some attorneys meet witnesses for the first time in courtroom hallways. The witness may not know what to wear, where to sit, that an oath must be taken, or how to articulate their version of the events in a clear, powerful way. I have seen witnesses in cut-off T-shirts, complete with beer belly, dirty hair, clothes that are too tight, all the while attempting to describe events that they have not rehearsed or thought about for years. I assist attorneys in witness preparation, which does not mean that I tell witnesses how to lie, but rather how to best articulate their experiences, knowing that coherent stories will be most effective.

Judge

Although the judge is supposed to be an impartial regulator/educator of courtroom procedure, he or she may have an effect on jurors none-theless. Jurors notice the judge's distracting nonverbal behaviors (e.g., reading through the yellow pages; Pettus, 1990). They might accidently "leak" their feelings to the jury in their facial expressions or vocal cues (Blanck, 1987). A researcher and I found that judges who appear to be highly involved (e.g., by leaning forward, nodding the head, taking notes) were perceived as more credible than judges appearing less involved. In general, jurors found male judges to be more credible than female judges (Badzinski & Pettus, 1994). In a follow-up study, it was concluded that jurors are likely to notice negative nonverbal behaviors ("He was totally bored," and "He didn't look too interested in the whole thing. It almost looked to me as if he had his mind made up about the defendant's sen-tence"; Burnett & Badzinski, 2005). Although we are not yet able to prove that judge behavior influences the verdict, if jurors watch judges for guidance, nonverbal behaviors, intentional or not, may play a role in jury decisions.

THE IMPORTANCE OF JURIES

Before discussing whether or not deliberations matter given what we know thus far, let us explore possible changes to the trial process that could assist with jury decision making.

Using Communication to Improve Decision Making

Communication truly plays a role in suggested alterations to the trial process. As mentioned earlier, jurors are not allowed to interact with trial participants; they must sit and listen. However, increasingly, jurors have been allowed to take notes during the trial (Heuer & Penrod, 1994; Penrod & Heuer, 1997, 1998). The notes are left with the court at the end of each day, and jurors are allowed to use them in deliberation. Notes can aid juror's memory of trial testimony, and although notes have a chance of being inaccurate, potentially other jurors' notes or memories can act as a check.

Perhaps more controversial is the option for jurors to ask questions of witnesses (Heuer & Penrod, 1994; Penrod & Heuer, 1997, 1998). The proposal usually calls for the jurors to write down their questions, and the judge screens them with the assistance of counsel. In this way, it is difficult to taint a trial with an errant question. Jurors might be less confused and more involved if they had the opportunity to ask questions. Still, attorneys might not wish to disallow a juror's question, and questions can suggest the way jurors are leaning. Although this option seems like a good idea, it has not been attempted in earnest.

Jury instructions are not usually user-friendly, and jurors may try hard to understand but still misinterpret them. As a result, one author has recommended using illustrated jury instructions (Dattu, 1998). Others have suggested that instructions be process-oriented, so that the jury first decides Step 1. If they answer the question "yes," they move to Step 2; if they answer the question "no," they move to Step 4 and so on. Researchers have found step-by-step instructions to be useful, and they have been implemented in some jurisdictions for case-specific trials (Taylor, Buchanan, Pryor, & Strawn, 1981). With innovative ways to assist juries and with their own set of decision-making faculties, how important are jury deliberations?

The Role of Deliberations

The quick answer to the above question is that jury deliberations are absolutely fundamental and necessary to our judicial system. Even if jurors make up their minds early in the trial, the deliberation process is essential. First, the group phenomenon of forging together with a common mind is an important process (Batiza, 1999). Second, despite any group frailty, jury decisions usually reflect what the judge would have done, with the advantage of having peers decide one's fate (Kalven & Zeisel, 1966; Simon, 1980). Third, the influence that occurs in a jury prior to the first ballot is strong and enough to negate individual preconceptions (Diamond, 2006; Sandys & Dillehay, 1995). In fact, for trials in which jurors are undecided, deliberations are essential; for trials in which jurors have already made up their minds, deliberations provide a testing ground for arguments in which they might be convinced to change their minds (Pettus, 1990). Finally, jurors take their role seriously (Bridgeman & Marlowe, 1979; Pettus, 1990). They are highly involved in the process, evaluating the evidence to create cogent stories of what happened.

SUMMARY

In this chapter, I have discussed the challenges associated with studying juries, and those challenges notwithstanding, I have discussed mathematical, cognitive, and communication-related explanations as to how juries function. Furthermore, this chapter has shown when jurors make decisions and how juries evaluate evidence, attorneys, witnesses, and the judge in the trial. It reviewed potential changes to the trial process to assist jurors, and concluded that they generally make good decisions in a necessary, deliberative process.

Communication scholars have knowledge that can be shared as consultants in court cases. For example, those knowledgeable about group communication can learn how to effectively facilitate focus group discussions such as those often used for complex court cases. Scholars of public speaking can use their knowledge of clarity and credibility to assist in preparing witnesses for trial. Scholars of argumentation and debate can assist attorneys as they develop opening statements and closing arguments. Those with interviewing skills can query jurors after a trial to discover what factors influenced their decisions.

Scholars who study jury decision making in particular have additional consulting skills, of course. For example, when I conduct jury focus groups, it helps that I understand the nature of argument and how stories create arguments; as a result, I am able to ask participants the kinds of questions that get to the heart of the case. I then work with the attorney to take the strongest arguments, constructing a clear story to articulate in court. Furthermore, knowing that jurors make their decisions early in the trial and that they build their argument based on what they hear has motivated me to conduct focus groups in phases. Information is added bit by bit, and jurors reflect in writing and as a group at each phase of the process. In this way, I have an idea of what actual jurors will be thinking as the trial progresses. The attorney and I can then consider the order and manner in which information is presented. In short, specialized knowledge of juries can provide an opportunity to play a role in litigation—a role that can be rewarding for the attorney and client as well as for the consultant.

REFERENCES

Apodaca v. Oregon, 406 U.S. 404 (1972).

Arnold, W.E. (1976). Membership satisfaction and decision making in six member and twelve member simulated juries. *The Journal of the American Forensic Association, 12*, 130–137.

Badzinski, D.M., & Pettus, A.B. (1994). Nonverbal involvement and sex: Effects on jury decision making. *Journal of Applied Communication Research, 22*, 309–321.

Barge, J.K., Schlueter, D.W., & Pritchard, A. (1989). The effects of nonverbal communication and gender on impression formation in opening statements. *The Southern Communication Journal, 54*, 330–349.

Batiza, P. (1999). One lawyer's inside look at the jury. *Practical Litigator, 10*, 9–18.

Bennett, W.L., & Feldman, M.S. (1981). *Reconstructing reality in the courtroom.* New Brunswick, NJ: Rutgers University Press.

Blanck, P.D. (1987). The "process" of field research in the courtroom: A descriptive analysis. *Law and Human Behavior, 11*, 337–358.

Bornstein, B.H. (1999). The ecological validity of jury simulations: Is the jury still out? *Law and Human Behavior, 23*, 75–91.

Boster, F.J., Hunter, J.E., & Hale, J.L. (1991). An information-processing model of jury decision making. *Communication Research, 18*, 524–547.

Bridgeman, D.L., & Marlowe, D. (1979). Jury decision making: An empirical study based on actual felony trials. *Journal of Applied Psychology, 64*, 91–98.

Burnett, A., & Badzinski, D.M. (2000). An exploratory study of argument in the jury decision-making process. *Communication Quarterly, 48*, 380–396.

Burnett, A., & Badzinski, D.M. (2005). Judge nonverbal communication on trial: Do mock trial jurors notice? *Journal of Communication, 55*, 209–224.

Dattu, F. (1998). Illustrated jury instructions: A proposal. *Law and Psychology Review, 22*, 67–102.

Davis, J.H., Holt, R.W., Spitzer, C.E., & Stasser, G. (1981). The effects of consensus requirements and multiple decisions on mock juror verdict preferences. *Journal of Experimental Social Psychology, 17*, 1–15.

Diamond, S.S. (2006). Beyond fantasy and nightmare: A portrait of the jury. *Buffalo Law Review, 54*, 717–763.

Ellsworth, P.C., & Mauro, R. (1998). Psychology and law. In D.T. Gilbert, S.T. Fiske, & G. Lindzey (Eds.), *The handbook of social psychology* (Vol. 2, 4th ed., pp. 684–732). New York: Oxford University Press.

Erickson, B., Lind, E.A., Johnson, B.C., & O'Barr, W.M. (1978). Speech style and impression formation in a court setting: The effects of "powerful" and "powerless" speech. *Journal of Experimental Social Psychology, 14*, 266–279.

Feigenson, N., & Dunn, M.A. (2003). New visual technologies in court: Directions for research. *Law and Human Behavior, 27,* 109–126.

Fisher, W.R. (1984). Narration as human communication paradigm: The case of public moral argument. *Communication Monographs, 51,* 1–22.

Fishfader, V.L., Howells, G.N., Katz, R.C., & Teresi, P.S. (1996). Evidential and extralegal factors in juror decisions: Presentation mode, retention, and level of emotionality. *Law and Human Behavior, 20,* 565–572.

Gelfland, A.E., & Solomon, H. (1977). Considerations in building jury behavior models and in comparing jury schemes: An argument in favor of 12-member juries. *Jurimetrics Journal, 17,* 292–313.

Grofman, B. (1976). Not necessarily twelve and not necessarily unanimous: Evaluating the impact of *Williams v. Florida* and *Johnson v. Louisiana.* In G. Bermant, C. Nemeth, & N. Vidmar (Eds.), *Psychology and law: Research frontiers* (pp. 149–168). Lexington, MA: Lexington Press.

Hastie, R. (1993). *Inside the juror: The psychology of juror decision making.* Cambridge, UK: Cambridge University Press.

Hastie, R., & Pennington, N. (1996). The O.J. Simpson stories: Behavioral scientists' reflections on *The People of the State of California v. Orenthal James Simpson. University of Colorado Law Review, 67,* 957–976.

Hastie, R., Penrod, S.D., & Pennington, N. (1983). *Inside the jury.* Cambridge, MA: Harvard University Press.

Heuer, L., & Penrod, S. (1994). Juror notetaking and question asking during trials. *Law and Human Behavior, 18,* 121–150.

Hong, P.B. (1997). A theory of final argument in civil trials. *Hamline Law Review, 21,* 31–63.

Isenberg, D.J. (1986). Group polarization: A critical review and meta-analysis. *Journal of Personality and Social Psychology, 50,* 1141–1151.

Kalven, H., Jr., & Zeisel, H. (1966). *The American jury.* Boston: Little, Brown.

Kaplan, M.F., & Miller, C.E. (1987). Group decision making and normative versus informational influence: Effects of type of issue and assigned decision rule. *Journal of Personality and Social Psychology, 53,* 306–313.

Kerr, N.L., & Bray, R.M. (2005). Simulation, realism, and the study of the jury. In N. Brewer & K.D. Williams (Eds.), *Psychology and law: An empirical perspective* (pp. 322–364). New York: Guilford.

Kessler, J.B. (1975). The social psychology of jury deliberations. In R.J. Simon (Ed.), *The jury system in America* (pp. 69–93). Beverly Hills, CA: Sage.

Landy, D., & Aronson, E. (1969). The influence of the character of the criminal and his victim on the decisions of simulated jurors. *Journal of Experimental and Social Psychology, 5,* 41–152.

Leigh, L.J. (1984). A theory of jury trial advocacy. *Utah Law Review,* 763–806.

LeVan, E.A. (1984). Nonverbal communication in the courtroom: Attorney beware. *Law and Psychology Review, 8,* 83–104.

Levett, L.M., Danielson, E.M., Kovera, M.B., & Cutler, B.L. (2005). The psychology of jury and juror decision making. In N. Brewer & K.D. Williams (Eds.), *Psychology and law: An empirical perspective* (pp. 365–406). New York: Guilford.

Linz, D., & Penrod, S. (1984). Increasing attorney persuasiveness in the courtroom. *Law and Psychology Review, 8,* 1–47.

Marder, N.S. (1987). Gender dynamics and jury deliberations. *The Yale Law
Journal, 96,* 593–612.

McAuliff, B.D., Kovera, M.B., & Nunez, G. (2009). Can jurors recognize missing
control groups, confounds, and experimenter bias in psychological science?
Law and Human Behavior, 33, 247–257.

McAuliff, B.D., Nemeth, R.J., Bornstein, B.H., & Penrod, S.D. (2003). Juror
decision-making in the twenty-first century: Confronting science and technology in court. In D. Carson & R. Bull (Eds.), *Handbook of psychology
in legal contexts* (2nd ed., pp. 303–328). West Sussex, England: Wiley.

Miller, G.R., Fontes, N.E., Boster, F.J., & Sunnafrank, M.J. (1983). Methodological issues in legal communication research: What can trial simulations tell
us? *Communication Monographs, 50,* 33–46.

Moscovici, S., & Zavalloni, M. (1969). The group as a polarizer of attitudes.
Journal of Personality and Social Psychology, 12, 125–135.

Nemeth, C. (1977). Interactions between jurors as a function of majority vs.
unanimity decision rules. *Journal of Applied Social Psychology, 7,* 38–56.

Pennington, N., & Hastie, R. (1981). Juror decision-making models: The gener-
alization gap. *Psychological Bulletin, 89,* 246–287.

Pennington, N., & Hastie, R. (1986). Evidence evaluation in complex decision
making. *Journal of Personality and Social Psychology, 51,* 242–258.

Pennington, N., & Hastie, R. (1991). A cognitive theory of juror decision making:
The story model. *Cardozo Law Review, 13,* 519–557.

Penrod, S., & Hastie, R. (1979). Models of jury decision making: A critical review.
Psychological Bulletin, 56, 462–492.

Penrod, S., & Heuer, L. (1997). Tweaking commonsense: Assessing aids to jury
decision making. *Psychology, Public Policy, and Law, 3,* 259–284.

Penrod, S., & Heuer, L. (1998). Improving group performance: The case of the
jury. In R. S. Tindale et al. (Eds.), *Theory and research on small groups*
(pp. 127–152). New York: Plenum.

Pettus, A.B. (1990). The verdict is in: A study of jury decision making factors,
moment of personal decision, and jury deliberations—from the jurors' point
of view. *Communication Quarterly, 38,* 83–97.

Saks, M.J., & Marti, M.W. (1997). A meta-analysis of the effects of jury size.
Law and Human Behavior, 21, 451–467.

Sandys, M., & Dillehay, R.C. (1995). First-ballot votes, predeliberation dispositions, and final verdicts in jury trials. *Law and Human Behavior, 19,*
175–195.

Simon, R.J. (1980). The rationality of jury deliberation and verdicts. In R.J. Simon
(Ed.), *The jury: Its role in American society* (pp. 49–71). New York: Lexington Books.

Stasser, G., & Davis, J.H. (1981). Group decision making and social influence:
A social interaction sequence model. *Psychological Review, 88,* 523–551.

Stockwell, L., & Schrader, D.C. (1995). Factors that persuade jurors. *University
of Toledo Law Review, 27,* 99–113.

Sunwolf. (2006). Decisional regret theory: Reducing the anxiety about uncertain outcomes during group decision making through shared counterfactual storytelling. *Communication Studies, 57,* 107–134.

Sunwolf. (2007, November). *Woulda/coulda/shoulda group talk: Counterfactual thinking in the jury room (an application of decisional regret theory).* Paper presented at the National Communication Association convention, Chicago.

Sunwolf, & Seibold, D.R. (1998). Jurors' intuitive rules for deliberation: A structurational approach to communication in jury decision making. *Communication Monographs, 65,* 282–307.

Taylor, K.P., Buchanan, R.W., Pryor, B., & Strawn, D.U. (1981). How do jurors reach a verdict? *Journal of Communication, 31,* 37–42.

Williams v. Florida, 399 U.S. 78 (1970).

Winter, R.J., & Greene, E. (2007). Juror decision-making. In F.T. Durson (Ed.), *Handbook of applied cognition* (2nd ed., pp. 739–761). West Sussex, England: Wiley.

Wright, D.B., & Hall, M. (2007). How a "reasonable doubt" instruction affects decisions of guilt. *Basic and Applied Social Psychology, 29,* 91–98.

6

Hindsight Bias, Juror Decision Making, and Courtroom Communication

Debra L. Worthington
Merrie Jo Pitera

People have a psychological tendency to exaggerate the *a priori* certainty of an event's outcome after the true outcome is known. For example, "I have a feeling Smith will lose this election" tends to become, after the fact, "See, I knew Smith would lose." The name for this kind of distortion is *hindsight bias*. It unconsciously affects most of us, including jurors, of course. For example, jurors in negligence cases might tend to believe an accident was obviously foreseeable now that they know it happened.

This chapter focuses on the impact of hindsight bias on juror decision making. We begin with an introduction to hindsight bias and its psychological foundations, outlining its application to the legal arena. We then introduce a variety of communication-based strategies for reducing the bias during civil trial proceedings, including developing appropriate case themes, using strategic witness examination, and designing effective visuals for demonstrative evidence. Throughout this discussion we demonstrate how these and other debiasing strategies may be integrated into attorney case preparation and presentation.

HINDSIGHT BIAS

Traditionally, psychologists have identified two types of hindsight bias. The first occurs when individuals make a decision or judgment they are later asked to recall. If, after their original estimate, they find out the right answer, they will recall their guess as having been more accurate than it really was. For example, if someone guesses the height of the Washington Monument to be 425 feet, but later learns the correct answer to be 555 feet, then he or she is likely to incorrectly recall the original estimate as having been closer to the right answer that it actually was (e.g., 475 feet).

The second type of hindsight bias occurs when people are given information about an event or situation, then asked to reconstruct the outcome while simultaneously attempting to ignore their knowledge of the outcome. For example, if a physician is provided symptoms for a hypothetical patient who is identified as having cancer, the physician will be more likely to interpret the symptoms as signs of cancer than if it had not been known the patient had cancer. Not only is it more likely that the diagnosis will be cancer, but also the diagnosis will be made more confidently.

Thus, central to hindsight bias is the tendency for people to "judge *a priori* decisions or actions in light of their *post hoc* knowledge" (Stallard, Price, & Dane, 2001, p. 109). Fischhoff, who conducted much of the early research into the hindsight bias, concluded that most people were unaware they engaged in it. Specifically, few individuals realize that they use outcome knowledge (hindsight) when asked to predict the "inevitability" of an event's outcome after the fact. Nor are we aware of its effects on our judgments—that is, that it gives us a stronger belief in the inevitability of the outcome, and it inflates our estimates of the probability of the outcome.

Psychological Foundations

Since Fischhoff's original work, a number of motives for hindsight bias have been suggested. Of these, Fischhoff's (1975) "creeping determinism" provides the most complete explanation, and has received substantial empirical support. The process of creeping determinism occurs when individuals integrate outcome information into what they "know" about the factual events that preceded the outcome (Fischhoff, 1975). In other words, when faced with an event "after the fact," the "retrospective judge attempts to make sense, or a coherent whole, out of all that he or she knows about the event" (p. 297). Essentially, people rewrite the events so that the "beginning and middle are causally connected to its end" (Wasserman, Lempert, & Hastie, 1991, p. 31). Using this backward-processing strategy, this mental "rewriting" subsequently makes it difficult for them to imagine how alternate outcomes could take place (Agans & Shaffer, 1994; Fischhoff, 1975; Schkade & Kilbourne, 1991). Additionally, facts that are in keeping with an event's outcome are rated as more significant and more relevant to the outcome (Baron & Hershey, 1988; Fischhoff, 1975).

Fischhoff's concept of creeping determinism may help explain how additional information can increase the strength of the bias and how an individual's perception of an outcome's inevitability will actually increase as additional antecedent information is integrated into an explanation of an event (Rachlinski, 1998). For example, after finding out that an investor lost money on a transaction suggested by her realtor, we might judge the realtor's advice as less sound than we might have judged otherwise. Ambiguous communication may be processed so that it is assimilated in keeping with the known outcome.

More recently, findings from a series of studies by Nestler, Blank, and von Collani (2008) suggest that creeping determinism is "not easy or automatic but rather effortful and resource demanding" (p. 1052). In other words, "the retrieval and evaluation of potential causal antecedents places demands on the limited pool of cognitive resources [available to people]" (p. 1052). Nester and his colleagues report that when individuals experience a high cognitive load, the effects of creeping determinism are significantly reduced. Their findings suggest that hindsight may not occur in every available instance, and this provides an additional explanation as to why the strength of the bias may vary.

Moderators of Hindsight

Research suggests that subjective experiences (i.e., personal awareness of how one is processing information) also can affect the magnitude of the bias for individuals at three junctures:

1. When learning of the initial outcome,

2. When thinking of the underlying causes of the outcome, and

3. When considering alternative outcomes (Sanna & Schwarz, 2007).

Essentially then, subjective cognitive experience may qualify the impact of accessible thought content, but only in situations in which the experience is considered informative for the judgment being made.

One of the most researched areas of hindsight bias addresses the impact of surprise on the extent and direction of the bias. For example, many people believe that lung cancer is a realistic outcome after an individual smokes two packs of cigarettes each day for 20 years. They are familiar with the situation (smoking) and the outcome (lung cancer) seems reasonable. Sanna and Schwarz (2007) argue that hindsight bias is likely to occur in situations of low surprise and higher familiarity, and when it is easy to recall or generate supporting evidence for a particular outcome. At the same time, however, hindsight bias will be reduced in opposite situations (e.g., surprising outcome, unfamiliarity, difficulty in generating support). They further argue that merely thinking about alternatives to a known outcome can reduce the hindsight bias, but only in circumstances as just noted (i.e., low surprise, high familiarity, obvious support). When the alternatives are difficult to generate, Sanna and Schwarz contend that the bias may actually increase (also see Sanna, Schwarz, & Small, 2002; Sanna, Schwarz, & Stocker, 2002). Thus, for example, it may be difficult for jurors to believe that working with asbestos-laden brake dust was the cause of a smoker's lung cancer, partly because cigarette smoking is a cause they are more familiar with. As Sanna and Schwarz (2007) suggest, the harder it is to see how events might have turned out otherwise, the more convinced we become that the outcome was inevitable (Fischhoff, 1982). Thus, the magnitude and direction of the bias is affected by the ease by which respective thoughts can be imagined. Accessibility to relevant cognitions, then, appears to have a significant impact on the bias.

Müller and Stahlberg (2007) qualify the impact of surprise, noting that it only attenuates the bias when a person does not question its informative value. Similarly, Schwarz (2004), in keeping with earlier work by Tversky and Kahneman (1973), suggests that the more examples one has, the easier it is to bring one or more to mind (and vice versa), thus the feeling of ease (or difficulty) leads people to infer that there are many (or few) reasons for an outcome.

It is no surprise, then, that although everyone engages in hindsight bias to some degree, people tend to be more prone to the bias when they lack topic-specific knowledge (Christensen-Szalanski & Willham, 1991; Klayman & Ha, 1987). Consequently, uninformed individuals are more likely to use hindsight in order to better process information, whereas individuals with case-specific or relevant knowledge are less likely to engage hindsight in their decision making (Christensen-Szalanski & Willham, 1991; Kelman, Fallas, & Folger, 1998; Klayman & Ha, 1987). Presumably, expertise increases the ability to imagine alternatives, increases familiarity, and reduces surprise that events led to a particular outcome (Nestler & Egloff, 2009).

More recent research by Ash (2009) suggests that surprise may be less significant. He argues that hindsight bias is driven by people's attempts to make sense of a situation, not by how surprising the outcome is. Thus, when sense-making is inhibited in ambivalent or incongruent situations, the bias should be attenuated, while it should be stronger in congruent situations. It should be noted, however, that at this time Ash's claim is only indirectly supported (Ash, 2009; Nestler et al., 2008).

Time may affect hindsight bias, as well. Initial surprise can fade over time, for example, and people may be better able to develop alternative explanations (independently, or with the help of others) as time goes on (Ofir & Mazursky, 1997; Robinson & Clore, 2002). In longer trials, for example, a known outcome may seem less surprising later in the trial than it was initially, thus reducing hindsight bias. (Moreover, jurors will have more time to identify and retrieve information relevant to the case as time increases.)

Hindsight bias may be affected also by visual cues and demonstrations of the sort commonly used in courtrooms. Roese, Fessel, Summerville, Kruger, and Dilich (2006), for example, have demonstrated that jurors are likely to be much more confident of the *a priori* predictability of an event after being shown simulations and reenactments depicting motion and trajectory effects. Although additional replication of their research is needed, the Roese et al. (2006) findings have important implications in the legal arena where computer animations of contested events (particularly accidents) are becoming the norm. Roese and his colleagues suggest that the "clarity" implied in an accident reconstruction may obscure the uncertainties inherent in such reconstructions, leading jurors to experience a heightened feeling of knowing that an event could lead to a particular outcome.

In legal proceedings, most jurors lack the specialized, topic-specific knowledge needed to evaluate complex evidence. Fiske and Taylor (1991) note that when faced with complex information, individuals often rely on cognitive shortcuts such as hindsight bias to assist in the decision-making process. These short cuts are created over time based on jurors' attitudes, experiences and beliefs. Ultimately, when dealing with ambiguous/complex information, fact finders will fill in the gaps using personal experiences and related attitudes to make a complete, coherent story.

Hindsight Bias in the Legal Arena

Much of the previous research has found that jurors generally find it difficult to ignore the known outcome of the event being disputed and subsequently engage in hindsight bias as part of their decision making (Casper,

Benedict, & Kelly, 1988; Casper, Benedict, & Perry, 1989; Christensen-Szalanski &Willham, 1991; Hastie, Schkade, & Payne, 1999; Hawkins & Hastie, 1990; Mandel, 2006; Stallard & Worthington, 1998; Sue, Smith, & Caldwell, 1973). A series of early studies illustrates the role of hindsight bias on mock juror decisions. In one, Casper et al. (1988) found that knowledge of a search outcome affected jurors' decisions in search and seizure cases. Mock jurors who knew that an improper search by police had found illegal drugs awarded smaller penalties for the illegal search than jurors who did not know its outcome. In a related study by Casper et al. (1989), participants provided with outcome information in an improper search case were instructed to ignore it. Results indicated that participants who knew that illegal material was found were unable to disregard this information and exhibited hindsight bias by awarding lower compensatory and punitive damages.

The courts recognize the existence of hindsight bias in judicial decision making and attempt to control for its effect in certain situation-specific cases such as medical malpractice and patent infringement (Rachlinski, 1998). For example, if a company has taken remedial action following an accident, the courts generally do not allow the jury to consider it in their decisions (Rachlinski, 1998). To do so simply by instructing jurors to ignore the information is probably futile, however (Lieberman & Arndt, 2000; Mandel, 2006, 2006–2007).

HINDSIGHT DEBIASING

Recent attempts to reduce jurors' tendency to engage in hindsight bias in the courtroom have met with mixed results. Wexler and Schopp (1989) suggested using jury instructions to address the bias in the courtroom, which Kamin and Rachlinski (1995) eventually tested. For their study, Kamin and Rachlinski used three conditions—foresight, hindsight, and hindsight debiasing. The case presented to each condition involved a negligence case regarding whether a city should have taken precautions to protect a river-front property owner from potential flood damage. In the foresight condition, participants received information set in an administrative hearing where one of the tasks was to determine the likelihood of a future flood. The hindsight and hindsight debiasing conditions were set in a courtroom context, in which participants of both conditions were given outcome knowledge (i.e., the town had flooded). In the hindsight debiasing condition, however, the judge asked participants to be conscious of the potential influence of outcome information and to consider alternative outcomes as they deliberate. Results indicated that subjects exposed to the hindsight condition provided higher probabilities that the flood would occur than subjects who participated in the foresight condition. The attempted debiasing technique (the jury instructions), however, failed to reduce jurors' tendency to engage in hindsight bias. The study concludes with an explicit call for the development of effective debiasing techniques for the courtroom, suggesting that "more intrusive procedures might be necessary to counteract the bias's influence" (p. 100). Similarly, Rachlinski (1998) noted "the bias is primarily a product of cognitive processes, and only procedures that alter the mental strategies used to make judgments in hindsight have any chance of producing unbiased evaluations" (p. 584).

As another approach to debiasing, Wexler and Schopp (1989) suggested that bias might be reduced by expert testimony about hindsight bias. Worthington (2008) tested this approach. Exposing mock jurors to a court-appointed expert, she found that jurors understood the concept of hindsight bias and how it could affect their decision making. However, although the expert testimony improved their understanding of the phenomenon, it did not reduce their hindsight bias. Nietzel, McCarthy, and Kern (1999) found that expert testimony that was "more specific and/or conclusive about the case at hand" had a significantly greater impact on juror opinions (p. 41).

As a result, Worthington (2008) suggests that expert testimony tied to the facts of the case at hand will likely be more effective, especially if reinforced during the attorney presentations.

Illustrating how specific arguments can effectively reduce the bias, Stallard and Worthington (1998) demonstrated that hindsight bias could be reduced with the introduction of a debiasing strategy into the defense attorney's argument. In this case, the defense, the Resolution Trust Corporation, a federal agency, was suing the Board of Directors of a failed Savings & Loan (S&L) for mismanaging the assets of the bank. Participants were exposed to three conditions: foresight, hindsight, and hindsight debiasing. In the foresight condition, participants were told the S&L was considering a new business plan and were asked to estimate the probability of the S&L's success if the plan was instituted. In the two remaining conditions, participants were given outcome knowledge that the S&L had failed. The hindsight debiasing condition also introduced strategic debiasing arguments by the attorney. For example, the attorney argued that jurors should focus on the information that was available to the Board members at the time the decisions were being made, and that they shouldn't be tempted to use hindsight, second-guessing the defendants. Mock jurors were asked if the board's actions were negligent. Next, they were asked to ignore the bank's failure, and predict the probability of the S&L's success. Results of the study indicated that the debiasing strategy was successful. Jurors in the hindsight debiasing condition were less likely to find the Board of Directors negligent and were better able to ignore the negative outcome, giving higher probability estimates the S&L would succeed. Arkes (1989) had earlier observed that defense attorneys who provide jurors with scenarios that do not implicate the accused used the same type of debiasing strategy. For example, in lung cancer cases it is not unusual for defense attorneys to point out other potential causes of a plaintiff's condition (e.g., family history, secondhand smoke, etc.).

When individuals have additional information of other potential alternatives or outcomes, they are less likely to rely on cognitive shortcuts such as hindsight bias. Arkes, Faust, Guilmette, and Hart (1988) were among the first to test the "consider-the-opposite-outcome" strategy to reduce hindsight, a strategy that appears to be successful in a variety of contexts (Agans & Shaffer, 1994; Arkes, 1989; Stallard & Worthington, 1998; Tversky & Kahneman, 1982). Their results indicated that asking participants not just to consider alternative outcomes, but rather specifically to consider the opposite outcome (e.g., the bank succeeding instead of failing) led individuals to assign increased probability estimates to the alternative outcomes, thus reducing hindsight bias. In other words, these alternative outcomes were more readily available to evaluate during the decision-making process. However, as noted earlier, recent research suggests that the subjective feeling of surprise may moderate the effectiveness of generating alternative explanations (Sanna & Schwarz, 2007; Sanna, Schwarz, & Small, 2002; Sanna, Schwarz, & Stocker, 2002). Thus, attorneys must keep in mind the ramifications of asking jurors to generate alternative outcomes—jurors should be able to easily generate alternative outcomes. Essentially, it is an attorney's responsibility to provide fact finders with viable alternatives that appear reasonable and that easily can be linked to antecedent events.

In short, debiasing studies suggest that stand-alone strategies, such as jury instructions, an expert witness, or providing plausible alternative outcomes, are rarely effective. Thus, we suggest the use of an integrated approach throughout the trial process.

SUGGESTED STRATEGIES FOR
INTEGRATING HINDSIGHT DEBIASING

An integrated approach to hindsight debiasing for jurors (or judges) might include inoculating them about hindsight bias in pleadings, voir dire, opening statements, witness testimony, and closing arguments. In the following section, we offer a number of suggestions to assist attorneys in developing hindsight-debiasing strategies into an integrated approach to their case development.

Bifurcation

Another strategy for reducing hindsight bias is bifurcation. That is, a judge may divide a trial into "parts" so that, say, one jury decides whether a corporation was negligent, and if yes, then another jury determines damages. The second jury obviously would know that something negative occurred, but could make its decision based on degree of injury or loss, without knowing potentially biasing specifics of the case.

An example of the effectiveness of bifurcation occurred in litigation involving the anti-nausea drug, Bendectin, prescribed for pregnant women. In this litigation, the plaintiffs claimed the drug caused fetal malformations ("Bendectin Litigation," 1988). The judge decided to bifurcate. During the first phase the only issue was causation, and the plaintiffs' children were not allowed to appear in court. After hearing only the causation issue, the jury decided that Bendectin did not cause the plaintiffs' alleged defects. It is reasonable to expect that the decision would have been different had the jury been able to see the malformed children who were the alleged "outcome" of taking the drug. That is, by excluding the children from the courtroom, the judge removed visual reinforcement of the "bad outcome" and presumably reduced the tendency for jurors to engage in hindsight bias when making their decision.

Some attorneys agree that bifurcation is a viable option for mitigating hindsight, particularly when addressing cases involving nonobvious decisions (such as may occur in patent cases, for example; Zura 2006). But there are reasons to be cautious with bifurcation. Critics note that it may not effectively debias since jurors are likely to be aware that a negative outcome led to the trial (Wexler & Schopp, 1989). Moreover, although some studies show bifurcation to reduce decisions and awards favoring the plaintiff, others show bifurcation to increase awards for the plaintiff (Greene & Bornstein, 2000; Landsman, Diamond, Dimitropoulos, & Saks, 1998). On the whole, bifurcation appears to favor the defense, (i.e., reduce hindsight bias), but this effect is not a consistent one.

Theme Development

As part of its case development, counsel will identify case themes. Expressed in an analogy, these themes are like billboards or newspaper headlines (i.e., short messages that capture the essence of each issue in the case). In addition to the main case themes, attorneys can develop and incorporate a theme that addresses the hindsight issue. This theme would be woven into the case strategy, ideally from the beginning, including pleadings, voir dire, openings, witness testimony, and closing arguments.

For example, one suggested case theme could be that "any action or decision could be made to look poor after the fact; therefore, one should judge the defendant's actions/decisions on the information available at the time." In the process of developing this theme, the attorney can develop examples using diverse but familiar subject areas as support (e.g., sports to politics to everyday events, etc.).

In conjunction with the thematic development, graphics can be created to bolster the hindsight case theme. For instance, the defense can design a time line of what was known when the decisions/actions were being made and juxtapose that against when the actual negative event occurred that gave rise to the litigation. However, as noted earlier, the presentation mode of the evidence (static vs. dynamic) can affect the extent and direction of the bias. This aspect is covered more fully in our discussion of demonstrative evidence.

Voir Dire (Where Applicable)

Where permitted by the court, counsel can question jurors during voir dire in an attempt to (a) educate jurors about hindsight bias, (b) reinforce trial themes, and (c) try to get commitments from jurors not to judge or punish their client based on hindsight bias. The following is an example of voir dire questioning that addresses these goals:

> How many of you have heard of hindsight bias—also known as Monday morning quarterbacking, or 20/20 hindsight? Well, for those of you not familiar, allow me to explain what it is. 20/20 hindsight occurs when the outcome of a person's decisions or actions look more obvious after the fact than if you had put yourself in the person's shoes prior to the decisions or actions being made. That's why it's called Monday morning quarterbacking (i.e., on Monday it is easier to criticize the decisions of the coach after the fact rather than before the game started). Thus, any decision after the fact can be made to look like a poor one. In this case, the decisions of my client are being viewed in hindsight (that is, after the fact), rather than viewed at the time when the decision/stock evaluation was being made. When you go back into that jury room and you hear someone "Monday morning quarterbacking" my client's decisions, will you be able to stand up to that person and remind them they are using 20/20 hindsight to judge my client's actions? Will you remind them that "Woulda, shoulda, coulda" has no place in this trial and they are to judge whether my

client's actions were reasonable at the time they were made, given the information provided to him?

Other sample questions will want to address not only these three goals but also relate hindsight bias to jurors' personal experiences and attitudes toward blaming others for their own mistakes (vs. accepting personal responsibility). For example:

> Has anyone here ever made a decision (at work, at home, in a group) that turned out badly and then you were second-guessed after the fact by your co-workers, etc.? [*Counsel can use a personal experience so that jurors will (a) understand the type of answer being sought, and (b) feel more comfortable admitting their bad decision. For example, "When I was in college I was in control of the fundraising money for our fraternity/sorority and after researching the stock market, I invested the money in some stocks to realize a return in our investment. However, the stocks I chose eventually fell and we lost the bulk of our initial investment. As a result, the frat brother/sorority sisters blamed me for the loss of their fundraising money."*] Has anyone experienced a similar situation where your decision was second-guessed? In your case, did people blame you for the bad outcome?

Opening Statements

As noted previously, research indicates the importance of individuals being able to imagine *plausible alternative* outcomes in order to reduce the influence of hindsight bias (Agans & Shaffer, 1994; Arkes, 1989; Tversky & Kahneman, 1982). Therefore, as another debiasing tactic, the attorney should offer the jurors alternatives to the actual outcome. This might help to weaken the focus on the bad outcome, and in turn, jurors may see other possible alternative outcomes by which to build and support alternative "stories" of the events that occurred. For instance, an attorney could argue, "on any given day, a stock broker offers research and advice for investing in the stock market, and the investor takes that advice and either makes money, loses money or maintains their investment without any change." [Ideally, counsel would show history of the specific investment in question to illustrate the likelihood of these three outcomes on any given day.]

Attorneys also should reinforce for jurors the information that was known *at the time* that led to the decision. Extending the stock example, "In plaintiff's case, the history of Stock X was on the rise (show history). In the time period this stock was researched, it was performing at X percent rate of return and had a history of stable growth. At the time the decision was made to invest, the information and research all pointed to the likelihood of a positive outcome." By incorporating these strategies into openings, attorneys will be working continually to reduce jurors' tendency to engage in hindsight bias.

Witness Testimony

Obviously, counsel will want to elicit testimony from their own witnesses to reinforce the information known at the time the decisions were being made. But counsel will also want to gain admissions from opposing witnesses that the bad event could not have been foreseen given the information that was known at the time. A defense counsel could, for example, gain an admission from plaintiff experts that the prominent financial advisors of the time were not predicting a down turn in the technology market. The defense could call as experts these same "prominent" advisors or have their own defense experts refer to these advisors' opinions at the time to reinforce the "unforeseeability" of the unexpected downturn in the value of the investment.

Expert Witnesses

As noted earlier, previous research suggests that expert testimony on the bias alone may not be enough to combat hindsight effectively and that debiasing is more effective when the expert testimony can be specifically tied to the case and/or draw specific conclusions about the case (e.g., links between asbestos and lung cancer, rates of false positives/negatives for a prostate cancer blood test, etc.; Nietzel et al., 1999; Worthington, 2008). The more that expert testimony can be linked to, and provide support for, attorney claims of a potential alternative outcome, the more likely it will be effective at reducing hindsight bias. Of course, problems arise when there are dueling experts supporting claims for differing alternative outcomes. One suggestion (where appropriate) for avoiding the conflicting information provided by dueling experts is the use of court-appointed experts (Goss, Worthington, Stallard, & Price, 2001; Worthington, Stallard, Price, & Goss, 2002). However, court-appointed experts are more likely to occur in larger, class-action types of cases (Goss et al., 2001; Worthington et al., 2002), and, as noted previously, such testimony should still be closely tied to the specifics of the case.

Demonstrative Evidence

It is not unusual for expert witness testimony to be accompanied by demonstrative evidence. As noted earlier, research by Roese et al. (2006)

found that in comparison to static displays, dynamic evidence *increases* the tendency of mock jurors to engage in hindsight bias. Thus, care must be taken when determining what to use as demonstrative evidence. Conceivably, there may be times when counsel may actually strive to augment, rather than mitigate hindsight bias. However, if the goal is to reduce the potential of dynamic evidence to increase juror bias, then the focal outcome and the defendant's or plaintiff's original decisions (foresight/antecedent judgments) should be presented as closely together as reasonably possible. On the other hand, if the temporal distance between the foresight judgments and the focal outcome is emphasized, there is a greater likelihood that mock jurors will engage in hindsight bias. If this type of design cannot be used, then counsel should consider static text and diagrams (Roese et al., 2006). Otherwise, counsel runs the risk that jurors will not only engage in hindsight bias, but will also have greater confidence in the dynamically presented events (e.g., auto accident portrayal, events leading up to a chemical spill, etc.; Roese et al., 2006). As noted earlier, Roese et al. suggest that the "clarity" suggested in an accident reconstruction may obscure the uncertainties inherent in such reconstructions. Subsequently, they may experience a heightened feeling of "knowing" that an event could lead to a particular outcome.

Closing Arguments

Similar to the goals of the opening statement, the closing argument serves as a case narrative to remind jurors of their commitment to avoid judging the defendant by looking backward with hindsight, to view the decisions at the time they were made, to consider the information known at the time, and to consider the other possible outcomes. For instance, an argument along the following lines could be used, "Your duty is to base a verdict not on speculation, not on what we know now, not on what *should have* happened, but on what did happen, given the information known at the time. Given what was known at the time, what subsequently occurred was not foreseeable by anyone, including my client."

CONCLUSION

Given the potential impact this enduring cognitive heuristic may have on trial verdicts, it is essential that researchers continue their efforts to identify components of the bias, as well as the effects it may have in this and other contexts. It is important to note, however, that although this chapter has focused on juror and jury decision making, a substantial amount of research indicates judges are just as prone to hindsight bias. For example, studies of judicial decisions in patent cases (Allison & Lemley, 1998; Guthrie, Rachlinski, & Wistrich, 2001; Mandel, 2006) found little or no difference in the amount of bias exhibited by judges and jurors. The good news is that many of the above suggestions can be adapted to judge trials, arbitration and mediation hearings, as well as criminal trials. Whether tried by a judge or a jury, ultimately, to reduce the tendency to engage in hindsight, attorneys must develop a comprehensive, integrative approach that attacks the bias throughout the hearing or trial. In doing so, attorneys can effectively address this common, potentially damaging juror decision-making error.

REFERENCES

Agans, R.P., & Shaffer, L.S. (1994). The hindsight bias: The role of the availability heuristic and perceived risk. *Basic and Applied Social Psychology,* *15*, 439–449.

Allison, J.R., & Lemley, M.A. (1998). Empirical evidence on the validity of litigated patents. *AIPLA Quarterly Journal, 26*, 185–277.

Arkes, H.R. (1989). Principles in judgment/decision making research pertinent to legal proceedings. *Behavioral Sciences & the Law, 7*, 429–456.

Arkes, H.R., Faust, D., Guilmette, T.J., & Hart, K. (1988). Eliminate the hindsight bias. *Journal of Applied Psychology, 73*, 305–307.

Ash, I.K. (2009). Surprise, memory, and retrospective judgment making: Testing cognitive reconstruction theories of the hindsight bias effect. *Journal of Experimental Psychology: Learning, Memory, and Cognition, 35*, 916–933.

Baron, J., & Hershey, J. (1988). Outcome bias in decision evaluation. *Journal of Personality and Social Psychology, 54*, 569–579.

"Bendectin Litigation," 857 F2d 290 (6th Cir. 1988).

Casper, J.D., Benedict, K., & Kelly, J.R. (1988). Cognition, attitudes and decision-making in search and seizure cases. *Journal of Applied Social Psychology, 18*, 93–113.

Casper, J.D., Benedict, K., & Perry, J.L. (1989). Juror decision making, attitudes, and the hindsight bias. *Law and Human Behavior, 13*, 291–310.

Christensen-Szalanski, J.J., & Willham, C.F. (1991). The hindsight bias: A meta-analysis. *Organizational Behavior and Human Decision Processes, 48*, 147–168.

Fischhoff, B. (1975). Hindsight ≠ foresight: The effect of outcome knowledge on judgment under uncertainty. *Journal of Experimental Psychology: Human Perception and Performance, 1*, 288–299.

Fischhoff, B. (1982). For those condemned to study the past: Reflections on historical judgment. In D. Kahneman, P. Slovic, & A. Tversky (Eds.), *Judgment under uncertainty: Heuristics and biases* (pp. 335–354). New York: Cambridge University Press.

Fiske, S.T., & Taylor, S.E. (1991). *Social cognition* (2nd ed.). New York: McGraw Hill.

Goss P.J., Worthington, D.L., Stallard, M.J., & Price, J.M. (2001). Clearing away the junk: Court-appointed experts, scientifically marginal evidence, and the silicone gel breast implant litigation. *Food and Drug Law Journal, 56,* 227–240.

Greene, E., & Bornstein, B. (2000). Precious little guidance: Jury instruction on damage awards. *Psychology, Public Policy & Law, 6,* 743–768.

Guthrie, C., Rachlinski, J.J., & Wistrich, A.J. (2001). Inside the judicial mind. *Cornell Law Review, 86,* 777–830.

Hastie, R., Schkade, D.A., & Payne, J.W. (1999). Juror judgments in civil cases: Hindsight effects on judgments of liability for punitive damage. *Law and Human Behavior, 23,* 597–614.

Hawkins, S.A., & Hastie, R. (1990). Hindsight: Biased judgments of past events after the outcomes are known. *Psychological Bulletin, 107,* 311–327.

Kamin, K.A., & Rachlinski, J.J. (1995). Ex post ≠ ex ante: Determining liability in hindsight. *Law and Human Behavior, 19,* 89–104.

Kelman, M., Fallas, D.E., & Folger, H. (1998). Decomposing hindsight bias. *Journal of Risk and Uncertainty, 16,* 251–269.

Klayman, J., & Ha, Y.W. (1987). Confirmation, disconfirmation, and information in hypothesis testing. *Psychological Review, 94,* 211–228.

Landsman, S., Diamond, S., Dimitropoulos, L., & Saks, M.J. (1998). Be careful what you wish for: The paradoxical effects of bifurcating claims for punitive damages. *Wisconsin Law Review,* 297–340.

Lieberman, J.D., & Arndt, J. (2000). Understanding the limits of limiting instructions: Social psychological explanations of the failures of instructions to disregard pretrial publicity and other inadmissible evidence. *Psychology, Public Policy, and Law, 6,* 677–711.

Mandel, G. (2006). Patently non-obvious: Empirical demonstration that the hindsight bias renders patent decisions irrational. *Ohio State Law Journal, 67,* 1391–1463.

Mandel, G. (2006–2007). Patently non-obvious II: Experimental study on the hindsight issue before the Supreme Court in *KSR v. Teleflex. Yale Journal of Law & Technology, 9,* 1–43.

Müller, P., & Stahlberg, D. (2007). The role of surprise in hindsight bias: A metacognitive model of reduced and reversed hindsight bias. *Social Cognition, 25,* 165–184.

Nestler, S., Blank, H., & von Collani, G. (2008). Hindsight bias doesn't always come easy: Causal models, cognitive effort, and creeping determinism. *Journal of Experimental Psychology: Learning, Memory, and Cognition, 34,* 1043–1054.

Nestler, S., & Egloff, B. (2009). Increased or reversed? The effect of surprise on hindsight bias depends on the hindsight component. *Journal of Experimental Psychology: Learning, Memory, and Cognition, 3,* 1539–1544.

Nietzel, M.T., McCarthy, D.M., & Kern, M.J. (1999). Juries: The current state of the empirical literature. In R. Roesch, S.D. Hart, & J.R. Ogloff (Eds.),

Psychology and law: The state of the discipline (pp. 25–53). New York: Kluwer/Plenum.

Ofir, C., & Mazursky, D. (1997). Does a surprising outcome reinforce or reverse the hindsight bias? *Organizational Behavior and Human Decision Processes, 69,* 50–57.

Rachlinski, J.J. (1998). A positive psychological theory of judging in hindsight. *University of Chicago Law Review, 65,* 571–625.

Robinson, M.D., & Clore, G.L. (2002). Belief and feeling: Evidence for an accessibility model of emotional self–report. *Psychological Bulletin, 128,* 934–960.

Roese, N.J., Fessel, F., Summerville, A., Kruger, J., & Dilich, M.A. (2006). The propensity effect: When foresight trumps hindsight. *Psychological Science, 17,* 305–310.

Sanna L.J., & Schwarz, N. (2007). Metacognitive experiences and hindsight bias: It's not just the thought (content) that counts! *Social Cognition, 25,* 185–202.

Sanna, L.J., Schwarz, N., & Small, E.M. (2002). Accessibility experiences and the hindsight bias: I knew it all along versus it could never have happened. *Memory & Cognition, 30,* 1288–1296.

Sanna, L.J., Schwarz, N., & Stocker, S.L. (2002). When debiasing backfires: Accessible content and accessibility experiences in debiasing hindsight. *Journal of Experimental Psychology: Human Perception and Performance, 3,* 497–502.

Schkade, D.A., & Kilbourne, L.M. (1991). Expectation-outcome consistency and hindsight bias. *Organizational Behavior and Human Decision Processes, 49,* 105–123.

Schwarz, N. (2004). Metacognitive experiences in consumer judgment and decision making. *Journal of Consumer Psychology, 14,* 332–348.

Stallard, M.J., Price, J.M., & Dane, F.C. (2001). Complex medical litigation and hindsight bias: Strategies to reduce fact finders' retrospective attributions of fault. In R. Roesch, R.R. Corrado, & R.J. Dempster (Eds.), *Psychology in the courts: International advances in knowledge* (pp. 109–120). Amsterdam: Harwood Academic.

Stallard, M.J., & Worthington, D.L. (1998). Reducing the hindsight bias utilizing attorney arguments. *Law and Human Behavior, 22,* 671–683.

Sue, S., Smith, R.E., & Caldwell, C. (1973). Effects of inadmissible evidence on the decisions of simulated jurors: A moral dilemma. *Journal of Applied Social Psychology, 3*(4), 345–353.

Tversky, A., & Kahneman, D. (1973). Availability: A heuristic for judging frequency and probability. *Cognitive Psychology, 5,* 207–232.

Tversky, A., & Kahneman, D. (1982). Judgment under uncertainty: Heuristics and biases. In D. Kahneman, P. Slovic, & A. Tversky (Eds.), *Judgment under uncertainty: Heuristics and biases* (pp. 3–20). Cambridge: Cambridge University Press.

Wasserman, D., Lempert, R.O., & Hastie, R. (1991). Hindsight and causality. *Personality and Social Psychology Bulletin, 92,* 683–700.

Wexler, D.B., & Schopp, R.F. (1989). How and when to correct for juror hindsight bias in mental health malpractice litigation: Some preliminary observations. *Behavioral Sciences & the Law, 7,* 485–504.

Worthington, D.L. (2008). Reducing the hindsight bias in mock-juror decision making: Assessing the effectiveness of a court-appointed witness. *Communication Law Review, 8*, 33–50.

Worthington, D.L., Stallard, M.J, Price, J.M., & Goss, P.J. (2002). Hindsight bias, *Daubert*, and the silicone breast implant litigation: Making the case for court-appointed experts in complex medical and scientific litigation. *Psychology, Public Policy, and Law, 8*, 154–179.

Zura, P. (2006, November 7). Experimenting with *KSR v. Teleflex*—Can hindsight be mitigated? (Part 1). *The 271 Patent Blog.* Retrieved from http://271patent.blogspot.com/2006/11/experimenting-with-ksr-v-teleflex-can.html.

7

Integrating Victims' Voices in the U.S. Criminal Justice System

Susan J. Szmania
Dan Mangis[1]

Since 1981, the President of the United States has issued a proclamation to designate a week in April as National Crime Victims' Rights Week (NCVRW). In 2009, President Barack Obama once again called on all Americans to raise awareness of crime victims' rights and services. In the proclamation, Obama reiterated the importance of the Victims of Crime Act of 1984 (42 U.S.C. 10601 et. 9 seq.), which laid the foundation for financial support to victims as well as victim participation in the legal system (Davis & Mulford, 2008). Through public awareness campaigns like the annual NCVRW and legislation like the Victims of Crime Act, crime victims have increasingly found a voice when it comes to justice in America. Yet, the struggle for victims to achieve this recognition both inside and outside the courtroom has raised new issues of fairness in the U.S. legal system.

In this chapter, we focus on victim participation in the courtroom from a communication perspective. We are interested in how victim communication is presented and occurs within, and subsequently impacts, the legal system. Although our discussion touches on legal precedents of victim inclusion in the U.S. legal system as well as several important vic-

125

tim advocacy concerns, our main goal is to consider the expanding role of victim participation in the criminal trial process. We also consider the growing influence of the victim experience outside the traditional justice system where victims have found a more visible role for raising awareness about victimization.

To organize our discussion, we explore three main claims about victims' communication in the U.S. legal system:

1. The legal participatory rights of victims are well established, but not all victims will want to or be able to participate in the legal process.

2. Victim participation in the courtroom makes an impact, but the extent to which victim participation directly influences the final verdict does not always follow a predictable pattern.

3. New initiatives aim to increase victim support through *formal* (e.g., therapeutic jurisprudence and Defense-Initiated Victim Outreach) and *informal* (e.g., restorative justice and truth commissions) legal processes.

We recognize that the promise of increased victim participation in courtroom settings is exciting to victim advocates, but at the same time, skeptics maintain that the criminal justice system should focus squarely on defendants' rights rather than victims. Although victim testimony may offer vivid and compelling narratives for the court to consider, this testimony often is considered overly emotional and not appropriate in a court of law. Finding common ground between these divergent viewpoints is fraught with challenge, and our intent in this chapter is not to weigh in on the debate about appropriateness of victim integration in the criminal justice system. Rather, we offer an overview of the expanding role of victims in the adversarial legal process by drawing on legal analysis and social science research. In the conclusion, we outline a set of suggested principles for victim participation in the criminal justice system.

THE RIGHT TO BE INFORMED, PRESENT, AND HEARD

It often comes as a surprise that victims of crime have traditionally had a passive role in U.S. courtroom proceedings. After all, as Gewirtz (1996) noted, we tend to believe that "the existence of a victim, of course, is what prompts the criminal trial" in the first place (p. 137). However, the adversarial legal system, on which U.S. criminal justice is based, pits criminal defendants against the state, which means that the state stands in to represent victims. In this sense, the crime is viewed as a crime against the community rather than any one particular victim (Gewirtz, 1996). Victims' rights are not explicitly stated in the U.S. Constitution; rather, it is defendants' rights that are outlined, such as in the Eighth Amendment limiting cruel and unusual punishment. For some victims, this omission amplifies feelings of marginalization and alienation in the legal process.

Yet, over the past 30 years, committed advocacy and important legislation have seen "the role of the crime victim . . . transformed from that of a passive witness to an active participant" in the legal system (Erez & Roberts, 2007, p. 277). In the United States, the push to bring about increased victim participation in the courtroom can be traced back to the advocacy of families of murdered children who wanted to have more of a role in the legal process. Beginning in the 1970s, parents fought to be present at the trials of their children's murderers and to have the opportunity to address the court about the emotional impact of their losses (Rentschler, 2007). Aligned with other movements such as those to protect rape victims, this advocacy was the precursor to what has become known as the Victim Rights Movement. The "universal concerns" of the movement are "the desire to be treated fairly and with understanding and the need to be heard as victims, not merely as witnesses" (Andrias, 1997, p. 22). Rentschler (2007) observed that today, "in the U.S., the movement comprises a network of grassroots activists and government institutions that organizes crime-victim families into visible agents in the wars on crime and terrorism" (p. 202).

Legislation at the federal and state levels has been essential for gaining greater victim participation in the legal system (Davis & Mulford, 2008). As Young, Herman, Davis, and Lurigio (2007) summarized, new laws haves established "the right to be notified of critical stages in the criminal justice process, to speak or present written statements at sentencing or parole hearings, and to receive restitution" (p. 3). At the federal level, this effort began with President Ronald Regan's support for a task force in the early 1980s to make recommendations about increasing victim participation in the legal system. This work resulted in the Victims of Crime Act of 1984, and more recently, the Crime Victim Rights Act in 2004 (18 U.S.C. § 3771), which outlines basic victims' rights, including the right for victims to be treated with fairness and respect. Additionally, Wood (2005) found that the National Victims' Rights Constitutional Amendment Network calls for the adoption of a federal Constitutional

Amendment regarding the national establishment of victims' rights. This amendment would provide uniformity in victims' rights across the nation although it has not been passed yet.

At the state level, the National Center for Victims of Crime reports that every state has passed some form of legal rights for victims. These rights are sometimes codified in what has been called a "Victim's Bill of Rights," and according to the National Center for Victims of Crime (n.d.), generally include the right to be present and notified about a trial, the right to compensation, the right to have their victim contact information kept confidential, and the right to be consulted if a case is dismissed. There also are other important protections for victims such as specially trained police officers who assist victims after a crime occurs and victim assistance units in prosecutors' offices to guide individuals through the legal system (Andrias, 1997).

Along with legislative changes and social support mechanisms, victim compensation funds also have become a widely used mechanism to provide financial support to victims of crime. Monetary payment is given to victims and/or surviving family members to make up for injuries, damages, lost wages, and other costs victims might incur following a crime. In some cases, victim funds are paid for by criminal offenders (known as "restitution"), and in other cases, the payment is provided for by taxpayers' contributions (known as "compensation"). However, receiving payments for suffering and loss of life has sparked a good deal of controversy even among victim's families. For example, Hadfield (2008), who surveyed people who filed for compensation from the 9/11 fund, found that if victim compensation was paid, then the victims and their families were bound by an agreement *not* to pursue further litigation. Hadfield concluded that, for some, finding out what happened and holding someone legally accountable were more important outcomes than receiving the financial payments.

VICTIM PARTICIPATION IN THE COURTROOM

Although we have stressed the increasing role of the victim in the criminal legal process, Erez and Roberts (2007) made the important point that very few victims actually take part in the criminal justice system. In addition to not being informed about their right to participate, victims face other barriers. Many crimes go unreported, and even when crimes are reported, most offenders enter guilty pleas, which means that a trial is not held, and thus there is no opportunity for a victim to participate in court hearings. Victims also may feel that their participation will not change the legal outcome. However, when victims do take part in the criminal legal process, it usually is divided between two stages: the guilt determination phase and the sentencing phase.

Guilt Determination

The purpose of the first phase of a criminal trial is to present enough evidence to determine whether or not an offender is guilty of the crime of which he or she has been accused. For victims of crime, this part of the trial can be an alienating process because the focus of the trial is on the offender, not on the victim's experience. Moreover, from a communication standpoint, the dynamics of interaction in the courtroom are unfamiliar to outsiders. Legal language is filled with jargon and specialized terminology (Tiersma, 1999). Legal professionals tightly control the legal process. The judge has the authority to grant permission to speak, to determine how long speaking exchanges will be, and to object to certain contributions. Lawyers play a key role in framing how information is presented, leaving little room for victims to express their feelings regarding the impact of the crime. Because this process can be especially difficult for victims, witness testimony often is the focus of scholarly discussions about courtroom communication.

During cross-examination of victim witnesses, Conley and O'Barr (2005) observed, "the lawyer's objective is to discredit opposition witnesses and minimize the impact of their testimony" (p. 22). One of the most widely studied areas where this occurs is in cases involving rape because a victim's credibility and previous behavior often are called into question (e.g., Borgida & White, 1978; Hackett, Day, & Mohr, 2008). This can be a painful and embarrassing process that asks victims to present many personal details in a public setting. Matoesian's (1993) research using conversational analysis uncovered some of the linguistic strategies that lawyers use to discredit witnesses in rape cases through the strategic use of silence, reframing, and questioning. These issues have led to the critique of power dynamics in the courtroom, which more often than not, places victims in a subordinate and passive position (Giacopassi & Wilkinson, 1985). In cases involving rape, "rape shield laws" have been put in place to protect rape victims from speaking about their past sexual behaviors, but these measures have not fully eliminated the imbalance in power that victims may feel in the court (Matoesian, 1995).

Another problem concerns how emotions should be properly displayed in the courtroom. The legal process is generally described as "impartial" and free from bias. Although this ideal may be more difficult to achieve in practice, it is seen as a fundamental tenant of the U.S. legal system. Victims of crime may challenge this impartial process by injecting emotionality into this process. This concern is further exacerbated by the jury system. As Lind (2008) observed, the jury can be "especially susceptible to external factors, such as compassion, sympathy, and empathy, which can greatly influence their verdicts" (p. 98). In this analysis, the author referred to examples where families of a murder victim wore buttons on their clothing with the victim's picture visible to all people in the courtroom, including the defendant. This practice has sparked debate about the use of expressive clothing and accessories in the courtroom because of their potential to sway the jury's decision-making process. This example also raises important questions about victim presence in the courtroom and the impact on legal decision making.

The role of victims' emotions in the courtroom also has been controversial when, for example, victims cry on the witness stand or physical fights erupt. A primary concern is that the emotions displayed in the courtroom will influence legal decision making (Tsoudis & Smith-Loving, 1998). The courtroom is often viewed as an objective and fair forum, and when this ideal image is threatened, such incidents are newsworthy. For example, a newspaper reported that during a courtroom hearing in Virginia, the fiancée of a murder victim attacked the alleged suspect, and the courtroom brawl ended in "swinging, grappling, yelling and pushing" (Doucette, 2006). To avoid negative encounters, judges often make arrangements so that victims and offenders enter and leave the courtroom at separate times, although victims sometimes report being surprised that they are often in close proximity to offenders and their family members in the courtroom (Hirsch, 2008).

Sentencing

Once an offender's guilt has been made by the criminal court, the next phase of the legal process involves the sentencing of the offender. During this portion of the trial, the court determines the offender's punishment. A primary goal is to assess the impact of the crime on the victim through allocution, most commonly called Victim Impact Statements (VIS). The purpose of the VIS is to give the victim a chance to explain the impact of the crime either by presenting an oral statement to the court or by writing a letter to the judge (Sanders, Hoyle, Morgan, & Cape, 2001). If the victim is deceased, family and friends may offer VIS to "fill the gap created by the victim's silence" (Gewirtz, 1996, p. 139).

The debate about the inclusion of VIS in capital punishment sentencing has been extensively analyzed in a trio of U.S. Supreme Court cases concerning the constitutionality of VIS (e.g., Logan, 2007). In these decisions, the Supreme Court decided whether or not "victim character-istics [introduced to the court through statements or by the prosecutor] can unfairly tip the scales in the penalty phase of a capital murder trial against the defendant" (Wood, 2005, p. 137). In *Payne v. Tennessee*, the Court upheld the right to include VIS at sentencing in death penalty cases in order to illustrate the "specific harm" of the crime and demonstrate that the victims "are not faceless strangers" (510 U.S. 808 [1991] at 825).

Because of the high stakes involved in death penalty jurisprudence, a good deal of research attention has focused what effect VIS presentation has on trial verdicts. One theory holds that VIS may result in harsher sentences for offenders because the emotionally intense testimony of vic-tims persuades the jury to impose a harsher punishment. Nadler and Rose (2003) found that criminal punishment is influenced by the extent to which emotional expression is given in VIS. The authors of the study had participants read descriptions of a crime and one of three VIS—one containing severe emotional injury, one containing mild emotional injury, and one containing no information about how the victim was coping with the crime. After reading one of these statements, participants were asked to indicate what prison sentence, if any, the defendant should receive. The results showed the stronger emotions in VIS resulted in more punish-ment and, conversely, that "*failure* on the part of the victim expressing mild emotional harm . . . was associated with *less* punishment (Nadler & Rose, 2003, p. 447).

The language describing the personal characteristics of victims and offenders also has been studied in the presentation of VIS. One experi-mental study claimed that VIS involving humanizing characterizations of victims might actually counter-balance harsh or dehumanizing language about criminal defendants. Although dehumanizing language about an offender by describing criminal acts as a "savage" or "animal-like" may increase a tendency for juries to impose harsher sentences, the authors noted that "humanizing language may make the value of life salient to jurors so that they may also place greater value on the life of the defen-dant" (Myers, Godwin, Latter, & Winstanley, 2004, p. 50). However, it is important to point out these results, like many other studies of VIS, were based on experiments using research participants and written vignettes and thus may not replicate actual courtroom dynamics.

Another line of research on VIS has examined what has been called the "expressive" function of VIS. This research highlights the "communi-cative element" of VIS and "represents the means by which legal censure is expressed" (Roberts & Erez, 2004, p. 230). Van der Merwe (2008), after reviewing a particularly violent case involving rape, concluded that VIS "have the power to make the court more aware of the true extent of human suffering involved and underscore the need for enhanced victim services" (p. 405). Others have shown that VIS allow victims and their families to provide a "historical record" of their loss in an official, public setting (Logan, 2008, p. 724). In a study of actual VIS presented at the sentencing of a notorious serial killer, victims' families memorialized the victims by recounting stories and memories of their loved ones (Szmania & Gracyalny 2006), illustrating that VIS were directed not only to the offender and the court but also to the community. In addition to having multiple goals in VIS, the need for victims to participate in the courtroom can be a very personal decision. Some victims may find that talking about their experience is healing, whereas others report that they feel worse after presenting a VIS because they are unsure about whether their statements made a difference in sentencing (e.g., Sanders et al., 2001).

Overall, rates of victim participation through the submission of VIS to the court are still quite low across federal, state, and municipal jurisdictions. Erez and Roberts (2007) noted that this is especially true for property crimes, where fewer VIS are presented as compared to criminal cases. One reason for this may be victims' perceptions of the severity of the crime. If a victim feels his or her claim is not important enough, then he or she may be less apt to take part in a criminal process. Other victims may find the courtroom to be intimidating. To overcome some of these barriers, victim services groups around the country have developed guidelines for how to construct victim impact statements, which are available from organizations such as Mothers Against Drunk Driving and the National Crime Victim Center. In addition to focusing crime victims on preparing a clear statement for oral or written presentation in a courtroom, victims also are given instructions about specific information to include so that they may increase the likelihood of receiving restitution. These instructions also may cover information about the "permissible bounds" of VIS, including who may present the statements and what information may be included (Logan, 2008).

Before turning to new approaches for victim participation in both formal and informal legal processes, we would be remiss not to mention the emerging role of technology in the courtroom. Through telephone and video conferencing, there are new ways for victims to participate at all stages of the criminal process (Wiggins, 2006). During the guilt determination phase, very young children may present their testimony by videotape, closed-circuit television, or in a separate room. These practices address concerns about victim safety in the presence of the offender, and in the case of children have been shown to maximize the "completeness and accuracy" of victim-witness testimony (Hill & Hill, 1987).

Technology also may help overcome physical barriers to victim participation. In one of the earliest uses of video victim testimony in U.S. courts, a man who was paralyzed after an automobile accident made video testimony over the Internet because he was not able to travel to the trial (DeMasters, 1998). Some U.S. states have recently begun to use video technology to assist victims who give statements at parole hearings. To date, however, most discussion about technology in the courtroom has centered on the permissibility of videotaped offender confessions and testimony as well as the extent to which the technology may impact legal principles, including due process and the right against self-incrimination (Wiggins, 2006).

NEW APPROACHES

In this section, we provide an overview of several new approaches for responding to victims' needs in their search for justice. Our discussion touches on several strategies used to support victims both inside and outside the formal legal system. To begin, we describe initiatives from within the legal profession that have sought to change the dynamics of the criminal legal process. Then, we look more broadly at programs providing victims and their surviving family members the opportunity to speak about how crime and victimization has affected them.

Therapeutic Jurisprudence

Therapeutic jurisprudence is a legal approach that redefines the role of the criminal defense lawyer as a "change agent" (Wexler, 2005). Developed in response to criticisms that the legal system does not always address underlying causes of crime such as drug dependency or joblessness, therapeutic jurisprudence calls for lawyers to divert their legal clients into appropriate treatment programs rather than taking the risk that the court will send their clients directly to prison with the highest sentence possible.

Although the main focus for therapeutic jurisprudence is the criminal defendant, lawyers actively work with their clients to display "genuine acceptance of responsibility" by offering apologies or providing proactive repayment to victims during sentencing (Wexler, 2005, p. 754). Apologies have been recognized by victims and their families to have a deep impact on how they view the legal system and the administration of justice, and hearing an apology may positively support a victim's healing process (Petrucci, 2002). To that end, a defense lawyer may encourage offenders to offer these apologies at the appropriate point in the trial. For critics, however, such actions may be viewed as attempts by the lawyer and the offender to receive a lighter sentence. Yet, therapeutic jurisprudence currently is debated by a growing number of international legal scholarship experts and has gained recognition as a important process for change within the practice of law (Wemmers, 2008).

Defense-Initiated Victim Outreach

Defense-Initiated Victim Outreach (DIVO) "address[es] the judicial needs of victim survivors through the justice process by providing a link between the survivors and the defense, especially in capital cases" (Armour & Frogge, n.d., p. 1). The goal is to give victims a chance to ask questions and understand the defense council. DIVO usually is initiated by a neutral victim liaison who contacts victims and their families. The victim liaison works to maintain communication between the defense council and the victim's family throughout the trial process in order to "engage the survivors, wherever they are, solely on the survivors' terms" (Branham & Burr, 2008, p. 1025).

Most notably, DIVO was used in the capital murder cases of Timothy McVeigh, the Oklahoma City Federal Building bomber, and Zacharias Moussaoui, convicted in the 9/11 terrorist attacks. Reflecting on these two cases, each involving thousands of victims, Branham and Burr (2008) observed that DIVO removed traditional communication barriers between victims and defense attorneys and demonstrated that "the interests of the defense team and the interests of the victims are far from being mutually exclusive" (p. 1023). Still in its formative phase, DIVO has been implemented in a small number of jurisdictions, although interest is growing for new program development.

Restorative Justice

Restorative justice programs have a common goal of bringing together individuals affected by crime to discuss what happened and what to do (Zehr, 1990). A restorative approach to justice places victims' needs squarely at the center of the process. Drawing on the community-based traditions of peacemaking and conflict resolution, restorative justice programs take a wide variety of formats and are offered to both youth and adult participants (Pranis, Wedge, & Stuart, 2003). The most well-known restorative justice program is victim offender mediation/dialogue in which victims of crime meet with convicted offenders post-sentencing for discussion with the aid of a trained facilitator (Szmania, 2006). Other restorative justice programs may take place as a diversion to sentencing through "conferencing" to bring together victims, offenders, and community members.

Restorative justice encounters allow victims and offenders to talk about what happened, to discuss the impact of the crime, to offer or receive an apology, and to negotiate restitution. Usually, these types of programs do not affect an offender's sentencing; however, other restorative justice programs, including conferencing and peacemaking circles, are scheduled prior to sentencing and do give victims, offenders, and community members an opportunity to discuss what happened and to decide what can be done to make things right. Outcome evaluations from a number of different types of restorative justice programs show that both victims and offenders are satisfied by their participation (e.g., Umbreit, Coates, & Lightfoot, 2005) and that participation in restorative justice may lower offender recidivism rates, particularly for juveniles (Bradshaw, Roseborough, & Umbreit, 2006). Today, restorative justice program are available in many communities in the United States and around the world.

Truth Commissions

Truth commissions have been organized in response to gross violations of human rights in countries around the world including Uganda, Argentina, and Sierra Leone. In the United States, a truth commission was established in 2005 in Greensboro, North Carolina, following racially motivated killings that took place in 1979. The South African Truth and Reconciliation Commission, one of the largest and most well-known initiatives, was authorized in 1995 and provided a forum for more than 20,000 victims of apartheid to give public statements and for some 8,000 perpetrators to explain what they had done. The hearings, although not official legal proceedings, provided a forum for victims to gain recognition for their suffering. Moreover, as Hatch (2006) suggested, they also laid a foundation for reconciliation to occur to at a national level.

Although truth commissions often are hailed for the ability to reach out to large numbers of individuals affected by crime, critics have noted public dissatisfaction in the process, citing the difficulty of achieving true reconciliation (Tepperman, 2002) or substituting what some have called "theatricality" for the "legal process" (Motsemme, 2004). Observing that the process of reconciliation takes time and cannot be achieved through commissions alone, Doxtader (2001) asserts that communication about crime is an essential step for moving a society from oppression toward democracy, a process that also has been called *transitional justice*. In societies that have experienced widespread human rights violations, transitional justice focuses on victim support by promoting peace, reconciliation, and democracy.

INTEGRATING VICTIMS' VOICES

We conclude by suggesting several principles to guide individuals working to integrate victims' voices both inside and outside of the U.S. criminal justice system, and we point to the important role of applied communication research in this endeavor. As should be clear from our overview, victims have already established their place in the U.S. legal process. Thus, our principles focus on *how* to help victims participate as fully as possible rather than arguing for or against *why* victims should take part. We recognize, however, that the debate over whether victims should have the power to influence legal decisions will continue to be the focus of some legal experts and scholars (e.g., Sanders et al., 2001).

First and foremost, legal professionals should ensure that victims are aware of their rights in the legal process. Victims should receive information about laws governing victim participation in the criminal justice system where they live. Victims also should be given clear instructions for how their participation will be used by the court. As discussed previously, this information is already widely available through many victim advocacy groups, but it is important that all victims receive this information. Victims should be notified about services that offer support. A growing number of cities offer victim services programs to offer help immediately following a crime, and similar services may assist victims who decide, for example, to take part in restorative justice programs years later. In this work, we see victim advocates playing an increasingly visible and important role, especially in preparing victims to prepare for new courtroom technology.

Although we have focused on victims who participate in the formal legal system, we also recognize that not all victims will want to or will be able to participate. For some victims, presenting oral testimony in a courtroom can be difficult, if not impossible, especially for those who have suffered deep trauma (Motsemme, 2004). Other victims may have practical reasons that prevent them from being fully involved in the court process. For these reasons, victims should be aware of alternate options for submitting information to the court such as through letters or by providing video statements to the court. Outside the legal process, memorialization projects, ranging from makeshift shrines at the site of an accident to the construction of permanent monuments or museums to commemorate tragedy, illustrate the variety of ways that victims may seek public recognition for their suffering (Barsalou & Baxter, 2007). We call for further recognition of the many ways that victims may find justice and healing following criminal victimization.

Finally, we urge communication scholars who aspire to apply communication research in the courtroom to take careful note of the complicated and conflicted performance demands placed on victims by the courtroom environment. Some basic communication coaching could be important in making the courtroom testimony experience a real option for victims saddled with communication apprehension. At the same time, the activities of the attorneys, judges, and other courtroom participants are also worth thinking about carefully when preparing for victim testimony. We suggest that the observations in this chapter formulate a good starting point for a practical application of communication theory to victim participation in the courtroom, but that the actual process of preparing a victim for courtroom testimony may never have a step-by-step instruction manual. Instead, scholars acting as consultants will need to adhere to the highest standards of professionalism, ethics, and maintain a strong sense of compassion in offering advice appropriate for each individual case.

NOTE

1. The opinions expressed here are the views of the authors and do not necessarily reflect the policies or positions of the U.S. Department of State.

REFERENCES

Andrias, R.T. (1997). Seeking justice for the victim. *Update on Law-Related Education*, 21(2), 22–23.

Armour, M., & Frogge, S. (n.d.). *Implementing defense-initiated victim-outreach in Texas*. Austin: Institute for Restorative Justice & Restorative Dialogue, School of Social Work, The University of Texas at Austin.

Barsalou, J., & Baxter, V. (2007). *The urge to remember: The role of memorials in social reconstruction and transitional justice*. United States Institute of Peace, Special Report, Stabilization and Reconstruction Series No. 5, January.

Borgida, E., & White, P. (1978). Social perception of rape victims: The impact of legal reform. *Law and Human Behavior*, 2(4), 339–351.

Bradshaw, W., Roseborough, D., & Umbeit, M.S. (2006). The effect of victim offender mediation on juvenile offender recidivism: A meta-analysis. *Conflict Resolution Quarterly*, 24(1), 87–98.

Branham, M., & Burr, R.H. (2008). Understanding defense-initiated victim outreach and why it is essential in defending a capital client. *Hofstra Law Review*, 36(3), 1019–1033.

Conley, J.M., & O'Barr, W.M. (2005). *Just words: Law, language, and power* (2nd ed.). Chicago: University of Chicago Press.

Davis, R.C., & Mulford, C. (2008). Victim rights and new remedies: Finally getting victims their due. *Journal of Contemporary Criminal Justice*, 24(2), 198–208.

DeMasters, K. (1998, October 4). Q & A: Getting a day in court via the Internet. *New York Times*, p. 9.

Doucette, J. (2006, April 19). Brawl erupts in courtroom as victim's fiancée attacks accused. *The Virginian-Pilot*. Retrieved May 3, 2009, from http://hampton-roads.com/node/92181.

Doxtader, E. (2001). Making rhetorical history in a time of transition: The occasion, Constitution, and representation of South African reconciliation. *Rhetoric & Public Affairs*, 4(2), 223–260.

Erez, E., & Roberts, J.V. (2007). Victim participation in the criminal justice system. In R.C. Davis, A.J. Lurigio, & S. Herman (Eds.), *Victims of crime* (pp. 277–297). Newbury Park, CA: Sage.

Gewirtz, P.D. (1996). Victims and voyeurs: Two narrative problems at the criminal trial. In P. Brooks & P. Gerwitz (Eds.), *Law's stories: Narrative and rhetoric in the law* (pp. 135–161). New Haven, CT: Yale University Press.

Giacopassi, D.J., & Wilkinson, K.R. (1985). Rape and the devalued victim. *Law and Human Behavior*, 9(4), 367–383.

Hackett, L., Day, A., & Mohr, P. (2008). Expectancy violation and perceptions of rape victim credibility. *Legal and Criminological Psychology*, 13(2), 323–334.

Hadfield, G.K. (2008). Framing the choice between cash and the courthouse: Experiences with the 911 victim compensation fund. *Law & Society Review*, 42, 645–682.

Hatch, J.B. (2006). The hope of reconciliation: Continuing the conversation. *Rhetoric & Public Affairs*, 9(2), 259–277.

Hill, P.E., & Hill, S.M. (1987). Videotaping children's testimony: An empirical view. *Michigan Law Review*, 85(4), 809–833.

Hirsch, S.F. (2008). *In the moment of greatest calamity: Terrorism, grief, and a victim's quest for justice* (2nd ed.). Princeton, NJ: Princeton University Press.

Lind, M.E. (2008). Hearts on their sleeves: Symbolic displays of emotion by spectators in criminal trials. *The Journal of Criminal Law and Criminology*, 98(3), 1147–1170.

Logan, W.A. (2008). Confronting evil: Victims' rights in an age of terror. *Georgetown Law Journal*, 96, 7217–776.

Matoesian, G.M. (1993). *Reproducing rape: Domination through talk in the courtroom*. Chicago: University of Chicago Press.

Matoesian, G.M. (1995). Language, law, and society: Policy implications of the Kennedy Smith rape trial. *Law & Society Review*, 29(4), 669–701.

Motsemme, N. (2004). The mute always speak: On women's silences at the truth and reconciliation commission. *Current Sociology*, 52(5), 909–932.

Myers, B., Godwin, D., Latter, R., & Winstanley, S. (2004). Victim impact statements and mock juror sentencing: The impact of dehumanizing language on a death qualified sample. *American Journal of Forensic Psychology, 22*(3), 39–55.

Nadler, J., & Rose, M.R. (2003). Victim impact testimony and the psychology of punishment. *Cornell Law Review, 88,* 419–456.

Petrucci, C.J. (2002). Apology in the criminal justice setting: Evidence for including apology as an additional component in the legal system. *Behavioral Sciences & the Law, 20*(4), 337–362.

Pranis, K., Wedge, M., & Stuart, B. (2003). *Peacemaking circles: From crime to community.* St. Paul, MN: Living Justice Press.

Rentschler, C.A. (2007). Victims' rights and the struggle over crime in the media. *Canadian Journal of Communication, 32*(2), 219–239.

Roberts, J.V., & Erez, E. (2004). Communication in sentencing: Exploring the expressive function of victim impact statements. *International Review of Victimology, 10*(3), 223–244.

Sanders, A., Hoyle, C., Morgan, R., & Cape, E. (2001). Victim impact statements: Don't work, can't work. *Criminal Law Review,* 447–458.

Szmania, S.J. (2006). Mediators' communication in victim offender mediation/dialogue involving crimes of severe violence: An analysis of opening statements. *Conflict Resolution Quarterly, 24*(1), 111–127.

Szmania, S.J., & Gracyalny, M.L. (2006). Addressing the court, the offender, and the community: A communication analysis of victim impact statements in a non-capital sentencing hearing. *International Review of Victimology, 13*(3), 231–249.

Tepperman, J.D. (2002). Truth and consequences. *Foreign Affairs, 81*(2), 128–145.

The National Center for Victims of Crime. (n.d). *Victims' Bill of Rights.* Retrieved September 29, 2009, from http://www.ncvc.org/ncvc/main.aspx?dbName=DocumentViewer&DocumentID=32697.

Tiersma, P.M. (1999). *Legal language.* Chicago: University of Chicago Press.

Tsoudis, O., & Smith-Lovin, L. (1998). How bad was it? The effects of victim and perpetrator emotion on responses to criminal court vignettes. *Social Forces, 77*(2), 695–722.

Umbreit, M.S., Coates, R.B., & Lightfoot, E. (2005). Restorative justice in the twenty-first century: A social movement full of opportunities and pitfalls. *Marquette Law Review, 89*(2), 251–304.

Van der Merwe, A. (2008). Addressing victim's harm: The role of impact reports. *Thomas Jefferson Law Review, 30,* 391–406.

Wemmers, J. (2008). Victim participation and therapeutic jurisprudence. *Victims & Offenders, 3*(2), 165–191.

Wexler, D.B. (2005). Therapeutic jurisprudence and the rehabilitative role of the criminal defense lawyer. *St. Thomas Law Review, 17,* 743–774.

Wiggins, E.C. (2006). The courtroom of the future is here: Introduction to emerging technologies in the legal system. *Law & Policy, 28*(2), 182–191.

Wood, J.K. (2005). Balancing innocence and guilt: A metaphorical analysis of the U.S. Supreme Court's rulings on victim impact statements. *Western Journal of Communication, 69*(2), 129–146.

Young, M., Herman, S., Davis, R.C., & Lurigio, A. (2007). Introduction to victims of crime: The interaction of research and practice. In R.C. Davis, A.J. Lurigio, & S. Herman (Eds.), *Victims of crime* (pp. 1–6). Newbury Park, CA: Sage.

Zehr, H. (1990). *Changing lenses: A new focus for crime and justice.* Scottdale, PA: Herald Press.

8

Pursuing Justice for Unwanted Pursuit

Stalking Research in the Courtroom

Charles Wesley Kim Jr.
Brian H. Spitzberg

In our daily interactions, communication occurs on many levels, verbal and nonverbal. Much of this communication is benign. When communication involves the crime of stalking, however, it may become a matter of life and death. This chapter examines some of the means by which stalkers communicate with their victims and the means by which victims communicate with their stalkers and first responders. It also explores the means by which law enforcement and prosecutors can convey to judges and juries the paralyzing fear and deep emotional trauma experienced by victims in stalking prosecutions.

Since the mid–1990s, extensive research has been conducted on stalking, and it is now possible to take stock of this process, both as a form of communication and as it is dealt with in the criminal justice system. This chapter summarizes what is known about stalking from a social scientific perspective, with emphasis on (a) the prohibition of stalking (i.e., the law surrounding stalking); (b) the process, prevalence and perpetration of stalking (i.e., the nature of the crime); (c) the protection of victims (i.e., the role that law enforcement and judicial processes play in responding to and managing stalking cases); and (d) the best practices and common pitfalls when prosecuting stalking. To date, far more is known about stalkers, their victims, and the process of stalking, than is known about how stalking fares in criminal justice contexts, so there necessarily is a degree of professional conjecture in drawing conclusions about the prosecution of stalking.

ANTI-STALKING LAWS

The idea of romantic obsession and threatening pursuit has been percolating in the narrative structures of romances and tragedies for centuries (Kamir, 2001). In the late 1980s, after the impact of movies such as *Play Misty for Me* (1971) and *Fatal Attraction* (1987), the idea of celebrity stalking began to intrude into the American cultural consciousness. The intersection of Hollywood, celebrity, and decades of consciousness-raising about domestic violence provided a natural spark for California to pass the world's first explicit anti-stalking law in 1990. Within a decade and a half, all 50 states, the U.S. government, Canada, Great Britain, Australia, The Netherlands, Germany, Japan, and a number of other countries had passed analogous legislation.

Stalking laws vary considerably from jurisdiction to jurisdiction (Beatty, 2003; Kapley & Cooke, 2007). There is considerable evidence that "layperson" definitions of stalking vary in systematic ways from legal definitions (Dennison & Thomson, 2005). Research also indicates considerable uncertainty and variability in defining stalking among helping professionals and police (e.g., Klein, Salomon, Huntington, Dubois, & Lang, 2009; Tjaden, Thoennes, & Allison, 2000). If victims do not recognize their experiences as stalking, and if the helping professions and criminal justice system do not recognize stalking as stalking, then stalking victims are unlikely to end up seeking redress through the courts.

Most legal and statutory definitions of stalking consist of some combination of the following elements: (a) an unwanted (b) purposeful or intentional (c) intrusive or harassing (d) course of conduct (e) that serves no other legitimate purpose, and (f) is fearful or threatening (g) to the victim or to a "reasonable person." Given the potential relevance of each of these components to the prosecution of stalking, each requires brief elaboration.

The role of fear, which is "the most fundamental justification for the existence of stalking laws" (Beatty, 2003, p. 2–10) is represented in statutes requiring that the victim or the victim's family be in fear of serious bodily injury or death. The model code recommends using a standard that includes "emotional distress" as a proxy for fear (National Center for Victims of Crime, 2007). Given the possibility that some victims should be afraid but are not, and others are afraid but have little legitimate reason to be, most jurisdictions apply a "reasonable person" standard: Would a reasonable person fear serious bodily injury or death in this circumstance? From a communication perspective, this provides options for constructing the case narrative both in the victim's voice, and in the minds of the judge or jury. The communication challenge is to impart, at a deep emotional level, the overpowering fear that often envelops stalking victims.

THE PROCESS, PREVALENCE, AND PERPETRATION OF STALKING

The Nature of the Crime

Stalking has been defined in a variety of ways, but most scholars define it as a process of unwanted and fear-evoking pursuit, intrusion, threat, and harassment. As the elicitation of fear or a sense of threat is a defining characteristic of stalking, stalking itself is a crime of communication. It is a course of criminal conduct over time in which a perpetrator communicates with a victim in a manner that evokes fear and apprehension, and in which a victim communicates that such conduct is unwanted (Mullen, Pathé, & Purcell, 2009). Therefore, it is an asymmetric relationship, in which two (or more) persons find themselves in interdependent interactions (Cupach & Spitzberg, 2008; Spitzberg & Cupach, 2007, 2008).

Rather than selectively reviewing individual findings from studies, it is possible to apply descriptive meta-analytic procedures to such research. A meta-analysis is a process by which different studies, conducted by different investigators, for different purposes, are aggregated. So, for example, one study may ask victims of stalking whether or not the pursuer had ever "threatened to kill you," whereas another study of police case files might use a coding system to identify the percentage of stalking cases that involved a "threat of bodily harm." These are two different ways of operationalizing "threat," but they also clearly refer to a largely similar set of behaviors. The estimates across these studies can be averaged to provide a more aggregate estimate of the percentage of stalking cases that involve "threats." When this procedure is applied across studies, it provides a variety of benefits over traditional literature reviews, including much larger and more generalizable sample sizes, and the ability to identify certain moderating variables.

The second author has been maintaining such a database (Dutton & Spitzberg, 2007; Spitzberg & Cupach, 2007). As of Fall 2010, the descriptive meta-analytic database has 268 studies of stalking, representing 306,644 subjects or cases. This does not mean that more than 300,000 cases of stalking have been studied, but that more than 300,000 persons or cases have been observed in regard to stalking. For example, some surveys have asked thousands of people whether or not they have been stalked, but only a small subset of those surveyed represent actual stalking victims.

Study populations may be divided into three broad categories clinical/forensic, general population, and college students. Studies of clinical and forensic populations typically involve domestic violence, stalking, or protective order samples. In contrast, studies of college students and more general populations represent a more "normal" end of a spectrum of disordered persons and relationships. These differences factor into the approaches mental health professionals, victim advocates, law enforcement, prosecutors, and the courts may take to terminate or at least mitigate the unwanted pursuit.

Prevalence of Stalking

Stalking is gendered. Men perpetrate about 80% of stalking in clinical/forensic samples, whereas women make up about 80% of victims in those samples. The evidence is mixed regarding whether female stalking victims feel more threatened than male victims (see Spitzberg, Cupach, & Ciceraro, 2010). One of the motives for the adoption of stalking legislation was that a pattern of behavior might cumulatively amount to a threatening and fearful pattern even with no explicitly threatening behavior. For example, finding a plastic baggie with sperm and pubic hair on the doorstep of one's home may not meet any ordinary definition of a "threat," but it is likely to evoke a sense of apprehension about the person who would leave such an item, and what that person is capable of doing. Similarly, a person who shows up at one's work, gym, school, parking lot, and in tandem pursuit on the highway is not enacting an obvious threat, but certainly may be perceived as capable of endangerment. None of these constitutes violence or assault, but they suggest the prospect of violence. The concern that a stalker's pattern of conduct may rise to the level of threat has provided a major impetus for passing stalking legislation.

Explicit threats and violence may not be necessary to the prosecution in every jurisdiction, but they are inevitably intertwined with decisions about prosecuting stalking. In the meta-analysis, threats occur for about

53% of the clinical and forensic samples of stalking victims, and a bit less so for the other samples. Physical violence also occurs more often in clinical and forensic samples, although sexual violence is equally uncommon for the three stalking populations. The correlation between threats and actual violence is substantial in the general population and college population (r = .64 and .74, respectively), but not in the clinical/forensic population. If these findings continue to be verified at the individual case level, it indicates that threats by those who currently come to the attention of clinicians, law enforcement, and the courts are not particularly diagnostic of actual victim risk. Although the use of threats may be persuasive as evidence, it is not very predictive of actual violence. This does not, however, diminish in any way the fear felt by victims, nor does it diminish the importance of clearly communicating to judge and jury the fear felt by victims. The goal of the stalker, after all, may be simply to control and place the victim in fear of what "might" happen. This may be an end in itself for the stalker, as we can see from the following ways in which stalkers communicate their threats to victims.

Perpetration

Stalking takes many forms. Figure 8.1 illustrates the types of behaviors that stalkers perpetrate on victims (Spitzberg, Dutton, & Kim, 2012; see also, Cupach & Spitzberg, 2004; Dutton & Spitzberg, 2007; Spitzberg & Cupach, 2007). Such a broad spectrum of behaviors can be used in highly creative and novel ways, and in the process, may run afoul of multiple types of nonstalking statutes (e.g., threatening communications, unwarranted invasion of privacy, breaking and entering, burglary, assault).

Stalkers may use violence as a tactic in their repertoire, but it is not at all certain that the use of violence is intended to harm. When victims or clinicians are asked to speculate on a stalker's motives, a broad range is revealed (Spitzberg & Cupach, 2007). High percentages of stalkers are perceived to be motivated out of intimacy (e.g., dependency, infatuation, jealousy, envy, obsession, sexual desire, relationship development, and reconciliation), aggression (e.g., anger, revenge, control, intimidation), disability (e.g., drug-based incompetence, mental impairment), or specific task (e.g., business dispute, neighborhood dispute, political dispute) motivations. As their campaign of pursuit can last for months or years, many stalkers traverse multiple motive states across the course of the relationship. Identifying the motive state of a stalker at a particular point in time can be important in prosecution in terms of demonstrating intent, and in demonstrating the potential threat of the stalker.

HYPER-INTIMACY: Inappropriate behavior masking as courtship, flirtation, or efforts to ingratiate target and/or pursue greater intimacy. Examples: sending gifts, symbols of affections, etc.

MEDIATED CONTACT: Use of technologies to establish or maintain contact and engage in communication. Examples: faxes, instant messaging, social network sites, etc.

INTERACTIONAL CONTACT: Efforts to engage in face-to-face communication. Examples: showing up at places, entering into conversation target is having with another person, joining common clubs or organizations, etc.

SURVEILLANCE: Efforts to obtain information about the target's life, location, or activities. Examples: driving by the target's home or work, following, use of technologies (e.g., GPS, computer Trojan horses), covert monitoring, etc.

INVASION: Unwarranted intrusions into the property or personal space of the target. Examples: trespass, breaking and entering target's property, solicitation of information from target acquaintances, etc.

HARASSMENT/INTIMIDATION: Efforts to influence target through infliction of minor irritants or costs. Examples: extraordinary persistence of contact, regulatory harassment, interference with everyday routines, etc.

COERCION/THREAT: Use of implicitly or explicitly threatening actions or objects to influence target reactions. Examples: verbal warnings, leaving startling objects in startling places, sending threatening images or messages, etc.

AGGRESSION/VIOLENCE: Use of physical force in the form of contact that has the potential to harm or injure the target, target's property or associates. Examples: kidnapping, physical assault, driving dangerously with or at target, etc.

PROXY PURSUIT: Use of third parties to facilitate any of these strategies or tactics. Examples: pursuer uses relatives or acquaintances, private detectives, or inveigling unwitting associates of the target.

Adapted from Cupach and Spitzberg (2004); Dutton and Spitzberg (2007); Spitzberg and Cupach (2007); Spitzberg et al. (2011)

Figure 8.1. Strategies and exemplary tactics of stalking.

One of the most problematic features of stalking, from a prosecutorial perspective, is that it usually emerges from an ongoing or preexisting relationship. Across all sample types, 80% of stalkers are known to their victims, and more than 40% are prior romantic partners. In cases involving prior romantic relationships, there often are inherent interdependencies (e.g., common property or children, workplace assignments, friendship networks) that continue to involve the stalker and the victim in each other's lives. It can be difficult to establish that a pattern of conduct is unwanted and fearful if the victim continues to permit interactions with the perpetrator to occur. This also has practical implications for the management of stalking cases, especially if the nature of the interdependencies changes across time as the victim attempts to establish new boundaries with the stalker. Sometimes breaking off communication itself sends an important message to the perpetrator that the victim is no longer willing to engage. The effectiveness of such strategies is affected, in part, by the nature of the underlying relationship between stalker and victim.

Ex-intimate stalking cases appear to be qualitatively different from stranger or acquaintance stalking cases (Logan & Walker, 2009; Roberts & Dziegielewski, 2006). Research indicates that it is the ex-partner stalking cases that are likely to be violent (e.g., Rosenfeld & Lewis, 2005; cf. McEwan, Mullen, MacKenzie, & Ogloff, 2009). Paradoxically, stalking by ex-intimates is probably the most dangerous type, yet these are the hardest to prosecute because of cultural notions about the complexity of intimate relationships.

Role of External Actors (Law Enforcement, Mental Health, Victim Services, Judiciary Response)

When justice system representatives and victim services representatives are asked what advice they would give stalking victims (Logan, Walker, Stewart, & Allen, 2006), the most common forms of advice are for the victims to enhance their personal safety, use the criminal court system, use law enforcement, go to a shelter, seek education about options, speak to a victim services representative, obtain mental health treatment, change their identity or relocate, collect documentation, and stay close to and inform others. Interestingly, none of the responses cited in the literature include specific recommendations for communication strategies to break the engagement cycle between stalker and victim or to build successful prosecutions. This may account, in part, for the difficulty that law enforcement officers have in investigating these crimes, and the difficulty that prosecutors face in obtaining convictions.

THE PROSECUTION OF STALKING

Law Enforcement Response to Stalking

"Little research has been conducted on prosecutorial behavior in stalking cases" (Brewster, 2003, p. 3–13), but it is clear that the vast majority of actual stalking cases never come to the attention of police, and when they do, police severely underidentify them as such. "Given the low number of stalking incidents identified by police, it is not surprising that stalking arrests are relatively few, constituting only a tiny fraction of all domestic violence arrests" (Klein et al., 2009, p. 6). Klein et al. found that for every incident identified by police as stalking during the study period, almost 21 other cases of stalking were not identified.

A national survey by Miller (2001) of 204 law enforcement agencies and 222 prosecutor offices within areas with large populations found that the vast majority of police departments handle stalking investigations through a domestic violence unit (about 40% overall). Stalking training appears wedded to domestic violence training, with only 13% to 15% of police agencies reporting specific training for stalking cases, and 33% reporting no in-service training on stalking—even though 57% of police agencies report having written policies and procedures for stalking cases. More than 80% of prosecutor offices reported some specific training on stalking, but only 50% had explicit written policies and procedures for handling stalking cases. It appears stalking enforcement and prosecution lack priority, evidenced by the fact that most states do not systematically record statistics specific to stalking (Miller, 2001).

Two large-scale national surveys provide some rough estimates of the criminal justice response to stalking. Tjaden and Thoennes (1998) conducted a random nationally representative survey of 16,000 U.S. adults. Of those identified as victims, 48% of men and 55% of women claimed the stalking was reported to the police, most often by the victim. The police arrested the suspect in about 21% of these cases. About 11% of these arrests resulted in a criminal prosecution, and 54% of those prosecuted were convicted of some crime. Police were considered helpful by 50% of victims. Results were similar in a very large subsequent study.

Stalking, especially in domestic or ex-partner contexts, is rarely a singular crime. Once stalking comes to the attention of law enforcement, the investigation may identify other crimes. As illustrated in Figure 8.1, stalking may be a collective charge, but any given stalking case presents the potential for ancillary charges.

A few studies of smaller samples have provided a more granulated understanding of the course of stalking cases through the criminal justice system. Jordan, Logan, Walker, and Nigoff (2003) examined 346 cases of men charged with stalking, comparing those found guilty with those whose cases were dismissed or found guilty at a later time. They considered a number of other charges (violent felonies, sex crimes, drug/alcohol crimes, property crimes, traffic crimes, etc.). Of all men charged with stalking in 1999 in the jurisdiction studied, 36% were charged with felony stalking, and 64% with misdemeanor stalking. Half of cases were dismissed (slightly more when considering final disposition of amended charges). Slightly more than one-fourth (28%) of felony charges were amended, most often to a misdemeanor count. Not surprisingly, those found guilty of stalking were more likely to have had multiple charges across multiple crimes, as well as prior convictions. The data also indicated that a prior protection order against a stalker is a significant predictor of other forms of involvement in the criminal justice system, and is likely to "signal an increased risk of other criminal activity" and "subsequent felony charges" (Logan, Nigoff, Walker, & Jordan, 2002, p. 550).

Another in-depth study on the judicial course of stalking cases comes from a case analysis of all stalking cases in Rhode Island between 2001 and 2005, including follow-up of re-arrests through July 16, 2008 (Klein et al., 2009). The study analyzed cases identified by police as stalking cases, and analyzed domestic violence cases to identify another group of "researcher-identified" cases of stalking that met the legal criteria of stalking but were not identified as such by police. The researchers compared these two groups with a large sample of nonstalking domestic violence cases. They found that almost three-fourths of stalking suspects had a prior criminal history, well over 90% were men, more than half had prior protective orders against them, and almost half had active orders against them. Victim demeanor was characterized as "afraid" in about 50% of the cases. Although physical assault was surprisingly rare, threats were common. "Almost half of the suspect stalkers continued to stalk their victims in defiance of a court no contact or protective order" (p. 45). Convictions were obtained on some charge (stalking or otherwise) for about 38% of the cases. Overall, however, only 8% to 10% of suspects were sentenced to incarceration, with most convicted stalkers being sentenced to *probation*. Approximately 50% of the stalkers in both groups were rearrested during the time of the study, and of the 683 charges filed among those rearrested, only 6% were for stalking, whereas 40% were for violation of protective or no contact orders. Overall, the data indicated that when police identify a case as stalking, the likelihood of arrest and prosecution increases, and the likelihood of subsequent rearrest and prosecution (at least for stalkers with no prior criminal or abuse history) decreases. The authors conclude: "the criminal justice response to stalking . . . is compromised by under identification by law enforcement, compounded by charge reduction and case dismissals by prosecutors" (p. 63). It also may be argued that these failures to aggressively and effectively prosecute the crime of stalking are, in large measure, a function of the absence of effective communication between victim and law enforcement, and between law enforcement and prosecutor. To quote the captain in *Cool Hand Luke,* "What we have here is a failure to communicate" with all that entails in terms of risk for the victim and society at large.

When statistics are summarized across samples in the meta-analysis, police are contacted in 43% of stalking cases, and are perceived to be helpful about as often as they are viewed as unhelpful. Protective orders are sought in about 30% of cases, are violated about 4 out of 10 times, and are perceived as escalating the problem in some way almost 30% of the time. Charges are initiated 41% of the time, arrests are reported in 43% of cases, 40% of cases prosecuted yield convictions for some stalking related crime, but almost 33% of the cases are dropped. These estimates represent disparate jurisdictions, sample sizes, operationalizations, and time periods, but still reflect much of what is currently known. The research is divided on whether stalkers are deterred when the victim contacts police (Botuck et al., 2009; Melton, 2004).

Challenges in Communicating the Crime of Stalking to Judges and Juries

Prosecutors face significant challenges when presenting stalking cases to judges and juries. A stalking case is like a mosaic. Each piece of evidence by itself may not appear threatening or fear-inducing, but when assembled into a pattern, and sequenced and framed into a coherent narrative by the prosecution, the finished product may justify the existence of threat or fear by the victim. It is difficult to convey this to judges or juries who are naïve to the stalking phenomenon. It requires close coordination between the victim, first responders, investigators, subject matter experts, counselors, and prosecutor to assure a successful prosecution.

Prosecutors must initially evaluate the viability of a stalking case. The "reasonable doubt" standard is challenging, considering the ambiguity inherent in the patterns of behavior constituting stalking. Judges or juries may view these behavior patterns as legitimate (or at least not unlawful) behaviors, especially in the context of ongoing relationships. Individuals separating after a relationship often send each other conflicting signals. Evidencing the precise point at which unwanted contact constituted a cumulative "threat" or evoked "fear" is part of the prosecution's challenge. Explaining why and how behaviors have over time become objectionable, many of which at one time were considered acceptable in an intimate relationship, requires communicating that the way in which former spouses or intimates interact can be transformed from legitimate behavior into criminal behavior—even if the objective behavior is the same. What has changed is the context and the manner in which the contact is perceived by the victim. This "reframing" of the context of behavior makes stalking an unusual crime, in that there often is no dispute about the facts; the dispute is over the interpretation of those behaviors.

Depending on the specifics of a given state's statutes, the prosecutor may be required to establish the following:

1. The existence of a threat (express or implied).

2. The threat is credible (i.e., the suspect is capable of carrying out the threat).

3. The defendant intended to induce fear on the part of the victim.

4. The victim unequivocally communicated a desire that the contact end.

5. "Reasonable fear" on the part of the victim necessitating an inquiry into the victim's mental state.

To establish these elements, the prosecution must consider whether or not research or expert opinion suggests ostensible danger or risk, whether the defendant's motivation was malicious (e.g., "Why did you stand outside her home and stare?" "I did it for love, not to induce fear"), the definitive break point or threshold at which the behaviors became unacceptable, and the reasonableness of the victim's fear. Victims often do not recognize the conduct they are subjected to as stalking, so in many cases, it is up to the first responder and investigator to identify the existence of a crime, and to start building the case long before the prosecutor is involved. Establishing criminal conduct "beyond a reasonable doubt" constitutes a high standard and that is exacerbated in cases where doubts or equivocation may exist even in the mind of the victim.

First responders must be trained to identify a possible crime. This may be difficult because stalking rarely involves a single event constituting cause for an arrest. Witness statements must be gathered and evidence preserved (physical evidence e-mails, text messages, etc.). The initial impressions of the first responder are important in developing the case because that individual is most likely to have observed, firsthand, the demeanor and apparent mental state of the victim (and in rare instances, the perpetrator). Did the victim appear afraid? How did the victim's behavior or statements indicate fear? Did the perpetrator seem puzzled at the victim's distress? These kinds of first impressions can be critical to the prosecution's evaluation of the case.

The old saying that, "Good witnesses make good prosecutions" is especially true in stalking cases, due to the victim-oriented nature of the crime. Good investigators will avoid cuing or leading any of the witnesses, instead taking a narrative approach and asking open-ended questions. In victim interviews, this offers the opportunity to gather information that may not be significant in the victim's mind, but may be of critical importance in tying the case together for purposes of prosecution. In suspect interviews, this offers the opportunity for the suspect to volunteer information that may be of use in formulating a management strategy (if the case has not yet risen to the level of a crime) or a prosecution or a defense. Videotaped interviews are especially useful, given that bodily communication, intonation, and demeanor often indicate more persuasive ostensible evidence of motive, fear, or credibility than written transcripts.

In assessing credibility, investigators must be attuned to the fact that in some cases the complainant is not the true victim. Sometimes the complainant is in fact the perpetrator, intent on abusing judicial process to further harass and intimidate the true victim. Given the high incidence of personality disorders identified in stalkers (and the difficulty in assessing the existence of such disorders), investigators must consider the plausibility of explanations about known objective conduct, identify and prioritize discrepancies, and seek third-party corroboration of alibis. Investigators must also remain alert to the possibility of "false victimization" (Schell, 2003; Sheridan & Blaauw, 2004; Tellefsen & Johnson, 2000), especially in cases where there are pertinent external events (e.g., civil lawsuit, divorce) that could provide some form of advantage by being a "victim."

If experts are needed, including mental health professionals qualified to comment on the victim's reasonable fear, they must be vetted by the prosecutor's office to avoid unpleasant surprises at trial. Although less common in the criminal arena, it is not unheard of for a purported "expert" to be found unqualified in *voir dire*. For this to happen to the prosecutor's expert in a jury trial can be fatal to the prosecution's case.

Presented with the work of the investigator, the prosecutor must determine whether or not he or she has a *prima facie* case of stalking. The prosecutor assesses the prospects for success or failure based on an evaluation of witnesses' credibility—especially the victim's—the quality of the evidence, the expert's anticipated testimony, any defenses the suspect may reasonably be expected to raise, and the existence of other more easily prosecuted crimes arising out of the same course of conduct supporting a stalking prosecution.

Prosecutors, especially in smaller offices, tend to be generalists. Even as training has increased for law enforcement and investigators, it has declined for prosecutors. This is to be expected, as prosecutor's offices are subject to public pressure to adapt their resources to the shifting concerns of the electorate. The public's perception, rightly or wrongly, is that stalking affects a small segment of the population (even though the data show that the prevalence of stalking is vastly greater than the number of arrests and prosecutions suggest). The practical significance of this for stalking prosecutions is that only the largest prosecutorial offices have the resources to train and commit to developing prosecutorial expertise in stalking crimes—assuming they assign a priority to it.

Vertically integrated prosecution units devoted to stalking crimes can streamline the response, investigation, and prosecution of stalking crimes (e.g., Boles, 2001; Dunn, 2008; Maxey, 2001, 2002). Such units can also "manage" cases that have not yet risen to the level of a prosecutable crime, especially with the assistance of external multiagency groups, that can provide expert resources (e.g., mental health professionals who can assist in evaluating the suspect's psychological issues and risk assessments). Specialized units are, of course, financially viable only in larger agencies, but they provide a model for how stalking investigations and prosecutions can be handled most efficiently.

Communication Strategies (Opportunities and Risks)

If all relevant factors align, then a stalking prosecution *may* ensue. It is more likely, however, that the case will plead out on some other crime(s) (e.g., burglary, breaking and entering, threats to commit a crime, and most commonly, violation of a restraining order). Prosecutors tend to go for low-hanging fruit because of the practical need to process as many cases as possible. It is easier to obtain a plea to a lesser crime than to contemplate a long, drawn-out stalking trial that may "re-victimize" or traumatize the victim—precisely the kind of process that some stalkers would relish. The likely course of the case thus serves the purposes of the prosecutor and may serve the purposes of the victim. Ultimately, the course of action should be directed simply at getting the stalker out of the victim's life for at least some period of time.

In the rare instance in which a stalking case goes to trial, the prosecutor must adhere to the rule, "Know thy judge" (i.e., the judge's biases and predilections, especially concerning unwanted romantic pursuit or continued interaction between former intimates over children). The prosecutor's message must be attuned to what the judge will hear and perceive about the case. This is especially true for bench trials, given that reversing a trial judge on appeal is extremely difficult.

Moreover, the prosecutor must consider the fact that jury trials are unpredictable. Even after *voir dire*, it is impossible to know whether or not one or more jurors will interpret actions by the stalker or victim in a radically different manner than the prosecutor intends. It is not enough that the prosecutor establish objectionable conduct by the defendant. The prosecutor must build sympathy for the victim, so that the judge or jury relate to the victim's situation and understand the gnawing fear and uncertainty that was tearing at the victim. A key challenge for the prosecutor is to develop a feeling of connection to, and identification with, the victim during the course of the case.

The prosecutor also needs to speak in terms the judge and jury can understand—to communicate the size, color, texture and meaning of the mosaic comprising stalking. The narrative must neither overstate nor understate the case, and the prosecutor must constantly observe and recalibrate the message to the jurors, individually and collectively. Each piece of evidence needs to be assembled in a linear and logical fashion, so the end result is a clear portrait of behavior that lacks a legitimate purpose and that would induce fear, threat or at least anxiety in even the most steadfast juror. Body language, eye contact, engagement with the jurors (or judge), and a professional but approachable demeanor all go into building a positive perception in the jurors, the prosecutor's witnesses (including the victim), and the prosecution's case. The goal is to build jurors' trust, respect and sympathy for the victim.

The prosecutor also must recognize that jurors expect certain things to happen in the courtroom, even if those things are gleaned from popular media and have little connection with reality. When in trial, the lawyers are on stage and must tailor their messages accordingly. Jurors notice everything. Attorneys on either side ignore this admonition at their own peril.

The prosecutor must acknowledge and address weaknesses in the case to inoculate the jury against thinking during cross-examination that the prosecution has not been completely forthcoming. No attorney wants the defects in a case to be highlighted by the other side. This is especially true where a victim has "baggage" affecting his or her credibility or character (e.g., substance abuse or prior convictions). Such weaknesses need to be acknowledged so the jury can move on and focus its attention on the stalker's behaviors and the negative impact that those behaviors would have on any "reasonable person," not just this particular victim.

Getting the jurors to envision themselves as the victim of the objectionable conduct can be the key to the case.

Given the high incidence of stalking by interdependent intimates, prosecutors must be careful to avoid aggravating preexisting conflicts between people who are going to have to interact into the future (especially parents). Deterring certain objectionable conduct is undesirable if it leads to worse conflict, and this can happen when the victim elects to pursue litigation against a stalker. Thus, if the stalker elects to accept a plea bargain the terms of the plea should contain safeguards for the victim (including limitations or prohibitions on communication, no-contact orders, stay-away orders, etc.) and meaningful enforcement should the defendant violate the terms of the plea.

Studies show that gender is an influential factor in the process and outcomes of the legal system, but the prosecutor needs to be very careful to keep the underlying argument gender-neutral to avoid offending the judge or any of the jurors. Despite the existence of significant data showing that men, especially intimates, are potentially more dangerous than other stalkers, the prosecutor cannot openly appeal to one group (women) at the expense of the other (men). This is a recipe for a hung jury and mistrial. The specific threat presented by this particular stalker and the specific fear of this victim must be the focus of the prosecution.

A further consideration is that if a stalker is acquitted, the Constitutional prohibition against double jeopardy will prevent use of the stalker's prior acts in a future prosecution for continued harassment. Given the difficulties of successfully prosecuting stalking cases and the importance of establishing patterns of behavior over time, the prosecutor must consider whether to pursue prosecution if the evidence of a pattern of criminal conduct may be needed later for a stronger case. Just because the case *can* be tried does not mean it *should* be tried.

The relative rarity of stalking prosecutions is partially a function of the relatively modest sentences. The vast majority of persons convicted of stalking receive probation. Only in cases where the stalker has escalated the level of violence (see Figure 8.1) resulting in physical injury is there a significantly heightened chance of a successful prosecution for stalking. Even in those cases, the penalties for stalking tend to pale in comparison with the penalties for burglary, battery, or other related crimes, including violation of a restraining order. If there is a possibility of a plea bargain, stalking will likely be one of the first charges dismissed due to the difficulty of prosecuting such cases. If the prosecutor does agree to this, then it is incumbent upon him or her to explain to the victim why it is being done and what the corresponding risks and benefits are for the victim.

A final consideration in stalking cases, an issue the literature has yet to explore in a meaningful way, is the danger of empowering the stalker. If the case is tried and the jury acquits or the case results in a hung jury, then there is a very real danger that the stalker will feel vindicated and empowered to engage in even more intrusive conduct. The purpose of prosecution is to protect the victim and stop the objectionable behavior, so the prosecutor needs to consider whether taking the case to trial might increase the risk of harm to the victim. In deciding whether or not to prosecute a stalking case, the prosecutor needs to have a frank discussion with his or her investigators, colleagues, and the victim about what can be reasonably expected to occur at trial—and in its aftermath. Regardless of the outcome of the case, it is extremely important to "close the loop" with the victim and first responders. Stalkers rarely fade away. They can be relied on to reinitiate communication with the victim periodically. Victims and law enforcement need to be ready to act when this occurs.

CONCLUSION

Stalking cases raise complex communication problems for victims in communicating the depth of their fear and emotional distress, for law enforcement in identifying the existence of and investigating this criminal conduct, and for prosecutors in communicating the gravity of the crime to judges and juries. The frequent presence of other crimes makes plea-bargaining an attractive option, especially if it achieves the underlying goal of giving the victim relief from harassment by the stalker. Trials are uncertain and if mishandled can have the disastrous outcome that the stalker will escape responsibility and continue or escalate a campaign of harassment toward the victim. Sentences for stalking are generally inadequate to deter future stalking behaviors. It is unsurprising that stalking prosecutions are rare.

These observations are not intended to diminish in any way the importance of the crime or the depth of the suffering experienced by victims, but rather to draw attention to the need for enhanced efforts on numerous fronts:

1. Increased public awareness about the behaviors constituting the crime;

2. Expanded stalking-specific training for first responders, investigators, prosecutors, and judges;

3. The creation of special vertical prosecution units closely linking first responders, investigators, and prosecutors;

4. Engagement with multidisciplinary, multiagency teams to provide the kinds of resources unavailable in most police agencies and prosecutor's offices;

5. Judicial education for judges who are naïve as to the behaviors that comprise stalking;

6. Education of the public regarding the nature of the crime and its impacts on victims, their families, and society at large; and

7. Enhanced sentencing and treatment to deter stalking.

Existing research on stalking can certainly inform all of these efforts.

Stalking researchers can be of value to actual cases, as well, by serving as an expert witness. Once in the courtroom, much will depend on how composed the victim is, and how well the prosecutor develops a coherent victim narrative. The victim's story needs to help a judge or jury to identify personally with the reasonable fear that anyone in the victim's place would experience. The questioning process should guide the victim's testimony to personalize the experience, provide tangible examples and descriptions of encounters, and demonstrate that she or he did nothing to invite such unwanted pursuit. The early involvement of an expert witness in evaluating the nature of the threat can significantly reinforce witness credibility. Moreover, an expert witness is better able to dispel certain myths about stalking; for example, the myth that it is the stranger, the mentally ill, or the celebrity stalker who pose the greatest threat, when virtually all of the research says it is the ex-intimate. Experts are more likely to be able to identify the conditions that make threats more credible and fearful. Stalking achieves fear through a communication process, and this process must be explained to the court. Our hope is that further research in this field will focus attention on the importance of identifying effective mechanisms for communication between victim and stalker to set clear boundaries, for communication between victim and law enforcement to promptly identify and properly investigate this unique crime, for communication between investigators and prosecutors to build solid cases, and for communication between prosecutors and judges and juries to obtain convictions. It is perhaps too much to expect that stalkers will receive the message, but this is an area that certainly bears further study as well.

REFERENCES

Boles, G.S. (2001). Developing a model approach to confronting the problem of stalking: Establishing a threat management unit. In J.A. Davis (Ed.), *Stalking crimes and victim protection: Prevention, intervention, threat assessment, and case management* (pp. 337–350). Boca Raton, FL: CRC Press.

Botuck, S., Berretty, P., Cho, S., Tax, C.A., Archer, M., & Cattaneo, L. B. (2009). *Understanding intimate partner stalking: Implications for offering victim services* (NCJ 227220). Unpublished NIJ-sponsored report available from http://www.ncjrs.gov/pdffiles1/nij/grants/227220.pdf.

Brewster, M.P. (2003). The criminal justice system's response to stalking. In M.P. Brewster (Ed.), *Stalking: Psychology, risk factors, interventions, and law* (pp. 3.1–3.21). Kingston, NJ: Civic Research Institute.

Beatty, D. (2003). Stalking legislation in the United States. In M.P. Brewster (Ed.), *Stalking: Psychology, risk factors, interventions, and law* (pp. 2.1–2.55). Kingston, NJ: Civic Research Institute.

Cupach, W.R., & Spitzberg, B.H. (2004). *The dark side of relationship pursuit: From attraction to obsession to stalking.* Mahwah, NJ: Erlbaum.

Cupach, W.R., & Spitzberg, B.H. (2008). Thanks but no thanks . . . : The occurrence and management of unwanted relationship pursuit. In S. Sprecher, A. Wenzel, & J. Harvey (Eds.), *Handbook of relationship initiation* (pp. 409–424). New York: Taylor & Francis.

Dennison, S.M., & Thomson, D.M. (2005). Criticisms or plaudits for stalking laws? What psycholegal research tells us about proscribing stalking. *Psychology, Public Policy and Law, 11*, 384–406.

Dunn, J. (2008). Operations of the LAPD Threat Management Unit. In J.R. Meloy, L. Sheridan, & J. Hoffman (Eds.), *Stalking, threatening, and attacking public figures: A psychological and behavioral analysis* (pp. 325–342). New York: Oxford University Press.

Dutton, L.B., & Spitzberg, B.H. (2007). Stalking: Its nature and dynamics. In S.M. Giacomoni & K. Kendall-Tackett (Eds.), *Intimate partner violence* (pp. 4.1–4.20). Kingston, NJ: CRI.

Jordan, C.E., Logan, TK, Walker, R., & Nigoff, A. (2003). Stalking: An examination of the criminal justice response. *Journal of Interpersonal Violence, 18*, 148–165.

Kamir, O. (2001). *Every breath you take: Stalking narratives and the law.* Ann Arbor: University of Michigan Press.

Kapley, D.J., & Cooke, J.R. (2007). Trends in antistalking legislation. In D.A. Pinals (Ed.), *Stalking: Psychiatric perspectives and practical approaches* (pp. 141–163). New York: Oxford University Press.

Klein, A., Salomon, A., Huntington, N., Dubois, J., & Lang, D. (2009). *A statewide study of stalking and its criminal justice response* (NCJ 228354). Unpublished NIJ-sponsored report available from http://www.ncjrs.gov/pdffiles1/nij/grants/228354.pdf.

Logan, TK, Nigoff, A., Walker, R., & Jordan, C. (2002). Stalker profiles with and without protective orders: Reoffending or criminal justice processing. *Violence and Victims, 17*, 541–553.

Logan, TK, & Walker, R. (2009). Civil protective order outcomes: Violations and perceptions of effectiveness. *Journal of Interpersonal Violence, 24,* 675–692.

Logan, TK, Walker, R., Stewart, C., & Allen, J. (2006). Victim service and justice system representative responses about partner stalking: What do professionals recommend? *Violence and Victims, 21,* 49–66.

Maxey, W. (2001). Stalking the stalker: Law enforcement investigation and intervention. In J.A. Davis (Ed.), *Stalking crimes and victim protection: Prevention, intervention, threat assessment, and case management* (pp. 351–374). Boca Raton, FL: CRC Press.

Maxey, W. (2002). The San Diego Stalking Strike Force: A multi-disciplinary approach to assessing and managing stalking and threat cases. *Journal of Threat Assessment, 2,* 43–53.

McEwan, T.E., Mullen, P.E., MacKenzie, R.D., & Ogloff, J.R.P. (2009). Violence in stalking situations. *Psychological Medicine, 39,* 1469–1478.

Melton, H.C. (2004). Stalking in the context of domestic violence: Findings on the criminal justice system. *Women & Criminal Justice, 15,* 33–58.

Miller, N. (2001). Stalking investigation, law, public policy, and criminal prosecution as problem solver. In J.A. Davis (Ed.), *Stalking crimes and victim protection: Prevention, intervention, threat assessment, and case management* (pp. 387–426). Boca Raton, FL: CRC Press.

Mullen, P.E., Pathé, M., & Purcell, R. (2009). *Stalkers and their victims* (2nd ed.). Cambridge: Cambridge University Press.

National Center for Victims of Crime. (2007, January). *The model stalking code revisited: Responding to the new realities of stalking* (NCJ 189192). Washington, DC: Author.

Roberts, A.R., & Dziegielewski, S.F. (2006). Changing stalking patterns and prosecutorial decisions: Bridging the present to the future. *Victims and Offenders, 1,* 47–60.

Rosenfeld, B., & Lewis, C. (2005). Assessing violence risk in stalking cases: A regression free approach. *Law and Human Behavior, 29,* 343–357.

Schell, B.H. (2003). The prevalence of sexual harassment, stalking, and false victimization syndrome (FVS) cases and related human resource management policies in a cross-section of Canadian companies from January 1995 through 2000. *Journal of Family Violence, 18,* 351–360.

Sheridan, L.P., & Blaauw, E. (2004). Characteristics of false stalking reports. *Criminal Justice and Behavior, 31,* 55–73.

Spitzberg, B.H., & Cupach, W.R. (2007). The state of the art of stalking: Taking stock of the emerging literature. *Aggression and Violent Behavior: A Review Journal, 12,* 64–86.

Spitzberg, B.H., & Cupach, W.R. (2008). Fanning the flames of fandom: Celebrity worship, Parasocial interaction, and stalking. In J.R. Meloy, L. Sheridan, & J. Hoffman (Eds.), *Stalking, threatening, and attacking public figures: A psychological and behavioral analysis* (pp. 287–321). New York: Oxford University Press.

Spitzberg, B.H., Cupach, W.R., & Ciceraro, L.D.L. (2010). Sex differences in stalking and obsessive relational intrusion: Two meta-analyses. *Partner Abuse, 1,* 259–285.

Spitzberg, B.H., Dutton, L.B., & Kim, C.W., Jr. (2012). The seductions of serial stalking: Persons, processes, and palliatives. In K. Borgeson & K. Kuehnle (Eds.), *Serial offenders: In theory and practice* (pp. 89–121). Sudbury, MA: Jones & Bartlett.

Tellefsen, L.J., & Johnson, M.B. (2000). False victimization in stalking: Clinical and legal aspects. *NYS Psychologist, 12*(1), 20–25.

Tjaden, P., & Thoennes, N. (1998). *Stalking in America: Findings from the National Violence Against Women Survey* (NCJ 169592). Washington, DC: National Institute of Justice and Centers for Disease Control and Prevention.

Tjaden, P., Thoennes, N., & Allison, C. J. (2000). Comparing stalking victimization from legal and victim perspectives. *Violence and Victims, 15*, 7–22.

9

Visual Forensics
Optimizing Graphics in the Courtroom

Shannon S. Dyer

We have all seen enough real and dramatized courtroom scenes on TV to know that visual aids often play a role in court cases. Whether as dramatic as the glove in the O.J. trial or as subtle as the tire track photographs in *My Cousin Vinny*, attorneys and expert witnesses sometimes rely on visual representations of their points. What is perhaps less obvious is that visual aids in the courtroom are becoming increasingly sophisticated as media technology continues to advance. These graphic tools can help communicate the complexities inherent in medical science, details of elaborate business contracts, or in recreating a sequence of events. There are specialists who concentrate on the preparation and presentation of visual aids specifically for the court context.

The term *visual forensics* is sometimes used to encompass the areas of specialization with regard to courtroom visual aids. Of the several areas and subareas of visual forensics, four are primary:

1. *Optical forensics* refers to evidence or testimony dealing with the eye, visual acuity, camera optics, ocular occlusions, and so on. For example, an expert in optical forensics might

testify as to a defendant's field of vision in a car collision or explain what a pilot should be able to see during particular weather conditions in a particular model of plane.

2. *Data analysis* (see Forte, 2009) is sometimes called visual forensic analysis or computer forensics. An expert in this area might graph the network trail left by a hacker using a destructive virus or discover how a computer identity theft was committed.

3. *Graphics* are visual aids used in court to clarify or represent evidence, supporting material, explanations, opinions, and so forth. Examples include crime scene photos, animated simulations, videos used by the court to instruct jurors in a case, graphs, charts, and so forth. A specialist in this area prepares the relevant visual aids to be used by attorneys and witnesses.

4. *Strategy.* Attention is paid to strategy when presenting graphics in the courtroom—how the media can be most effective, the relative advantages of one medium over another, and so forth. Graphics strategy examines how the human mind processes visual images, how jurors use these images in decisions, and media theory to help decode visual argumentation and persuasion.

Examples of the four areas of visual forensics are represented in Table 9.1.

Although the first two categories, optical and computer data analysis can be critical elements in some court cases, this chapter explores the other two categories—graphics and strategy—that is, the selection of supporting media and the strategies behind their application. As an introduction to those areas, we first discuss *visual cognition*, or how jurors process visual information, *forensic graphics*, or the visual media used in court, and finally, *optimizing graphics* through visual forensics.

VISUAL COGNITION

To plan which visual aid is appropriate for a case, it is helpful to begin with an understanding of visual cognition, that is, how jurors process visual information. Visual cognition is the foundation of strategic choices for forensic graphics. Theories of visual cognitive processing include primacy and recency effects, the beneficial use of chunking and chaining

Table 9.1. The Four Areas of Visual Forensics

Optics	Data Analysis	Graphics	Strategy
Camera lenses	Video reconstruction	Photographs	Inoculation
Fields of vision	Computer reconstruction	PowerPoint	Primacy/Recency
Cockpit view	Viruses	Charts and graphs	Narrative structure
Eye disorders	Hacking	Simulations	Chunking/Chaining
Eye injuries	Identity theft	Video confessions	Learning styles
Ocular diseases	Intellect property theft	Surveillance video	Media effects
Obstructions	Media piracy	Virtual crime scene	Color/Motion

in cognitively complex learning, narrative and schemas, the importance of color and motion in visual preference, and visual and verbal learning styles, among others.

Primacy and Recency

The timing of the presentation of visual material in a trial can matter. Primacy studies suggest that we favor first exposure to information in learning and recency suggests we also favor the last information presented. Early studies from this robust line of research found that the order in which information is received about a person can strongly influence the impression formed about the person (Luchins, 1958). Timing information at the first and last part of a trial may influence how well a juror forms explanations, orders the information, and remembers facts. There are, however, several factors that can limit the effects of primacy and recency.

Distinctions between effects on verbal and visual primacy and recency are important for lawyers who want to add visual aids to their verbal evidence (Tremblay, Parmentier, Guerard, Nicholls, & Jones, 2006). Visual data presented *vividly* in the middle of the trial may be just as memorable as spoken information that is presented first or last. Vivid visuals may carry as much cognitive power as the primacy and recency effects. But their vividness is critical, as not just any visual will have this effect. For example, pictures are more powerful than visually depicted words (Allik & Siegel, 1974). A PowerPoint presentation that solely uses words on a screen may not be as effective as a photo image or even speech. Regardless of the power of the visual image, however, graphic images do not persuade us in isolation. The brain requires a logical, semantic analysis to make judgments about those images (Storbeck, Robinson, & McCourt, 2006).

Cognitive complexity also can lessen the effects of primacy (Marsh & Woo-Kyoung, 2006). Increasing the number of alternative explanations that the defense provides a juror may blunt the primacy effect of the first explanation given in an opening statement. Thus, the length of the trial, and the vivid visual evidence during it, may have an effect on how a juror emphasizes information in memory. Over time, recency may even shift to a primacy response bias in retention level (Kerr, Ward, & Avons, 1998). A juror may find the first explanation of the defendant as jilted lover compelling, but as they hear about his violent temper, recency may make this second explanation more compelling. As subsequent potential suspects are revealed providing additional competitive explanations, each recent primed explanation is replaced, and the juror may fall back to the first explanation of jilted lover. In sum, first and last ordering can increase impact in juror perception formation, but vivid, visual and cognitively complex information can limit these effects.

Chunking and Chaining

Chunking is the grouping of items or environmental aspects together into one unit (Sargent, Dopkins, Philbeck, & Chichka, 2010). Humans navigate through environments by relying on internal representations of those environments. When a juror is shown a crime scene photo, for example, all of the various details of the scene are stored in the brain as one unit. When a witness' testimony contradicts a single detail, those internal representations are updated or challenged in chunks.

Chaining is the association of linked items learned in a particular order to assist in learning. By traveling down this chain of associations (Tulving & Craik, 2000) one can recall an entire list of items or events. Just as the classic commercial listing the ingredients to a Big Mac ("two all beef patties, special sauce, lettuce, . . ." etc.) was an effective advertising strategy, there is evidence that sequential learning through chaining is effective in learning generally (Giurintano, 1973). Linking events in a subtle but memorable list may be an effective way for case items to be communicated throughout the trial.

Narrative and Schemas

Narrative processing is one of the longest studied areas of personality and cognitive development (Singer & Bluck, 2001). A juror using narrative processing would bring a lifetime habit of processing information in a story form containing a sequence of events (plot), characters, vivid imagery, and often centering on a theme or conflict. As Donald Polkinghorne (1988) argues in *Narrative Knowing and the Human Sciences,* "narrative is a scheme by means of which human beings give meaning to their experience of temporality and personal actions" (p. 11). These schemata, or mental organizational structures, are based on our previous understanding of the world of scripts and stories (Mandler, 1984). With events, such as a trip to the grocery store, individuals may have a script of loosely related ideas or expectations about such an event. Individuals can then use that script as a basis for comparing how this trip is similar or different from the grocery store trip script. Story schemas are built through the building blocks of scripts based on previous experiences.

This perspective suggests that as we study how humans know information, we should focus on how we live, experience, and interpret our world. Narratives are how we interact with friends, work through gathering knowledge, structure experiences, and store information in memory (Schank & Berman, 2002). Going to work, listening to television, having a discussion with a friend, all rely on organizing the information that we need in a fluid, natural manner. Stories allow us to actually build our knowledge base by making information storage and retrieval more efficient. Each time we recall a favorite movie or childhood memory, it is easier to recall or relay the information in a short predictable narrative form.

Nancy Pennington and Reid Hastie (1992) provide a story-based model to apply narrative thinking to the courtroom and to explain juror decision making. Their study tested which stories affected the jurors' judgments and impacted the credibility of the evidence. The model found that stories that were constructed with ease and completeness had a significant influence on juror decisions. Stories are how jurors piece together the evidence presented at trial to make sense of what happened. This story organization allows jurors to enter jury deliberations with an organized understanding of what they think happened.

Color and Motion

Color can have symbolic association in a juror's mind. Even the most innocent use of color may trigger various associations—from fear to school spirit to a favorite person or place. Colors in graphics can be associated in a way that links the content of the graphics for the jurors. This association comes from the cognitive tendency for efficiency by compressing new information through associations with representations already in memory (Brady, Konkle, & Alvarez, 2009). In a visual field that is filled with many competing bits of information, color can help us choose what to focus on. Color is one factor in selective attention that assists an individual when distinguishing information from its surroundings (Kastner & Ungerleider, 2000). Color and motion can work separately or together as attention factors (Holcombe & Cavanagh, 2008). When we are driving, we can respond to the white rabbit darting across the road even while we are reaching down to turn on the radio. Color and motion can provide vividness in a complex or lengthy trial.

Visual and Verbal Learning Styles

Individuals may vary in their preferences for visual or verbal learning through cognitive ability, cognitive style, or learning preference (Mayer & Massa, 2003). Individuals with a strong visual learning style will benefit the most from visual input (Smith & Woody, 2000), whereas verbal learners may not benefit or may learn less. Jurors who prefer a more visual learning style will likely get more out of an emphasis on visual presentations. The visual–verbal divide, however, may not be as strong as other individual differences such as sensing versus intuitive learners or sequential versus global learners in predicting satisfaction with learning experiences (Choi, Lee, & Jung., 2008). Jurors see and hear visual and verbal information differently, but when designing visual aids, other learning style dimensions may be even more relevant.

FORENSIC GRAPHICS

The unique expertise required at the intersection of science and media has created a new industry in legal support services. Forensic graphic specialists create a wide range of multimedia messages for legal practitioners to bring visual support into the courtroom. Forensic graphics include charts and graphs, photographs and images, PowerPoint and multimedia presentation technologies, video and films, and animation and gaming formats.

Charts and Graphs

Graphs are visual depictions of numbers and categories that help the receiver understand via visual and analytic tools. Although graphing a set of numbers or relationships between categories is one of the more simple graphic representations used in the courtroom, the cognitive tools used to understand graphs are not simple at all. There are three main analytic processes used to comprehend graphs: pattern recognition, the interpretation of qualitative and quantitative information from those patterns, and the decoding of referents from the graph's labels and titles (Carpenter & Shah, 1998). So we not only use visual recognition of the pie chart as a way to divide up the whole, but we determine the sizes of the slices and their relative proportion to each other as well as independently reading the labels and taking in legend information. This complex three-step process organizes the information more efficiently than orally presented statistics alone. However, these processes can get more complicated as we increase the inferences a viewer has to make when interpreting the graph. That is, more efficient graphs maximize pattern recognition, chunk the quantitative information, and minimize the inferential processes required to interpret the information (Shah, Mayer, & Hegarty, 1999).

The notion that jurors have a specific process of visually decoding the information on graphs is the basis of *graphical perception theory* (Cleveland & McGill, 1984). The idea is that specific types of graphs are more effective than others, whereas the processes underlying how a juror makes sense of quantitative information remain constant.

Photographs and Images

In general, the effect of photography on jurors can be marked. Color photographs are more evocative and persuasive than black-and-white photographs, and any photograph is more influential than no photo at all (Douglas, Lyon, & Ogloff, 1997; Whalen & Blanchard, 2006).

A visual hindsight bias suggests that a juror cannot disregard present knowledge when judging what someone in the past *should have* seen. An example of visual hindsight bias would be a malpractice case where a radiologist views the x-ray of a seemingly healthy patient, and then, a few years later when that patient passes away from a tumor, subsequent radiologists testify in court that the tumor is identifiable on the original x-ray (Harley, 2004). Visual hindsight bias includes interpreting photos through the lens of outcome knowledge, even while attempting to disregard that knowledge.

PowerPoint and Multimedia Presentation Technologies

The ubiquitous nature of PowerPoint as a dynamic presentational tool has spurred a flood of intuitive, artistic, and practical sources of advice on constructing effective displays. However, there is only nascent theoretical grounding and study of the medium (Katt, Murdock, Butler, & Pryor, 2008). These few early studies have explored the recall effects of text in visuals, limiting the number of lines per slide, and display features.

Visual rhetorical strategies have been suggested in the construction of PowerPoint presentations as well. Rather than viewing it as merely a subset of visual aids, it may be approached as a merging of the verbal and visual narratives in order to provide memorable images and create a personal conversation with the audience (Cyphert, 2004). This requires a fundamental shift from oratory as an outlined speech to relying on a visual storyboard for speech structure.

Video and Film

Video recordings in the courtroom are varied both in content and purpose. Videos are used as evidence, such as a crime caught on a security camera, an eyewitness' cell phone video, a recreation of a chain of events, a medium for expert testimony, a recorded confession, a way to give the jury instructions, and more. The prevalence of video cameras in the world and in the courtroom makes an analysis of the medium and its pitfalls critical. However, there is a surprising paucity of research in the forensic context relative to the prevalence of video media in the courtroom (Schwartz, 2009).

One study found that mock jurors exposed to videotaped testimony had a greater emotional reaction than those who read transcripts, and the liability assessments were higher in the video recreation condition (Fishfader, Howells, Katz, & Teresi, 1996). It appears that jurors make damage assessments based on the facts of the case, and make liability assessments based on emotions associated with that evidence. Few of us can be immune to the emotional intensity that can be captured on an eyewitness video such as those used in police cars these days.

Production values of film can become a part of the case. Resolution of the digital film, special effects, audio features, camera angles, lighting, mood-setting colors, and editing choices have potential ethical and evidentiary implications. For example, the angle of the camera can be influential to a juror. Because the juror is looking through the view of the camera operator or pre-set camera angle, there is a bias that emerges toward the viewpoint of the camera (Ratcliff, Lassiter, Schmidt, & Snyder, 2006). If the camera is pointing at the suspect in an interrogation room, and the detective is behind or beside the camera, the juror may be more sympathetic to the detective and more negative toward the defendant. Nonetheless, videos can be an invaluable source of instruction, a richer and denser source of information, and a more accurate source of learning than an exclusively oral presentation (Goodman-Delahunty & Hewson, 2009). Videos help simplify information in a setting that tests the cognitive load of jurors, such as a complex trial.

Animation

Animation, or the use of dynamic motion and trajectory in illustrating an event, is a powerful tool in the courtroom. There are three basic categories: animation, scientific animation, and simulation (Fisk, 2008). Basic animation provides a moving, three-dimensional illustration. Scientific animation is governed by facts and physics. These technical graphics conform to specific facts of the case and physical laws. A simulation relies on scientific data, but is used for prediction. Many complicated topics such as cases involving complex medical evidence naturally lend themselves to the visual-spatial ease of an animated illustration (Fisk, 2008). Jurors with little background in biology or chemistry reap a particular benefit from these vivid illustrations.

One of the reasons that these media are persuasive to jurors is their ability to dramatically increase hindsight bias via simulation (Roese,

Fessel, Summerville, Kruger, & Dilitch, 2006). That is, after seeing the animation jurors feel that an individual should have known a certain outcome was possible or probable. Because of the powerful effects of visual media—including color, motion, narrative, and vividness—visual hindsight bias is an important part of the effective and ethical construction of visual aids and graphically presented evidence (Harley, 2007). Animation can create such a certainty about hindsight that it can lead to a "propensity effect" (Roese et al., 2006). After seeing an animation about an event, a juror could feel that a certain outcome was inevitable, based on a gut-level intuition, just before the critical moment appears in the animation. Animation, uniquely, can let us relive an event such as a split-second car accident, as well as feel emotions that we imagine would have been felt by the actual participants in the actual situation. We can predict that the car is going to hit, for example, even if the animated information and mental anticipation was not, in fact, available to the actual participants in the real-life accident.

Animation can be more powerful than orally presented evidence alone. For example, one study conducted with mock jurors found that there is a greater impact on subjects who are allowed to see a computer-animated display than on subjects just being told the same information (Kassin & Dunn, 1997). Jurors watched either a pro-plaintiff or pro-defendant version of an animation depicting a case debating whether a man fell from a building or jumped, and they were verbally given the information from the opposing side. Animation led to judgments that contradicted the physical evidence. On the other hand, another study found that the animation had varying effects on decision outcome depending on the case (Dunn, Salovey, & Feigenson, 2006). Where there was no effect on persuasiveness, the researchers suggest that the jurors' *expectation* for persuasiveness of the animation was high, and thus, jurors may have corrected for this perceived influence. Or possibly, the familiarity with the case, a car accident, may have rendered the animation less impactful—or even less necessary—for the visualization of the event depicted. With the less common case of a plane crash, jurors found the animation very influential in the decision.

Forensic animation has advantages for trials. Trial length can be reduced when verbal explanations are compressed into images, and animation can improve jurors' recall, attentiveness and understanding of the evidence (Schofield, 2009). Cognitive chunking is more effective when animation accompanies instruction and the resulting organization reduces the cognitive load (Munyofu, Swain, & Ausman, 2007). Video and animation are used frequently and are especially valuable in complex trials with complex evidence. In a time of high media stimulation, there is a potential disadvantage to presenting complex information to a jury orally without media support.

OPTIMIZING GRAPHICS

Optimizing graphics in the courtroom involves strategic choices informed by media effects research. For example, the following communication strategies could assist in forensic graphics choices made by legal professionals: visual reinforcement, visual argumentation, and anticipating media effects.

Visual Reinforcement of Verbal Information

Individual differences in affect and cognition can determine preferences for visual stimulus versus a combination of visual and verbal stimuli (Sojka & Giese, 2006). If a juror is more emotional than logical in the way life is approached, a visual aid alone may have more impact than a careful logical explanation accompanying a graphic. With abstract concepts, however, graphics can increase recall and understanding closer to the level of concrete concepts (Prabu, 2006). So, although a juror may understand the specific monetary loss better than a complex contractual agreement, a graphic that visually depicts the relationships described in the contract can go a long way in providing clarification. Vividness—that is, being concrete, image-provoking, and detailed—is associated with persuasiveness in the courtroom (Bell & Loftus, 1985, 1989). And visual aids sometimes can provide vividness that oral testimony alone cannot.

On the other hand, sometimes "colorful language, picturesque examples and provocative metaphors" can undermine the message and distract from the essential meaning of the message (Frey & Eagly, 1993, p. 32). Smith and Shaffer (2000) determined that message congruity between the vivid elements introduced and the general theme of the message is effective. If an inappropriately vivid or extreme metaphor, for example, were used to describe a crime, it may be incongruent with the rest of the case. Visual aids should be thoughtfully and appropriately selected and designed to reflect and integrate the other messages presented in the case.

Although the purpose of visual aids usually is to represent reality, it is certainly possible to construct graphics intended to misrepresent reality. It will be an increasing responsibility of attorneys and judges to become vigilant in monitoring for unreliable videos and to make careful decisions about the probative value of forensic graphics in the courtroom (McAuliff, Nemeth, Bornstein, & Penrod, 2003). Graphic evidence and information should be understood and screened just as oral and written communication is.

Thus, part of visual forensic strategy is to assist in designing, selecting, and barring particular graphics to be used in the courtroom. In today's environment of media literacy, to avoid video or animation as an effective tool to communicate would ignore a very important area of courtroom communication. Generation X jurors comprise more than 40% of jury pools (Morse, 2009). Although older and younger adults tend to make similar decisions when given similar information (Higgins, Heath, & Grannemann, 2007; Weinstock & Cronin, 2002), it is not as clear how differences in media literacy will influence juries with large age differences among jurors. One certainty is that the level of media expected in today's courtroom will only rise in the years to come as the new e-generations enter the jury pools.

Visual Argumentation

Visual forensics allows for a more concrete direction in the way that the story unfolds in the jury's mind. Mental images are built and maintained in the human brain in a manner similar to the way actual visually perceived stimuli are seen in the environment (Kosslyn, 1994). When we imagine how a crime scene might have unfolded, our mind creates that image in a manner similar to actually seeing it. When a speaker relies on verbal argumentation alone, jurors rely on their own imagined experiences and story to fill in the blanks. So a lawyer might address the jury with a statement, "imagine a quiet night" and each juror might have a completely different conceptualized context for the story that follows. A visual illustration leads the jury into the story together with a more concise and consistent viewpoint for the narrative. Video images are a more concrete and directional way to simulate or re-enact a past event.

Visual argumentation takes place in the mind of the juror. For example, in the actor–observer effect, jurors tend to explain their own behavior as situational, but the behavior of others is attributed to person or personality traits (Jones & Nisbett, 1971). This is particularly common when making attributions to someone whose behavior was highly idiosyncratic, or when the behavior or event was negative, or when the event is hypothetical (Malle, 2006). For trials, these conditions are common. For example, jurors may certainly be exposed to extreme and/or negative descriptions or explanations of a situation, person, or place. It would be expected, therefore, for a juror to assume the negative events or actions were caused by the person or personality in question, whereas they might explain their own behavior as situational. In verbal presentations, this effect might be countered by warning of the hazard of this human tendency. By planting this seed of counterargument, the counsel is emulating through argumentative strategy elements of attitudinal inoculation theory (Compton & Pfau, 2005). Much like a medical administration of an inoculation, a message is provided and then time must pass for jurors to construct counter-arguments to build up a resistance against the threat of the existing or unknown attitudes. On the other hand, using videos which animate the scene is a more vivid way to describe the perspective and narrative one wishes to present.

Media Effects

Jurors bring with them scripts and schemas for the courtroom. They have expectations as to what criminals look like, how lawyers and judges should act, and how a trial will unfold. Often, these are unrealistic expectations based on media portrayals that they have watched for years in actual and dramatized movie and TV presentations. With the perpetual popularity of crime and law TV shows and films, the legal community has begun to acknowledge the importance of popular media in understanding jurors (Elkins, 2007).

SUMMARY

Visual media are an integral part of our everyday lives, and today's jurors have a high degree of media literacy. The accessibility of technology makes some of the most sophisticated media forms feasible for almost any case or courtroom presentation. Visual forensics is the strategic use of forensic graphics in the courtroom based on a communication perspective. By understanding the cognitive visual processes that a juror uses, legal professionals and graphics consultants are able to make fundamental choices among the various graphics and visual aids available. An awareness of media literacy and visual effects of certain approaches to those visual aids, as well as familiarity with or pursuit of related research, can optimize the use of these important forensic communication tools.

REFERENCES

Allik, J.P., & Siegel, A.W. (1974). Facilitation of sequential short-term memory with pictorial stimuli. *Journal of Experimental Psychology, 103*(3), 567–573.

Bell, B.E., & Loftus, E.F. (1985). Vivid persuasion in the courtroom. *Journal of Personality Assessment, 49*(6), 659–664.

Bell, B.E., & Loftus, E.F. (1989). Trivial persuasion in the courtroom: The power of (a few) minor details. *Journal of Personality & Social Psychology, 56*(5), 669–679.

Brady, T.F., Konkle, T., & Alvarez, G.A. (2009). Compression in visual working memory: Using statistical regularities to form more efficient memory representations. *Journal of Experimental Psychology: General, 138*(4), 487–502.

Carpenter, P.A., & Shah, P. (1998). A model of perceptual and conceptual processes in graph comprehension. *Journal of Experimental Psychology: Applied, 4*(2), 75–100.

Choi, I., Lee, S.J., & Jung, J.W. (2008). Designing multimedia case-based instruction accommodating students' diverse learning styles. *Journal of Educational Multimedia and Hypermedia, 17*(1), 5–25.

Cleveland, W.S., & McGill, R. (1984). Graphical perception: Theory, experimentation, and application to the development of graphical methods. *Journal of the American Statistical Association, 79*(387), 531–554.

Compton, J.A., & Pfau, M. (2005). Inoculation theory of resistance to influence at maturity: Recent progress in theory development and application and suggestions for future research. *Communication Yearbook, 29*, 97–145.

Cyphert, D. (2004). The problem of PowerPoint: Visual aid or visual rhetoric? *Business Communication Quarterly, 67*(1), 80–84.

Douglas, K.S., Lyon, D.R., & Ogloff, J.R.P. (1997). The impact of graphic photographic evidence on mock jurors' decisions in a murder trial: Probative or prejudicial? *Law and Human Behavior, 21*(5), 485–501.

Dunn, M.A., Salovey, P., & Feigenson, N. (2006). The jury persuaded (and not): Computer animation in the courtroom. *Law & Policy, 28*(2).

Elkins, J.R. (2007). Symposium: Popular culture, legal films, and legal film critics. *Loyola Los Angeles Law Review, 40*, 745–782.

Fishfader, V.L., Howells, G.N., Katz R.C., & Teresi, P.S. (1996). Evidential and extralegal factors in juror decisions: Presentation mode, retention, and level of emotionality. *Law & Human Behavior, 20*, 565–572.

Fisk, G. (2008). Using animation in forensic pathology and science education. *Labmedicine, 39*(10), 587–592.

Forte, D. (2009). Visual forensics in the field. *Computer Fraud & Security, 5*, 18–20.

Frey, K.P., & Eagly, A.H. (1993). Vividness can undermine the persuasiveness of messages. *Journal of Personality and Social Psychology, 65*(1), 32–44.

Goodman-Delahunty, J., & Hewson, L. (2009). *Improving jury understanding and use of DNA expert evidence.* Canberra: Criminology Research Council.

Giurintano, S.L. (1973). Serial learning process: Test of chaining, position, and dual-process hypotheses. *Journal of Experimental Psychology, 97*(2), 154–157.

Harley, E.M. (2004). The "saw-it-all-along" effect: Demonstrations of visual hindsight bias. *Journal of Experimental Psychology: Learning, Memory, and Cognition, 30*(5), 960–968.

Harley, E.M. (2007). Hindsight bias in legal decision making. *Social Cognition, 25*(1), 48–63.

Higgins, P.L., Heath, W.P., & Grannemann, B.D. (2007). How type of excuse defense, mock juror age, and defendant age affect mock juror decisions. *Journal of Social Psychology, 147*(4), 371–392.

Holcombe, A.O., & Cavanagh, P. (2008). Independent, synchronous access to color and motion features. *Cognition, 107*, 552–558.

Jones, E.E., & Nisbett, R.E. (1971). *The actor and the observer: Divergent perceptions of the causes of behavior.* Morristown, NJ: General Learning.

Kassin, S.M., & Dunn, M.A. (1997). Computer-animated displays and the jury: Facilitative and prejudicial effects. *Law and Human Behavior, 21*(3), 269–281.

Kastner, S., & Ungerleider, L.G. (2000). Mechanisms of visual attention in the human cortex. *Annual Review of Neuroscience, 23*, 315–341.

Katt, J., Murdock, J., Butler, J., & Pryor, B. (2008). Establishing best practices for the use of PowerPoint as a presentation aid. *Human Communication, 11*(2), 189–196.

Kerr, J., Ward, G., & Avons, S.E. (1998). Response bias in visual serial order memory. *Journal of Experimental Psychology: Learning, Memory, and Cognition, 24*(5), 1316–1323.

Kosslyn, S. (1994). *Image and brain.* Cambridge, MA: MIT Press.

Luchins, A.S. (1958). Definitiveness of impression and primacy-recency in communications. *Journal of Social Psychology, 48*, 275–290.

Malle, B.F. (2006). The actor-observer asymmetry in attribution: A (surprising) meta-analysis. *Psychological Bulletin, 132*(6), 895–919.

Mandler, J.M. (1984). *Stories, scripts, and scenes: Aspects of schema theory.* Hillsdale, NJ: Erlbaum.

Marsh, J., & Woo-Kyoung, A. (2006). Order effects in contingency learning: The role of task complexity. *Memory & Cognition, 34*(3), 568–576.

Mayer, R.E., & Massa, L.J. (2003). Three facets of visual and verbal learners: Cognitive ability, cognitive style, and learning preference. *Journal of Educational Psychology, 95*(4), 833–841.

McAuliff, B.D., Nemeth, R.J., Bornstein, B.H., & Penrod, S.D. (2003). Juror decision-making in the twenty-first century: Confronting science and technology in court. In D. Carson & R. Bull (Eds.), *Handbook of psychology in legal contexts* (2nd ed., pp. 303–327). West Sussex: Wiley.

Morse, G.J. (2009). Techno-jury: Techniques in verbal and visual persuasion. *New York Law School Law Review, 54*, 241–558.

Munyofu, M., Swain, W.J., & Ausman, B.D. (2007). The effect of different chunking strategies in complementing animated instruction. *Learning, Media and Technology, 32*(4), 407–419.

Pennington, N., & Hastie, R. (1992). Explaining the evidence: Tests of the story model for juror decision making. *Journal of Personality and Social Psychology, 62*(2), 189–206.

Polkinghorne, D. (1988). *Narrative knowing and the human sciences.* Albany: State University of New York Press.

Prabu, D. (2006). News concreteness and visual-verbal association: Do news pictures narrow the recall gap between concrete and abstract news? *Human Communication Research, 25*(2), 180–201.

Ratcliff, J.J., Lassiter, G.D., Schmidt, H.C., & Snyder, C.J. (2006). Camera perspective bias in videotaped confessions: Experimental evidence of its perceptual basis. *Journal of Experimental Psychology: Applied, 12*(4), 197–206.

Roese, N.J., Fessel, F., Summerville, A., Kruger, J., & Dilitch, M.A. (2006). The propensity effect: When foresight trumps hindsight. *Psychological Science, 17*(4), 304–310.

Sargent, J., Dopkins, S., Philbeck, J., & Chichka, D. (2010). Chunking in spatial memory. *Journal of Experimental Psychology: Learning, Memory, and Cognition, 36*(3), 576–589.

Schofield, D. (2009). Animating evidence: Computer game technology in the courtroom. *Journal of Information Law & Technology, 1*, 1–20.

Schank, R.C., & Berman, T.R. (2002). The pervasive role of stories in knowledge and action. In M.C. Green, J.J. Strange, & T.C. Brock (Eds.), *Narrative impact: Social and cognitive foundations* (pp. 287–314). Mahwah, NJ: Erlbaum.

Schwartz, L-G. (2009). *Mechanical witness: A history of motion picture evidence in U.S. courts.* New York: Oxford University Press.

Scott v. Harris, 550 U.S. 372 (2007).

Shah, P., Mayer, R.E., & Hegarty, M. (1999). Graphs as aids to knowledge construction: Signaling techniques for guiding the process of graph comprehension. *Journal of Educational Psychology, 91*(4), 690–702.

Singer, J.A., & Bluck, S. (2001). New perspectives on autobiographical memory: The integration of narrative processing and autobiographical reasoning. *Review of General Psychology, 5*(2), 91–99.

Smith, S.M., & Shaffer, D.R. (2000). Vividness can undermine or enhance message processing: The moderating role of vividness congruency. *Personality & Social Psychology Bulletin, 26*(7), 769–780.

Smith, S.M., & Woody, P.C. (2000). Interactive effect of multimedia instruction and learning styles. *Teaching of Psychology, 27*(3), 220–223.

Sojka, J.Z., & Giese, J.L. (2006). Communicating through pictures and words: Understanding the role of affect and cognition in processing visual and verbal information. *Psychology & Marketing, 23*(12), 995–1014.

Storbeck, J., Robinson, M.D., & McCourt, M.E. (2006). Semantic processing precedes affect retrieval: The neurological case for cognitive primacy in visual processing. *Review of General Psychology, 10*(1), 41–55.

Tremblay, S., Parmentier, F.B.R., Guerard, K., Nicholls, A.P., & Jones, D.M. (2006). A spatial modality effect in serial memory. *Journal of Experimental Psychology: Learning, Memory, and Cognition, 32*(5), 1208–1215.

Tulving, E., & Craik, F.I.M. (Eds.). (2000). *The Oxford handbook of memory.* Oxford: Oxford University Press.

Weinstock, M., & Cronin, M.A. (2002). The everyday production of knowledge: Individual differences in epistemological understanding and juror-reasoning skill. *Applied Cognitive Psychology, 17*, 161–181.

Whalen, D.H., & Blanchard, F.A. (2006). Effects of photographic evidence on mock juror judgement. *Journal of Applied Social Psychology, 12*(1), 30–41.

II

Communication Applications

Expert Witness Testimony

Content

10

Effects of Sexually Oriented Messages on Individuals and Communities

A History of Challenging Assumptions in the Courtroom

Daniel Linz

Rule 702 of the Federal Rules of Evidence allows an expert to provide scientific, technical, or other specialized knowledge that will assist a judge or jury to understand evidence presented at trial. Over the past 20 years, my colleagues and I have testified as expert witnesses in cases involving sex communication. We have offered expert testimony on the effects of pornography on individuals, obscenity and the scientific measurement of community standards, the impact of adult bookstores and exotic dancing establishments on communities, and other sex-related communication effects.

Although attorneys hired the expert opinions described here, they can be thought of more broadly as *challenging commonplace legal assumptions about sex-related communication through reliance on empirical evidence.* The conflicts that manifest themselves in courtrooms when an expert is called are not about "He said" versus "she said." They are about "Everybody knows that . . ." versus "no way!" Our testimony almost always offers an opportunity to challenge conventional wisdom about the effects of sex-related communication.

Informing the courts also presents an opportunity to make theoretical and methodological contributions to the sex-related communication effects literature. Consequently, the implications for communication theory and research will accompany the description of some of the testimony we have given.

Sex-related communication testimony sometimes involves a "battle of the experts." American law uses an adversarial procedure for settling both criminal and civil disputes. Both sides are responsible for finding and producing witnesses to bolster their position at trial. Research shows, however, that jurors and certainly judges do not automatically defer to the opinions of experts, and that their verdicts appear to be generally consistent with external criteria of performance (Vidmar, 2005).

In an adversarial system judges and juries take from experts what they need to make a decision. This means that in the end it does not matter if the expert is on the winning or losing side of a case. What is important is that the expert offer the court information based on the best science available so that judges and juries can make informed decisions. A few adversarial moments involving debates between experts are described here to illustrate that competing expert testimony may lead to improvements in legal contexts especially when the competing experts exchange *reasons and explanations* for their opinions.

Giving expert testimony is also an opportunity to provide information to the court about basic science methodology. As Vidmar (2005) points out, experimental studies have raised questions about juror abilities to understand basic science principles. Jurors are confused by statistical and methodological testimony. Sometimes the judge protects the jury from confusion, but we should not assume that judges are immune from misunderstandings involving social science methodology (Kovera & McAuliff, 2000). Expert testimony can sensitize fact finders, judges, and juries to these issues.

Our expert opinions are based on studies or tests employing empirical observations. There are guidelines available to scientists that allow them to be confident about the reliability of their claims. The expert testimony described here is part of a effort by me to shift sex communication and First Amendment questions to empirical grounds so that there is a reliance on social science evidence of harm before fundamental rights are curtailed.

CHALLENGING LEGAL ASSUMPTIONS ABOUT SEX-RELATED COMMUNICATION

Testimony Concerning the Effects of Pornography: Shifting the Debate From Sex to Violence Against Women

In 1986 Edward Donnerstein, Neil Malamuth (leading experts in the effects of pornography), and I presented testimony to Attorney General Edwin Meese III and the Attorney General's Commission on Pornography. Meese's mandate was to examine the impact of sexually explicit materials on individual viewers and society. The Commission operated on the commonly held assumption that exposure to explicit sex was the problem. But we wanted to make the point that violent films similar to those viewed by our subjects in laboratory experiments and field studies were substantially more harmful than explicit pornography.

We testified that films portraying sexually violent images (e.g., rape) consistently produce strong antisocial effects on adults, including increased callousness toward rape, negative evaluations of victims of sexual assault, and increased aggression toward women in a laboratory setting (see Donnerstein & Linz, 1995; Imrich, Mullin, & Linz, 1990; Linz & Donnerstein, 1990; Linz & Malamuth, 1993; Linz, Penrod, & Donnerstein, 1987).

Moreover, a film does not have to be sexually explicit to contain violence against women. Studies indicated that movies containing violence against women in sexually nonexplicit contexts (e.g., "slasher" films with female victims and films depicting women as "consenting" to rape) are capable of producing many of the same antisocial effects as violent pornography.

The U.S. attorney general used this testimony and concluded that the level of violence in a film should be emphasized and not just the amount of sexual content. The Attorney General's Commission on Pornography, despite its original assumptions about the harmfulness of sexually explicit materials on individual viewers and society, concluded that violent films might be substantially more harmful than explicit pornography. According to the Commission (p. 329):

> The so-called slasher films, which depict a great deal of violence connected with an undeniably sexual theme but less sexual explicitness

than materials that are truly pornographic, are likely to produce the consequences discussed here to a greater extent than most materials available in "adults only" pornographic outlets.

Challenging the Conventional Wisdom That Explicit Sex Depictions Are Not Tolerated in the Community

Despite the potentially greater harmful effects stemming from viewing violence, obscenity law has been universally geared toward sexually explicit materials and the community's acceptance of them (e.g., *Miller v. California*, 1973). In judging sexually explicit materials that may be obscene, the judge or jury must take the viewpoint of an average person applying contemporary *local community standards*.

Prosecutions for obscenity in the United States have involved hardcore sex. Potentially vicious, violent, degrading depictions are fully protected by the First Amendment as long as they do not contain strong sexual content. The basic assumption of obscenity law is that people see explicit sex as filthy, offensive, disgusting, and shameful and as a breech of the accepted moral standard. But the assumption is that the community does not feel this way about violence. Obscenity law may draw its legitimacy from the fact that it presumably reflects community values. Certain depictions of sex can be regulated through prosecution because they are intolerable to community members. Thus, it is fundamental that the Court be "right" about community disapproval in order for decisions to be just.

Edward Donnerstein and I were asked to testify about our study of adult residents in western Tennessee (Linz et al., 1995). We designed the study to measure whether community members believed that sexually explicit films charged in a certain court case appealed to a shameful, morbid, or unhealthy (prurient) interest in sex and were patently offensive. Community standards were measured using a representative sample of western Tennessee residents who were randomly assigned to view either the sexually explicit films charged in the case, violent materials that would never be the target of an obscenity prosecution, or other control materials.

The study demonstrated that despite the federal prosecutors' assumptions, the sexually explicit films charged in the case *did not* appeal to a shameful, morbid, or unhealthy (prurient) interest in sex, and were not patently offensive. It is difficult to know what impact the testimony had on the jury, but we wondered about a larger question: What is the effect of the law being "wrong" about community standards and morals?

We found that although a majority of community members accepted nonviolent sexually explicit films, there was no evidence that a majority of community members accepted violent "slasher" films. Or, more to the point, these violent films appeared to exceed community standards, whereas the sexual materials did not. Furthermore, participants indicated that they believed the majority of *others* in the community tolerated the violent films they had viewed while they personally did not.

Our data suggested that the law often might be "wrong" about community disapproval of explicit sexual materials. Community members tolerate consenting hard-core sex by an overwhelming majority. They disapprove of sex juxtaposed to violence in "slasher" films. Our findings indicated that to be true to community standards, sex tied to violence should have been the subject of prosecution in western Tennessee and not consenting hard-core pornography.

What are the consequences for the law when persons not considered blameworthy by the community are punished (pornographers) and those blameworthy (producers of violence) are *not* punished as we found in our study? Discrepancies between the obscenity code and community tolerance may tend to undercut the law's moral credibility, which in turn undercuts the law's power as arbiter of proper conduct in this and other domains.

Testimony on the Impact of Indecency on Children: Another Challenge to the Idea of Media Harmfulness

In 1993, the FCC notified the Infinity Broadcasting Corporation that they might be liable for a $600,000 fine for the broadcast of allegedly *indecent* material on the "Howard Stern Show," asserting a threat to children listeners. In this case we were asked by Howard Stern's counsel to review the social science evidence and give an opinion as to whether the harm done to children listening to the show justified punitive fines (Donnerstein, Wilson, & Linz, 1992). Although the government's interest in protecting the well-being of children is compelling, when it conflicts with fundamental parental rights and First Amendment rights, case law requires that the government show some evidence of harm.

We concluded that children listening to the "Howard Stern Show" would not understand the vast majority of the references to sex because they were, for the most part, indirect or vague. Children under 12 years of age do not fully understand sexual terminology and sexual metaphors. Without such understanding, we reasoned that the harmful impact of these terms on children's attitudes and behaviors is likely to be quite limited.

At that time, Howard Stern relied on sexual innuendo rather than explicit statements about sex in his radio act. Part of the offending broadcast cited by the FCC as evidence of indecent remarks was a discussion of Pee Wee Herman who had been arrested for indecent exposure in a movie theater in Florida. Stern referred to Pee Wee euphemistically as "spewing his junk." In fact, nearly every reference to sex in the Stern shows cited by the FCC as indecent was in the form of an innuendo, metaphor, or veiled reference.

Because studies show that children do not understand metaphorical or nonliteral language, we testified that there was little evidence that Stern's sexual references would affect children. The prohibition of broadcast indecency was therefore, in our opinion, not justified by social scientific evidence.

BATTLE OF THE EXPERTS

Many scholars are concerned about the increasing complexity of jury trials and question whether the testimony of competing experts helps unsophisticated jurors to make informed decisions. Recent research suggests that competition in the courtroom is actually more elucidating than confusing under the right conditions (Boudreau & McCubbins, 2009), especially when the competing experts exchange *reasons for why their statements may be correct.*

When experts exchanged reasons, they consistently helped unsophisticated subjects to make decisions that are comparable to those of sophisticated subjects. This result is encouraging. It suggests that competing expert testimony may lead to improvements in the information given to judges and juries when experts are careful to give *reasons and explanations* for why their statements may be correct.

Pornography in the Workplace

In an effort to prevent sexual harassment, the Los Angeles Fire Department banned *Playboy* magazine and other sexually oriented magazines from fire stations. A fire captain sued, claiming he had a First Amendment right to possess, read, and consensually share his *Playboy* magazine at his fire station. The City of Los Angeles, the defendant in the case, asked me to provide testimony to substantiate the city's claim that reading and viewing pictures in *Playboy* magazine may influence the way male firefighters treat female firefighters.

I testified that, in my expert opinion, the reading of *Playboy* in the workplace could lead to discrimination and possibly sexual harassment. The reason reading of *Playboy* leads to sex-role stereotyping is that research has shown that sex-role stereotyping often is the first step to sexual harassment. Furthermore, I said that work in the laboratory indicated that men would treat women as sex objects if they already have gender-schematic attitudes and viewed pornography (McKenzie-Mohr & Zanna, 1990).

In our studies, we replicated these findings and extended them to situations where men and women work together (Jansma, Linz, Mulac, & Imrich, 1997; Mulac, Jansma, & Linz, 2002). In our studies, men were shown films divided into three categories: sexually degrading, sexually educational (i.e., sexually explicit, but not degrading), and neutral. After watching the film, the men interviewed two female job applicants. The study showed that the sexually degrading films had no effect on the manner in which the men evaluated or remembered the female applicant. At the same time, both the sexually degrading as well as the sexually educational films heightened the possibility that the men would classify the female applicants as untrustworthy, incompetent, or incomprehensible.

The plaintiff offered Dr. Neil Malamuth's testimony to rebut my testimony. He acknowledged that asserting a connection between reading *Playboy* and "sexual stereotyping" is reasonable, but argued that based on the present state of scientific studies, we could not be sure. He gave several reasons for his opinion:

1. The laboratory studies involved films that included explicit intercourse, whereas *Playboy* merely contains photographs of solitary nude women.

2. The studies were based on college-age men, whereas most male firefighters were older.

3. The laboratory studies used a small number of subjects and questionable control groups.

4. The two studies were inconclusive, with some of the results actually supporting the claim that reading *Playboy* has no impact on a male firefighter's treatment of his female co-workers (e.g., pornographic films had no influence on men's ratings of a female job applicant).

The court found the testimony of Dr. Malamuth to be credible and persuasive, and found accordingly that the defendants failed to prove a connection between reading *Playboy* and "sexual stereotyping," and between "sexual stereotyping" and sexual harassment. Was this the right decision? It doesn't matter. What is important is that the experts offered the court information based on the best scientific evidence available at the time so that the judge could make an informed ruling.

Alcohol Consumption Combined With Adult Entertainment: Experts Battle Over How Best to Measure Crime

Another example of a battle of the experts in court involved expert opinion on whether states may legally regulate sex-related communication in alcohol-serving establishments. The justification for regulation of adult entertainment in taverns and bars businesses is based on the idea that the combination of liquor and erotic dancing leads to more "secondary effects" than either one. Using this as a justification, the Ohio General Assembly passed a law in 2007 closing adult businesses from 12 midnight to 6 a.m., and restricted nude performances in any establishment that had a liquor permit.

Ohio adult nightclub owners and other adult businesses owners challenged the law. The adult business owners sought a preliminary injunction on the basis of secondary effects to stop enforcement of the new law. I was called as an expert on behalf of the adult nightclub owners and testified there were no more secondary crime effects in establishments that combine liquor service and adult entertainment than either one alone. The testimony was supported by a statewide empirical study of Ohio cities Toledo, Columbus, Dayton, and Cleveland, which demonstrated no correlation between the presence of crime and liquor-serving establishments featuring nude or semi-nude dancing (Linz, Yao, & Byrne, 2007). The results of the study challenged the assumption that the combination of liquor and erotic dancing lead to uniquely harmful secondary crime effects.

Dr. Richard McCleary testified on behalf of the defense and challenged our methodology of measuring crime, specifically, our use of Calls for Service to the police. Dr. McCleary opined that Calls for Service were not a reliable measure of the secondary crime effects of sexually oriented businesses because they are based on 911 and most criminal incidents are not discovered through these calls. He said that the Uniform Crime Reports (UCRs), National Incident-Based Reporting System, or Incident-Based Reports are better measures of crime because they are based on crime incident reports, that is, where a police officer has investigated a crime and filed a report on the crime, which is then entered into the police department's statistical reporting system is a better measure.

There are many ways to scientifically measure crime. Each has its own advantages. Although it is correct that criminologists often used UCRs in their studies, 10 years of "hands-on" real-world experience at town hall meetings and legislative hearings in states and local communities across the country have led me to a different preference. Calls for Service are an important indicator in debates about the secondary crime effects of adult businesses. Municipalities and police departments use them as a measure of crime and disturbance. When police are asked to testify before legislatures or city counsels regarding adult businesses, they rely on them for evidence. They also measure community disorder and mischief, and lesser levels of crime that would not be reflected by the UCRs.

During this battle of the experts we were able to draw sharp distinctions that informed the court—by providing explicit justifications for our research choices. The court noted that the competition between expert witnesses and their fundamental disagreement about methodological standards was important in the judge's decision. The evidence I presented shows that the General Assembly of Ohio may have reached a different conclusion regarding the relationship between alcohol, secondary effects, and sexually oriented businesses.

MAKING METHODOLOGICAL AND THEORETICAL ADVANCES

Using Survey Evidence to Determine What is "Obscene"

Surveys often are used in criminal prosecutions to establish community standards of obscenity. One criticism of this approach is that it does not involve responses to the allegedly obscene materials charged by the prosecution, because the survey respondent does not have a chance to look at the materials.

In the case *State of North Carolina v. Cinema Blue of Charlotte, Inc.* (1989) we conducted a study of residents of Mecklenburg County, North Carolina, where we were able to make methodological advancements by taking a cross-section of residents and randomly assigning them to view either a control film or the sexually explicit materials charged in the case (Linz et al., 1991). The results demonstrated that on the whole, the materials did not appeal to a shameful, morbid, or unhealthy (prurient) interest in sex, and were not patently offensive.

The legal outcome of this case was peculiar. The judge said that the jury could determine what the community standard was without expert testimony. Consequently, the defense attorneys could *not* use our study as evidence and the defendant was convicted and went to jail. The case was appealed to the federal court in *St. John v. State of North Carolina Parole Commission*, 764 F. Supp. 403 (W.D.N.C 1991) and now, ironically, stands for the proposition that it is appropriate to exclude survey evidence on community standards because the jury brings the community standard to the trial, thus no evidence is necessary to establish it.

What would have happened had the jury been able to hear about our study and the fact that a cross-section of the community did not find the materials obscene? Obscenity cases are unique criminal proceedings in that they are virtually the only cases where a jury is asked to take into account the consensus of the community before making a judgment. Jurors by law have the responsibility of articulating community standards, although not even local or state legislative bodies are allowed to usurp this function.

As social scientists, we know that there is no guarantee that once a jury is selected, it is representative of the average person in the community. Our study showed the average person's opinion can be calculated by randomly selecting people from the community, having them view the materials being prosecuted and taking an "average" of their responses. Because they are called on to make a sociological assessment of the standards of the community, it is imperative that the jury has access to this social science methodology. Our study should not override the jury's final determination, but the methods used to collect our calculation of the "average" person should be considered by the jury to determine whether the materials are obscene.

A Theoretical Contribution

Interestingly, when we asked the individuals in our study what they thought the community at large tolerated, they believed others would be *in*tolerant of the same materials they personally found acceptable. This belief in empirically false propositions about other in the society exemplifies the theoretical concept of "pluralistic ignorance" (O'Gorman 1988). Usually, people are motivated to *overestimate* support for their values among others (e.g., Fields & Schuman 1976–1977)—an effect known as the "egocentric bias." However, we found individuals perceiving *less*, rather than more, support for their beliefs about sexually explicit materials.

By what process might the social environment have misinformed its inhabitants? We proposed that the discrepancy between perceptions of the community standard and the individual adults' own standards were the result of recent legal events in Mecklenburg County. During the 2 years before the trial, several arrests for obscenity were made and defendants were tried and found guilty in well-publicized trials. Community members in our study may have assumed that because there had been a large number of arrests and several guilty verdicts, most people in the community did not tolerate these types of materials (a phenomenon we call *prosecution-induced intolerance*). The greater the attention by the media to obscenity prosecutions in a community, the more the average observer may assume that citizens of the community are intolerant. However, when members of the community were individually questioned, they expressed a much higher level of tolerance.

This misperception also may have consequences for interpersonal interactions, which in turn also influence perceptions about community beliefs. The erroneous belief in lack of tolerance for sexually explicit materials in the community may lead people to be hesitant to speak out honestly about their own opinions. Here, another theory of public opinion may come into play. This unwillingness to speak out may be an example of the more general tendency toward a "spiral of silence," whereby a silent majority falsely perceives itself to hold a minority opinion and, thus, remains quiet in order to avoid personal ridicule (Noelle-Neumann 1974, 1984).

PROVIDING COURTS WITH BASIC SCIENTIFIC PRINCIPLES

Research indicates that in many instances judges do not know how to distinguish reliable from unreliable expert testimony. Kovera and McAuliff (2000), for example, provided a sample of 144 Florida circuit judges with the abbreviated version of an award-winning sexual harassment study. Most of the judges were not sensitive to factors that affect the validity of such research. Judges who had had some training in scientific methods tended to perform better than those who had not, but even many of those were not sensitive to such obvious methodological problems as lack of control groups or experimenter bias.

Much of our testimony has been about informing judges and juries about basic science and its power in asking and answering questions. In the case *City of Erie, et al., v. PAP's A.M.* the Supreme Court held that cities and states may ban nude dancing as a way of combating the crime and other "negative secondary effects" associated with adult establishments. The decision was horribly fractured, as many are in the area of sex communication. A plurality (four justices, Justice O'Connor, joined by the Chief Justice, Justice Kennedy, and Justice Breyer) said a city might rely on the experience of (i.e., "studies" done by) other cities as evidence of these harmful effects.

Justice Souter dissented. In an earlier case, he had stated that the government could essentially assume that "pernicious secondary effects" would result from the presence of nude dancing establishments. But he changed his mind. Justice Souter stated now that cities must prove that nude dancing is actually causing them harm (secondary effects).

In explaining his change of mind, Justice Souter deflected the potential embarrassment of a public recantation by a graceful turn of phrase (Greenhouse, 2000), saying, "I should have demanded the evidence then, too." His revised position was that a city should have to provide evidence both of "the seriousness of the threatened harm" and "the efficacy of its chosen remedy." Because Erie failed to provide this evidence, the case should be sent back to the lower courts to permit the city to do so.

Justice Souter said that there was arguably no relationship between adult businesses and crime. He said harmful secondary effects could not be presumed to exist from past studies. The city's failure to conduct their own study was even more damaging in light of a brief we submitted, arguing, on the one hand, that scientifically sound studies show no correlation between adult business and crime and, on the other hand, the studies commonly used by cities to justify their regulations are not scientifically sound, but rather are flawed and inconclusive. We collected more than 120 "studies," analyzed them both in regard to their conclusions and their "methodological rigor," and found that with few exceptions, the most frequently used studies are seriously and often fatally methodologically flawed (Linz, 1999; Paul, Linz, & Shafer, 2001).

We also developed a list of criteria for evidence of adverse secondary effects to be objectively sound. Most important was the idea that quasi-experimental designs or equivalent procedures should be used to ask a critical question: "Compared to what?" Because most studies of secondary effects attempt to uncover increases in crime or neighborhood economic deterioration, we argued that professional standards dictate that adult and non-adult (control) sites must be compared with regard to crime and neighborhood deterioration, and that before/after time-series designs should be employed when possible.

The plurality (Justice O'Connor, joined by Chief Justice Rehnquist, Justice Kennedy, and Justice Breyer) rejected Justice Souter's dissenting opinion that empirical proof must be required. They said our methodological suggestions amounted to a Dauber-based secondary effects standard and that was too strict (1999 WL 805047, app at A.1). The plurality flatly rejected the idea that legislatures must invoke academic studies claiming to show that threatened harms are not real.

But the court did come to the conclusion in a later decision that the evidence of secondary effects relied on by municipalities must be held to some minimal standard (City of Los Angeles vs. Alameda Books, Inc., 2002). In this decision, the court reiterated that governments may regulate sexually oriented businesses on the basis of studies done in other communities, however, the cities may not engage in shoddy data collection or reasoning in coming to the conclusion that adult businesses cause these effects. They added that if plaintiffs succeed in casting doubt on a municipality's rationale in either manner, the burden shifts back to the municipality to supplement the record with evidence renewing support for a theory that justifies its ordinance.

By the time he wrote his dissenting opinion in *Alameda*, Justice Souter was so convinced as to the value of empirical research he argued for a standard based entirely on it. Further tests of this assumption on a community-by-community basis are not tremendously difficult, Justice Souter noted and:

> stress should be placed on the point that requiring empirical justi-
> fication of claims about property value or crime is not demanding
> anything Herculean. Increased crime, like prostitution and muggings,
> and declining property values in areas surrounding adult businesses,
> are all readily observable, often to the untrained eye and certainly to
> the police officer and urban planner. These harms can be shown by
> police reports, crime statistics, and studies of market value.

And precisely because this sort of evidence is readily available, Justice Souter noted:

> Reviewing courts need to be wary when the government appeals, not
> to evidence, but to uncritical common sense in an effort to justify such
> a zoning restriction. It is not that common sense is always illegitimate
> in First Amendment demonstration. The need for independent proof
> varies with the point that needs to be established, and zoning can be
> supported by common experience when there is no reason to question
> it. But we must be careful about substituting common assumptions for
> evidence, when the evidence is as readily available as public statistics
> and municipal property valuations, lest we find out when the evidence
> is gathered that assumptions are highly debatable.

In fact, in the *Alameda* case, Justice Souter has formulated a legal test based on empirical verification. He argues that the weaker the empirical evidence concerning secondary effects, the more likely the governmental action is not content neutral. He states:

> The lesson is that the lesser scrutiny applied to . . . zoning restrictions
> is no excuse for government failure to provide a factual demonstration
> for claims it makes about secondary effects; on the contrary, this is
> what demands the demonstration. And finally the weaker the demon-
> stration of facts distinct from disapproval of the adult viewpoint, the
> greater the likelihood that nothing more than condemnation of the
> viewpoint drives the legislation. The danger is that without empirical
> verification the city has a right to experiment with a First Amendment
> restriction in response to a problem of increased crime that the city
> has never shown to be associated with adult businesses.

In the next section I suggest there is evidence that lower courts are taking seriously Justice Souter's advice to consider scientific evidence presented by experts.

SHIFTING FIRST AMENDMENT
QUESTIONS TO EMPIRICAL GROUNDS

The Seventh Circuit Court of Appeals has directly tackled the implications of *Alameda* and the standard of proof for secondary effects in an opinion written by Chief Judge Frank H. Easterbrook. Easterbrook is noted for his depth of knowledge and sophistication in the area of social science and economics and is one of the most cited appellate judges in the United States. The opinion provides a set of methodological requirements or principles for determining when an empirical link between the presence of an adult business in a community and adverse secondary crime effects has been reliably demonstrated. The central question regarding the presence of crime in and around adult businesses is, according to the court, "compared to what?"

In this decision, the Seventh Circuit Court of Appeals struck down an amendment to an ordinance in Indianapolis as unconstitutional that required certain time, place and manner restrictions upon adult business because the city of Indianapolis relied on inconclusive evidence when drafting the regulation. In this opinion, Judge Easterbrook provides the standard for a sound methodological demonstration of adverse secondary effects. Specifically, he stated that in order for the ordinance to be constitutional, the city must provide evidence that these restrictions actually have public benefits great enough to justify any curtailment of speech. And, this evidence must be more than just the government's "reasonable" belief that secondary adverse effects exist in relation to adult businesses. In his opinion in *Annex Books* he states:

> Indianapolis has approached this case by assuming that any empirical study of morals offenses near any kind of adult establishment in any city justifies every possible kind of legal restriction in every city. That might be so if the rational relation test governed, for then all a court need do is ask whether a sound justification of a law may be imagined. But because books (even of the "adult" variety) have a constitutional status different from granola and wine, and laws requiring the closure of bookstores at night and on Sunday are likely to curtail sales, the public benefits of the restrictions must be established by evidence, and not just asserted.

The court also said that studies of secondary effects could not be simple cross-sectional studies because such studies do not allow for a high level of internal validity—the ability to establish a causal relationship. The Court said with regard to the evidence introduced by the city:

> Nor do the studies show that an increase in adult businesses' operating hours is associated with more crime; the studies are simple cross-sectional analyses that leave causation up in the air. (In other words, they may show no more than that adult businesses prefer high-crime districts where rents are lower.)

The Court said that before/after time-series designs are especially helpful in determining if adult businesses are a source of criminal activity because they allow for the deduction of causality. Referring to the Los Angeles study at issue in the *Alameda Books* case (discussed earlier) the court notes:

> But the fact that *crime rose as adult establishments entered the area* (see 535 U.S. at 435 [describing the study]) implied that the causal arrow ran from adult businesses to crime, rather than the other way. That could happen because adult establishments attract a particular kind of clientele that is emboldened by association with like-minded people, so that prostitution and public masturbation (for example) are more acceptable near congeries businesses than they would be elsewhere.
> Plaintiffs (in the Annex Books case) offered a study by Daniel Linz, a professor at the University of California, Santa Barbara. Linz first examined the relation between crime and adult establishments in Indianapolis. . . . He found little relation—*and he added a time series, while the City relied on a cross section.*
> In other words, Linz conducted the same kind of analysis as the Los Angeles study in *Alameda Books*, asking whether crime went up in a given census tract when new adult establishments opened, or down when they closed. Linz concluded that these openings and closings did not materially affect crime.

Most importantly, the court insisted that the "compare to what" question be asked. The court required that a comparative analysis be undertaken so that crime in and around adult businesses could be put into some perspective relative to crime at other businesses in the community. The Court even went so far as to suggest that alcohol-serving businesses would serve as the best control or comparison points. The Court noted:

Nor can we tell whether 41 arrests at one business over the course of 365 days is a large or a small number. *How does it compare with arrests for drunkenness or public urination in or near taverns,* which in Indianapolis can be open on Sunday and well after midnight? If there is more misconduct at a bar than at an adult emporium, how would that justify greater legal restrictions on the bookstore—much of whose stock in trade is constitutionally protected in a way that beer and liquor are not.

Finally, Judge Easterbrook made a specific recommendation for statistical analysis noting that multivariate regression analysis may provide a better foundation for determining secondary crime effects than either a time series or a cross-sectional analysis. The court notes:

> One may doubt that Linz's work is the last word; a multivariate regression would provide a better foundation than either a time series or a geographic cross-section. See Daniel L. Rubinfeld, *Reference Guide on Multiple Regression,* Reference Manual on Scientific Evidence (2d ed.) (Federal Judicial Center 2000).

Judge Easterbrook said to send it back to the lower courts and let the empirical findings fall where they may. Specifically:

> Counsel for Indianapolis conceded at oral argument that none of the studies that the City has offered in defense of its ordinance deals with the secondary effects of stores that lack private booths. Nor do the studies assess the effects of stores that sell as little as 25% adult products. These shortcomings, plus Linz's work, call the City's justifications into question and require an evidentiary hearing at which the City must support its ordinance under the intermediate standard of *Alameda Books*. See also *Abilene Retail #30, Inc. v. Dickinson County,* 492 F.3d 1164 (10th Cir. 2007) (reaching the same conclusion on a similar record).

The expert testimony provided to the court in *Annex Books* was helpful in shifting sex communication and First Amendment questions to empirical grounds. This represents a long-standing effort to provide the court with social science evidence of harm before fundamental rights of speech are curtailed.

REFERENCES

Boudreau, C., & McCubbins M.D. (2009) *Competition in the courtroom: When does expert testimony improve jurors' decisions?* Paper presented at the

Third Annual Conference on Empirical Legal Studies Papers, Working Paper Series.

City of Erie v. Pap's A.M., 529 U.S. 277, 289 (2000).

Cinema Blue of Charlotte, Incorporated; Jim St. John; Curtis Rene Peterson, Plaintiffs-appellees, v. Peter S. Gilchrist, III, Defendant-appellant, United States Court of Appeals, Fourth Circuit. - 887 F.2d 49

Donnerstein, E., & Linz, D. (1995). Media. In J.Q. Wilson & J. Petersilia (Eds.), *Crime: Twenty-eight leading experts look at the most pressing problem of our time* (pp. 237–266). San Francisco CA: Institute for Contemporary Studies.

Donnerstein, E., Wilson, B.J., & Linz, D. (1992). On the regulation of broadcast indecency to protect children. *Journal of Broadcasting and Electronic Media*, 36(2), 111–117.

Fields, J.M., & Schuman, H. (1976–1977). Public beliefs about the beliefs of the public. *Public Opinion Quarterly*, 40, 427–428.

Gatowski, S., Dobbin, S., Richardson, J., Ginsburg, G., Merlino, M., & Dahir, V. (2001). Asking the gatekeepers: A national survey of judges on judging expert evidence in a post-Daubert world. *Law Human Behavior*, 25, 433–458.

Greenhouse, L. (2000, March 30). A change of mind and a deft mea culpa. *New York Times*.

Imrich, D., Mullin, C., & Linz, D. (1990). Sexually violent media and criminal justice policy. In R. Surette (Ed.), *The media and criminal justice policy: Recent research and social effects* (pp. 103–128). Springfield, IL: C. C. Thomas.

Jansma, L., Linz, D., Mulac, A., & Imrich, D. (1997). Men's interactions with women after viewing sexually explicit films: Does degradation make a difference? *Communication Monographs*, 64(1), 1–24.

Kovera, M., & McAuliff, P.B. (2000). The effects of peer review and evidence quality on judge evaluations of psychological science: Are judges effective gatekeepers? *Journal of Applied Psychology*, 85, 574–586.

Linz, D. (1999). *City of Erie v. Pap's A.M.*, 529, U.S. 277 (2000). 1999 WL 805047, app. at A1.

Linz, D., & Donnerstein, E. (1990). The relationship between exposure to pornography and anti-social behavior. *The Expert Witness, the Trial Attorney and the Trial Judge*, 5, 26–30.

Linz, D., Donnerstein, E., Land, K., McCall, P., Scott, J., Klein, L.J. et al. (1991). Estimating community tolerance for obscenity: The use of social science evidence. *Public Opinion Quarterly*, Spring, 80–112.

Linz, D., Donnerstein, E., Land, K., McCall, P., Shafer, B.J., & Graesner, A. (1995). Measuring community standards for sex and violence: An empirical challenge to assumptions in obscenity law. *Law and Society Review*, 29(1), 127–168.

Linz, D., & Malamuth, N.M. (1993). Communication concepts 5: Pornography. In S. Chaffee (Ed.), *Communication concepts series*. Newbury Park, CA: Sage.

Linz, D., Penrod, S., & Donnerstein, E. (1987). The Attorney General's Commission on Pornography: The gap between "findings" and facts. *Law and Social*

Inquiry: The American Bar Foundation Research Journal, 1987(4), 301–324.

Linz, D., Yao, M., & Byrne, S. (2007). Testing Supreme Court assumptions in *California v. la Rue*: Is there justification for prohibiting sexually explicit messages in establishments that sell liquor? *Communication Law Review,* 7(1), 23–53.

McKenzie-Mohr, D., & Zanna, M.P. (1990). Treating women as sex objects: Look to the (gender schematic) male who has viewed pornography. *Personality & Social Psychology Bulletin, 16,* 296–308.

Miller v. California, 413 U.S. 15 (1973).

Mulac, A., Jansma, L.G., & Linz, D. (2002). Men's behavior toward women after viewing sexually explicit films: Degradation makes a difference. *Communication Monographs, 69*(4), 311–328.

Noelle-Neumann, E. (1974). Spiral of silence: A theory of public opinion. *Journal of Communication, 24,* 43–51.

Noelle-Neumann, E. (1984). *The sprial of silence: Public opinion—Our social skin.* Chicago: University of Chicago Press.

O'Gorman, H.J. (1988). Pluralistic ignorance and reference groups: The case of ingroup ignorance. In H.J. O'Gorman (Ed.), *Surveying social life: Papers in honor of Herbert H. Hyman.* Middletown, CT: Wesleyen University Press.

Paul, B., Linz, D., & Shafer, B.J. (2001). Government regulation of adult businesses through zoning and anti-nudity ordinances: Debunking the legal myth of negative secondary effects. *Communication Law and Policy,* 6(2), 355–391.

Vidmar, N. (2005). Expert evidence, the adversary system, and the jury. *American Journal of Public Health,* 95(suppl 1), S137-S143.

St John v. State of North Carolina Parole Commission, 764 F. Supp.403 (W.D.N.C 1991).

Wells, G. (1992). Naked statistical evidence of liability: Is subjective probability enough? *Journal of Personal and Social Psychology, 62,* 739–752.

11

Semantics in Court

Providing Opinions on
Likely Meanings of Messages

Michael T. Motley

My first expert witness case involved a man who was injured using a chin-up bar designed to fit within a door frame. The bar has rubber suction cups at each end, and its length is adjusted by twisting its two sections together or apart for a telescoping effect. On vacation in Europe, the man placed the bar within the door frame of his hotel room, twisted it out enough to get a tight fit, and began to do chin-ups. In order to do his chin-ups through a full range of motion while hanging above the floor, he had to bend his legs back at the knees. As he did his chin-ups, the bar slipped, his knees were first to hit the marble floor, and both kneecaps were shattered, one being dislodged about 3 inches into his thigh. He sued (*Cala v. Best Products*, 1985). The defense responded that the rubber ends were not suction cups, that metal brackets had been packaged with the bar, that proper use of the bar required the brackets to be screwed into the door frame to support the bar, and, moreover, that the instructions stated this. The man claimed that after having purchased the device, he opened one end of its rectangular box, dumped out the bar, threw away

197

the box with no brackets or instructions having come out of it, and used the bar unaware of the need for brackets.

One issue in the case, therefore, was that of who was at fault because the brackets were not used. The attorney for the plaintiff looked over the door-bar box (he had bought a new one to examine), and noticed the phrase, "Portable and Convenient for Pullups at Home or Office." He felt certain that the meaning of "Portable and Convenient" is contradicted if brackets have to be screwed out of one door frame and into another in order for the bar to be used in different locations (e.g., "at Home or Office"). Deciding that he had a good argument, and feeling that it would be even more persuasive if it were endorsed by a communication professor, he phoned his local university, got me by chance, and asked me to testify that if a product is described as "portable and convenient for use at home or office," then that means that it does not require the nuisance of frequently installing and removing brackets.

My answer disappointed him. Like any good semantics student, I explained that meanings are in people, not in words, that for every expert witness he found to agree with his meaning of "portable and convenient," the other side could find an expert witness to agree that screws and brackets are very portable, that using a screwdriver is not inconvenient, and that ". . . at home or office" might indeed imply multiple locations, as he insisted, but that the other side could argue just as effectively that it implies a stationary location (e.g., "home or office" versus "home and office"). In short, I said that I could not under oath endorse a single exclusive meaning for the target phrase.

Fortunately, that did not terminate our discussion. Eventually we agreed that it would be wise to frame the question as one of whether the need for brackets had been communicated well or poorly—by the box as a whole, and/or by the instructions (even though the client said he never saw them). I agreed to examine the box and instructions, easily came to the opinion that the need for brackets was communicated very poorly, was retained as an expert witness, supported my opinion with an experiment comparing the original box with variations I hypothesized would communicate the brackets message more clearly (see Motley, Chapter 15, this volume), and went through the various remaining steps of an expert-witness assignment for the first time (e.g., Motley, Chapter 16, this volume).

I have chosen the door-bar example to introduce this chapter on litigation concerning semantics partly because it is chronologically where my experience began, but also because it demonstrates a principle that seems to apply to virtually all of the 30 or so semantics-related, or mean-ing-interpretation, cases in which I have been involved: Usually it is not productive to claim a specific meaning for a specific word or phrase in isolation. About the only time this is preferred is when asked for a lay "translation" of specific passages in legal or technical documents. Instead, it usually is more effective to identify one or more messages that one side claims to have been communicated (e.g., "This bar is to be used only with accompanying brackets for support"), and then ask whether that meaning was communicated relatively well or relatively poorly by the composite of verbal and nonverbal information to which a client was (or was supposed to have been) exposed. Usually, the opinion comes not from a direct translation of given phrases, but rather from interactions of messages, message placement, verbal and physical context, accompanying metamessages, and so forth (e.g., Foss & Hakes, 1978; Hayakawa, 1962, 1972; Nierenberg & Calero, 1981).

This chapter attempts especially to introduce semantics-based litigation consulting to readers who may wish to venture into this kind of work for themselves. But it hopes to also serve attorneys who may not be aware that some communication scholars will have expertise in this area.

For the most part, the chapter simply provides several examples of the kinds of meaning-related issues that can come up in court cases, along with descriptions of how they might be approached by an expert witness with a communication background. When possible, recurrent themes or principles are pointed out, but these are fairly rare, as virtually every case is different. The organization is according to the semantic issues involved.

WARNINGS AND DISCLAIMERS: WAS THE PLAINTIFF INFORMED?

Case 1: Door-Bar Gym

Let us simply continue with the door-bar case. One of the legal issues was whether the defendant should be liable for the injury because the plaintiff did not use the bar with the supporting brackets provided, and because—at least according to the defense—the need for the brackets was communicated to consumers. Among the expert witnesses on various issues was the communication professor mentioned above, me, who was asked for an *opinion on the clarity with which the packaging and instructions communicated the need for supporting brackets.* Inspections of the box and the instructions were performed.

The Box. The box was rectangular (~ 22" × 2" × 2") with two opposite long sides containing the same information, the other two long sides blank, and the two ends blank. The information contained on the box is presented in Fig. 11.1. The reader is invited to examine the box via Fig. 11.1 to formulate an independent opinion before reading the opinion rendered and its rationale. Is the message about needing brackets communicated well? Why or why not?

The opinion rendered, of course, was that the need for brackets was communicated very poorly. Here are some of the reasons for that opinion:

- Most obviously, perhaps, brackets are not mentioned at all on the box. There is nothing saying, "Brackets enclosed," "Use only with enclosed brackets," "Screwdriver needed for installation," or anything of the sort.

- The photograph of the man doing chin-ups contains no brackets.

- The end panels did not say "open this end," or "open at other end." If opened at the end containing the brackets and instructions, they would have had to come out with the bar, precluding the possibility of their getting stuck in the box and the consumer never knowing they existed.

- "Instructions enclosed. Please read carefully." This is a weak admonition in any case, but especially for devices that are ostensibly intuitive in their operation (e.g., unscrew the two sections until a snug fit is made with the suction cups, and do chin-ups). And "please" suggests ". . . but only if you want to" rather than ". . . do it for your own good." Compare the original with a revision such as, "Important safety and mounting instructions enclosed. Read before using bar to avoid injury."

- "Capable of holding up to 200 pounds when properly secured to door frame" is irrelevant if the user is 200 pounds or less and *believes* (even if incorrectly) he or she knows how to "properly secure" the bar. Much better would be, ". . . when secured to door frame with enclosed brackets," for example.

- "Portable and convenient for use at home or office" does not necessarily preclude the use of brackets, as the attorney had originally wanted to argue. But something like "Portable and convenient for use at home or office; brackets and screws included" or ". . . mounting hardware included" would be more accurate about portability and more clear about brackets.

- Adjustable from 21" to 32"
- Portable and convenient for pullups at home or office
- Capable of holding up to 200 pounds when properly secured to door frame
- Instructions enclosed. Please read carefully before using product.

Figure 11.1. Mock-up of door bar gym box.

Not all readers will necessarily agree with all of these points, but I think most will agree that it is very easy to support an opinion that the target message was communicated poorly. More specifically, it is easy to argue that it *would NOT be unusual or unexpected for a consumer, after having seen the box, to be unaware that supporting brackets were required.*

The Instructions. Even though the plaintiff said that he never saw the instructions, his attorney asked that an expert witnesses evaluate them. The instructions are represented by Fig. 11.2. Again, the reader is invited to formulate an opinion on whether the need for brackets is communicated well, and why or why not, before reading on.

The expert opinion was that the instructions communicated poorly the need for brackets. That is, it would not be out of the ordinary for a consumer to be unaware of the need for brackets even if he or she had seen the instructions, and maybe even if he or she had read them, for the following reasons:

- The page of "instructions" is presented as a "Door Bar Gym Course" emphasizing the variety of exercises that can be done with the bar. It does not appear at first glance to be instructions for proper and/or safe use of the bar. In this context, there is no reason for the reader to expect safety instructions or mounting instructions, so it would be easy to miss them unless highlighted (which they weren't). For example, if the consumer had purchased the bar only for pull-ups (which for some reason is not among the exercises shown with this "Course"), he or she might be expected to dispose of the "Door Bar Gym Course" sheet upon first glance because it would appear to be merely a list of irrelevant exercises. It would seem that a better heading and objective for this page would be something like, "Door Bar Gym Installation Instructions and Exercise Options."

- The seven exercises shown are illustrated without brackets.

- The seven illustrations show two different bar positions. And a third position would be necessary for pull-ups where the head and chin come over the bar and under the top of the door. The implication of these various bar positions is similar to the "portable and convenient" point raised earlier. Three or so viable bar locations within the door frame suggests that using the bar involves the rather considerable nuisance of moving the bracket locations, or suggests that brackets are not necessary.

- The Warning section is formatted almost like an eighth exercise (or an appendix to exercise 7) and is easy to miss if the reader is not interested in learning a complete repertoire of exercises.

DOOR BAR GYM COURSE

1. UPPER BODY STRETCH
Grasp the bar firmly, bend knees slowly and let your head hang forward. Lift feet slowly from floor and hold this position for a moment or two.

2. SPINE ARCH STRENGTH
Grasp the bar firmly bend knees slowly let your heels together with weight resting on front of toes. Lean forward as far as possible, with head well back, arch your back.

3. HIP AND KNEE STRETCH
Grasp bar with hands alternated as shown. Bend knees and let arms stretch full length. Slowly raise knees keeping knees and heels together.

4. WAIST AND HIP STRETCH
By bending knees allow arms to stretch full length, gradually raise feet from floor heels well together. Stretch legs as high as possible.

5. FULL BODY STRETCH
In straight standing position facing forward, grasp bar with palms back with elbows bent forward. Keep feet firmly in place, flat on floor and with heels together, twist body at hips slowly.

6. SIT UPS
Lying flat on back, feet locked beneath bar and with palms held behind head, sit up as far as possible, touching elbow to opposite knee.

7. POWER DEVELOPING
Sitting on a low bench or chair with feet under bar extend arms and slowly lower and raise body, bend back as far as possible.

WARNING:
- Check with your physician before starting this exercise program.
- Don't use the door bar gym if your weight is over 200 LBS.
- Please make sure to secure the door bar gym on a door frame with a metal bracket at each end tightly.

Figure 11.2. Instructions for door bar gym course.

- The bracket section of the warning is placed as the third and final warning and is thus de-emphasized.

- The bracket section of the warning is preceded by one routine warning, "Check with your physician," and one redundant warning (the 200-pound limit already mentioned on the box). This relatively unnecessary information can discourage reading the remainder of the section, functioning instead as a meta-message to suggest that an experienced reader is not the intended audience.

- The strange syntax of the brackets section distracts and thus weakens the warning: "Please make sure to secure the door bar gym on a door frame with a metal bracket at each end tightly."

- There are no instructions or diagrams for mounting the brackets or using them to support the bar. Even if the proper installation is fairly obvious or intuitive upon inspecting the brackets, a diagram and mounting instructions certainly would be expected to communicate the importance of brackets better.

- The seven exercises are explained with no reference to brackets. By contrast, suppose each of the seven exercises began with "After securing the bar within the brackets, . . ." or some such.

Again, not all readers will agree with each point, nor that this list is exhaustive. And some may find it to be a bit too critical, bordering on "overkill." In practice, of course, the consultant should mention everything that might be worth mentioning, and let the attorney decide what will ultimately be used and discarded.

In any case, the lists provide a series of examples to support the opinion that the target message was communicated poorly. Notice that if asked, "poorly communicated compared to what," or "poorly by what standard" one can frame the issue in various ways. At the least, perhaps, one can simply ask whether the target message ("brackets are needed," in this case) is communicated well enough to satisfy the defendant's claim that it was provided (or, in some cases, to satisfy the legal requirement that it be provided, e.g., Peters & Peters, 1999). By that standard, the original door-bar instructions might or might not pass the test, and even the box might pass because it admonished the consumer to "Please read carefully" the instructions that did indeed mention brackets. At the other end of the continuum, however, we can ask whether a hypothetical box designer or instructions designer, if *making a serious attempt* to communicate the importance of using the brackets, would be likely to do so more effectively, less effectively, or about the same.

That is, imagine that you, the reader (or you, the jury member if we were in court) were asked to design the box (or the instructions) hypothetically, and that directions from your superior included the following: "Remember—people can get hurt using this product if they try to use it without the brackets, so try to make sure that everyone who sees your box (or instructions) knows that they have to use the brackets so that nobody gets hurt." Now, do you think you would have handled the brackets message(s) differently than the original did? Mock jurors answer virtually unanimously that they would have done a much better job, even without seeing the list of criticisms of the original. And after seeing the list, confidence that they would have done a better job increases significantly. In effect, the impression formed when one compares one's own hypothetical design to the original is that very, very little effort went into communicating the original target message.

Apparent lack of effort is persuasive, of course. *And this seems to occur in case after case where the relative effectiveness of a communication message is challenged.* Sometimes the intuitive impression is that the creator of the package or instructions was not made aware of the need for the target message; sometimes it seems that a reasonable effort was made, but badly; and sometimes the impression is that an intentional effort was made to disguise or conceal the target message. Any of these is damaging, of course. We see another instance of questionable communicative effort in the next case.

Case 2: Haulster Police Vehicle

These days the vehicle driven by a parking patrol officer is likely to have four wheels, or a single front wheel situated within a safety frame that prevents the vehicle from tipping over. Not too long ago they were simpler three-wheeled vehicles, much like a large golf cart with a roof. The change was largely because of the following case.

A parking patrol officer in central California was doing her job, a car pulled in front of her, and she swerved to avoid it. The sharp turn caused the vehicle to begin tipping over, she lost her balance and began to fall out, the vehicle continued to tip all the way over on its side, falling on her and killing her. Her family sued the manufacturer of the vehicle (*Fleming v. Cushman*, 1988). The major issue in the case was not communication, but rather the design of the vehicle, and accordingly the primary expert witnesses were engineers on both sides. Communication became an issue, however, when the defense emphasized that a warning was posted on the dashboard—a warning that instructed operators of the vehicle to avoid hard turns. An explicit claim by the defense was that the accident would not have happened if that warning had been heeded, and thus the victim was blamed for swerving hard in defiance of the instructions. An expert-witness opinion was solicited on whether the danger of sudden hard turns was communicated adequately. Before finding out which side solicited the opinion and what the opinion was, you be the judge (or expert witness, that is). The text of the warning is provided here. Is the danger of hard turns communicated well? If so, how so; if not, why not?

SAFETY WARNING

> *While operating vehicle*: Remain seated, use both hands for steering. Keep arms and legs within vehicle body. Avoid sudden starts and stops. Sudden hard turns can cause upset. Regulate speed to meet road and weather conditions. Do not operate near an explosive environment. If a malfunction occurs, cease operation. Do not operate vehicle until condition is corrected.

The safety warning does indeed warn against sharp turns, saying, "Sudden hard turns can cause upset." But the expert opinion for the plaintiff was that overall, and for several reasons, the warning against hard turns was inadequate.

First, "sudden hard turns can *cause upset*" seems a strange way to make the warning. "Rollover" or "flip" seem preferable to "upset," except that this vehicle probably cannot realistically fall to the side more than 90 degrees, so "rollover" and "flip" are perhaps technically inaccurate (both implying at least 180 degrees, one could argue). Still, "rollover," "flip," "tip over," "fall over," "fall on its side," or the like, seem preferable to "upset." (By the way, in response to interrogatories, the relevant defendant was asked "whether the word 'upset' was intended to mean roll over," and answered, "Yes.") Notice also that "Sudden hard turns can cause upset" is the only nonimperative statement in the entire section, and that it contains the "weasel word," *can* (i.e., might or might not). In combination, this makes for a weak admonition (compared with "Do *not* attempt sharp turns; the vehicle tips over easily," for example).

Second, notice the placement of the hard-turn message within the list, and notice what precedes it. It is the fifth of nine or so warnings.[1] This is bad enough; it should be higher on the list. But to make matters worse, it is preceded by extremely obvious warnings of the type found on children's rides at zoos and kiddie amusement parks: "Remain seated. Use both hands for steering. Keep arms and legs within vehicle body." There is a meta-message (Nierenberg & Calero, 1981) or relational-dimension message (Watzlawick, Bevin, & Jackson, 1967) here to the effect that the operator is assumed to be ignorant. (Moreover, there is a contradiction between keeping arms inside and doing a job that requires reaching out to put chalk marks on tires.) It is easy to imagine a reader seeing these first few unnecessary warnings—which, in effect, constitute violations of the "relevance" and/or "quantity" maxims (Grice, 1975)—and deciding to read no further, assuming the remainder to be equally frivolous.

Finally, recall that one of the defendant's claims was that the warning label advised the operator to avoid hard turns and that *had the advice on the warning label been heeded, the accident would not have happened.* For the sake of argument, let's imagine that the warning label had indeed communicated very effectively regarding the danger of hard turns. Now, notice what comes immediately before the hard-turn warning: "*Avoid sudden starts and stops.*" Using the defendant's own logic (i.e., that the warnings should have been heeded), what was the woman supposed to have done when the car pulled in front of her? She had been instructed to not hit the brakes ("Avoid sudden stops") and to not swerve away ("[Avoid] hard turns"). And colliding with the car was not an option because the vehicle had no seat belt. Thus, the "*Avoid sudden . . . stops*" warning contradicted the defendant's claim that the warning-label instructions should have been followed.

Ultimately, "Avoid sudden starts and stops" was even more damaging to the defendant's case. It seemed curious that operators of this vehicle would be warned to avoid sudden starts and stops. The communication consultant wondered what could possibly be the danger of starting suddenly (assuming a clear path, of course), or stopping suddenly, and why these warnings were included. Upon investigation, it turned out that the manufacturer of the parking meter vehicle produced two models of its "Radial Frame On-Road Haulster," both sharing the same frame, engine, transmission, and thus treated as simply two models of the same vehicle. One was Haulster Model 898434, the "Police Vehicle," as it was called. That is the one we have been discussing. But the other was Haulster Model 898435, the "Flatbed." This is a three-wheel, no-cab, miniature flatbed truck used for hauling stacks of crates and boxes around factories and warehouses. Aha! In the context of that flatbed vehicle being stacked high with crates, admonitions about sudden stops, sudden starts, hard turns causing the load to become *upset*, and so forth, might seem like fairly good communication. (The otherwise irrelevant information about heavy loads in a "Before Starting Engine" section takes on a new frame as well.)

It became apparent that someone had written a decent warning for the Model 898435 Flatbed, and then he, she, or someone else simply slapped the same decal onto the dashboard of the Model 898434 parking meter patrol vehicle with no consideration of the fact that it would not be carrying cargo loads and that its having a tall cab made it susceptible to tipping over. To put it another way, it was obvious that very little or no effort had gone into warning operators of Model 898343 about the dangers of hard turns (or anything else specific to that model), defense claims to the contrary notwithstanding. The case ended with a very large settlement in favor of the plaintiff.

Case 3: Vacation Company Liability Clause

The defendants in the first two cases claimed that they had provided a warning to users of their product, that the warning was ignored, and that an accident was the result. An accident is behind the next case, as well, but this time the defendant denied liability not because of a warning, but because of a disclaimer.

A newlywed couple went on their honeymoon in Cancun, Mexico. Their local travel agency made transportation, lodging, and several other arrangements through a large vacation-planning company. The couple paid the vacation company an extra fee to receive personal transportation between the airport and hotel, both ways, via "private transport"—a car and driver similar to a taxi or limousine service. At the end of the honeymoon, on the way from the hotel to the airport for the return flight, the private transport car collided with a bus and both the driver and the groom were killed. The bride sued the vacation company (*Stevens v. Atkinson & Mullen*, 2007), Apple Vacations (no relation to Apple computers).

The vacation company defense included a claim that the private transport company was an independent contractor hired by Apple Vacations, that its drivers were not employees of, or otherwise under control of Apple Vacations, and that the plaintiff had agreed to a contract containing a "liability clause" that released Apple Vacations from liability over problems with their independent contractors. The plaintiff responded that she and her late husband had missed the liability clause, but that this did not matter because they had assumed the private transport company to be run by, or at least approved by, Apple Vacations. That is, even if they had read Apple's liability disclaimer regarding independent contractors, they would not have recognized the private transport company to be an independent contractor.

As for the liability clause, it is contained in a document called the Apple Vacations Fair Trade Contract. Several of the brochures, vouchers, itineraries, and other documents distributed to Apple Vacation clients mention the Fair Trade Contract and instruct clients to read it. The Fair Trade Contract is a document of approximately 2,000 words, most in extremely tiny print, on a single 8.5" × 11" page. It is organized into two major sections. The first of these is "Your Contract with Apple Vacations," and contains seven subsections—Bookings and Payments, Amendments and Cancellations, Air Carriers, Luggage, and so forth.

The second major section is "What We Provide in Return," and contains eight subsections—Price Guarantee, Flight Information, Amendments and Cancellation, Refunds, Our Responsibility to You, Handicapped Facilities, Security, and Apple's Total Vacation Insurance Plan. Within the subsection titled "Our Responsibility to You," is the following "liability clause":

WHAT WE PROVIDE IN RETURN

[Four Previous Subsections]

Our Responsibility to You: Apple Vacations has made arrangements with airlines, hotels and other independent suppliers to provide you with the services you purchase. We have taken all reasonable steps to ensure that proper arrangements have been made for your vacation. However, we do not accept and expressly disclaim any liability for the actions or omissions of these independent suppliers, over whom we have no direct control. If you have any dispute with such persons, however, we will give you as much reasonable help as we can in resolving this. [The remainder of the subsection does not concern independent suppliers. Rather, it disclaims liability for terrorism, severe weather phenomena, flight delays, and other matters unrelated to the case.]

The communication issue was not whether the liability clause was clear, but rather whether it would be relatively easy or relatively difficult for the average client to have missed it, as the plaintiff claimed to have done. According to an expert witness in communication retained by the plaintiff, there were a few relatively minor points to criticize with respect to the placement of this liability clause. First, it comes under a major heading, "What We Provide in Return," along with presumably relevant subheadings such as Price Guarantee, Refunds, Security, Flight Information, and Handicapped Facilities. The communication witness suggested that a reader who is not particularly interested in "what Apple Vacations provides in return"—perhaps because all of his or her concerns already had been addressed by the travel agent or by Apple Vacation brochures and advertisements—might skip all or most of this section and thus miss the liability clause.[2] The second criticism was that not only is the liability statement listed under an inappropriate major heading, "What We Provide in Return," but moreover is under an inappropriate subheading—"Our Responsibilities to You." The argument was that because the subsequent information is in fact about what Apple Vacations is *not* responsible for, the placement of the liability clause "What We Provide in Return: Our Responsibilities to You" was misleading. That is, the liability clause would be more appropriately placed *not* as a subsection under "What We Provide in Return" *nor* within a "Our Responsibilities to You" subsection, but rather under a separate and equal main heading—"Liability Limitations," or some such, with a subheading "Liability Disclaimer," or some such.

There was a more serious criticism of the Apple Vacation documents with respect to the liability disclaimer, however. Among the documents received by Apple Vacations clients is an 8.5" × 14" page of fine print with two distinct halves. The top half deals with passengers whose ultimate destination is not the same country as their original departure point, and with baggage liability limitations. The bottom half uses highlighting (special heading and fonts) to appear as the more important half (which, for most travelers, it indeed is). It begins as follows:

APPLE VACATIONS

APPLE VACATIONS FAIR TRADE CONTRACT

Please read this Apple Vacations Contract to give you a clear idea what you can expect. These vacations are operated by: **Apple Vacations, 7 Campus Boulevard, Newtown Square, Delaware County, PA 19073**, as principle and tour operator.

AMMENDMENTS AND CANCELLATIONS

[Etc. for three 6" columns]

This is an approximately 1,450-word document with the same format as the approximately 2,000 word Fair Trade Contract just discussed, and containing much identical information under identical subheadings. Indeed 9 of its 12 subsections are verbatim duplications. But it does not contain the liability clause! The plaintiff's communication witness presented an opinion that under the heading, "Apple Vacations Fair Trade Contract," the statement, "Please read *this* Apple Vacations Contract . . ." implies "*this* contract you are looking at," and that it would be natural to assume that reading this present document would satisfy the admonitions in brochures and other Apple Vacations literature to read the Fair Trade Contract. That is, a client who read this document and then later came across the "true" Fair Trade Contract, might, because of the extensive verbatim overlap between the two, dismiss the "true" Fair Trade Contract as having already been read and thus would miss the liability clause.

To put it another way, the defendant argued that "APPLE VACA-TIONS FAIR TRADE CONTRACT: Please read *this* Apple Vacations Contract" really meant something like this: "APPLE VACATIONS FAIR TRADE CONTRACT: Please read *the* contract referenced in the preceding heading. The document you are reading now is not it." It is easy to argue that if that was the meaning, it was not communicated well. Much better, according to the plaintiff's expert witness, would have been something like, "APPLE VACATIONS CONTRACTS: It is important that you read the Apple Vacations Fair Trade Contract, which you will find on page [page number] of [document name or description]. It contains very important information that is not presented here."

Recall that the plaintiff claimed that reading the contract would have made no difference because she and her late husband did not know the private transport company to have been one of the independent contractors addressed in the liability clause. Rather, they had assumed Apple Vacations ran the company. Thus, a second communication issue was whether this would have been a reasonable assumption by a typical Apple Vacations client. The available data were a bit nebulous, but were sufficient to allow both sides their arguments.

The defense argued that the couple should have known the private transport to be an independent contractor for any of several reasons. The auto, a white Dodge Stratus, had no Apple Vacations logo on it, while all of the many Apple Vacations buses and vans in the airport area where they met the car did have the Apple Vacations logo, so the couple should have known this was not an Apple-operated vehicle. Also, the car's driver had a different kind of shirt than the airport greeters and Apple Vacations bus drivers, and this identified him as a non-Apple employee. Finally, there is lettering above the wheel well on both sides of the car that identifies it as being operated by a different company than Apple Vacations.

The communication consultant for the plaintiff formulated an opinion based on more than 900 pages of documents including photos of Apple airport greeters, Cancun airport bus and taxi areas, Apple vans and buses, the wrecked Dodge Stratus, and so forth; depositions by plaintiff and defendant spokespersons; brochures, itineraries, and other documents provided by Apple Vacations to its clients; accident scene police reports; and more. The opinion was that an ordinary client might very well assume the private transport to have been operated by, or at least endorsed by, Apple Vacations. Reasons included responses to the defense arguments as well as additional observations:

1. Granted, the buses and vans did indeed have the hard-to-miss Apple Vacations logo painted on them, and the Dodge Stratus did not. But there were no vehicles smaller than a van (i.e., no Dodge Stratus-sized vehicles) that did have the Apple logo, so the absence of one on this Dodge Stratus does not necessarily communicate independence from Apple. That is, if one were to notice the missing logo, the conclusion might be that Apple does not paint the logo onto its smaller vehicles.

2. By the time Apple Vacations clients at the Cancun airport enter their private hotel transportation, they have encountered at least two different shirt designs worn by ostensible employees of Apple Vacations. If one notices that the Dodge Stratus driver is wearing yet another shirt design it might communicate independence from Apple, or it might be interpreted as representing a different role or rank within the Apple Vacations organization.

3. There is indeed lettering on the Dodge Stratus identifying it as belonging to a different company. It is four short lines of print (the company name and three lines of registration codes) easily legible at distances under about 6 feet. But it is in Spanish, so someone who does not read Spanish might ignore it, and without unusually close inspection it appears to be consistent with the lettering on the sides of the Apple Vacations vans and buses. Moreover, even if one does read Spanish, the company name, Transportacion Turistica y Mas (Tourist Transportation and More) could be taken as an identifier for the way Apple Vacations uses these vehicles instead of taken as the name of a different company.

4. The brochures that offer private transportation between the airport and hotel happen to present the option of private transportation—along with optional spa treatments, jungle excursions, and so forth—within a list labeled "Apple Extras." In fact, one itinerary uses the term "Apple Extras" within its heading (Add Apple Extras to your Vacation) and then twice again within the first two sentences. It is not unreasonable to assume these "Apple Extras" to be truly Apple extras, that is, owned by, run by, and/or endorsed by Apple Vacations.

5. Even if the liability clause had been read, it may not have communicated what is meant by "independent contractors." Recall the introduction to the disclaimer: "Apple Vacations has made arrangements with airlines, hotels and other independent suppliers. . . ." The only examples provided are airlines and hotels. But all clients would certainly know that the airline they are using is independent of Apple Vacations, and with rare exceptions, likewise for their hotel. One implication is that the "independent suppliers" referenced in the disclaimer will be obviously independent, as in the airline and hotel examples, but this is not the case. Much better would have been something like, "Apple Vacations has made arrangements with independent spa services, taxi companies, limousine and transportation companies, excursion and adventure services and other independent suppliers and contractors."

Of the two communication issues in this lawsuit, the support for an opinion on whether a client would assume the private transport to be independent is probably less well supported than the opinion that the liability clause was easy to miss. But the attorneys for both sides apparently agreed that if taken together, a jury could be persuaded that the plaintiff was being truthful in her claims about the liability clause and about her assumptions regarding the private transport's affiliation, and that although these were mistakes, they were reasonable mistakes caused or allowed in part by the defendant's verbal and nonverbal messages in literature sent to its clients. The day before the trial was to begin, they reached a settlement.

Advertising: Is the Product or Service Accurately Represented?

We see so many instances of false or misleading advertising these days that it may be difficult to imagine the veracity of an advertisement as an issue that makes it all the way to court. Court cases concerning advertisements are not uncommon, however. One familiar form is that in which someone becomes ill or injured using a product and then blames the corresponding advertisements. Some of these are intuitively frivolous, such as the man who blamed his obesity on the advertisements of the donut shop where he consumed more than two-dozen donuts per week. (The models in the advertisements were slim, so he saw no connection between donuts and weight gain; or so he claimed.) Others seem more legitimate, as in a person becoming ill after taking a drug whose advertising fails to mention negative interactions with other drugs the person is taking. These cases are similar to some of the warnings and disclaimers cases discussed here, in that the defense claims that the consumer was provided with information that allowed the problem to have been avoided, whereas the consumer-plaintiff argues that insufficient information was provided.

A second common form of litigation over advertising is that in which a customer claims that a product does not live up to the promises made by its advertising. Often, these evolve into class-action suits. This time, the communication roles are somewhat reversed. The plaintiff complains, in effect, that the defendant provided too much information—because it led to strong but incorrect assumptions about the product's features.

In my experience, both types of litigation usually are fairly straightforward for the expert witness in communication. In the warning-adequacy cases, an opinion is sought on whether the probability of certain dangers or side effects was presented well enough for a typical alert consumer to have noticed. In the missing features cases, the matter of whether the product or service indeed delivered the features in question usually is made by an expert witness in engineering, psychology, or some other area. Likewise, experts in areas other than communication are enlisted for assessment of how disappointed or distraught the typical consumer would be to find the feature missing. For the communication expert, however, the typical task is to formulate an opinion on whether the advertising would lead the ordinary consumer to expect the feature to be present. In either type of case, the communication expert examines the advertising in question, of course. If the position of the potential hiring attorney is unknown, an unbiased opinion can be formulated (see Motley, Chapter 16, this volume). If not, an objective opinion can be attempted and can be empirically tested if desired (see Motley, Chapter 15, this volume).

Warnings Example: Ephedrine in Diet Pills

In a case similar to some of the warnings cases discussed here, a woman suffered a serious stroke and heart attack after taking Metaboburn—an over-the-counter "dietary supplement" and "metabolism booster"—in an effort to lose weight. Her family claimed that the heart attack and stroke occurred because the pills contained a dangerous amount of ephedrine, and sued (*Santa Maria v. Jahn d/b/a Metaboburn*, 2006).

A physician testified for the plaintiff about the known properties of ephedrine: Ephedrine originally was used for treating asthma, but this practice had been abandoned several years earlier because of known risks. Among other things, ephedrine stimulates the nervous system and increases blood pressure, heart rate, and cardiac contractility—dangerously so if taken in sufficient amounts or if combined with caffeine (which was ingested frequently by the stricken woman). Its association with severe adverse reactions—including life-threatening cardiac arrhythmia, cerebral hemorrhage, and stroke—had been known for at least 10 years prior to the present case. It can cause life-threatening or debilitating effects even with short-term use of doses in the range of 20 to 60 mg per day. (The Metaboburn bottle recommends up to eight capsules per day, equaling 96 mg per day.)

As for the communication issue of whether warnings were adequate, it was easy for the communication witness to formulate an opinion. One brochure for the product lists several ingredients and their *positive* effects—improved immune system, stamina, vitality, and so forth—but makes no mention whatsoever of ephedrine, associated risks, increased risk with caffeine, seizure, heart attack, stroke, or anything related to these matters. Similarly, a "Dietary Weight Loss Supplement Sheet" not only lists a number of exotic ingredients with no mention of ephedrine or risks, but also describes the pills as "medically tested to be . . . safe," adding, "the standards have been set by scientists for the safe . . . ratios and quantities that should be used." (Set by scientists, yes, but not followed by Metaboburn, apparently.)

The label on the bottle at least mentions "ephedra," a less familiar (and thus communicatively inferior) name for ephedrine, and lists the per-capsule dosage—12 mg. But there is absolutely no acknowledgment or warning of *any* associated risks, much less of exacerbating risks via caffeine. Nor was there any mention of FDA-recommended dosage limits (24 mg per day, 7-day maximum). Instead, the label's "Suggested Use" advises up to two capsules every 4 hours (i.e., 10 capsules equaling 120 mg, or five times the FDA recommendation for someone who arises at 6 a.m. and goes to bed at 10 p.m. and fails to interpret the earlier "up to eight capsules per day"—96 mg—as a maximum).

The communication witness quibbled with a few related matters on the bottle, as well, such as an apparent effort to portray the product as safe (e.g., "Natural . . . ," "Herbal formula . . . ," "Super Effective . . ."), and a very badly worded warning implying that only persons with certain conditions—pregnancy, diabetes, and so on (none being relevant to the plaintiff)—need be the least concerned. But the blatant absence of warnings about known risks of ephedrine, and the apparent disregard for safe dosage levels made this opinion something of a "slam dunk" as semantics issues in litigation go.

Advertised Features Example: Implications of an SDIO Slot

Usually, when an opinion is solicited as to whether certain features of a product have been delivered as promised by its advertising, the consultant

or expert witness in communication simply examines the relevant advertising and makes an educated guess as to what the advertising messages
would lead the typical consumer to expect. Most often this is a simple
matter. But less so in the next example, partly because the communication witness for the plaintiff was completely unfamiliar with the product
and implications of some of its high-tech claims, and partly because the
defense had hired an expert witness in marketing who claimed to have
shown that actual consumers of the product were happy with it.

In 2006 a class-action suit was brought against the manufacturer
and distributor of the "Treo 600," an early predecessor to contemporary
PDAs such as the Blackberry, Palm, and iPhone (*Casaburi & Werksman
v. Palmone*, 2006). The plaintiffs claimed that advertisements for the Treo
600 implicitly promised a feature that did not in fact exist. Specifically,
advertising highlighted the Treo's SDIO (Secure Digital Input–Output)
expansion slot that would accept accessory cards (to be purchased separately) giving the Treo additional capabilities, possibly including wireless
capability via Bluetooth and/or WiFi. In fact, although the expansion
slot did exist, expansion cards for Bluetooth and WiFi did not, and were
not forthcoming, as both sides acknowledged. The defense conceded that
Bluetooth/WiFi were mentioned explicitly in certain promotional material
but insisted that this material was a minor part of its advertising effort,
and that it reached a relatively small number of potential or eventual
customers. The plaintiffs claimed, however, that Bluetooth/WiFi were
promised, albeit implicitly, in *all* advertising for the Treo 600. That is to
say, all advertising highlighted the SDIO expansion slot, and, according
to the plaintiffs, an SDIO slot implies Bluetooth and/or WiFi capability
to potential buyers.

Thus, one issue was whether advertising that mentioned the Treo
600's expansion slot, but without explicit reference to Bluetooth or WiFi,
nevertheless implied Bluetooth/WiFi as a natural connotation of the SDIO
slot. The plaintiffs retained an expert witness in communication for whom
"SDIO" had virtually no connotative meaning, so an opinion based merely
on the usual examination of advertising materials would have been biased
by the plaintiffs' and attorney's account. An opinion was formulated,
however, essentially by building a denotative meaning (i.e., a hypothetical
standard meaning) based on others' connotations for "SDIO expansion
slot."

As one indicator of these connotations, discussions of SDIO within
independent technical material tend to mention "Bluetooth," "WiFi,"
"wireless capability," and/or "wireless networking" within their explanations (with no exceptions among a dozen or so cases). For example,
from Miller (2003), "What is SDIO? . . . With SDIO you can use WiFi,

Bluetooth, GPS." From Unknown (n.d.) regarding a rival PDA, ". . . will work with SDIO expansion cards. This means you'll be able to easily add Bluetooth, WiFi."

As another indicator, a casual and admittedly nonscientific survey of some of the expert witness's high-tech–oriented acquaintances asked, "If you read an advertisement back in 2003 or so for a PDA and email device that has an SDIO expansion slot, what kinds of ways would you think that you could use that SDIO slot?" All (n = 11) replied with some version of "wireless capacity," with most mentioning Bluetooth specifically. These connotations fit the few denotations available via technical glossaries, all of which (n = 4) mentioned wireless capacity. In short, an opinion evolved to the effect that common connotations of "SDIO" or "SDIO expansion" include the assumption of wireless capability.

Thus, on the one hand, the plaintiffs could argue that the Treo 600 advertising led customers to expect wireless capacity that in fact did not exist and was not forthcoming—the classic false advertising argument. But on the other hand, the defense had evidence that customers who purchased the Treo 600 were not disappointed by the absence of wireless capability. A defense expert witness in marketing performed a very extensive survey of Treo 600 owners, including questions such as these:

- Did you buy the Treo 600 partly because it had Bluetooth capability? ("No" favors defense, "Yes" favors plaintiff, Majority = "No")

- Is the Treo 600 supposed to have WiFi and Bluetooth capability? ("No" favors defense, "Yes" favors plaintiff, Majority = "No")

- Did you ever have any complaints about optional add-on features the Treo 600 was supposed to have? ("No" favors defense, "Yes" favors plaintiff, Majority = "No")

Responses to these questions and a number of others like them favor the defense, obviously. The implication is that most actual Treo 600 owners did not particularly expect wireless capacity and/or were not bothered or disappointed by its absence. The communication witness for the plaintiffs countered, however, that the wording of these and several other survey questions were biased toward "No" responses favoring the defense. (Readers may wish to reread the example questions to test for agreement.)

Recall that the advertising did not say or imply that the Treo 600 was Bluetooth/WiFi capable, per se. Rather, it implied, allegedly, that it could be made Bluetooth/WiFi capable via an expansion card for the SDIO slot. So, presumably, everybody knew the Treo 600 was not wireless-capable straight out of the box. The communication witness claimed, therefore, that even a dissatisfied customer might give an answer favoring the defense when asked the survey questions in the form they were presented. For example, "Did you buy the Treo 600 partly because it had Bluetooth capability" may very well be answered "No" by someone who bought it looking forward to adding Bluetooth (i.e., "No, I bought it knowing it didn't have Bluetooth capability yet"). Thus, notice the difference between the original (strikethrough) version of the survey questions and the version preferred by the plaintiffs' communication witness (italicized):

- Did you buy the Treo 600 partly because ~~it had Bluetooth capability?~~ *you would be able to add Bluetooth to it?*

- Is the Treo 600 supposed to have ~~WiFi and Bluetooth capability?~~ *an expansion slot for adding WiFi or Bluetooth?*

- Did you ever have any complaints about optional add-on features ~~the Treo 600 was supposed to have?~~ *that were supposed to be available or become available for the Treo 600 but were not?*

Whether the revised questions would have received significantly different answers is an empirical question, of course. Indeed, so is the overall matter of whether, by highlighting the SDIO slot, the advertising led prospective Treo 600 buyers to expect wireless capacity as an especially attractive feature (although the 2003 condition would be difficult to replicate). There was not enough time and money to test either question, but the communication witness's opinion and prediction on the hypotheses were, among other factors, persuasive in reaching a settlement satisfactory to the plaintiffs.

Legalese and Other Gobbledygook: What Does It Mean in Simple English?

It is no surprise that legal language is sometimes confusing to the layperson. It may be surprising, however, to know that it is sometimes confusing to the courts, as well. The norm is for attorneys to rely on their own interpretations of contracts, wills, and other legal documents. But occasionally an outside opinion is sought, and sometimes from someone in the communication discipline.

This may be as simple as interpreting a single sentence (e.g., "I hereby certify that the procedures indicated by date have been completed and that the fees submitted are that actual fees I have charged and intend to collect for those procedures"; *Consumer Cause v. Western Dental*, 1997). Or they may involve the translation of sizable documents from legalize to simple language.

Although these can be tedious, they are such procedurally straight-forward tasks that a single brief example should suffice. The example case concerns the translation of an indemnification clause from a contract when a company called Industries sold one of its companies, called Manufactur-ing, to a company called General (*El Paso CGP v. SPX*, 2005). Some years after the sale, General began receiving lawsuits over exposure to asbestos from one of the valves made by Manufacturing. General sought reimburse-ment from Industries, claiming that the valves were made prior to the sale, and that their contract pledges Industries to secure General against this kind of loss or damage. Industries claimed that various features of the case constituted an exception to the contract, and hired a communication consultant to translate the contract's indemnification clause.

In cases such as this, the hiring attorney will determine the degree of simplification sought. The attorney in this case asked for extreme simpli-fication. Figure 11.3 shows the attempted translation. Note in particular the side-to-side, font-coded organization. I have found this to be a very helpful approach to visual presentation in similar cases.

ISSUES OF SEXUAL CONSENT: BEYOND BASIC SEMANTICS

Unlike most other chapters in this volume, the expert-witness work described thus far in this chapter has not depended on a primary research area of its author. Rather, I have discussed work that could be available to most any of the many communication scholars who have studied, or who are interested in and sensitive to, subtleties of language and mean-ing. That is to say, these cases do not necessarily require research and publication in semantics, per se. In this final section, however, as in most other chapters in this volume, the interested reader is briefly introduced to a particular research specialty area that has applications to litigation issues. Again, the idea is to invite the reader both to consider joining the pursuit of relevant issues via research, and to consider applying findings to litigation issues.

As an example, although the cases discussed so far in this chapter have been civil cases, recent research on male–female communication pat-terns during physical intimacy has allowed expert-witness contributions to criminal cases. More specifically, certain research (e.g., Motley, 2008a; Motley & Reeder, 1995) has explored the common ways in which women, during any phase of physical intimacy, communicate that they wish to go

ORIGINAL	TRANSLATION
18. Indemnification of General by Industries	18. Indemnification of General by Industries
(a) Industries will indemnify and hold harmless General, Manufacturing, and each of the Subsidiaries (the "indemnified Parties"), from and against any losses arising out of any claimed or asserted liabilities of Manufacturing or any of the Subsidiaries of any nature, whether accrued, absolute, contingent or otherwise, based upon any event, occurrence or act, or failure to act, prior to the Time of Closing, including, without limitation, all federal state and foreign tax liabilities of Manufacturing and of each of the Subsidiaries due or to become due with respect to any period prior to the Time of Closing, other than	(a) We will secure them against losses due to virtually anything prior to closing except --
(i) liabilities reflected or adequately reserved against on the consolidated balance sheet of Manufacturing included in the Manufacturing Financial Statements;	(i) liabilities already acknowledged;
(ii) obligations for performance subsequent to the Time of Closing, which obligations were incurred prior to the Time of Closing, under contracts and commitments either listed in Schedules C, D, E, F, H and I or not required to be listed therein, unless such obligations under contracts or commitments not required to be so listed **are the result of any circumstances existing prior to the Time of Closing which, if known at that time, would have required a reference in a balance sheet or related notes thereto dated as of the Time of Closing of any Business Unit of Manufacturing to enable certification by independent public accountants as to the financial condition of such Business Unit in accordance with generally accepted accounting principles;**	(ii) obligations incurred before closing but already acknowledged, **except for things not required to be acknowledged but that still should have been;**
(iii) for any liability covered by product liability insurance in force or which would have been in force had insurance coverage no less extensive than that set forth in Schedule J hereto been maintained in force;	(iii) anything covered by insurance (in the amounts on Schedule J);

Figure 11.3. Legalese translation example.

(iv) liabilities of Manufacturing or any of the Subsidiaries, not covered by product liability insurance as set forth in clause (iii) of this subsection (a), which arise out of any event, occurrence or act subsequent to the Time of Closing **and are claimed or asserted to have been caused by any product manufactured or sold by Manufacturing or any of the Subsidiaries prior to the Time of Closing, except to the extent the aggregate losses from all such liabilities which arise out of any event, occurrence, or act taking place within a period of five years subsequent to the Time of Closing** *and are occasioned by no fault of Manufacturing or any of the Subsidiaries subsequent to the Time of Closing,* **exceed $100,000 in the aggregate;**

(v) certain other matters referred to in an agreement between Industries and Manufacturing, a copy of . . .

(iv) things not covered by insurance that come up after closing **but supposedly happened because of something we made or sold before closing,** *except to the extent that* **the corresponding losses exceed $100,000** *and weren't their fault;*

(v) [Etc.]

Figure 11.3. Continued.

no further, and the degree to which most males understand those various messages to mean "stop." It turns out that there are very direct ways that women resist (e.g., "Please don't do that"), slightly indirect ways (e.g., "I'm not sure about this"), and very indirect ways (e.g., "I'm seeing someone else"). And it happens that although most males understand the direct resistance messages to mean "stop," they misinterpret the indirect messages to have other meanings (e.g., "I'm not sure about this so reassure me that you're committed to me," or "I'm seeing someone else so don't interpret what we're about to do as a commitment to you"; Motley, 2008a; Motley & Reeder 1995). Similarly, studies have examined intimacy situations in which the more eager partner is well aware of the other's resistance, yet tries to talk or otherwise "coerce" the other into yielding to reluctant escalation of the intimacy (Motley, 2008b) that is, yielding to unforced but unwanted intimacy similar to the altruistic intimacy discussed in earlier research (e.g., Meston & Buss, 2009; VanWey, 2004).

There is an obvious potential application of this and related research to alleged date rape cases. If it is established that the victim used direct resistance messages, and/or that the intimacy was forced, then this favors the prosecution. And if it is established that only indirect messages were used by the victim, with no physical or verbal force or abuse present, then this might warrant doubt that could favor the defense.

The two date rape cases on which I have served as an expert witness both happened to have been for the defense. The two cases were very similar, so a single example should suffice. In the example case (*Lester v. [Withheld]*, 2008),[3] a well-known NFL football player left a strip club with two of the dancers and a male friend who drove them to a hotel using the car of one of the dancers. During the drive, the football player was in the back seat with both dancers, who openly groped and fondled him. The friend left them at the hotel, and the football player took the women to his room, where he had sex with one woman while the other watched, and then had sex with the second woman while the first watched.

The women left the room a bit later, both quite intoxicated, and went to their car. On their way out of the parking lot a hotel security guard stopped them and asked if they were OK to drive. One of the women said that they had just been raped, giving the room number and the alleged perpetrator's name. The guard recognized the NFL star's name, phoned the authorities, and waited with the women for their arrival. Both sides agreed on everything described here thus far.

The NFL player claimed that the sexual activities were consensual, and that not only did neither woman say "no," but in both cases as he had sex with one, the other cheered them on. He and his attorney speculate that the rape allegation was an attempt to deflect the guard's attention away from the fact that both the driver of the car and her passenger were quite intoxicated.

The defense wanted an expert witness in communication to give an opinion on "whether anything was inconsistent with consensual sex." Documents included the two women's independent statements to police, the NFL player's statement, the examining physicians' medical forensic reports (examined also by an expert witness in medicine, of course), and the police report. The communication witness assumed that the task would be to analyze the resistance messages used or alleged by the women, and/or to see whether the player's statement alluded to things the women said that should have been recognized to be resistance or, according to the research, might not have been recognized as resistance even though probably intended as such.

As it turned out, the opinion was that there was nothing in the documents inconsistent with consensual sex. Neither woman's statement claimed that she or the other woman had said "no" or "stop" directly or indirectly, nor that either fought or struggled during their sex acts. Nor did the guard or police officers report the women to have reported that they had said any version of "no" or "stop" directly, indirectly, verbally, or nonverbally. As would be expected, the statement of the accused did not describe any direct resistance. But nor did it include anything that might have been intended resistance yet not recognized as such. Moreover, the medical reports indicated that sexual intercourse had occurred but that all irritations were consistent with consensual sex with no signs of atypical force or roughness.

The defense attorney had told the communication witness privately that his client was married, famous, wealthy, and willing to pay "a reasonable but not excessive amount" to settle out of court and "make this go away" without publicity or embarrassment. And that is exactly what happened. Not even the local newspaper reported on it.

Again, the point of this example is not that it represents an area that would be easily pursued by the typical reader, as would be the case with the earlier examples in this chapter. Rather, the point is that the typical reader may want to consider whether his or her own research specialties can be applied to courtroom issues, and/or whether the research specialties described in this or other chapters might be interesting to pursue.

CONCLUSION

As we have seen, there are a number of ways in which issues of semantics and meaning come up in court cases. In all of the examples discussed here, the question has been whether a message or set of messages would be expected to be interpreted as one side claims or as the other side claims. Sometimes the answer is so obvious that one hardly needs a degree in communication to formulate an opinion that a jury would almost certainly agree with (although a credentialed communication witness will sometimes be used for credibility purposes). Other times the answer depends on subtleties that probably are better analyzed by someone with experience in, or at least sensitivity to, communication, language, and meaning. And finally there are times when the question probably is better informed by someone whose primary research area is closely related to the issues at hand. In any case, the application of communication research or skill to questions of the likely interpretation of target messages can be valuable to the courts. And it can be a worthwhile, enjoyable, and sometimes exciting endeavor for the communication scholar.

NOTES

1. Notice the similarity of this problem with that of the placement of the warning information within the "instructions" of the Door-Bar Gym.

2. Notice the similarity to the critique of the dashboard warning for the parking patrol vehicle.

3. The name of the accused is being withheld in this chapter for obvious reasons. Under certain circumstances the true case name might be available from the author.

REFERENCES

Casaburi and Werksman, et al. v. Palmone, Sprint Spectrum. (2006). State of California, County of San Francisco, Case No. 04-435844.

Consumer Cause v. Western Dental. (1997). State of California, County of Los Angeles, Case No. 36225425.

Cala, P. v. Best Products, et al. (1985). State of California, County of Sacramento, Case No. 321866.

El Paso CGP Co. v. SPX Corp. (2005). State of Texas, Harris County, 164th District, Case No. 2005-04660.

Fleming, F. v. Cushman Motor Sales, et al. (1988). State of California, County of Stanislaus, Case No. 201599.

Foss, D.J., & Hakes, D.T. (1978). *Psycholinguistics: An introduction to the psychology of language.* Englewood Cliffs, NJ: Prentice-Hall.

Grice, H.P. (1975). Logic and conversation. In P. Cole & J.T. Morgan (Eds.), *Syntax and semantics: Speech acts* (Vol. 3, pp. 41–58). New York: Academic Press.

Hayakawa, S.I. (1962). *The use and misuse of language.* Greenwich, CT: Premier.

Hayakawa, S.I. (1972). *Language in thought and action* (3rd ed.). Englewood Cliffs, NJ: Prentice-Hall.

Lester v. [Withheld]. (2008). State of California, County of Fresno.

Meston, C.M., & Buss, D.M. (2009). *Why women have sex.* New York: Holt.

Miller, M. (2003). What is SDIO? In *Articles.* Retrieved December 2006, from http://www.geek.com/search/?section=term=SDIO.

Motley, M.T. (2008a). Unwanted escalation of sexual intimacy: Pursuing a miscommunication explanation. In M.T. Motley (Ed.), *Applied interpersonal communication research: Original studies* (pp. 121–144). Boston: Sage.

Motley, M.T. (2008b). Verbal coercion to unwanted sexual intimacy. In M.T. Motley (Ed.), *Applied interpersonal communication research: Original studies* (pp. 185–203). Boston: Sage.

Motley, M.T., & Reeder, H.M. (1995). Unwanted escalation of sexual intimacy: Male and female perceptions of connotations and relational consequences of resistance messages. *Communication Monographs, 62,* 356–382.

Nierenberg, G.I., & Calero, H.H. (1981). *Meta-talk: Guide to hidden meanings in conversations.* Grand Rapids, MI: Cornerstone.

Peters, G.A., & Peters, B.J. (1999). *Warnings, instructions, and technical communications*. Tuscon, AZ: Lawyers & Judges Publishing.

Santa Maria v. Jahn d/b/a Metaboburn. (2006). State of Idaho, County of Ada, Case No. CV PI 0400264D.

Stevens v. Atkinson & Mullen Travel, t/a Apple Vacations. (2007). State of Pennsylvania, County of Philadelphia, Case No. 003096.

Unknown. (n.d.). PDAs. In *Reviews*. Retrieved December 2006, from http://www.gizmodo.com/infosynch-review.

VanWey, L.K. (2004). Altruistic and contracted remittances between male and female migrants and households in rural Thailand. *Demography, 41,* 739–756.

Watzlawick, P., Bevin, J.H., & Jackson, J.J. (1967). *Pragmatics of human communication: A study of interactional patterns, pathologies, and paradoxes*. New York: Norton.

12

Forensic Linguistics

Gerald R. McMenamin

The purpose of this chapter is twofold: to provide a brief introduction to the emerging field of forensic linguistics and then to outline the theory and practice of forensic stylistics as a technique that uses the linguistic analysis of writing style for the purpose of authorship identification.

FORENSIC LINGUISTICS

Forensic linguistics is the scientific study of language as applied within forensic contexts. One of the oldest and most developed areas of forensic linguistics is that of forensic phonetics. With the exception of forensic phonetics, forensic linguistics is a relatively new application of general linguistics and therefore a growing area of modern applied linguistics. Although the subareas of forensic linguistics and their classification are evolving as the field grows, they generally follow given taxonomies for the study of the structure and function of language. Recent research and practice in forensic linguistics include analyses of various modes of language:

- *Spoken Language*: auditory and acoustic voice identification, dialect identification, oral interlanguage interpretation—as in cases of bribery, solicitation, extortion, threats, and so on.

- *Written Language*: stylistics and authorship identification, written interlanguage translation, legal language—as in cases of product labeling, advertisements, defamation, contracts, hazard warnings, contracts, written confessions, and plagiarism.

- *Spoken or Written Language*: semantics, pragmatics, discourse analysis—as in jury instructions, analysis of slander, fraud, and so on.

- *Transcribed Language:* transcripts of recorded language and of recorded testimony—as in cases of child sex abuse, police interrogations, confessions, perjury, and the like.

Many research studies have been done in forensic linguistics, starting with the pioneering work of Roger Shuy in the 1980s and continuing to the present with Shuy's prolific work, and constantly increasing contributions by others. (For the most current compilation of work in the field, see Coulthard & Johnson, 2010.)

During the 1990s, various university courses in forensic linguistics were developed, and full university programs in forensic linguistics have more recently started up in various countries. An important impetus to the advancement and scientific growth of forensic linguistics was the University of Birmingham's 1994 initiation of *Forensic Linguistics: The International Journal of Speech Language and the Law*, and the simultaneous founding of the *International Association of Forensic Linguistics*.

The classification of subareas in forensic linguistics is evolving as the field develops. The research and casework of forensic linguists presently define the field in a taxonomy that includes the following subfields:

- *Auditory phonetics* is the study of speech sounds based on what is heard and interpreted by the human listener. This is sometimes used in combination with dialect studies that, for example, might help to identify the geographic origin or social-group membership of a speaker.

- *Acoustic phonetics* is the study of the physical characteristics of speech sounds as they are vocalized by the speaker. This requires laboratory equipment, specialized computer analysis, and significant preparation on the part of the analyst. Acoustic analysis is used primarily for speaker identification, but also for group assignment of speaker (height, weight, regional/social/language group), voice and accent disguise, and effect of intoxication on speech.

- *Semantics* is the study of meaning as expressed in and represented by words, phrases, sentences, and texts; *Pragmatics* is the study of intended meaning within distinct contexts of language use and is a frequently applied extension of research on meaning. The focus of semantics and pragmatics in forensic contexts is the comprehensibility and interpretation of language that is difficult to understand. These areas of linguistic research primarily are used to disambiguate texts and laws, or to interpret meaning in spoken discourse, such as reading of rights, police warnings and interviews, and jury instructions.

- *Discourse analysis* is the study of units of language that are larger than the sentence, such as narratives and conversations. Sometimes a speaker's intended meaning can only be interpreted successfully by reference to a context much broader than the specific words or sentences used. Forensic discourse analysis involves the interpretation of spoken and written language in specific contexts, such as dictation, conversations, and hearings; in the language of the courtroom itself (lawyers, witnesses, questioning, and jury instructions), and in the language of specific speech acts such as threats, promises, warnings, and so on.

- *Linguistic stylistics* is the examination of writing style and is used in the forensic determination of authorship. Stylistics first identifies and describes the qualitative features of a piece of writing, then moves to a complementary quantitative analysis when certain linguistic indicators of style are identified and can be measured. A more recent development in forensic stylistics is its application to the identification of author-specific computer code in proprietary programming. Present areas of forensic research in stylistics include the development of new methods of analysis and large language corpora to establish what weight to assign particular style markers that appear in systematic fashion in the writing of individuals or groups.

- *Language of the law* is an area of study that goes back at least as far as David Melinkoff's work in 1963. It relates to the need for clarity and brevity in the languages of laws, insurance policies, and consumer literature. Present research is extended to the emphasis on plain language, language rights, and the pragmatics of legal and courtroom language.

- *Language of the courtroom* relates to the study and analysis of the language of courtroom personae—witnesses (witness examination, victims, children, men vs. women); lawyers (trial language, legal debate, closing arguments); and judges (trial dialogue, jury instructions).

- *Interpretation* refers to the complex skill of orally translating the native language of a speaker (e.g., Lao) into the language of the judicial system (e.g., English). Present forensic research is focused on interpretation tasks specific to questions and answers in testimony, the perceived role of the interpreter, interpreter education and experience, the right to interpretation, and the like. Some of the important questions relate to pretrial interpreting, courtroom interpreting, interpretation with cultural and dialect differences, questioning in interpreted testimony, and the absence of interpretation.

- *Translation* of written materials in the legal context requires more than a literal, word-for-word matchup of two languages. Good translations are constrained by the intended meaning of the author, the new text created by the translator, and the meaning given the translated text by its reader.

LINGUISTIC STYLISTICS

Language is the internal system human speakers and writers develop and use to communicate. A *dialect* is a variety of language that appears when a particular group of speakers develops consistent patterns of language use, called "class characteristics" in forensic linguistics. An *idiolect* (Bloch, 1948) is a variety of language developed by the individual speaker as a uniquely patterned aggregate of linguistic characteristics observed in his or her language use.

Linguistics is the study of the nature, development, and use of the internal system of language within its communicative contexts. One area of linguistics that is necessary for the understanding of stylistic analysis is the study of *linguistic variation*. With respect to group diversity, the individual creates systems of verbal behavior to resemble those of the groups he or she identifies with, but then may diverge from the norm based on such factors as the need for distinctiveness, breaks in communication networks, and the individual's process of language acquisition and learning (Labov, 2002).

Style is seen as that part of human behavior that reflects individual variation in activities that are otherwise invariant. Think about the way we dress. Although the conventions of a particular social context may narrowly constrain sartorial choices (e.g., what actors may wear to the Academy Awards), individual variation is allowed. The elements of language are likewise available to all members of a speech community and are what enable communication. Yet, a linguistic style is observed as the result of what an individual selects to use from the array of linguistic elements available to his or her group of speakers. The development of such style in children and adults is related to the ongoing acquisition of personal criteria for making individual choices, a lifelong process of learning and development. Style in all realms of human activity is acquired early by children, and once acquired has significant staying power.

Style in language is not always unambiguously defined. In spoken language, style is used to refer to linguistic variation that is directly related to the social context of conversation. Style in written language, in contrast, reflects both a writer's conscious response to the requirements of genre and context as well as the result of his or her unconscious and habituated choices of the grammatical elements acquired through the long-term experiential process of writing. A writer's style is, then, the sum of the recurrent choices he or she makes in the process of writing.

Stylistics is the study of style in language. Traditionally, the focus of literary stylistics was the esthetic quality of expression or the prescriptive conformity of language to the rules of grammatical correctness and social propriety. *Linguistic stylistics*, in contrast, is the systematic interpretation of *style markers* as observed, described, analyzed, and often measured in the language of groups and individuals. Style markers are the observable result of the habitual and usually unconscious choices an author makes in the process of writing. There are two general types:

1. Choice of optional forms: *I give you my heart. / I give my heart to you. / I give to you my heart.*

2. Deviation from a norm: *I am working today.* or *I'm working today.* versus *I be working today.*

Stylistic variation is reflected as class characteristics observed in the writing of distinct social and geographical groups, and also as individual features observed in the idiolect of single writers who share a language or dialect. Among the most common class features are those that appear as deviations from the norm and are common to careless or undereducated writers, for example, mixing homonyms such as *its/it's*, *effect/affect*, or *their/there* (see Example 12.1).

On the other hand, markers of group or individual style may simply demonstrate variations of form that are not thought of as mistakes. Consider the many ways in which Americans transcribe phone numbers. In a corpus study of 514 California letter writers who recorded a phone number, more than 11 variants appeared. The table in Example 12.2 shows the frequency distribution of their phone number forms. Note the sharp drop off in frequency of formats other than the most commonly used, that is, 000-000-0000 and (000) 000-0000, thereby making them more telltale the lower their frequency.

The analysis of style is carried out using one or a combination of three models outlined by Wachal (1966): resemblance, consistency, and population. The so-called *resemblance model* is used when external factors narrow candidate authors so that the authorship task is to exclude or identify just one or a few suspect writers. The *consistency model* is used to determine if various writings were written by the same author. Establishing the consistency of a group of writings is frequently the first step in a resemblance case when circumstances do not allow an assumption of common authorship for questioned writings. The *population model* is used in forensic contexts when the pool of candidate authors is not able to be limited by circumstances. In this instance, the resemblance model is used repeatedly on one possible author after another until all are excluded.

In the discussion of models of analysis for questions of authorship, I have used the terms *Questioned* and *Known*. In the forensic sciences, there

---

Known Writings of Suspect

```
K12:11        ... I am answering there question ....
K26:11        ... to seek their approval ....
K32:12        ... forwarded there letter to you ....
K54:16        ... on there Companies involvement
```

Questioned Letter

```
Q1:10         ... submitting there full Application ....
Q1:12         ... as part of there D/A ....
Q1:15         ... as part of there paperwork ....
Q13:24        ... bells on there cats ....
```

Example 12.1. Spelling of homonyms *their* vs. *there*.

No.	Format	n	%
1	000, 000-0000	1	0.20
2	0000000000	3	0.58
3	Misc. Forms	3	0.58
4	1+000+0000000	7	1.36
5	000 0000000	7	1.36
6	000.000.0000	11	2.14
7	000/000-0000	15	2.92
8	000 000-0000	29	5.64
9	000 000 0000	29	5.64
10	000-000-0000	159	30.93
11	(000) 000-0000	250	48.64
	TOTAL	514	99.99

Example 12.2. Phone number formats (USA).

is a bullet, fingerprint, blood stain, fiber, email, and so on, whose origin is questioned. The forensic case becomes viable if and when a possible reference source is found for the questioned item (i.e., a gun, fingerprint, DNA sample, piece of clothing, computer, etc. from a possible suspect). The same requirements must be met in the linguistic analysis of style: a Questioned writing, one whose authorship is in doubt or unknown is tested vis-à-vis Known exemplars, writings attested to have been produced by one or more of its possible authors.

THE DESCRIPTION AND MEASUREMENT OF STYLE

Rigor in language description requires careful framing of research questions, systematic observation, data from observation, reliable methods of description and analysis, valid interpretation of results, and a statement of the basis for every conclusion (Johnstone, 2000). Sometimes the data can be quantitative; that is, used in tests of the statistical probability of their occurrence. Descriptive findings are often more "demonstrable" than quantitative results, however, because descriptive findings appeal to the nonmathematical but structured sense of probability held by judges and juries (Cohen, 1977). All of the examples provided in this chapter are descriptive presentations of linguistic data (although Example 12.2 goes a bit beyond by presenting the raw data for further quantitative assessment).

The measurement of variation in written language is an all-important complement to description and is necessary when using the occurrence of linguistic units to draw statistically valid conclusions relative to authorship. Quantification of data makes decision making related to hypothesis testing easier and more precise, and it meets linguistic and judicial criteria for scientific findings and evidence.

Various researchers (e.g., Grant, 2007; Grant & Baker, 2001) have been working on aspects of quantification of textual elements, especially those related to the selection and significance of style markers. I also outline basic tests for evaluating the significance of the relationship of variables across comparison writings (McMenamin, 2002).

THE LINGUISTIC VARIABLE

The most important step for systematic observation in both the description and subsequent measurement of linguistic variation is the identification of the *linguistic* variables of interest. The analyst isolates structural linguistic units that carry significance with respect to group or individual writing style. Preferred variables, as first articulated by Labov (1966a) are those that are high in frequency, immune from total suppression (e.g., conscious change or disguise), codable, and widely distributed throughout a particular population (and I would add, individual).

The linguistic (dependent) variable is a class of variants ordered along a continuous dimension as determined by extralinguistic (independent) variables, one of which is the particular individual author. The linguistic variant is a specific instance of the dependent variable, and a shift in the distribution of variants reflects a change in extralinguistic factors affecting the variable (Labov 1966a), for example, different authors if applied to stylistic analysis. Labov (1966a) indicates further:

> The variable is of course an abstraction. In actual texts, we meet with variants only. However, the move from variant to variable is the basic step which must be taken here. It implies that the speech performance of the individual or group is best explained through the assumption of an underlying linguistic continuum, in which categories form, reform and dissolve. (p. 21)

FORENSIC STYLISTICS

Linguists observe the language of groups and individuals to study the habitual variation represented in their speaking and writing. The constellation of the patterned forms and uses of language of an individual represents a unique set of features and is thereby used to identify the language of that single writer. When applied to samples of written language in dispute, the analysis of linguistic variation is referred to as *forensic stylistics*.

It is worth mentioning two ostensibly related activities that are not included in forensic stylistics, namely, examination of handwriting, typewriting, ink, and so on, and psychological profiling based on language. The former is considered to be the concern of *forensic document examination*, and the latter is known to be called *forensic psycholinguistics*.

Cases of questioned authorship typically present the linguist with a questioned writing to be first contrasted, for possible exclusion of the author, then compared, for possible identification of the author, to a set of exemplar writings known to have been written by a writer suspected of authoring the questioned material. The author's style is exhibited in a writing sample large enough to demonstrate the individual variation present in the underlying linguistic patterns internal to the habitual language used by the author.

Individual differences in writing style are related to individual choices of alternative forms made available to the writer by the large stock of linguistic alternatives held in common by all the speaker/writers of the author's group (i.e., the speech community). Thus, individuality in writing style results from a given writer's unique position within the group, as represented by his or her individual aggregate set of habitual linguistic choices.

Some case examples of variables may help to make the concept of *style marker* clear:

The Zodiac Killer: This is a spelling example resulting from work done for the recent movie, *Zodiac*, produced and directed by David Fincher. The serial killer calling himself the Zodiac physically separates the diagraph -gh- in words like *right* and *night* so they appear on the page as *rig ht* and *nig ht*. Fincher suspected one Arthur L. Allen, who also demonstrates this habit, as the writer of the threatening letters sent by the Zodiac (see Example 12.3). (Note: no authorship conclusion was possible due to the paucity of known writings from Allen. Other examples appear at the movie's Web site http://www.zodiacmovie.com/.)

Peeping Tom: This punctuation example comes from a criminal matter related to a peeping tom who wrote letters to the very victim he spied on through her bedroom window. In the Questioned as well as Known writings, numerous unmotivated parentheses appear around underlined words. These words, far from being parenthetical, are instead meant by the writer to be emphasized by the use of the parentheses and underlining (see Example 12.4). (There are more examples confirming the same pattern, but they are potentially offensive and have been omitted.)

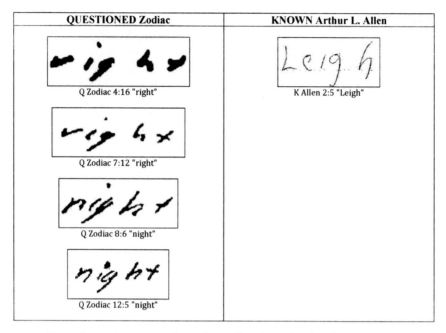

QUESTIONED Zodiac	KNOWN Arthur L. Allen
Q Zodiac 4:16 "right"	K Allen 2:5 "Leigh"
Q Zodiac 7:12 "right"	
Q Zodiac 8:6 "night"	
Q Zodiac 12:5 "night"	

Example 12.3. Separation of graphemic units in digraph -gh-.

"Who loved mom most?" A woman's adult children disputed the apparent provisions of their mother's Will, with the son living closest to his mother being suspected of adding provisions favoring only him. Known typed writings of the deceased mother demonstrated an invariable punctuation pattern in the use of end quotes: quote marks enclosing stated words and phrases appear with punctuation *before* (inside) the quotes, but quote marks used for emphasis appear with punctuation after (outside) the quotes. In contrast, the punctuation in the Questioned Will and in the Known writings of the suspect son occurs only *before* (inside) the quote marks in all cases. For just a few of the many instances of this to appear in the writings, see Example 12.5.

In the same case, the spelling of *already* vis-à-vis *all ready* also varied between the suspect son, his mother, and her purported Will, as can be seen in the data of Example 12.6.

"Who wrote the Will?" A speaker of English as a second language was said to have concocted a Will for a decedent whose first language was English. The Questioned Will shared the same syntactic variation in sequencing tenses as the Known writings of the suspect author (see Example 12.7).

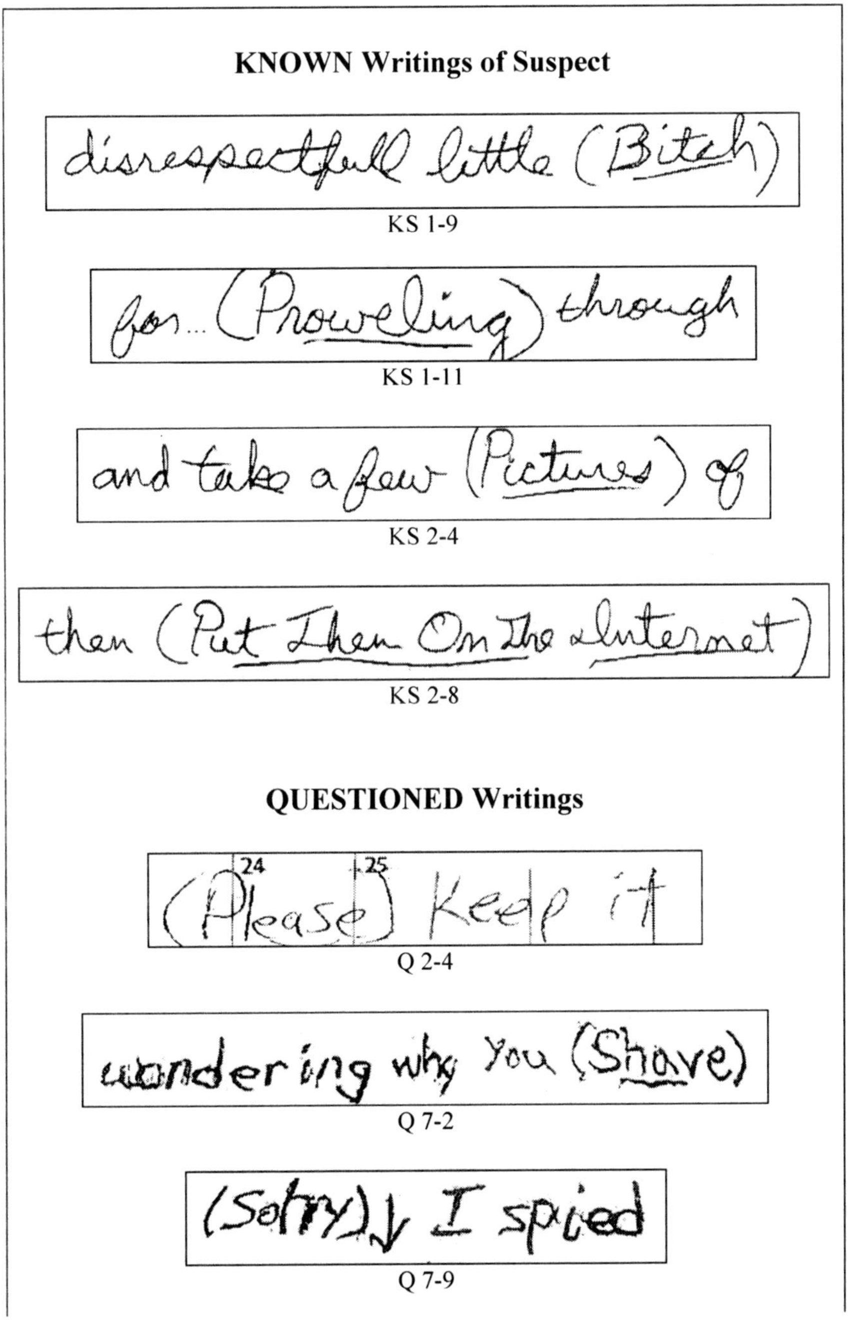

KNOWN Writings of Suspect

disrespectfull little (Bitch)

KS 1-9

for... (Proweling) through

KS 1-11

and take a few (Pictures) of

KS 2-4

then (Put Them On The Internet)

KS 2-8

QUESTIONED Writings

(Please) Keep it

Q 2-4

wondering why You (Shave)

Q 7-2

(Sorry) I spied

Q 7-9

Example 12.4. Punctuation: Parenthesis + underlining for emphasis.

```
                      KNOWN WRITINGS of Deceased Mother

End-quotes used for statements
        232    , wrote a terse/"Is this yours?"  and sent it to her chagrine
        479    off the line, get off the/line."   The electricity was develop
        511    /for some tools from the house!"  He was a new hired man, no
        531      and put some more peas on it.   My father did not smoke, an

End-quotes used for emphasis
        520    ing B E E R.  (Idaho was "dry",  Wyoming "wet)  I was so su
        569    ather always went "first-class".  Even on a short train trip
        715    er she ran so did the "Indian".  He at last caught up with
        742    Idaho was "dry", Wyoming "wet".  My mother worked for Presby

                      KNOWN WRITINGS of Suspect Son
End-quotes used for statements
        65     88 you repeatedly cried "Wolf!"  to/your family and friends,
        71     the/former love of your life,"  James D. Flinner, of various
        545    Instead of saying, "How nice!"  Marie deftly inserted her/fi

End-quotes used for emphasis
        15     s for his "final arrangements."  Previously, Ernest/had writt
        67     Linford. Your "other brother,"  Floyd Whiting, as usual, did
        90     t, and the "love of your life,"  James D. Flinner,/suffered at
        94     Avenue, the Winterland "cabin,"  the house at 1940 Juniper St.

                          QUESTIONED WILL
End-quotes used for statements
        50     mind, but I can make YOU mind!"  Starting I 1984 I had orgina
        66     man said,"The buck stops here."  I also have to/cite the old
        168      might as well have the game."  From what I am able to piece

End-quotes used for emphasis
        124    and/a Ph.D. from this "school,"  evidently without having tak
        245    pregnant with her "love child."  We were living in Laramie in
        309    Floyd for this absurd "advice,"  and he gently reminded Lloyd
        326    , and me about her "situation."  Larry himslef told me next to
```

Example 12.5. Position of end-quote marks relative to sentence-final punctuation.

```
Known Writings of Deceased Mother
  47    get to work.  Since Erne was  all ready  fit to be tied
  47    to be tied because we hadn't  all ready  left for Laramie, I
  84    I were Dorothy/Sayres I would  all ready  have the solution to

Known Writings of Suspect Son
  209   by 1997 she estimated he had  already  extracted his "1/3"
  295     two required meetings have  already  been held. All of the
  312  since Tom Long's law firm was  already  engaged with the legal
  565   /stopped.  It also makes the  already  unpleasant job for the

Questioned Will
  06       seems to be over.  We had  already  been thoroughly soaked
  18    be stopped. It also makes the  already  unpleasant job for the
  36    at 22 months of age, Judy was  already  bossy.  Our second/
```

Example 12.6. Spelling of adverb *already*.

```
Known Writings of Suspect
1:8    I told him that I am a very good cook and   [was]
1:17   James kept asking me when am I coming back. [was]
1:18   He was saying that he is very attracted to me [was]
1:23   he promised that he will help me look for a job [would]
2:17   He told me that he will make a Will which [would]
2:18   He added that all I had to do is love him. [was]

Questioned Writings
1:16   I made sure that she will be taken care. [would]
1:18   Frank told me their wedding will be next year. [would]
1:25   He also said that he has a Will that says .... [had]
2:8    he called Cela his wife, because that's what she is to him [was]
2:28   He said she is the only one that is worth of it. [was]
2:34   he said that his Will is perfectly good. [was]
```

Example 12.7. Past-tense verb in main clause followed by present-tense verb in subordinate clause.

Husband or daughter: A woman's existing Will directed her estate to a daughter from a first marriage. After the death of the testatrix, a more recent Will appeared, naming her husband as beneficiary. The data presented three ways to position direct objects (DO) and indirect objects (IO) within a sentence, as in the following table:

Form 1	I	give	John	my estate.
	S	V	IO	DO
Form 2	I	give	my estate	to John.
	S	V	DO	to IO
Form 3	I	give	to John	my estate.
	S	V	to IO	DO

The Known Will only places the *to* + *IO* elements at the end of the sentence, whereas the Known writings of the husband and the Questioned Will both contain instances of the *to* + *IO* elements placed before the DO (see Example 12.8).

```
Known Existing Will
EW1:7        I give and bequeath all tangible property to my daughter.
EW2:2        All the rest I give to my daughter.
EW2:7        [It is my wish that] she provide my husband a monthly allowance.
EW2:16       I specifically give all of the powers enumerated to my Executrix.
EW3:4        I hereby give my fiduciaries the power to allocate the expenses.

EW1:7        S         V              DO    to    IO
EW2:2        DO        S              V     to    IO
EW2:7        S         V              IO          DO
EW2:16       S         V              DO    to    IO
EW3:4        S         V              IO          DO


Known Writings of Suspect
KS389:24     Please send to me, a copy of any letter you send.
KS39:6       She will return to the office, the telephone and the fax.
KS297:10     I give to my accountant freedom to ....
KS302: 11    I give to my beloved husband authority to ....
KS348:12     The management company will send to you the money.

KS389:24               V              IO          DO
KS39:6       S         V      to      IO          DO
KS297:10     S         V      to      IO          DO
KS302: 11    S         V      to      IO          DO
KS348:12     S         V      to      IO          DO


Questioned Will
QW1:3        I give and bequeath all personal property to my husband Thomas.
QW1:9        I give and bequeath to my daughter Clarice, nothing.
QW1:13       I give to my nephew Marvin one hundred thousand dollars.

QW1:3        S         V              DO    to    IO
QW1:9        S         V      to      IO          DO
QW1:13       S         V      to      IO          DO
```

Example 12.8. Order of indirect and direct objects within sentences.

Mad at the boss: A disgruntled employee wrote anonymous letters to the board of directors of his firm. All of his known work-related correspondence demonstrated a sequential format of sentences and paragraphs drawn from a unique internal template he had developed over time. Unfortunately for him, he used this same format, demonstrably not used by other employees, to write the questioned letters to his board (see Example 12.9).

Town Council Approval: A land developer who wanted to represent official approval of his large land development to potential investors produced a letter of support from the local town council. Unfortunately, many of the stylistic characteristics of this letter matched those of his own writings and at the same time contrasted with those of the supposed author. One of the stylistic features common to both sets of writings was the use of very long periodic sentences containing multiple levels of sentence coordination and embedded subordination (see Example 12.10).

```
Known Letters of Suspect
K5:13      Should you have any queries pertaining to the enclosed please do
           not hesitate to contact the undersigned ....
K6:13      Should you have any queries pertaining to the enclosed please do
           not hesitate to contact the undersigned.
K9:14      [Identical]
K14:11     [Identical]
K17:12     [Identical]
K25:14     [Identical]
K27:19     [Identical]
K30:28     [Identical]
K31:20     [Identical]

Questioned Letters
Q1:6       Should you have any queries pertaining to the enclosed please do
           not hesitate to contact the undersigned.
Q2:21      Should you have any queries regarding this enclosed letter please
           don't hesitate to contact the writer ....
Q5:6       Should you have any queries pertaining to the enclosed please do
           not hesitate to contact the undersigned.
```

Example 12.9. Identical content of letter-closings.

```
Known Writings of Suspect [one example; structure of embedding levels not shown]

K1:26 "I have been asked to step aside from all day to day operations within
the Forest property, there is lots of items to be completed regarding the
property and even just last week end, your house and equipment was damaged in
a freak hail storm no one from Smith Lawyers came out to inspect the
property, but I helped out and looked after tenancy and covered all the
broken windows to your premise and other tenants houses, this is even that I
have not been paid this month and even your staff member was not paid until
last week and other creditor have not been paid and lots of cheques have
bounced and you can just think of all the bad rumors going around."

Questioned Writings [one example; structure of embedding levels not shown]

Q3:17 "We would like to make recommendation for approval on the 31st May 2000
for Council to approve the Coastal Stage 1 after it has been on public
exhibition for two weeks this is different to what we told you before but
legally council has to, before approving your DA and then the remaining total
stages would be approved after Council adopts the full LES  and LEP and this
will not be until mid September 2000 as we had no difficulties in approving
the company's Development Application, however, we feel it is important that
we address all legal and government authority issues prior to releasing your
DA approval from council."
```

Example 12.10. Periodic sentences with patterned levels of embedded coordination and subordination.

LIMITATIONS OF FORENSIC STYLISTICS

Linguistic Limitations

Linguistic limitations to the theory and practice of forensic stylistics have been identified in recent years and have long been studied in authorship attribution research (McMenamin, 1993, 2002). Specific concerns presently center around four principal questions:

1. Is the selection of stylistic variables objective, or arbitrary and subjective?
The selection of stylistic variables is objective and is based on the theory of variation analysis developed by William Labov and others, and proposed as far back as 1966. Labov (2008) outlines the process for defining the linguistic variable:
Step 1. Notice variation—alternative ways of saying the same thing.
Step 2. Define the envelope of variation—the largest environment in which the variation occurs.
a. Accompany reports of occurrences of a variant with reports of all nonoccurrences.
b. Set aside neutral cases: environments where it is not possible to distinguish variants.
c. Note exclusions—individual items that behave in idiosyncratic fashion.
Step 3. Define the (independent) constraints on the variable (e.g., writing context or author).

2. Can the frequency of occurrence of stylistic variables be well defined statistically?
Frequency of occurrence is, in fact, well defined if one follows the steps just outlined for coding variants of style variables. Successful statistical approaches to the general and forensic analysis of style go back decades (see McMenamin, 1993). More recently, Grant and Baker (2001) describe the statistical and linguistic bases of Principal Component Analysis, a method for measuring the collective range of variation needed for authorship identification. Additionally, I outline some basic measures in McMenamin (2002). Among the many researchers now working to develop more reliable measures of style, the work of Tim Grant (2007) is the most promising, wherein he proposes a text-sampling strategy to identify potentially useful, reliable, and valid style markers.

3. Are linguistic norms accessible enough to be used as a basis for the analysis of variation within or away from specific norms?

Recall that style variables can be of two types: deviations from a norm and variations within a norm. The clear cases, often those not requiring reference to a corpus, are variables that are prescriptive errors (i.e., deviations from the conventions of a clearly established norm). However, many useful style markers represent variation within a norm (i.e., multiple error-free ways of saying the same thing). It is here that corpus-based determination of style-marker significance is important.

Another seldom mentioned linguistic limitation of current practice in authorship attribution is the inability to clearly differentiate between group versus individual variation, commonly referred to in the forensic sciences as class versus individual features. A corpus-based approach to style markers can first help identify group variables and then make it possible to assign remaining variables to a set of individuating style markers (i.e., those associated with individual identification) based on relative frequencies of occurrences of identified linguistic variables.

With respect to the need to refer to a community norm in order to establish individual variation, it has long been clear that such work is indispensable to successful stylistic analysis. As Labov (1996) said, sociolinguistics has established the community as the stable and systematic language unit against which the behavior of individuals must be judged.

Other more detailed accounts of the need to use linguistic corpora, especially to describe and establish group norms, are found in Coulthard (1994), McMenamin (2004), and Solan and Tiersma (2004).

Recognition of the need for a reference corpus does not mean that establishing a norm for any given analysis is in any way easy. The corpus for a given case should match as much as possible the context of writing of the text(s) under scrutiny. That is, an ad hoc corpus may have to be assembled in the event that one enabling a representative analysis does not already exist.

4. Assuming that the most telltale markers are those least consciously used, is it possible to determine levels of conscious intervention in the writing process?

It would, of course, be very useful to find a method to test a writer's level of consciousness at any given point in the writing process. However, a performance approach appears to be as adequate for the analysis of writing as it is for the description of spoken language. Labov's research related to levels of style (casual to formal) has demonstrated that variation is more consistent in casual speech, so this may be a place to begin research on writing, that is, attempting to study an individual's writings that are grouped by level of attention paid to the process of writing itself or to other aspects of the writing context that would result in text that is formal (more conscious) or casual (less conscious).

Legal Limitations

Legal limitations to forensic stylistics relate to the standards for the admissibility of scientific evidence. Forensic stylistics presents no real limitations in countries or venues that rely on a "general acceptance" test like that first laid out in the United States by the District of Columbia Court of Appeals in *Frye v. United States* (1923), wherein expert opinion based on a scientific technique was admissible if the technique was generally acceptable in the relevant scientific community.

However, starting with the U.S. Supreme Court's decision in *Daubert v. Merrell Dow Pharmaceuticals* (1993), the reliability of scientific evidence in federal and many state venues is now to be judged on five specific factors:

1. whether the theory or technique can be tested;

2. whether the theory or technique has been subjected to peer review and publication;

3. the known or potential rate of error;

4. the existence of standards controlling the operation of the technique; and

5. general acceptance in the relevant scientific community.

Stylistic analysis stands up to the *Daubert* criteria (Coulthard, 2004; McMenamin, 2004), although the research area of immediate need is the establishment of error rates for stylistic analysis. The fact that forensic stylistics meets to a greater or lesser extent all but one of the *Daubert* criteria makes the technique reliable even while error-rate research is being done. In fact, in the later decision of *Kumho Tire v. Carmichael* (1999), the U.S. Supreme Court emphasized flexible application of the *Daubert* criteria as opposed to rigidly applying any particular *Daubert* factor in a given case.

On the other hand, this does not mean that judicial criteria external to the academic discipline of forensic linguistics, such as those set out in *Daubert*, cannot provide impetus for improvement in the methodology of forensic stylistics. On the contrary, Grant (2007), for example, correctly observes, "Because of the American pressure [from *Daubert*] it is likely that the number and variety of quantified approaches will increase in forensic authorship analysis" (p. 3).

Additionally, I would stress the importance of resolving another thorny problem—the reconciliation of distinct approaches to the identification of style markers and the resulting process of analysis. If the judicial requirements are to be fully realized, that is, having standards controlling the analysis of style, and achieving general acceptance of forensic stylistics in the scientific community (linguistics), it will be necessary to find a middle ground between those who preselect style markers for analysis based on a given set of *a priori* criteria, versus those who hold that the style markers used for analysis of a particular set of writings must be first observed as linguistic variables in those very writings. I have previously referred to these respective approaches as *top–down* vis-à-vis *bottom–up*, my position being that the basic data for linguistic analysis is language as it is used by speakers and writers as they communicate with each other.

REFERENCES

Bloch, B. (1948). A set of postulates for phonemic analysis. *Language*, 24(1), 3–46.

Cohen, L. J. (1977). *The probable and the provable*. Oxford: Clarendon.

Coulthard, M. (1994). On the use of corpora in the analysis of forensic texts. *Forensic Linguistics*, 1(1), 27–43.

Coulthard, M. (2004). Author identification, idiolect, and linguistic uniqueness. *Applied Linguistics*, 25(4), 431–447.

Coulthard, M., & Johnson, A. (2010). *Routledge handbook of forensic linguistics*. Oxford: Routledge.

Grant, T. (2007). Quantifying evidence in forensic authorship analysis. *The International Journal of Speech, Language and the Law*, 14(1), 1–25.

Grant, T., & Baker, K. (2001). Identifying reliable, valid markers of authorship: A response to Chaski. *Forensic Linguistics*, 8(1), 66–79.

Johnstone, B. (2000). *Qualitative methods in sociolinguistics*. New York: Oxford University Press.

Labov, W. (1966). *The social stratification of English in New York City*. Washington, DC: Center for Applied Linguistics.

Labov, W. (1996). When intuitions fail. In L. McNair, K. Singer, L. Dolbrin, & M. Aucon (Eds.), *Papers from the parasession on theory and data in linguistics* (pp. 77–106). Chicago: University of Chicago, Chicago Linguistic Society.

Labov, W. (2002, August). *Driving forces in linguistic change*. Paper presented at the 2002 International Conference on Korean Linguistics, Seoul National University, Seoul, Korea.

Labov, W. (2008). Quantitative reasoning in linguistics. Posted as notes for Linguistics 563, http://www.ling.upenn.edu/~wlabov/Papers/QRL.pdf.

McMenamin, G.R. (1993). *Forensic stylistics.* Amsterdam: Elsevier.

McMenamin, G.R. (2002). *Forensic linguistics: Advances in forensic stylistics.* Boca Raton, FL: CRC Press.

McMenamin, G.R. (2004). Disputed authorship in U.S. law. *International Journal of Speech Language and the Law, 11*(1), 73–82.

Melinkoff, D. (1963). *The language of the law.* Boston: Little Brown.

Solan, L.M., & Tiersma, P.M. (2004). Author identification in American courts. *Applied Linguistics, 25*(4), 448–465.

Wachal, R.S. (1966). *Linguistic evidence, statistical inference and disputed authorship.* Unpublished doctoral dissertation, University of Wisconsin, Madison.

CASE REFERENCES

Daubert v. Merrell Dow Pharmaceuticals, Inc., 951 F.2d 1128 (1991)

Frye v. United States, 293 F. 1013 (App. D.C. 1923)

Kuhmo Tire Company, Ltd., v. Carmichael, 119 S.Ct. 1167 (1999)

13

Forensic Technology

Computers and Digital Media as Sources of Evidence

Raymond Hsieh
Patricia Paola

Computer forensics is a set of investigation and analysis techniques used to obtain legal evidence from a computer. A computer specialist attempts to discover data in a computer system and recover deleted information, encrypted information, and damaged files with the aid of special software designed to read the computer's hard drive. The software gives a hard drive the ability to access deleted documents and render them undeleted. A basis for computer forensics is that many electronic files—emails, databases, calendars, images, photos, and audio files—are difficult if not impossible to destroy completely. Floppy diskettes, DVDs, CDs, flash media, and thumb drives are the other computer devices that are examined by computer forensics. A forensic specialist can discover all files on a computer system including deleted files, hidden files, and encrypted files, as well as password-protected files. Computer forensics is an autopsy of the hard drive.

Cybercrime—any criminal activity or offense involving a computer—has facilitated the need for computer forensics. A computer specialist may assist in a police investigation by acquiring and analyzing evidence and by reporting the findings. The Internet permits expanded freedom throughout the world resulting in a massive amount of cybercrime.

This chapter explains computer forensics, and explores and discusses a few cybercrimes, including fraud, cyberstalking, and pornography. The legal and ethical rights of the suspect and the forensic specialist also are examined.

Technology has given society the gift of the computer. Unfortunately, it also has brought out some of the ugliness that the world has to offer. In respect to this element of life, computer forensics has become necessary to analyze computers and help in the fight against cybercrime. Computer forensics, also referred to as digital evidence, is the use of computer investigation and analysis techniques to obtain legal evidence from computers. A computer forensic specialist can perform the recovery of information for different types of situations such as helping to recover lost information for businesses, trace computer traffic to assist in a missing person case, or assist law enforcement in pre-search preparation for warrants and then the handling of the computer after the arrest.

Computer forensics conducts an analysis on the physical and the logical level of the computer. The physical level is looking at the operating system for master or allocation file tables that are accessible to the user. The logical level boots the computer and looks through the information that the user sees. In the analysis, the forensic computer specialist makes an exact copy of the hard drive. This copy contains information that a normal backup of the computer does not have the capability to copy. A copy of the hard drive is always made using software and/or hardware writer blockers to assure the original evidence is never changed or tainted throughout the examination. Although the use of a writer blocker is designed to prevent modification of the evidence, there always is a possibility that evidence could become tainted or lost. This can happen, for example, through the use of special software tools used to help crack passwords on the computer. In conjunction with the analyses of the computer's hard drive, the specialist also may investigate all floppy diskettes, DVDs, CDs, flash media, and thumb drives associated with the computer.

Computer forensics is used to discover data on computer systems and recover deleted information, encrypted information, and damaged files. Magnetic fields and electronic pulses are collected and analyzed using special tools and techniques.

Again, a forensic computer specialist may examine any electronic information storage device for files. Electronic files may include emails, databases, calendars, images, photos, and audio files. Any past activity on such a device may have left evidence. For example, the Internet is used extensively for communication, shopping, research, and so forth. And cell phones and other devices are used to transmit, store, and retrieve information. It is the mindset of most users that this information is private. But it is not. The information is stored on servers on the Internet, at work, and on the hard drive of their personal computers. At times, sensitive and incriminating material becomes a digital fingerprint that the computer forensic expert obtains to be used as evidence in a courtroom.

COLLECTION

Electronic (digital) evidence is information stored on or transmitted to another electronic device, therefore making it latent evidence in court. Testimony is required in court to explain the examination and any limitations because the digital information is contained in the device that cannot be seen as physical evidence. This latent evidence is extracted from the device by the aid of special software and equipment. To meet the challenges of presenting electronic evidence in court, proper forensic procedure requires four phases: collection, examination, analysis, and reporting. Documentation continues from the beginning to the end of the evidence-collection effort.

The most important requirement at a crime scene, with respect to collecting digital evidence, is that the first responder must have the necessary legal authority to search and seize the suspected evidence at the scene. In most cases, law enforcement must obtain a warrant that allows the investigation of all electronic devices within the premises or crime scene. There are situations where a paperless warrant is applicable while still protecting the Constitutional rights of the individual(s) being investigated.

The collection phase is in real time at the scene and involves recognizing and collecting while documenting all electronic evidence. The state of evidence is documented, and it is important that the equipment stay in the condition in which it was found. When documenting elements of the scene the examiner observes and documents the physical scene such as the location of the computer and the position of the mouse. Also, the state of the system is documented, including the power status of the computer (on, off, or sleep mode). The front of the computer or monitor is photographed (on, off, or sleep mode) to document the status of the screen at time of the collection. Most importantly, the equipment is never turned on or off in this phase as data can be lost or date stamps can be changed.

The collection of digital evidence at a crime scene starts with the first law enforcement responder. He or she must decide whether to collect and preserve all the electronic evidence or contact a computer forensic expert who is trained and can transport and store the evidence. First responders encounter electronic devices in almost every case, therefore creating the need for officers to train in the collection of evidence. If not trained, or if the case is extensive, a forensic computer examiner may be summoned to the crime scene to perform the collection tasks. Training is essential in the procedures of collection and preservation of the evidence, due to the fragile nature of electronic evidence that can be easily damaged, altered, or destroyed. For example, damage causing a missing date could result in all other collected evidence being successfully challenged.

When the first responder enters a crime scene, he or she must secure the scene by removing all people from the vicinity of possible evidence. The next step is to document, with drawings, a written summary, and photographs, all electronic devices before performing any tests on them. The electronic equipment may have latent fingerprints, but these need to be processed after the evidence recovery is complete because the chemicals used in processing latent prints can damage equipment and data (Ashcroft, 2001).

First responders and forensic examiners are challenged by the speed with which technology is changing, and this requires training to be an ongoing process. For example, the rapid changes in cell phone technology makes extracting evidence from them a challenge. Moreover, when a cell phone is part of the evidence at a scene, there are legal requirements regarding unopened emails and unread text messages, as well as for incoming calls after the seizure, so it is much preferred that the examination be conducted in a short amount of time.

After securing the scene, the examiner conducts interviews to find out possible passwords, user names, and the name of the Internet service provider. The examiner also tries to find out the purpose for the system, whether there is any off-site storage, and what hardware or software is installed on the system. The examiner must document the location of the computer and all other connections and electronic devices with notes, photos, and a sketch of the scene. With the risk for contamination, gloves must be used before handling any electronic devices. A computer forensics specialist must identify all of the different components to be processed as well as determine the power source, as a battery-operated device needs to be processed before the battery runs out to avoid the possibility of information being lost.

The investigation of a computer reveals what user-created files exist and which files may contain important evidence of criminal activity. These usually include address books, email files, database files, calendars, image or graphic files, and Internet bookmarks and favorites. The computer consists of the central processing unit, a monitor, keyboard, data storage devices, and a mouse. A computer may stand alone, or can be connected to a network, and/or have other components such as modems, scanners, printers, and docking stations.

All computers contain an operating system. Digital evidence may be found in the operating system because the user does not realize that data are being written in more than one area. This sometimes allows temporary files, passwords, and Internet activity to be recovered for examination. Computer-created files can consist of back-up files, cookies, history or hidden files, configuration files, and system files. However, there are other data that can be discovered such as bad clusters; free space; deleted files; computer date, time, and password; lost clusters; slack space; and unallocated space. This information is obtained with the assistance of software and forensic training.

Technology keeps creating many electronic devices that are faster and better than the model already on the market. Some of these devices contain perishable data that must be immediately secured, documented, and photographed. Many of these devices are listed in Table 13.1, with an asterisk (*) indicating devices that are battery or electrically operated and thus require immediate attention when processing the evidence so as to not lose information if the device were to shut down.

There is a tremendous amount of information that can be stored on digital media (CD, DVD, external drives, etc.), making this a critical part of the examination as well. The forensic expert must take specific care to protect digital media from physical damage, vibration, magnetic fields, electrical static, and large variations of temperature and humidity (SWGDE, 2006). Media are transported in antistatic packaging, and care is taken to avoid heated car seats, excessive vibration, radio transmitters, and other sources of potential damage.

The examination phase is the most critical for collecting evidence because the evidence may be visual, hidden, and obscured. The analysis of the evidence is viewed by the investigative team, not just the forensic examiner, or law enforcement person performing the examination. Once collection, examination, and analysis are completed, a written report outlines the complete procedure and is used in discovery or for testimony in court.

LEGAL PROTECTION

The forensic examiner must be an unbiased and ethical individual with the vision to always uphold the rights of all individuals in the investigation.

Table 13.1. Electronic Devices or Attachments

Smart card	A small, handheld device containing a microprocessor that is capable of storing a monetary value, digital certificate, encryption key, or authentication information (password)
Dongle	A small device that plugs into a computer port that contains information similar to a smart card
Biometric scanner	A device connected to a computer system that recognizes an individual's characteristics such as voice, fingerprints, and retina
Answering machine*	Part of the telephone using magnetic tapes or is a digital recording system. Most machines have caller ID, names and telephone numbers of callers, as well as deleted messages, last number called, and memos
Digital camera	Camera that transfers images and video to computer media allowing for potential evidence such as images, removable cartridges, sound, time and date stamp, and video
Personal Digital Assistant (PDA)* systems	A small device used as a personal organizer that can synchronize data with another computer by use of a cradle and is able to include computing, telephone/fax, paging, and networking features. A PDA can contain an address book, documents, appointment information, email, passwords, telephone numbers, text messages, and voice messages.
Memory card	A removable electronic storage device that can store hundreds of images and is used in computers, digital cameras, and PDAs; does not lose information when power is removed
Modems	Internal and external, wireless analog, DSL, ISDN, cable used to facilitate electronic communication by allowing the computer to access other computers and/or network via a telephone line, wireless, other communication mediums
Network components	Local Area Network (LAN) card on Network Interface Card (NIC) used to connect to computers, and allow for the exchange of information and resource sharing
Routers, hubs, and switches	Used in a networked computer system to provide a means of connecting different computers or networks
Servers	Provide some service for other computers connected to it via a network to share resources such as file storage or email
Network cables and connectors	Connect components of the computer network

Device	Description
Removable storage devices and media	Store magnetic, digital, or electrical information; examples are floppy disks, CDs, DVDs, cartridges, and tape
Pagers*	Handheld electronic device that contains telephone numbers, voice mail, and email
Printers*	Contain a memory buffer allowing them to receive and store multiple-page documents while they are printing, and some models contain a hard drive. It is possible to get network identity or information, superimposed images on the roller, time and date stamp, and user usage log from the printer
Scanners*	An optical device that is connected to the computer and scans images to the computer as a file, used to convert documents and pictures to electronic files that can be viewed, or transmitted and manipulated on a computer
Telephone*	Connected directly to a land-line system or remote base station that is wireless; two-way communication using land lines, radio transmission, cellular systems, or a combination. Telephones contain caller ID, emails, pages, and text messages
Copiers*	Contain user-access records as well as history of copies made
Credit card skimmers	Used to read information contained on the magnetic stripe on plastic cards, includes expiration date, user's address, name, and card number
Digital watches	Several types are pagers that store digital messages and they may contain address books, appointment calendars, notes, and emails
Facsimile (Fax) machine	Can store preprogrammed telephone numbers and the history of transmitted and received messages; some machines have the ability to store hundreds of faxes, either incoming or outgoing or at least a log of the faxes.
Global Positioning System (GPS)	Provides information on previous travel; some automatically store the previous destinations that include travel logs
Games: Xbox, Playstation3	Game consoles and other devices provide a convenient means to store data of all kinds, including images, video, audio, and text files
IPod/mp3	Handheld music device that holds calendar entries of dates of crimes or related to crimes, contact information of perpetrators or victims, stores photos and documentation

*Indicates devices requiring immediate attention

The examiner must understand and uphold the First and Fourth Amendments of the U.S. Constitution along with many acts of law that have been passed to protect rights. The use of the Internet has opened the scope of crime to encompass the entire world, thus compelling the U.S. legal arena to pass new laws in order to protect all citizens.

Warrants

A warrant is the authorization to enter a domicile or business of an individual during an investigation. A judge or magistrate will issue a warrant only if all rights of the accused are protected under federal, state, and local laws.

According to the Supreme Court, a warrantless search does not violate the Fourth Amendment if one of two conditions is satisfied. First, if the government's conduct does not violate a person's "reasonable expectation of privacy," then formally it does not constitute a Fourth Amendment "search" and no warrant is required. Giving consent to search relinquishes a reasonable expectation of privacy, as does having incriminating evidence in plain view, for example. Second, a warrantless search that violates a person's reasonable expectation of privacy will nonetheless be "reasonable" (and therefore constitutional) if it falls within an established exception to the warrant requirement—breaking passwords or encryption on a suspect's computer, for example. Computer searches must take these factors into account, of course.

The investigator must first obtain a valid search warrant based on probable cause to "search" (which, in the case of computer forensics translates to "analyze") personal technological devices and electronic data for evidence of a crime or criminal activity. There are cases where a valid search warrant is not obtained and the responder must make a careful and valid determination that a warrantless search is reasonable because the situation falls under a recognized exception to the warrant requirement. An example would be viewing the evidence with consent or the evidence being in plain view (Galves & Galves, 2004).

Courts often treat electronic devices as being analogous to closed containers in the physical world, the owners of which maintain a reasonable expectation of privacy therein. For example, obtaining a warrant to look on a hard drive solely for Excel spreadsheets is similar to getting a warrant to look only in a certain container for certain information. This seems simple enough, but many issues may arise. Armed with a warrant to search for specifically labeled information, what would occur if an investigator searched every labeled and nonlabeled file and document on a computer, perhaps all Word, PowerPoint, or pdf files? Courts differ in their approaches to this scenario. Some would allow the entire search of all files in that particular computer, whereas others would require the warrant to be more specific in its scope, mentioning the precise computer files and programs to be searched and seized. To avoid potential judicial overrulings, prosecutors and investigators sometimes work together to establish clear search and seizure policies for electronic evidence in their particular jurisdictions.

The potential for confusion regarding the expectation of privacy is high. Sometimes a warrant is not even necessary, not because of an exception, but because the suspect maintains no legitimate expectation of privacy in the computer files in the first place. For example, if a suspect uses a computer that is openly available, with no password protection, or one in a workplace to which the employer's system administrator has direct access and can monitor all of the computer activity, he or she may have abandoned all Fourth Amendment rights with respect to that computer because it is used in such an open and public way.

Other issues could emerge if a person took a computer to a third party for repair and, while working on it, a technician stumbled across incriminating information and reported it to authorities. Generally, obtaining and reporting information in these circumstances would be valid as long as there was some manifestation that the suspect relinquished his or her reasonable expectation of privacy in the computer by placing it in the hands of a third party. Because the Fourth Amendment requires "state action," it does not apply to nongovernmental persons who might conduct searches on their own and report evidence of potential criminal activity, as long as they were not acting in any way as agents of the government. But sometimes it is not as easy as that. Some courts would probably opine that a computer owner leaving a computer with a technician did not totally abandon all reasonable expectations of privacy because the "exposure" to the public was limited to the repair shop, and it should have gone no further.

Investigators thus need to be aware of the Fourth Amendment and the warrant requirement demonstrating probable cause as a protection of a suspect's reasonable expectation of privacy. Both investigators and prosecutors must be especially aware that search warrants cannot be used for fishing expeditions. The warrant should specifically describe all the things to be searched and all the items to be seized. On the other hand, although it needs to be particular and specific, the warrant should be as broad as the probable cause will allow, so that the investigator is not boxed in and has flexibility during the search to locate all possible incriminating information. If care is not taken with the warrant protocols, the fruits of the search may well be rendered inadmissible at trial (Galves & Galves, 2004).

Electronic Communications Privacy Act

In preparing the investigation, it is imperative not to violate the Electronic Communications Privacy Act (ECPA) or the Privacy Protection Act The ECPA sets out the provisions for access, use, disclosure, interception, and privacy protection of electronic communications. Enacted in 1986, ECPA covers electronic communication and prohibits the unlawful access and disclosure of communication contents. The plans for the investigation must be developed in compliance with departmental policy, as well as federal, state, and local laws. In particular, under the Privacy Protection Act, with certain exceptions, it is unlawful for an agent to search for or seize certain materials possessed by a person reasonably believed to have a purpose of disseminating information to the public. For example, seizure of First Amendment materials such as drafts of newsletters of web pages may implicate the Privacy Protection Act (Ashcroft, 2001).

The First Amendment

The First Amendment guarantees the right to freedom of expression to free people everywhere. The First Amendment reads:

> Congress shall make no law respecting an establishment of religion, or prohibiting the free exercise thereof; or abridging the freedom of speech, or of the press, or the right of the people peaceably to assemble, and to petition the government for a redress of grievances.

The Supreme Court has held that obscene speech, defamation, incitement of panic, incitement of crime, fighting words, and sedition are not protected by the First Amendment. The forensic expert often finds that obscene speech and defamation are particularly relevant to obtained evidence.

Cable Communication Privacy Act

The Cable Communication Privacy Act (CCPA) prevents a cable company from releasing personally identifiable information about a subscriber unless the government offers clear and convincing evidence that the subscriber is a suspect and the subscriber is given an opportunity to contest the issue at an adversarial hearing. Data collection is limited to that which the system regards as necessary to maintain daily operations, such as billing records, maintenance and repair orders, premium service subscription information, and subscriber complaints. Access to this information is restricted to system personnel, businesses that provide services for the system (accountants), program and program guide providers, service auditors, and franchising representatives. It has been amended by the USA Patriot Act (Newman, 2007).

USA Patriot Act

The September 11 terrorist attacks on the United States have made the need for amendments of the ECPA and CCPA. The act punishes and attempts to deter terrorist activities in the United States and around the world, and enhances law enforcement investigation tools. It expands federal agencies' powers in intercepting, sharing, and using private telecommunications, especially electronic communication. It also sets out procedures and limitations to seek redress for individuals who feel their rights have been violated. It also is used to detect and prosecute other alleged potential crimes such as providing false information on terrorism. The act was renewed on March 2, 2006 (Newman, 2007).

Communications Decency Act

A 1973 Supreme Court case, *Miller v. California*, determined that obscene language was not protected under the First Amendment, setting the standard for language permitted on the Internet. However, differentiating between adults and children created a problem with freedom of speech, forcing the U.S. government to manufacture laws to protect the children. Embedded in the Telecommunication Act was the Communications Decency Act (CDA). The CDA became law in 1996 and was designed to protect children from online pornography. It imposed large fines and prison terms for transmitting indecent material over the Internet. However, another lawsuit, *Reno v. ACLU*, challenged indecency on the Internet, forcing the case to the Supreme Court, which ruled that the law unconstitutionally restricted free speech and that the Internet is protected under the First Amendment. The Supreme Court said in its ruling that freedom of expression in a democratic society outweighs any unproven benefit of censorship. The ruling also acknowledged the phenomenal growth of the Internet, but declared government regulation of communication content more likely to interfere with the free exchange of ideas than to encourage it (Reynolds, 2007). Had the court ruled the CDA to be constitutional, the Internet would have been opened to many aspects of legal scrutiny and the reality would have changed today's growth dramatically.

Child Online Protection Act

The Child Online Protection Act (COPA) was signed into law in 1998. This law protected children from harmful material on the Internet. This includes exposure to offensive graphic or verbal material, as well as to coercive or misleading advertising. Again, the federal courts ruled the law violated First Amendment rights. Following several appeals, the Supreme Court stated there is a potential for extraordinary harm and a serious chill upon protected speech if the law were to go into effect. The ruling made it clear that the COPA was unconstitutional and could not be used to shelter children from online pornography (Reynolds, 2007).

The Electronic Communication Privacy Act

The ECPA sets out the provisions for access, use, disclosure, interception, and privacy protections of any electronic communication. The law was enacted in 1986 and covers various forms of wire and electronic communications. According to the U.S. Code, electronic communication means any transfer of signs, signals, writing, images, sounds, data, or intelligence of any nature transmitted in whole or in part by a wire, radio, electromagnetic, photo electronic, or photo optical system that affects interstate or foreign commerce. The ECPA prohibits unlawful access and certain disclosures of communication contents. Additionally, the law prevents government entities from requiring disclosure of electronic communications from a provider without proper procedure.

The Fourth Amendment

Searching and seizing computers without a warrant are limited by the Fourth Amendment. The Fourth Amendment states that no one can violate the right of people to be secure against unreasonable searches of their persons, houses, papers, and effects; and that a warrant for such a search can be issued only if there is probable cause and a description of the specific places or persons or things to be searched or seized.

The Fourth Amendment limits the ability of government investigators to search for evidence. The courts apply the same test to electronic information as they do to any other reasonable expectation of privacy. Law enforcement is restricted from investigating a person's private computer files without probable cause. When probable cause is proven absent, the evidence obtained is suppressed under the exclusionary rule.

Exclusionary Rule

The Exclusionary Rule is the right to be free from unreasonable searches and seizures by law enforcement, as declared by the Fourth Amendment. It pertains to the methods by which evidence is obtained rather than in what the evidence represents. It rules that if the evidence is not legally obtained, then it is not admissible in court. Theoretically, there are several alternatives to the exclusionary rule. There may be illegal searches and seizures that would be criminally actionable, with the officers undertaking them being subject to prosecution, but examples of officers being criminally prosecuted for overzealous law enforcement are extremely rare (Edwards, 1955). Likewise for internal discipline of officers whose search and seizure might have been illegal (Goldstein, 1967). Persons who have been illegally arrested or who have had their privacy invaded will usually have a tort action available under state statutory or common law, however.

The Computer Fraud and Abuse Act

The Computer Fraud and Abuse Act was passed into law in 1986 to help reduce hacking of computer systems. Since its induction, this act has been amended three times, the last time being with the USA Patriot Act.

The Computer Fraud and Abuse Act makes it illegal to obtain government-classified information from a computer and then use that information to do harm to the United States or make profit for oneself or defraud others, or to cause damage to a government computer, or to provide a government computer password to others who might use it to harm the government or its computers or its people.

The use of these amendments and acts are carefully examined and adhered to in all forensic investigations. A warrant will not be issued if not in accordance with these laws. The Internet has opened the crime arena to all corners of the world; however these laws with the exclusion of the USA Patriot Act are only enforceable in the United States. For this reason, it is another challenge for law enforcement and forensic examiners when evidence is found in another country that is not as law abiding or as moral as one would hope.

COMPUTER CRIMES

Crimes on a computer are as vast as one's imagination, and criminals are coming up with different scams and crimes daily. Again, the use of the

Internet is permitting crime to spread like a wildfire. Too many crimes are committed to discuss them all, but a few common examples of computer crimes would be cyberstalking, fraud, and pornography.

Cyberstalking

Cyberstalking creates a monumental problem as with stalking in the physical world. The notion that Internet stalkers are harmless is false and can be a dangerous misperception. Some cyberstalkers have encountered or observed their victim before the stalking began. Others obtain information about their victim on the Internet—sometimes by information a person puts on social sites, but other times by information put on by someone else. The stalkers can be women, men, or children who desire to control their victims, many of whom are former intimates (Swanson, Chamelin, & Taylor, 2005).

The image most of us have of a stalker or a pedophile is not true. The majority of pedophiles are highly intelligent, respected, middle-age men. These family men have strong ties to their religion and work hard for a living. Many of these predators have the means to spend hours at their computers, often at work. The image of a sloppy old man lurking and viewing pornographic photos is not who these stalkers and pedophiles really are. Arrests have included coaches, teachers, school bus drivers, firemen, policemen, clergy, physicians, and school counselors (Frangos, 2005). Cyberstalking is a major problem with teenagers today, leading to many teenage suicides by victims who don't know where to turn to get away from their torture.

With the increasing popularity of social networking, the need for monitoring by law enforcement increases as well. Social networking fosters sites that can jeopardize one's security and privacy. Although these sites were intended to facilitate contact among acquaintances, they have become a breeding ground for bullying and sexual predators. For instance, with the use of photo imaging and picture enhancement a picture can be produced that is entirely false, then placed on a networking site for all to see. Moreover, one's site may be viewed by sexual predators, thus putting the user at risk. Photos and postings that start out as a prank can turn into cruelty that can cause embarrassment, and in some cases even suicide, of innocent victims. As technology advances, crime finds yet another method to create victims and to create the need for new laws to police the Internet.

Fraud

Fraud has always been an enormous problem in business. But the advent of the computer allows criminals to scam victims they do not know, as well as people they do know, because they can contact them anonymously. One prominent example that is spreading fast today is identity theft.

Computers are used by criminals to access victims all over the world via the Internet. Scams are commonplace on the Internet and as quickly as one is exposed another one takes its place. Because no one is exempt from computer fraud, it spreads fast and makes a horrific job for law enforcement. Fraud takes many forms. An email hoax is a form of fraud that can be costly to the victim, for example. Or, as suggested earlier, a hacker can obtain information from a computer and steal one's identity.

There are laws against intentionally defrauding computer users, and against intentionally accessing computers without authorization. These laws are meant to protect Internet users from freely giving information to others without consequences if the other party uses the information to benefit themselves. Nevertheless, Internet users should make sure they know what they are getting into before any information is given to another, and should be skeptical of deals on the Internet and requests for personal information (Kastor & Forness, 2002).

Pornography

Pornography is the explicit depiction of sexual subject matter to bring sexual excitement and pleasure to the viewer. When it depicts children, it is illegal. With use of the Internet, the crime of child pornography is spreading because the perpetrators and pedophiles are now able to communicate with anyone in many different countries. As technology increases, the devices that perpetrators use for storing photographs has changed to now include PDAs, DVDs, X-Boxes, and cell phones, in addition to the computer itself. It is important for the forensic computer examiner to recover all electronic devices in order to encompass any and all hiding places for this matter. The statistics for pornography is daunting and displays why this crime is flurrying at a frightening rate. The statistics are as follow:

- Internet sexual predators are predominately White and educated. Internet predators usually are male, however the fact cannot be ignored that this type of crime crosses many profiles.

- Internet predators spend large amounts of time gaining the confidence of children, sometimes taking months to build a child's trust. As the predator strengthens the relationship with the child, he works to place a wedge between parents and children. Using the insecurities of childhood, predators befriend children by listening to problems in an unbiased, nonjudgmental manner. Parents are the disciplinarians, and when children are angered by parental discipline, the predator is there to talk to, to offer understanding, and to continue strengthening the bond.

- In 1995, the FBI formed a group called Innocent Images to uncover individuals attempting to develop illicit sexual relationships with minors through use of the Internet. As of 2003, Innocent Images has convicted more than 2,000 individuals. But lest that seem impressive, if 6.8 million children are going to be a victim of Internet crime, then 2,000 convictions is only .03% of crime committed (Frangos, 2005).

- In 2002, the FBI unveiled Operation Candyman, which forced Internet provider Yahoo! to disclose email addresses. Until this court-ordered action, email addresses had been protected from disclosure. This gave the FBI the ability to trace the trails of three individuals involved in child pornography using the names of Shangri_la, Candyman, and Girls 12–16. Using this information, the FBI obtained search warrants for the three individuals and found email address of more than 11,000 users who frequented these three groups. This operation resulted in 608 searches and 131 indictments. From the 131 indictments came 125 arrests with 69 convictions upheld. Most distressing is that 16 of the convicted predators admitted to the molestation of 58 children.

FORENSIC TOOLS

Commercial software applications known as "All-in-One" tools are used to aid with extracting information from the computer. Not all of the tools are available outside of law enforcement, thus they cannot fall into the hands of someone on the wrong side of the law.

One example of this software, by New Technology, Inc., is a suite of tools often used in corporate and government investigations and reviews of security risks. These include software that can assess activity on a computer hard drive without the user needing a forensic background, and can help identify whether or not a targeted computer system was used to access inappropriate information. Another application allows an examiner to remove information from a drive and cross-validate that the information has been removed. Another gives the investigator a listing of files that could store information in a compressed or graphic format, whereas yet another makes exact copies of hard drives.

As another example, Encase Forensic is one of the standard tools for capturing, analyzing, and reporting on digital evidence. Powerful filters and scripts enable investigators to build a case on forensically sound evidence. It contains a full suite of analysis, bookmarking, and reporting features.

A particularly versatile tool is DriveSpy, a DOS-based forensic tool, developed by Digital Intelligence, Inc. DriveSpy provides many of the functions necessary to copy and examine contents of a hard drive. All activities are logged, optionally down to each keystroke. The examiner can analyze DOS and non-DOS partitions and retrieve extensive architectural information for hard drives or partitions. The software also allows the user to select files based on name, extension, or attribute; unerase files; search a drive or partition or selected files for text strings; or view sectors or clusters, to name but a very few of its capabilities.

There are many other software tools available to the forensic computer examiner, each with its own specialized uses and features. These include Forensic Replicator by Paraben Forensic Tools, Forensic Toolkit Imager from AccessData, X-ways Forensics, FastBloc by Guidance Software, and Maresware by Mares and Co.

SUMMARY

Computer forensics is a field of science that acquires, collects, preserves, and presents latent electronic evidence in crimes. The first responder at the crime scene may be trained to collect electronic evidence or may need to contact a computer forensic examiner. A thorough chain of custody must be maintained in the collecting, packaging, and transporting of all evidence and electronic equipment. A chain of custody records the route the evidence takes from the crime scene through investigation until the trial so that everyone who takes possession of the evidence is recorded. Improper care of the evidence as well as an unlawful seizure can make the gathered information inadmissible in a court of law.

> Computer forensics specialists and examiners are trained in specific techniques applicable to the field. It is important to remember that experts in other computer-related fields are not generally trained in forensics. For example, experts in computer hardware, software, or data recovery will not have the expertise necessary to successfully retrieve, analyze, and report accurate findings from electronic media without specific forensic training. (Newman, 2007, p. 45)

Computer forensics is the autopsy of a computer, that is, finding hidden or erased information in the heart of the device. This requires the use of special hardware and software in order to extract information from digital devices or media. A forensic examiner can recover information that the user thought was erased or deleted, because in fact the information can be in the hard drive until it is written over. The forensic examination starts at the crime scene and includes all electronic devices at the scene—not just the computer but also cell phones, PDAs, printers, and so forth. The first step is to photograph all equipment, including the screen of the computer if it is on, and then to draw a sketch of the scene. Special attention must be given to all devices that are powered by batteries so that the information is not lost if the device powers down. The notes recorded by the examiner will indicate the mode in which the devices were found before being packed and shipped for extraction of the evidence.

All citizens—whether victim or perpetrator—have rights under the law and the forensic examiner must abide by the law at all times without bias. All citizens have the right of a legal search and seizure of evidence, which, under the Fourth Amendment, requires a search warrant to have a probable cause. If evidence is seized without a search warrant then the evidence collected is not admissible in a criminal trial.

> Evidence resulting from a computer forensics investigation can mean the difference between winning and losing a case. Often the only evidence that exists, aside from circumstantial, is the evidence found as the result of a computer forensics investigation. Witnesses can forget the facts as they occurred or use "selective memory" on the stand. Computer and electronic forensics evidence cannot be refuted, as it is the result of a scientific process and exists in an obviously tangible form. (Newman, 2007, p. 45)

The Internet, via chat rooms, and other direct communication opportunities, allows ways for a predator to reach young children. Moreover, it has opened the world of crime to include locations all over the world, many of which have no laws to protect the innocent or to impede the criminal. Computer crimes such as cyberstalking, fraud, and pornography are at epidemic levels and as law enforcement takes care of one crime another one takes its place. Computer forensics plays a huge role in aiding law enforcement in the fight against cybercrime, and helping to convict criminals by extracting digital evidence that was once unattainable.

REFERENCES

Ashcroft, J. (2001, July). http://www.ncjrs.gov/pdffiles1/nij/187736.pdf. Retrieved December 14, 2009, from www.ncjrs.gov.

Edwards, R. A. (1955). *Criminal liability for unreasonable searches and seizures.* Retrieved November 13, 2009, from http://caselaw.lp.findlaw.com/data/constitution/amendment04/06.html.

Frangos, A. (2005). *No child is safe from internet crime.* Thonotosassa, FL: DDR Publications,.

Galves, C., & Galves, F. (2004, Spring). Ensuring the admissibility of electronic forensic evidence and enhancing its probative value at trial. *Criminal Justice Magazine, 19.* Retrieved November 30, 2009, from http://www.abanet.org/crimjust/cjmag/19-1/electronic.html.

Goldstein, H. (1967). Police policy formulation: A proposal for improving police performance. *65 Michigan Law Review, 1123.* Retrieved December 2, 2009, from http://caselaw.lp.findlaw.com/data/constitution/amendment04/06.html#t158.

Kastor, G., & Forness, M.J. (2002, August 2). *Computer fraud.* Retrieved November 30, 2009, from http://www.ed.uiuc.edu/wp/crime-2002/fraud.htm.

Newman, R.C. (2007). *Computer forensics evidence collection and management.* Boca Raton, FL & New York: Auerbach.

Reynolds, G. (2007). *Ethics in information technology* (2nd ed.). Boston: Thomson Course Technology.

Swanson, C.R., Chamelin, N.C., & Taylor, R.W. (2005). *Criminal investigation* (9th ed.). New York: McGraw Hill.

SWGDE. (2006, July). *Best practices for computer forensics.* Retrieved from http://www.oas.org/juridico/spanish/cyb_best_pract.pdf.

Presentation

14

The Effect of Direct, Nonphysical Evidence on Trial Outcomes

Confessions and Eyewitness Testimony

Franklin J. Boster

Communication scholars have argued that communication is inherently persuasive (Berlo, 1960; Boster, 2006), and from Aristotle (1909) to Kruglanski (Kruglanski & Thompson, 1999) social influence experts have emphasized the importance of evidence in gaining audience conformity to the recommendations made in persuasive messages. Although some contemporary theorists claim that the impact of evidence on persuasive message effectiveness is contingent on factors such as outcome-relevant involvement such that the effect is observed only under conditions of high outcome-relevant involvement (e.g., Chaiken, 1980; Petty, Cacioppo, & Goldman, 1981), and although some emphasize its importance more strongly than others, they all *agree* that evidence is relevant in the matter of convincing audiences.

The legal environment abounds with persuasive messages. It is obvious that attorneys attempt to convince legal decision makers, but more subtle influence attempts occur as well. Interrogators may strive to extract confessions from suspects, albeit unconsciously at times. The police may seek to influence eyewitnesses to select a prime suspect from a lineup, again perhaps unconsciously at times. Confessions and eyewitness identifications may subsequently become evidence at trial, and these types of evidence have a strong persuasive impact (Kassin, 2005; Wells et al., 2000).

McCroskey's (1969, p. 170) familiar definition of evidence as "factual statements originating from a source other than the speaker, objects not created by the speaker, and opinions of persons other than the speaker that are offered in support of the speaker's claims," emphasizes the forms that evidence might assume. Presuming that the speaker is an attorney, this definition is a relatively useful way to think of legal evidence. So, for example, confessions and eyewitness identifications can be classified as factual statements originating from a source other than the attorney, expert witness testimony can be construed as opinions of persons other than the attorney, and physical evidence can be thought of as objects not created by the attorney.

Generally, legal definitions are kindred in spirit with McCroskey's definition, but focus more commonly on the functional aspects of the construct. Evidence is construed broadly as anything presented in court for the purpose of convincing a legal decision maker or a legal decision making group, as when Thayer (1898) asserts that evidence "is a term of forensic procedure [which] imports something put forward in a court of justice" (p. 264).

Logicians view arguments as being composed of propositions, some of which can be classified as premises and at least one of which can be classified as a conclusion. A valid deductive argument is one in which the conclusion follows necessarily from the premises, given some rules of syntax (e.g., definition of implication, negation, etc.); a strong inductive argument is one in which the conclusion follows from the premises with high likelihood. A sound deductive argument is a valid argument in which the premises are true, and a sound inductive argument is a strong argument in which the premises have a high probability of being true.

Conventional wisdom has it that evidence functions to make the premises of an argument more believable, so that it contributes to the soundness of already valid/strong argument forms. McGuire (1960), Hample (1977, 1978, 1979), Wyer and Goldberg (1970), and others have demonstrated consistently that when arguments are logically valid, the addition of information that increases (or decreases) the extent to which audiences find the premises true yields a concomitant increase (or decrease) in the judgment of the truth of the conclusion. This increase (or decrease) in probative value may be more or less than is predicted by the theorems of probability theory, but it does increase (or decrease).

Numerous distinctions among types of evidence have been drawn in the communication literature (see Reinard, 1988). A different set of distinctions is generally drawn among those who study social science and the law, largely because the distinctions have specific applications to legal practice. Thus, matters of inadmissible evidence, expert evidence, and physical evidence might be distinguished because of debates concerning the rules of admitting evidence and the decisions to admit evidence, the standards required to establish someone as an expert, and the complex science involved in finding certain kinds of physical evidence admissible.

Quite correctly, philosophers have challenged the notion that science can achieve the status of a value-free intellectual enterprise. Despite this challenge, the goal of preventing one's values from biasing one's scientific conclusions remains a common pursuit and concern in the scientific community. Nonetheless, scientists are members of a larger community that has strong value concerns, and when pressed or induced by members of that community to perform research that addresses select matters of value, social scientists do let their values intrude without concern for bias in at least one important way; namely, the problem they choose to investigate.

Some matters of law, in general, and matters of legal evidence, in particular, fit this description. It has been known for some time—recently it would be reasonable to claim that it has become painfully evident—that two cornerstones of the evidentiary system, the veracity of eyewitness testimony and the veracity of confessions, were not laid on a foundation as solid as the legal system might prefer. Eyewitnesses may be in error; confessions may be false. These observations have led to substantial and important research programs inspecting the structural integrity of these cornerstones.

The remainder of this chapter examines these observations and research programs. In particular, a review of the scientific literature documents the frequent fallibility of both eyewitness testimony and confession evidence. Moreover, the nuance of these literatures is addressed. The aim of these investigations is a matter of social engineering; specifically, how is evidence to be gathered and admitted into depositions and trials so as to avoid the error of convicting those not guilty of the crime for which they were tried, while not favoring those who were actually guilty of the crime for which they were being tried? That goal is very much, and unashamedly, value-laden, the value being to improve legal decision making.

Surprisingly, although communication was among the disciplines to make important and relatively early contributions to the scientific study of the legal system (e.g., Miller & Fontes, 1979), and although evidence is a seminal construct in a seminal portion of its scholarly agendum—persuasion—communication scholars have not been among the most active in the evidence debate. Instead, applied social psychologists have led the majority of these efforts. Doubtlessly, the issues raised in this chapter will suggest opportunities for communication scholars to contribute to the ongoing process of knowledge generation concerning both eyewitness and confession evidence.

THE DIRECTNESS OF EVIDENCE

Evidence employed in a trial may be based on more or less direct observation. Confessions and eyewitness identifications involve observations that are very much direct, and hence are direct forms of evidence. A police officer may claim to have heard a suspect confess to a crime, and may have that confession on audio- or videotape. A rape victim may claim to be able to identify her assailant, and may do so in a court of law.

Alternatively, imagine walking into a home, hearing a shot, walking into the kitchen, observing a dead male body on the floor, and seeing a woman holding a smoking gun while standing near the body. These observations do *not* provide direct evidence that the woman holding the smoking gun shot the man lying on the floor, nor for that matter do they provide direct evidence that a gunshot was the cause of death. They do create circumstances, however, that would lead many persons to that conclusion in the absence of a strong rebuttal.

Neither direct nor indirect evidence are flawless. As has been noted, and as is emphasized again subsequently, direct evidence such as confessions may be false and direct evidence such as eyewitness identifications may be mistaken. Moreover, the inferences made from indirect, or circumstantial, evidence may be unwarranted as well.

Nevertheless, it is a separable matter as to how much legal decisions makers are influenced by these various kinds of evidence. It is possible that certain types of evidence have a suasory impact much greater than is warranted; the converse being possible as well. Such matters are empirical questions, and can be determined only by examining the results of experiments designed to answer them.

CONFESSIONS

Stipulating that false confessions do occur, a reasonable goal of forensic interviewing would be to maximize the ratio of true confessions to false confessions. This ratio cannot, however, be estimated accurately because certainty of guilt cannot be settled definitively in all, or perhaps even most, cases. Nevertheless, there is a subset of cases that can be used to gauge the magnitude of the phenomenon. The Innocence Project (n.d.; see Scheck, Neufeld, & Dwyer, 2000) estimates that in approximately 25%

of the cases in which persons were convicted, but were later exonerated by DNA evidence, suspects pled guilty, confessed, or provided incriminating information to legal personnel. Given that a substantial number of suspects confess to crimes, if the 25% estimate is accurate, it implies that a substantial number of innocent persons are or have been incarcerated, and in the absence of changes in the manner in which confessions are elicited, that a substantial number of innocents will be incarcerated in the future. It also implies that a substantial number of persons guilty of these crimes have not been identified.

The legal system is sensitive to the matter of self-incrimination under the Fifth Amendment. For example, physical beatings or threats of physical beatings are prohibited as a means of obtaining confessions. Moreover, the legal system addressed the issue in the well-known 1966 Supreme Court decision, *Miranda v. Arizona (1966)*. The wording of the well-known Miranda rights that emerged from this decision was not fixed by the Supreme Court, but rather guidelines were outlined. Minimally, they include:

1. The right to remain silent with the understanding that anything said might be used in court.

2. The right to have an attorney present before talking with the police, as well as having one present during questioning.

3. The right to have an attorney provided in the event that one cannot afford an attorney.

Interestingly, suspects rarely invoke their Miranda rights. Some scholars estimate that 80% of suspects waive them (Leo, 1996a; Leo & White, 1999). Innocent suspects may believe that there is no need to protect against self-incrimination because they have committed no crime; guilty suspects may waive them as a means of appearing innocent. Regardless of motive, this system safeguard may not function as effectively as intended, or as believed commonly.

The fact that Miranda rights are not invoked regularly is not troublesome if interrogators can distinguish true and false confessions, perhaps because the interrogation process is assumed to be effective at promoting the emergence of the truth concerning the suspect's innocence or guilt. The ample deception detection literature, however, suggests that persons' ability to detect deception does not exceed chance probability (e.g., Bond & DePaulo, 2006, 2008). Furthermore, there is no corpus of strong and consistent evidence indicating that interrogators differ substantially from other people in their ability to detect deception (e.g., Aamodt & Custer, 2006; Bond & Uysal, 2007; see also Kassin, 2005, for a brief review) or that training improves matters (Kassin & Fong, 1999; Meissner &

Kassin, 2002). Nevertheless, some evidence has emerged indicating that law enforcement investigators exhibit a lie bias, that is, they are more likely than others to presume that the suspect is lying, and that they are more confident in their judgments than others (Meissner & Kassin, 2002). Notably, the increased confidence fails to translate into improved accuracy (Aamodt & Custer, 2006).

Coupled with the suspect's innocence, typical interrogation procedures compound this limitation. Law enforcement investigators enter the interrogation setting highly confident that the suspect is lying, and innocent suspects are more likely to waive their rights than are others (Kassin & Norwick, 2004; Leo, 1996b). They may follow the procedures known as the Reid Technique, which capitalizes on three powerful social and psychological forces to extract confessions (Kassin, 2005).

1. The technique mandates isolating suspects, thus increasing their stress. Coupled with isolation, interrogations may be of long duration so that suspects become fatigued and their cognitive capacity to resist is depleted.

2. The interrogator is advised to confront the suspect with the claim that the suspect committed the crime. Not infrequently, confrontation may be accompanied by the presentation of false evidence as it is legal for interrogators to lie to suspects (the reverse not being the case).

3. Interrogators are coached to minimize the crime, that is, provide suspects with reasonable and moral explanations for why the crimes were performed, and perhaps why they cannot remember committing them.

The outcome of this technique may be to create a self-fulfilling prophecy. The confrontational nature of the interrogation can result in suspects responding in ways that lead interrogators to become more convinced of their guilt, for example, they present less coherent accounts or exhibit nonverbal displays indicating extreme nervousness. Increased certainty of guilt in turn can reinforce the confrontational nature of the interaction leading to a deviation-amplifying spiral that results in a false confession.

Although some false confessions are given voluntarily and without coercive interrogator pressure, the self-fulfilling prophecy described in the preceding paragraph may lead to what is best termed *coerced confessions*. Using distinctions made commonly between types of social influence (e.g., Festinger, 1953; French & Raven, 1968; Kelman, 1961) suspects may either privately accept or not privately accept their own account. Put differently, some innocents, on the one hand, may confess as a means of escaping what is perceived as a punishing interrogation, perhaps believing that because they are innocent, and because it is a just world, the truth eventually will come out (e.g., at trial). Others, on the other hand, confused by what appears to be overwhelming evidence that they committed the crime (as when interrogators present false evidence), may actually come to believe that they did commit the crime.

Interrogator motives in this process are not well understood. From the standpoint of law enforcement because a false confession leads to a twofold problem of convicting an innocent person and allowing a guilty one to go free, one would expect interrogators to be overly sensitive to false confessions. One might speculate, however, that other forces might function to oppose such sensitivity. For example, interrogations might evolve into perceived competitions in which interrogators come to perceive extracting a confession as a "win" in a battle of wills. The desire for closure, particularly when accompanied by pressure to find the guilty party, or to move on to the next case, might provide a competing motive. The desire to confirm that their initial impression was correct may provide yet another motive.

Regardless of suspect or interrogator motive, the consequences of a false confession are clear. Confessions, even when accompanied at trial by exculpatory evidence, have high probative value, and often lead to convictions (see Kassin, 2005, for a brief summary). Confessions are clearly messages that are not in the self-interest of the suspect, and despite the skepticism of some public figures (e.g., Lippmann, 1922) and scholars (e.g., Cialdini, 1984) about naively accepting the veracity of such statements, people appear likely to believe them. Possibly it is a difficult cognitive task to generate compelling reasons for a statement against self-interest, save that it is true.

Reducing the number of false confessions requires an analysis of their cause(s), and Kassin's (2005) review identifies three primary factors.

1. The duration of the interrogation matters, as more false confessions are produced as interrogation length increases.

2. The interrogator practice of introducing false evidence (e.g., "Then why did we find your fingerprints on the murder weapon?") increases the likelihood of a false confession.

3. The practice of minimizing the offense, stopping just short of implying leniency in exchange for a confession, increases the likelihood of a false confession.

Notably, each of these factors is structural, and could be eliminated by changes in interrogation procedure. Kassin (2005) advocates such modifications, adding one additional suggestion. Specifically, he recommends,

1. Limiting the duration of interrogation.
2. Prohibiting the introduction of false evidence.
3. Prohibiting the use of minimization.
4. Requiring that interrogations be videotaped.

Research has not determined what might be reasonable and unreasonable duration, a distinction likely moderated by numerous factors (e.g., time of day, age of suspect, etc.). Additional research also is required to better understand any factors that might moderate the impact of introducing false evidence and minimization.

Although the videotaping requirement might be viewed as a method of controlling the three preceding factors, Lassiter, Diamond, Schmidt, and Elek (2007) demonstrate that the videotaping process is not straightforward. In their experiment, judges and police officers were exposed to a videotaped confession and asked to judge the extent to which it was given voluntarily. The experiment varied as to who was shown on the videotape—the suspect, the interrogating detective, or both equally. Mean voluntariness ratings are provided in Table 14.1, representing a 9-point scale with lower numbers indicating more voluntariness.

The data in Table 14.1 indicate a substantial focus effect. Specifically, when the camera is trained on the suspect, confessions are perceived to be much more voluntary than when both the suspect and the detective are in the frame or when the detective only is in the frame (the former difference being statistically significant, but not the latter). There was no significant difference between the ratings of the judges and police. These results can be presented in a more stark fashion if the voluntari-

Table 14.1. Mean Voluntariness Ratings

		Focus	
	Suspect	Equal	Detective
Judges	3.17 (83%)	4.33 (67%)	5.56 (43%)
Police	2.50 (100%)	3.75 (67%)	4.63 (43%)

ness measure is dichotomized. Lassiter et al. (2007) do so by presuming that those with ratings in the 1 to 4 range believe that the confession was voluntary, those with ratings in the 6 to 9 range believe that the confession was not given voluntarily, and those with a rating of 5 are excluded. The percentages presented in parentheses in the table indicate the percentage of participants in each condition who judged the confession as voluntary, and these figures demonstrate dramatically the magnitude of the camera-perspective effect. Clearly, a simple prescription advocating videotaping interrogations will be insufficient to eliminate the problem, or likely reduce it substantially. Instead, factors such as camera perspective will have to be incorporated as well.

To conclude this section reviewing the type of direct evidence that is obtained from confessions, it is instructive to consider a piece of anecdotal evidence. At times, case studies may serve to exemplify how false confessions occur and how they become translated into convictions, and to emphasize the magnitude of their consequences. The case presented here is from the Innocence Project (n.d.).

Eddie Joe Lloyd

> Innocence Project client Eddie Joe Lloyd served 17 years in a Michigan prison for a murder and rape he did not commit before DNA testing proved his innocence and led to his release in 2002.
>
> Lloyd was convicted of the brutal 1984 murder of a 16-year-old girl in Detroit. While in a hospital receiving treatment for his mental illness, Lloyd wrote to police with suggestions on how to solve various murders, including the murder for which he was convicted. Police officers visited and interrogated him several times in the hospital. During the course of these interrogations, police officers allowed Lloyd to believe that, by confessing and getting arrested, he would help them "smoke out" the real perpetrator. They fed him details that he could not have known, including the location of the body, the type of jeans the victim was wearing, a description of earrings the victim wore, and other details from the crime scene. Lloyd signed a written confession and gave a tape recorded statement as well.
>
> At trial, the prosecution played the confession to the jury and claimed that Lloyd had killed the victim in order to get away with the rape. The forensic evidence consisted of a semen stain on longjohns used to strangle the victim and a bottle that was forced into the victim, and a piece of paper with a semen stain that was stuck to the bottle. The only testing presented at trial consisted of confirming the presence of semen and other biological matter.
>
> Lloyd was represented during pretrial by a court-appointed attorney who received $150 for pretrial preparation and investigation.

This attorney gave $50 of this to a convicted felon, who conducted no investigation into Lloyd's mental state or confession.

This lawyer withdrew from the case 8 days before trial, but another attorney was appointed and the trial was not postponed. The trial attorney did not meet with the pretrial attorney. He did not question the details of the investigation and did not cross-examine the police officer most directly involved in the coerced confession. He called no defense witnesses and gave a 5-minute closing argument. The jury deliberated for less than 1 hour before convicting Lloyd of first-degree felony murder in May 1985.

Lloyd's attorney lamented in the press that his client would not permit an insanity defense, saying, "With a psychiatric plea, we might have had a chance. If he's not goofy, there's not a dog in Texas." Lloyd insisted that, despite his mental illness, he was innocent.

At the time of sentencing, Judge Leonard Townsend complained that the court's hands were tied because he could only sentence Lloyd to life imprisonment rather than what he believed was the "only justifiable sentence," which was "termination by extreme con[striction]" (i.e., hanging). With regard to Michigan's repeal of the death penalty, Townsend added, "And on account of this case, a lot of people who had reservations about capital punishment have been convinced that they should jump over the fence and sign petitions. The sentence the statute requires is inadequate. I cannot impose the sentence that the facts call for in this matter."

When asked if he had anything to say, Lloyd answered, "Into each life tears must fall. That means on both sides. MJ [the victim] had a right to live, as we all do . . . she said goodbye . . . and disappeared in the darkness never to be seen again alive. One day later she was found in a vacant garage. Cold, alone, and lifeless . . . Eddie Lloyd was focused on as a suspect while he was a mental patient and somewhere along the line he was charged and convicted of the crime, a heinous crime, brutal. What I want to say to the court is that, to the family, MJ, to the city of Detroit, to everybody who was involved with the case, I did not kill MJ. I never killed anybody in my life and I wouldn't."

An attorney appointed to file Lloyd's direct appeal did not visit Lloyd in prison or raise a claim of ineffective assistance of counsel. Lloyd wrote to the court saying his appellate assistance was lacking, and the appellate attorney wrote that Lloyd should not be taken seriously because he was "guilty and should die."

All of Lloyd's appeals failed. Lloyd contacted the Innocence Project in 1995, seeking assistance in having the biological evidence subjected to DNA testing. For years, Project students searched for the evidence. Finally, a number of evidence items were found with assistance from the Wayne County Prosecuting Attorney's Office.

DNA testing conducted by Forensic Science Associates, and confirmed by the Michigan State Crime Lab, found the same unknown male profile from sperm cells on the broken glass bottle, the piece of paper, the stain on the longjohns, and samples collected from the victim's body during the autopsy. Each of these profiles excluded Eddie Joe Lloyd.

He was exonerated and released on August 26, 2002, after serving 17 years in prison for a rape and murder he did not commit. Sadly, he passed away just 2 years later.

A strong criterion of success would be to adopt procedures that reduce or eliminate confessions such as Lloyd's without decreasing the number of true confessions. A weaker, but still useful, criterion would be to reduce or eliminate confessions such as Lloyd's regardless of the effect on the number of true confessions so long as the number of guilty persons convicted is unaffected. The extent to which Kassin's recommendations would meet these standards remains to be determined.

EYEWITNESS IDENTIFICATION

Eyewitness identification is one of the earliest examples of the application of social science to the law. Specifically, in 1908 Munsterberg noted that eyewitness testimony might be critiqued at trial. Subsequently, however, scholars have focused on reducing errors in eyewitness testimony prior to the testimony being presented in court. This advantage is important, given that cross-examination does not appear to be effective in correcting eyewitness-testimony errors.

As with confessions, it is safe to stipulate that eyewitness identification errors occur, but it is difficult to estimate their magnitude. Nevertheless, some idea of the frequency of the problem can be inferred. For instance, Wells et al. (1998) report that in 36 of the first 40 (90%) DNA exoneration cases, mistaken eyewitness identification was an important factor in the erroneous conviction. In Scheck et al.'s (2000) analysis of 62 such cases, 52 (83.9%) involved mistaken eyewitness identification. Outside the realm of DNA exoneration cases, Rattner (1988) claimed that mistaken eyewitness identification accounted for a substantial number of convictions in a large sample of cases examined.

Two common distinctions made in these cases deserve careful consideration so as to frame the issue precisely. First, a distinction can be drawn between memory for events (Loftus, 1979) and memory for a perpetrator (Cutler & Penrod, 1995). The former process is termed *event memory* and the latter *identification memory*. Second, there are factors affecting either event memory or identification memory that can be controlled by the legal system and there are others that cannot be. The former are termed *system variables*, and the latter, *estimator variables* (Wells et al., 2000). For example, Loftus, Loftus, and Messo (1987) discuss the weapons effect. That is, when perpetrators have weapons, less attention is paid to their faces, and eyewitness identification accuracy decreases. The effect of this factor cannot be controlled by the legal system, but it can be estimated from carefully conducted experiments. Thus, it exemplifies an estimator variable. Alternatively, the manner in which a lineup is conducted can be controlled by the legal system, and hence exemplifies a systems variable.

Given these distinctions, the focus of this section is on system factors that impact on identification memory. Initially, however, it is instructive to pursue briefly a false lead—the impact of a particular system variable on memory for events.

The traditional police interviewing technique has been shown to be less than effective at eliciting comprehensive and accurate information about events, and one of the primary reasons is the nature and structure of the traditional interview. Specifically, interviewers frequently ask many questions, the questions are predominately close-ended, interviewers interrupt often, and they tend to be loath to depart from a predetermined question order. The cognitive interview (Fisher & Geiselman, 1992) overcomes these problems by asking few questions, asking predominately open-ended questions, and by using other techniques that enhance memory.

Although the cognitive interview has demonstrated to be effective in increasing the quantity and accuracy of information provided by eyewitnesses to events, it has not been of particular benefit in improving eyewitness identification (Wells et al., 2000). Instead, research programs focusing on the nature of the lineup have proven more fruitful, and it is this matter that is considered here.

Initially, a profitable distinction can be drawn between lineups and showups. The former involves presenting a series of possible perpetrators to the eyewitness and asking that eyewitness to make an identification. The latter involves presenting one suspect to the eyewitness and asking that eyewitness if the suspect is the perpetrator. Wells et al.'s (2000) review suggests that the preponderance of the empirical evidence indicates that showups fail to protect innocent suspects as well as competently conducted lineups do.

Lineups may be conducted in such a manner that the suspects are presented physically or by photo array. In either case, three structural factors have been shown to affect the accuracy of eyewitnesses when presented with a lineup: fillers, method of presentation, and communication. Each of these issues is discussed briefly.

The set of possible perpetrators in a lineup will include the person suspected by police of having committed the crime. The other members in the lineup, however, may vary. In some cases, all or some subset of them may be other suspects. In the extreme case in which all members of the lineup are suspects, the task may become akin to taking a multiple-choice test, and, as with multiple-choice tests, guessing may produce inaccurate answers (Wells & Turtle, 1986).

Alternatively, a lineup might be composed of one suspect and a set of fillers, *filler* referring to a person known to be innocent. Generally, this lineup composition strategy results in fewer innocent suspects being identified, but this conclusion is contingent on the manner in which fillers are selected. If, for example, fillers are selected so that only the suspect fits the description of the perpetrator, then innocent suspects have a relatively high probability of being identified (e.g., Lindsay & Wells, 1980). But if all lineup members are very similar to one another, then identification accuracy drops as well (e.g., Luus & Wells, 1991). Wells et al. (2000) argue that the fillers should fit the description of the perpetrator given by the eyewitness because otherwise innocent persons are likely to be identified; however, fillers should not be similar in other ways because this strategy provides no additional protection for the innocent while infirming the ability of eyewitnesses to make an accurate identification.

Interestingly, occasionally suspects have features so distinct that it is difficult or impossible to find fillers who are sufficiently similar. Photo arrays, however, may be modified to allow the possibilities of either concealing such features or replicating them across fillers. Recent research has indicated that replication produces more correct identifications than concealment, and that it does so without increasing incorrect identifications (Zarkadi, Wade, & Stewart, 2009).

Lineups can be conducted so that suspects and fillers are presented either simultaneously or sequentially. Simultaneous presentation refers to a procedure in which eyewitnesses view suspects and fillers, either physically or via photo array, at the same time. As Wells et al. (2000) point out, this procedure allows eyewitnesses to make comparative judgments (e.g., to select the lineup member who most resembles the perpetrator). Alternatively, sequential presentation involves showing the eyewitness one suspect/filler at a time and requiring the eyewitness to judge if that person was the perpetrator. If the eyewitness reports that the person was not the perpetrator, then a second suspect/filler is presented. The total number of suspects/fillers in the lineup need not be revealed to the eyewitness. Therefore, relative judgment becomes unlikely; the next suspect/filler might more closely resemble the perpetrator than the preceding suspect(s)/filler(s). As Lindsay and Wells (1985) demonstrate, when the perpetrator is in the lineup, no difference in correct identifications is found between the two procedures. But, when the perpetrator is not in the lineup, a substantial difference is found. Specifically, false identifications are substantially higher in the simultaneous presentation condition.

Finally, the instructions communicated to the eyewitness also might affect outcomes. The most pivotal instruction found thus far involves informing the eyewitness that the perpetrator may or may not be in the lineup. In a thorough review, Steblay (1997) reports that when the perpetrator is in the lineup there is little difference in correct identifications as a function of including or not including this instruction. When the perpetrator is not in the lineup, however, Steblay reports that adding the instruction decreases false identifications by more than 40%.

In addition to these structural factors, it is important to emphasize one process factor. Sporer, Penrod, Read, and Cutler's (1995) review of the relationship between eyewitness confidence and eyewitness accuracy produced evidence of decidedly modest correlations between the two variables, albeit a correlation moderated by other variables. This finding is troublesome in light of the judicial system's common conflation of certainty and accuracy. It is even more troubling when coupled with the fact that feedback from law enforcement officials to eyewitnesses (e.g., "you picked our suspect") may inflate confidence independently of accuracy. It may be reasonable to heed the advice of Wells et al. (1998) and Wells et al. (2000) and to require that the law enforcement personnel conducting the lineup be unaware of who is (are) a suspect and who is (are) a filler.

CONCLUSIONS

Extensive bodies of research suggest that two types of direct evidence—confessions and eyewitness identifications—lead more frequently than most realize to identifying innocent persons who did not commit the crime for which they were convicted. Nevertheless, these research programs also identified some of the reasons for these errors. Consequently, they have recommended structural changes that might decrease the incidence of obtaining false confessions and mistaken eyewitness identifications.

Two common features of these two types of evidence deserve emphasis. First, certainty and confidence are important components in both cases. Their correlation with accuracy is not always substantial. Interrogator confidence may interfere with accurate judgment and contribute to producing false confessions. Eyewitness certainty may result in more compelling testimony, even when the identification was incorrect.

Second, creating a video- and audiorecording of the event may contribute to the solution in both cases. As the Lassiter et al. (2007) research program indicates, the manner in which the recording is created matters. Nevertheless, a well-constructed video- and audiorecording has the potential to reveal the manner in which a confession was forced or ways in which law enforcement personnel might have influenced an eyewitness judgment.

Despite what might be fruitful recommendations for structural change, room for improvement remains, providing a set of opportunities for those wishing to contribute to the improvement of legal decision making. Certainly, subsequent research efforts have the potential to expand on the factors that to date have been demonstrated to affect the accuracy of confessions and eyewitness testimony. But, a clear understanding of these literatures also might provide opportunities to testify as an expert witness in specific cases about the potential consequences of procedures used to gather confession evidence, eyewitness testimony, or both. Thus, both research and practice may serve to reduce the incidence of convicting people innocent of a given charge, and, by extension, increase the probability of convicting those who are guilty of those charges.

REFERENCES

Aamodt, M.G., & Custer, H. (2006). Who can best catch a liar? A meta-analysis of individual differences in detecting deception. *Forensic Examiner, 15,* 6–11.

Aristotle. (1909). *The rhetoric of Aristotle: A translation.* Cambridge: University Press.

Berlo, D.K. (1960). *The process of communication.* New York: Holt, Rinehart & Winston.

Bond, C.F., Jr., & DePaulo, B.M. (2006). Accuracy of deception judgments. *Personality and Social Psychology Review, 10,* 214–234.

Bond, C.F., Jr., & DePaulo, B.M. (2008). Individual differences in judging deception: Accuracy and bias. *Psychological Bulletin, 134,* 477–492.

Bond, C.F., Jr., & Uysal, A. (2007). On lie detection "wizards." *Law and Human Behavior, 31,* 109–115.

Boster, F.J. (2006). Communication as social influence. In G.J. Shepherd, J. St. John, & T. Striphas (Eds.), *Communication as . . . Perspectives on theory* (pp. 180–186). Thousand Oaks, CA: Sage.

Chaiken, S. (1980). Heuristic versus systematic information processing and the use of source versus message cues in persuasion. *Journal of Personality and Social Psychology, 39,* 752–766.

Cialdini, R.B. (1984). *Influence: How and why people agree to things.* New York: William Morrow.

Cutler, B.L., & Penrod, S.D. (1995). *Mistaken identification: The eyewitness, psychology, and the law.* New York: Cambridge University Press.

Festinger, L. (1953). An analysis of compliant behavior. In M. Sherif & M.O. Wilson (Eds.), *Group relations at the crossroads* (pp. 232–256). New York: Harper.

Fisher, R.P., & Geiselman, R.E. (1992). *Memory-enhancing techniques for investigative interview: The cognitive interview.* Springfield, IL: Charles C. Thomas.

French, J.R.P., Jr., & Raven, B. (1968). The bases of social power. In D. Cartwright & A. Zander (Eds.), *Group dynamics* (pp. 59–69). New York: Harper & Row.

Hample, D. (1977). Testing a model of value argument and evidence. *Communication Monographs, 44,* 106–120.

Hample, D. (1978). Predicting immediate belief change and adherence to argument claims. *Communication Monographs, 45,* 219–228.

Hample, D. (1979). Predicting belief and belief change using a cognitive theory of argument and evidence. *Communication Monographs, 46,* 142–146.

Innocence Project. (n.d.). [False confessions]. Retrieved March 17, 2010, from http://www.innocenceproject.org/fix/False-Confessions.php.

Innocence Project. (n.d.). [Content]. Retrieved March 17, 2010, from http://www.innocenceproject.org/Content/201.php.

Kassin, S.M. (2005). On the psychology of confessions: Does innocence put innocents at risk? *American Psychologist, 60,* 215–228.

Kassin, S.M., & Fong, C.T. (1999). "I'm innocent!": Effects of training on judgments of truth and deception in the interrogation room. *Law and Human Behavior, 23,* 187–203.

Kassin, S.M., & Norwick, R.J. (2004). Why suspects waive their *Miranda* rights: The power of innocence. *Law and Human Behavior, 28,* 211–221.

Kelman, H.C. (1961). Processes of opinion change. *Public Opinion Quarterly, 25,* 57–78.

Kruglanski, A. W., & Thompson, E. P. (1999). Persuasion by a single route: A view from the unimodel. *Psychological Inquiry, 10,* 83–109.

Lassiter, G.D., Diamond, S.S., Schmidt, H.C., & Elek, J.K. (2007). Evaluating videotaped confessions: Expertise provides no defense against the camera-perspective effect. *Psychological Science, 18,* 224–226.

Leo, R.A. (1996a). Inside the interrogation room. *The Journal of Criminal Law and Criminology, 86,* 266–303.

Leo, R.A. (1996b). *Miranda's* revenge: Police interrogation as a confidence game. *Law and Society Review, 30,* 259–288.

Leo, R.A., & White, W.S. (1999). Adapting to Miranda: Modern interrogators' strategies for dealing with the obstacles posed by Miranda. *Minnesota Law Review, 84,* 397–472.

Lindsay, R.C.L., & Wells, G.L. (1980). What price justice? Exploring the relationship between lineup fairness and identification accuracy. *Law and Human Behavior, 4,* 303–314.

Lindsay, R.C.L., & Wells, G.L. (1985). Improving eyewitness identification from lineups: Simultaneous versus sequential eyewitness presentations. *Journal of Applied Psychology, 70,* 556–564.

Lippmann, W. (1922). *Public opinion.* New York: Harcourt.

Loftus, E.F. (1979). *Eyewitness testimony.* Cambridge, MA: Harvard University Press.

Loftus, E.F., Loftus, G.R., & Messo, J. (1987). Some facts about "weapons focus." *Law and Human Behavior*, *11*, 550–562.

Luus, C.A.E., & Wells, G.L. (1991). Eyewitness identification and the selection of distracters for lineups. *Law and Human Behavior*, *15*, 43–57.

McCroskey, J.C. (1969). A summary of experimental research on the effects of evidence in persuasive communication. *Quarterly Journal of Speech*, *55*, 169–176.

McGuire, W.J. (1960). A syllogistic analysis of cognitive relationships. In C.I. Hovland & M.J. Rosenberg (Eds.), *Attitude organization and change* (pp. 65–111). New Haven, CT: Yale University Press.

Meissner, C.A., & Kassin, S.M. (2002). "He's guilty!": Investigator bias in judgments of truth and deception. *Law and Human Behavior*, *26*, 469–480.

Miller, G.R., & Fontes, N.E. (1979). *Videotape on trial: A view from the jury box*. Beverly Hills: Sage.

Miranda v. Arizona, 384 U.S. 436 (1966).

Munsterberg, H. (1908). *On the witness stand*. New York: Doubleday.

Petty, R.E., Cacioppo, J.T., & Goldman, R. (1981). Personal involvement as a determinant of argument-based persuasion. *Journal of Personality and Social Psychology*, *41*, 847–855.

Rattner, A. (1988). Convicted but innocent: Wrongful conviction and the criminal justice system. *Law and Human Behavior*, *12*, 283–293.

Reinard, J.C. (1988). The empirical study of the persuasive effects of evidence: The status after fifty years of research. *Human Communication Research*, *15*, 3–59.

Scheck, B., Neufeld, P., & Dwyer, J. (2000). *Actual innocence*. New York: Doubleday.

Sporer, S., Penrod, S.D., Read, D., & Cutler, B.L. (1995). Choosing, confidence, and accuracy: A meta-analysis of the confidence-accuracy relationship in eyewitness identification studies. *Psychological Bulletin*, *118*, 315–327.

Steblay, N.M. (1997). Social influence in eyewitness recall: A meta-analytic review of lineup instruction effects. *Law and Human Behavior*, *21*, 283–298.

Thayer, J.B. (1898). *A preliminary treatise on evidence at the common law*. Boston: Little, Brown.

Wells, G.L., Malpass, R.S., Lindsay, R.C.L., Fisher, R.P., Turtle, J.W., & Fulero, S.M. (2000). From the lab to the police station: A successful application of eyewitness research. *American Psychologist*, *55*, 581–598.

Wells, G.L., Small, M., Penrod, S., Malpass, R.S., Fulero, S.M., & Brimacombe, C.A.E. (1998). Eyewitness identification procedures: Recommendations for lineups and photospreads. *Law and Human Behavior*, *22*, 603–647.

Wells, G.L., & Turtle, J.W. (1986). Eyewitness identification: The importance of lineup models. *Psychological Bulletin*, *99*, 320–329.

Wyer, R.S., Jr., & Goldberg, L. (1970). A probabilistic analysis of the relationships among beliefs and attitudes. *Psychological Review*, *77*, 100–120.

Zarkadi, T., Wade, K.A., & Stewart, N. (2009). Creating fair lineups for suspects with distinctive features. *Psychological Science*, *20*, 1448–1453.

15

Testing Expert Opinion via Standard Empirical Methods

Michael T. Motley

"No, I did not have sexual relations with that woman, Ms. Lewinsky." Although this was not the lie that led to Bill Clinton's impeachment, it was certainly the claim most widely discussed by the public. Even after the facts became known regarding what behaviors Clinton and Lewinsky did and did not engage in, debate continued over the veracity of Clinton's denial. He claimed that merely having received oral sex did not qualify as "sexual relations." Some agreed. Some disagreed and argued that he had lied to the public.

Because connotations are subjective, the veracity of Clinton's statement is a question of definition, not one of fact. Whether Clinton's definition is relatively unique or relatively common is, however, an empirical question. It would be fairly easy to test. For example, heterosexual men could complete a questionnaire containing a large number of bogus filler questions to disguise the target questions; which on, say, Item 11 asks participants to specify the number of women with whom they have had sexual relations; then asks on, say, Item 25 how many women they have been with where the intimacy went no further than receiving oral sex; then asks on Item 26 whether the women in Item 25 were included in the

Item 11 count. The higher the number of participants who say no, the more common and therefore legitimate the Clinton connotation, and the more who say yes, the more unique is Clinton's connotation. No version of that empirical test was ever conducted, as far as I know, although it could have been informative. But many legal questions like this one and others in this volume can indeed be tested via empirical tests of the type with which social scientists are intimately familiar.

This chapter discusses the potential to apply basic empirical research methods to issues of courtroom litigation. Essentially, the idea is that usually *expert opinion, although expert, is still opinion; these opinions often represent mere hypotheses; and sometimes these hypotheses are empirically testable.*

Whether or not to actually perform an empirical test is at the discretion of the hiring attorney, of course. On the negative side, from the attorney's point of view, an empirical test will add to the expert's fees. More importantly, it may fail to support the expert's position. (If asked the standard finishing question in a deposition, "Do you have any other information that bears on this case," the expert would have to admit an unsuccessful test of his or her opinion, of course.)[1] On the positive side, good empirical evidence can add considerable credibility and support to the expert's opinion.

Independent of these perhaps obvious pros and cons, the attorney's personal attitude toward science versus opinion may come into play, as well. For example, in the first expert-witness case I ever assisted, I formed an independent opinion consistent with the opinion the soliciting attorney was hoping for. Being empirically oriented, I offered to run a lab experiment to test the opinion. I remember quite well the attorney's response to that suggestion: "No science! You are an expert; your *opinion* is sufficient." I responded that I could not feel as confident under oath with hypothesized opinion as I could with empirically tested opinion and would like to run the test for my own conscience, free of charge. He allowed the test, the results provided overwhelming support of the opinion, he changed his mind and used the data in court, gladly paid for the study, and went on to recommend to colleagues the "expert witness who runs experiments." Since then, about half of the attorneys with whom I have worked have wanted to run empirical tests of the opinion/hypothesis when possible; for various reasons about half have not.

This chapter demonstrates, through examples,[2] the *variety* of communication-related litigation issues to which empirical methods can be applied. The chapter assumes a basic familiarity with quantitative methods, but keeps it simple nevertheless.

EXAMPLE 1: IS "GIRL" A DEROGATORY TERM FOR AN ADULT FEMALE?

Although it never got as far as the courtroom, I remember being fascinated in about 1978 by a female colleague's formal complaint that a male colleague (not me) continually referred to her and other adult females as "girls." She was quite adamant that "girl" carried negative connotations absent in "woman," her preferred label. The male colleague, once confronted, said that he would try to begin using "woman," but that it would be difficult because it would require changing a lifelong habit. He also excused his lexical choice by claiming that the dialect where he grew up considers "woman" to have the more negative connotation, implying a female of considerably advanced age and reduced vitality.

Although the complaint was being settled reasonably amicably, an experiment was commissioned to compare the connotations of "girl" and "woman." Approximately 30 male and 60 female college students completed a set of 7-point semantic differential scales on written descriptions of four adult individuals—two females, Jane and Joan, for the target data, and two males, John and Jack, for bogus filler data to disguise the purpose of the study. Each description was about five sentences long with different details for each person's college major, number of years since graduation, current job, hobbies, and marital/family status. A manipulation check confirmed that the study had been successfully disguised as an effort to compare impressions of various majors, jobs, and hobbies. In fact, however, there were two randomly assigned versions of the questionnaire. On one, the descriptions of Jane and Joan began, "Jane is a woman who . . ." and "Joan is a woman who . . ."; whereas the other began "Jane is a girl who . . ." and "Joan is a girl who . . ." Otherwise the two questionnaires were identical. (Both John and Jack were "a guy" on both versions, with data for these items ignored.) Subjects rated the four persons described on the following semantic differential scales (with poles randomly ordered): fun–dull, young–old, serious–frivolous, attractive–unattractive, competent–incompetent, and interesting–uninteresting. As for the results, virtually none of the girl–woman comparisons showed a significant difference or even came close. This was the case whether male and female subjects were combined or separated, whether Jane and Joan were combined or separated, and whether the individual semantic differential scales were combined or separated. (The only exception was that female subjects ranked Joan as significantly more interesting—$p < .05$—when described as a girl.)

In short, the study failed to support the complainant's claim that "woman" has a more positive connotation, and also failed to support her colleague's claim that "girl" has a more positive connotation. Although it is not clear that either party accepted it as such, the study ended up merely demonstrating the old general semantics adage that meanings are "in people," not "in words" (e.g., Korzybski, 1994).[3]

This girl–woman experiment has been used as the initial example partly because of chronology, partly for simplicity, and partly because of assumed familiarity with the issue by many readers. Although this complaint was handled internally by the university's judicial process, subsequent examples are from actual court cases.

EXAMPLE 2: WAIVER AND RELEASE—
LITERAL CONNOTATION OR "COMMON SENSE"?

Suppose you are the administrator of a high school track meet or band contest or dance recital, and one of the out-of-town student participants shows up and submits the required "Participant's Waiver and Release," but the line marked "Parent's Signature" is blank. You witness the participant's coach, band director, dance teacher, or similar adult representative signing and submitting the form. Do you allow the student to participate because a presumably responsible adult has accepted the conditions of the waiver, or do you interpret "Parent's Signature" literally and refuse to allow the student to participate because the parent is not present to sign?

Essentially, this was the decision facing the director of a wrestling tournament in California in 1992. Knowing that the student wrestler's coach had signed the waiver and release form on the "Parent's Signature" line, he allowed the student to compete. Unfortunately, the student suffered a serious neck injury. His mother sued the wrestling association that had sponsored the tournament, claiming that she specifically had not wanted her son to wrestle in this tournament and had intentionally refused to sign the waiver on the assumption that the absence of her signature on the "Parent's Signature" line would preclude his being allowed to participate (*Johnson v. USA Wrestling, et al.,* 1995).

Unlike most court cases where the meaning of a word or phrase becomes an issue (e.g., see Motley, Chapter 11, this volume), the plaintiff's challenge was not that the waiver was so ambiguous as to allow multiple interpretations, or that the intended meaning was not adequately communicated, but rather the opposite. The challenge was that the phrase, "parent's signature" is so clear and unambiguous that the substitution of the coach's signature should not have been allowed. The response of the defendant (the sponsoring wrestling association and others) was not that the denotative meaning of "parent" is unclear, but rather that the tournament director's decision to allow the coach's signature to suffice was normal, natural, and reasonable.

A simple experiment with 55 student participants was able to shed a bit of light on the question. Essentially, the participants played the role of tournament director. They were given the following instructions: "Imagine that you are the administrator of a wrestling tournament. Before the tournament, you received [the following] relevant information from the national association that will be sponsoring the tournament." The information included two excerpts from literature provided to the actual tournament directors, as well as a copy of the actual "Participant's Waiver and Release." Together, this constituted about 500 words of fine print, among which were two statements that the form "should be" signed by a "parent or guardian" for wrestlers under the age of 18, and a signature line labeled "Signature (parent sign if under 18)." About half the subjects read this original information; the other half read identical information except that "adult representative" was substituted for "parent."

Participants in both groups were asked to imagine a scenario whereby, on the day of the tournament, (a) one or more wrestlers under age 18 show up expecting to wrestle; (b) they do not have a waiver and release form, but the tournament director provides one; and (c) one or more of them are unable to obtain a parent's signature at this time.

Three kinds of questions were asked of the subjects. First, two questions asked whether it would be consistent with the guidelines if they, as tournament director, allowed the wrestlers to compete with no signed form. Subjects in both groups recognized overwhelmingly that the guidelines called for a signed form. Second, two questions asked whether it would be consistent with the guidelines if they allowed the wrestlers to compete with a form signed by their coach. Overwhelmingly, subjects with the "parent" form said no, and subjects with the "representative" form said yes.

Third, subjects were asked to "Suppose that (a) an under-18 wrestler produces a form signed by his coach, and (b) you know that the form is signed by the coach. Describe what you think *you* would *actually* do in this situation," where Likert-scale responses allowed (a) Would *not* let him wrestle; would hardly consider otherwise, (b) Would *not* let him wrestle, but regretfully, (c) Uncertain, (d) *Would* let him wrestle; but reluctantly, and (e) *Would* let him wrestle; would hardly consider otherwise. This time, the differences were not so overwhelming. Almost half the participants in both groups said that they would allow the student to wrestle, with no significant difference between the groups.

In short, this simple experiment suggested that although a form signed by a coach but not a parent precludes a wrestler's participation according to virtually anyone's *literal* interpretation of the guidelines for this tournament, nevertheless, many ordinary people (including many jurors, presumably) might very well elect to ignore the guidelines in favor of a more "humane" or "commonsense" decision. The case was settled out of court.

EXAMPLE 3: LIABILITY—PACKAGING IMPLICATIONS?

One of the more popular home exercise devices over the years has been a chin-up bar for use in door frames. Early versions of the device had a suction cup at both ends of a telescoping bar that could be twisted out for a snug fit in the door frame. Contemporary versions have safety brackets that are screwed into the door frame to support the bar.

During the transition between the two styles, a young man was doing chin-ups using a bar without brackets. In order to hang from the bar for a full extension of his arms, he had his legs bent back at the knees. The bar slipped and both kneecaps were shattered when they hit the floor. He sued, saying the bar was unsafe (*Cala v. Best Products*, 1985). The defense responded that metal brackets had been enclosed and were supposed to have been used. The plaintiff claimed that he never saw any metal brackets—that he opened the rectangular box, dumped out the bar, and no brackets (or instructions) came out with it, presumably having been lodged within the box if indeed they were packaged in the box.

It happens that the outside of the box made no mention of brackets. Rather, it only stated the name of the product (Adjustable Door Bar Gym), showed a picture of a man using the bar for chin-ups (with no brackets!), and gave four bulleted statements, as follows:

- Adjustable from 21" to 32"

- Portable and convenient for use at home or office

- Capable of holding up to 200 pounds when properly secured to door frame

- Instructions enclosed. Please read carefully before using product

Apparently, either brackets had always been part of the product but had never been mentioned on the package; or, probably more likely, the product had been sold originally without brackets, accidents were reported, and brackets were added but without altering the box to mention them. One issue in the case was whether the box could have been easily and inexpensively altered (e.g., perhaps by addition of a simple sticker) in such a way that (a) consumers would have been more likely to use the brackets, and/or (b) would have been more likely to read the instructions, and (c) less importantly, would have been no less likely to purchase the product.

It was the opinion of an expert witness in communication that either of the two primary goals could have been achieved via any of several modest and inexpensive alterations to the box. To test his opinion, a simple experiment was conducted. The study was disguised as a marketing study to determine "how consumers get certain impressions of a product just from examining the package." Subjects were asked to examine one of seven mock-ups of the Door Bar Gym box—the original and one of six hypothesized improvements ($n \sim 20$ per group)—and then answer two primary questions. One was open-ended: "Imagine that you have just purchased this product, have taken it home, and want to use it for the first time. Please describe what you would do in preparing the product for use. Include briefly everything from the time you open the package to the time you first use the product. Please do not refer back to [the mock-up]." Later, the answers to this question would be examined to see if the subject mentioned reading the instructions and/or mentioned installing brackets, with the number of subjects doing so being compared for the seven versions of the box. The other primary question was a 7-point Likert item (*Definitely would* to *Definitely would not*): "What is the likelihood that you would want to purchase the product [represented by the mock-up]?" Answers to this question were compared across the seven versions, as well.

The six suggested improvements involved editing the original package in one of the following ways:

1. Adding a separate bullet item, "safety brackets and mounting screws enclosed,"

2. Editing the original bullet item, "Capable of holding up to 200 pounds when properly secured to door frame," to include "(Safety brackets enclosed.),"

3. Changing "Instructions enclosed" to "Important safety instructions enclosed,"

4. Adding safety brackets to the picture of the man using the bar,

5. A combination of "1" and "3" from this list, and

6. A combination of "1" and "4" from this list.

When participants' responses to the original box were compared with responses to the six variations, results showed that all six revisions significantly ($p < .01$) increased the likelihood that a consumer would read the enclosed directions before using the bar. (Of participants who saw the original box, only about 40% said that they would read the instructions, whereas for all other groups this ranged from 75% to 90%.) As for mentioning brackets, all six alterations were improvements, three at the .01 level of confidence, one at the .05 level, and two not significantly. Essentially, large numbers of subjects described using brackets if their box mentioned brackets verbally, that is, "1," "2," "5," and "6" above, whereas fewer did so in the other modification groups, that is, "3" and "4" above, *with zero doing so in the original-box group.* As for likelihood of purchasing the product, none of the alterations had a negative effect, and one had a statistically significant positive effect (specifically, changing "Instructions enclosed" to "Important safety instructions enclosed").

In short, the results showed that the original box was extremely ineffective in making clear the importance of reading the instructions[4] or using the brackets, and demonstrated that any of several very simple minor alterations could have made a very big difference in this regard (and without decreasing the attractiveness of the product). The attorney for the plaintiff later said that the experiment played a major role in obtaining a very favorable settlement for his client.

EXAMPLE 4: ADVERTISING—MISLEADING OR NOT?

In a class-action suit claiming misleading advertising, plaintiffs alleged that consumers had been misled by the packaging for the "SoundBlaster" sound card with respect to its processing capacities. (A sound card is a device inserted into a computer to allow, among other things, recording and converting sound input—e.g., from a microphone, CD, etc.—into digital audio files that can be edited and then played back through speakers or headphones.) The plaintiffs claimed that the packaging implied an impressive 24-bit recording, editing, and playback sampling size and 96 kHz sampling rate when in fact the sound card was disappointing for its mere 16-bit, 48 kHZ sampling. The defense claimed that some of the sound-card applications did indeed live up to the higher standard; conceded that recording, editing, and playback did not; but claimed that the package said so.

An expert witness in communication filed a detailed report agreeing with the plaintiff that the higher sampling capability was implied for all applications, including recording, editing, and playback. Although the report was solid, it was very lengthy, technical, and contained evidence and arguments that were potentially difficult for jurors to follow, as it outlined more than 20 reasons and ways that the package exaggerated the sound card's true capabilities and/or hid accurate statements of its capabilities. Much easier to understand, presumably, would be data showing simply what the typical consumer's expectations would be upon examining the package.

Accordingly, a study was conducted in which 105 student subjects with above-average grade point averages were asked to play the role of consumer on four products—the SoundBlaster and three "filler" products, the latter included to disguise the study as one on packaging style preferences (rather than false advertising), and to deflect attention off the SoundBlaster package as being of special interest.[5] For each product, subjects were given a brief description of the generic product, followed by a set of criteria they should look for on a hypothetical shopping trip for that product. Subjects then examined the product's box for as long as they wished in order to determine if the product satisfied the assigned criteria. Finally, subjects answered written questions as to whether the assigned criteria were indeed satisfied by the product, and then repeated the process for the next product.

For the SoundBlaster, subjects were introduced to what a sound card is, including a brief explanation of the concept of sampling size being measured in bits and sampling rate in kHz; and were asked to play the role of a shopper concerned especially about recording, editing, and playback capabilities, and seeking the criteria of 24-bit, 96 kHz processing. They then examined all six sides of the Audigy SoundBlaster box for as long as they wanted (typically about 2 to 3.5 minutes). Then they answered a series of questions as to whether the product would satisfy their shopping criteria.

The first question tested whether they remembered the 24-bit, 96 kHz criteria accurately—97.1% did. The next four questions asked whether the product satisfied those criteria—generally, for recording, for editing, and for playback. Multiple-choice responses identified the product to be exactly the same, slightly better, much better, slightly worse, or much worse than the target criteria. Results showed that as for general specifications, 91.4% thought the product was exactly as specified, 3.8% thought it was slightly better, and only 4.8% thought (correctly) that it was worse. For recording in particular, 95.2% thought (incorrectly) the product met or exceeded the criteria. Likewise for editing (91.4%) and playback (96.2%). Results were virtually identical when subjects were limited to computer science and electrical engineering majors.

The implication, of course, is the same as the expert-witness opinion, namely, that consumers were indeed misled by the packaging. That is, they would not be likely to notice the accurate but buried statement about 16-bit, 48 kHz sampling and would instead be influenced by the several overt references to far more desirable 24-bit, 96 kHz processing. But although the opinion and the empirical test matched, the empirical test was judged to be much more easily understood than the expert-witness report's descriptions of more than 20 exaggerations among more than 570 pieces of information on the box. Indeed, the judge in the case said as much.

EXAMPLE 5: LIABILITY—CLEAR WARNING?

Not too long ago, the vehicle used by most parking patrol officers had three wheels and resembled a golf cart with an enclosed cab. One reason for the more contemporary designs—four wheels in most cases—is a 1987 accident in California. While an officer was driving her three-wheeled cart, a car pulled in front of her, and she swerved to avoid collision. Her vehicle was top heavy and the hard turn caused it to tip over. As it was tipping, she fell out and the vehicle landed on top of her and killed her.

Her estate sued (*Fleming v. Cushman*, 1988). Although most of the liability issues concerned the engineering design of the vehicle—whether it could have been easily designed to withstand hard turns, and so forth—the defense introduced a communication issue by noting that there was a warning sticker on the dashboard that instructed operators to not swerve hard, and suggested that had the warning been heeded, the accident would not have happened.

The warning read as follows:

WHILE OPERATING VEHICLE: Remain seated. Use both hands for steering. Keep arms and legs within vehicle body. Avoid sudden starts and stops. Sudden hard turns can cause upset. Regulate speed to meet road and weather conditions. Do not operate near an explosive environment. If a malfunction occurs, cease operation.

The attorney for the plaintiff thought that "Sudden hard turns can cause upset" was not a sufficient warning of the danger of hard turns, and called a communication scholar for an expert-witness opinion. The expert witness agreed and pointed out that there are several ways that the warning seemed inadequate:

1. It begins with childish and obvious warnings that discourage further reading;

2. The warning to keep arms inside is contradicted by the job of marking tires, thus reducing the credibility of the warning;

3. The warning to avoid sudden stops seems unwarranted for this vehicle and thus is potentially confusing;

4. If, as the defense contended, the operator was supposed to heed the posted warning(s), then the instruction to avoid sudden stops, together with the instruction to avoid hard turns leaves no reasonable course of emergency action except to crash (but there was no seat belt) or jump out;

5. Again, "cause upset" is a weak warning for the potential consequences of hard turns (compared with "roll over" or "flip over," for example); and

6. The "sudden hard turns" warning is buried in the middle of relatively unimportant and unnecessary warnings, instead of being highlighted (e.g., by leading the list).

To test this opinion, an experiment was performed to compare the original warning against a simple modification hypothesized to communicate more clearly. Subjects were randomly assigned to one of three groups, one reading the original warning, and the others reading either of two hypothesized improvements.[6] Otherwise, the groups' tasks were identical.

Subjects were led to believe that several products' packaging and labeling information was being tested and that they had been assigned a three-wheeled utility vehicle like the one used by parking patrol officers. Subjects read a general description of the vehicle, saw a picture of it, read instructions for using it, including the warning decal; and were given a hypothetical scenario in which they are driving the vehicle when a car suddenly pulls in front of them.

The subjects answered an open-ended question, "What do you think you should do in this situation," and completed a 7-point Likert scale (*very safe* to *very dangerous*) on each of five potential courses of action, including "slam on the brakes" and "swerve hard to one side."[7] Responses were compared between the original warning decal and each of the two hypothesized improvements.

The results were as predicted. On the open-ended question, subjects swerved with the original warning, but not with either modification, the latter preferring overwhelmingly to hit the brakes. And on the Likert items, subjects with either modification rated swerving to be significantly more dangerous than subjects with the original warning.

In short, the experiment provided empirical support for the expert's opinion that the original warning was inadequate in communicating the danger of swerving hard, and that this could have been corrected with minor modifications.

FINAL OBSERVATIONS

Other examples are available, but by now the point probably has been made that some (not all) of the opinions one might be asked to render as a consultant or expert witness can be tested and supported empirically, and that this kind of support can be persuasive in the courtroom. Although all of the examples given here have been from my experience in cases dealing with questions of meaning in messages, it is easy to imagine conducting empirical tests of other kinds of expert opinion, including several of those discussed in this volume. For example, to support an argument for a change of venue, mock-juror subjects could be used to test the effect of pretrial news stories to which actual jurors are likely to have been exposed.

Moreover, although all of the examples given here have had an expert witness testing his own opinion, there are other possibilities. An expert witness with insufficient research-methods training could hire a colleague to conduct a test of his or her opinion, for example.

Although the example experiments discussed here have supported their hypotheses with least at a .05 level of confidence, as is the norm in the social sciences, it is worth noting that less-stringent confidence levels may sometimes suffice in court if necessary. Although I have not yet needed to try it, one can imagine that a jury might be much more persuaded by empirical evidence where there is, say, only a 10% chance that the observed effects were due to chance (i.e., a .10 level of confidence) than they would be by an unsupported expert opinion alone.

In any case, this chapter has introduced an idea that is both novel and highly effective, according to all attorneys with whom I have spoken, but is at the same time very simple, at least for most academicians in the social and behavioral sciences. The idea, again, is that expert-witness opinions often represent empirical questions and often these can be tested empirically, via standard social science research methods, as part of the preparation for a trial. Assuming that the design is solid and the opinions are supported, empirical evidence can boost the confidence of the expert witness, can weaken the opposition's challenges to the expert, and can be a very important piece of evidence in persuading jurors.

NOTES

1. Granted, one could argue that a failed test does not support the null and thus provides no evidence for either side, but this would probably do one's case more harm than good in court.

2. Readers may imagine and prefer different experimental designs for one or more of these examples, of course, as is often the case in social science research.

3. It stands to reason, of course, that in matters of labeling people, the preferences of the one being labeled usually should prevail.

4. As discussed in Chapter 11 (this volume), the instructions communicated about the brackets very poorly anyway.

5. The products were GE Soft White Light Bulb, Sony ICD-B7 Digital Voice Recorder, Audigy SoundBlaster sound card, and Sensodyne toothpaste, in that order.

6. Specifically, these were bulleted and straight versions (with no significant difference found between the two) of the following: Avoid sudden hard turns, as rollover can occur. This vehicle flips more easily than a four-wheel vehicle when cornering. Avoid sudden starts in confined areas, as collision can occur. Regulate speed to meet road and weather conditions. Remain seated. Use both hands for steering. Keep arms and legs within vehicle body. Do not operate near an explosive environment. If a malfunction occurs, cease operation until condition is corrected.

7. Other courses of action included simultaneously hitting the brakes and swerving, letting off the accelerator and colliding with the car, and jumping from the vehicle before it collided with the car.

REFERENCES

Cala, P. v. Best Products, et al. (1985). State of California, County of Sacramento, Case No. 321866.

Korzybski, A. (1994). Science and sanity: An introduction to non-Aristotelian systems and general semantics (5th ed.). Fort Worth, TX: Institute of General Semantics.

Hayakawa, S.I. (1972). Language in thought and action (3rd ed.). Englewood Cliffs, NJ: Prentice-Hall.

Johnson, J. v. USA Wrestling, et al. (1995). State of California, County of Alameda, Case No. 713933-0.

16

Friendly Advice for the Expert Witness in Communication

Michael T. Motley

One of the objectives of this book is to interest readers in the possibility of applying their expertise in communication to courtroom litigation situations. Assuming that many readers have not yet had that sort of experience, this chapter attempts to give advice to the novice consultant or expert witness. Although this chapter is designed primarily to acquaint the scholar with the ways of attorneys and litigation, it can serve attorneys as a reminder of the ways in which novice consultants or experts may be naïve and in need of a little guidance.

The chapter is organized chronologically. I begin with the initial contact by an attorney regarding a particular question or case, and proceed through reviewing the case, preparing the report, giving a deposition, and providing courtroom testimony, with a few intermediate steps along the way. Thus, in addition to providing advice in the sense of "do's" and "don'ts"—some of which admittedly will seem obvious—the chapter also serves to give the first-time expert witness an idea of what to expect from the process.

A couple of caveats are in order. First, although I lay out an orderly start-to-finish set of steps and procedures, real cases may not always be this formulaic. Some will evolve as described here, whereas others will not. Second, and more important, advice and directions from the attorney who hires you trumps the advice offered here. He or she may have different preferences in general, or the particulars of the case might dictate a deviation from the norm.

While we proceed through various phases of the process, there is one particular piece of advice that applies throughout all phases and thus is mentioned at the outset. It seems to be against the basic nature of many academics to reply to a question with, "I don't know," or "That isn't within my area of expertise," or "I'm sorry but I have no informed opinion on that," and the like, even when that is indeed the case. Rather, many academics, when not knowing the answer to a question, believe that they know, nevertheless; and many who realize they don't know the answer will happily provide a best guess without qualifying it as such. When in the role of expert witness, however, it is highly advisable, if not imperative, to stick to the specific issue(s) that one has been asked to examine, and to stick to the opinions that have been carefully prepared. Speculation often is fine in private conversations with the hiring attorney, but questions from opposing counsel should be answered with well thought-out specificity. That is to say, responses such as "I don't know," "I was not asked to form an opinion on that," "That is not a matter that I have studied," "That is not within my area of expertise," and the like very often are the correct answer for the expert witness in depositions, the court room, and even in casual conversation with the opposing attorney. If an individual is very well prepared on one or more very specific issues, then he or she can maintain credibility and confidence and optimize clarity by limiting the testimony to those specific issues.

THE INITIAL CONTACT

Typically, an expert witness or litigation consulting job begins with an informal phone or email query from the attorney, in which he or she tries to determine in very general terms whether the prospective expert is willing and able to assist with a particular case or question—the desired assistance usually being to provide an "expert opinion" on one or more specific questions or issues. Attorneys use various methods for finding a prospective expert in the first place. For example, the attorney may consult commercial expert-witness directories, phone the local university's public relations office, phone the nearest communication or psychology department chair or department secretary, rely on word-of-mouth advice of other attorneys, check the law firm's files for names of experts who have offered their services, and so forth.

In any case, the initial contact is usually a very general "feeling out" regarding interest and ability. Sometimes the attorney will reveal the position he or she represents, which of course, wittingly or not, biases the response of the prospective expert who is willing to assist. There is a preferred alternative, however, and the prospective expert can initiate it if the attorney has not. Specifically, the two parties can agree that the attorney will specify the issues in question, but without revealing which position he or she represents. Then, if the question seems to be within the expert's area, the attorney sends part or all of the materials that need to be examined in order to formulate an opinion, specifies the question(s) on which an opinion is being solicited, and the prospective expert examines the materials (sometimes relatively casually at this point) and informally reports his or her opinion. If that opinion is the one that the attorney wants to argue then the expert may be hired. (Sentiments vary on whether the expert should bill the attorney for time spent in developing an unwelcome opinion that precludes being hired. My view is that the expert should not charge in this situation except in the rare event that formulation of the preliminary opinion was extremely time-consuming and this possibility was recognized at the outset and overtly negotiated with the attorney.)

Note also that once the initial impression and opinion is formulated, many attorneys prefer that it be reported informally and orally. Indeed, it is not unusual for almost all contact with the attorney to be by phone until a final formal report is delivered. Because email messages between attorney and expert witness are discoverable in some states, it is advisable to put in writing only what the attorney asks to be put in writing (e.g., Wiesen, 2007).

At some point early in this process—either at the initial contact or right after the preliminary opinion has been offered—the prospective expert or consultant will be asked to provide a vita and a rate sheet. Although not always requested, it is worthwhile to begin developing a summary list of consulting experience, as well.

Some attorneys offer a retainer during the initial contact; others don't happen to mention one. Although some consultants would disagree, I avoid the matter and decline retainers even if offered.

It is advisable also that in the initial review of the case, and through-out the entire job, the expert witness should refrain from being overly concerned about the merits of the case or its likely outcome, remembering that he or she is not an attorney, but more importantly remembering that the assignment is restricted to providing an opinion on one or more very specific questions. Although it is certainly the expert's job to determine and represent the truth regarding those questions, it is not his or her job to be an advocate for the attorney's client (that being the attorney's job), nor to ensure justice (that being the court's role).

THE RESEARCH

Depending on the nature of the case, the question, and the nature of one's expertise, the formulation of the expert's opinion might be based on a wide variety of information. In some cases, it might consist only of reexamining the original materials received after the attorney's initial query. In others, it will require examination of additional—sometimes voluminous—documents (medical reports, police reports, advertising brochures, photographs, instruction manuals, etc.). Although rare for communication-related consulting, on-site examination of physical evidence of one sort or another may be required in some cases.

Assuming that one is billing by the hour, it becomes worthwhile at this point to log all time spent on researching the case, as well as all time spent phoning or corresponding with the attorney, taking notes on documents reviewed, outlining, drafting and writing reports, and so forth. There is no standard way to log time or to report it on the eventual invoice, but the suggestion here is that for each segment of work on the case one should log the date that the work occurs, the start time, end time, location of the work (e.g., home, Starbucks, airplane to Denver, etc.), and nature of the work (e.g., examination of Smith deposition, pp. 65–108). It can be helpful to have all of these details in one's records even though the final billing may contain only a fraction of this information (e.g., probably only date, task, cumulative time for each segment, and total time for the job; plus, of course, mailing address and social security number). Although there are anecdotal reports of expert witnesses billing for casual "thinking time"—ideas about the case that arise while showering, washing dishes, driving, and so forth—my opinion is that this is inappropriate. Although some experts prefer to bill at various intervals during the research and subsequent phases, I prefer to bill once at the end of the case unless the attorney prefers otherwise.

It is advisable also to log all documents, photographs, locations, and items examined, with two purposes in mind. First, this list probably will be required in any formal report submitted. Second, in situations where the opinion is based on only a fraction of a large amount of material examined, a log can aid in identifying those specific parts that may be needed later for exhibits, visual aids, references in the report, and the like.

Notes and comments should not be written on originals of the documents examined, as this contaminates them in the event of subsequent examination by jurors, opposing experts, and so forth. Rather, notations should be made on copies of the documents or on detachable notes affixed to the documents or on separate logs. It also is wise to retain all notes, calculations, citations of sources consulted, and so forth in case they are needed to support one's opinions (Kolczynski, 1997). Also, there always is the possibility that these notes may be subpoenaed, in which case care should be taken as to their contents. (I have never been asked to provide notes made while working on a case, but apparently it can happen in some states; Kolczynski, 1997. It can't hurt to ask the attorney about this possibility before beginning.)

Finally, recognize the possibility of supporting or challenging the emerging opinion(s) with information beyond that provided by the attorney. Although expert opinions constitute evidence in the courts, they often are, technically, mere hypotheses or guesses. And the more support one can gather for those hypotheses, the better. In most cases, for example, it is possible to at least see if one or more colleagues are willing to listen informally to your evidence and opinion (presented with appropriate discretion and respect for the privacy of the parties involved) and then offer feedback. This kind of informal feedback may not be admissible in court, but informed feedback often is instructive, of course. In other cases, one may wish to conduct and report formal interviews with other experts, potential users of a product in question, potential readers of a document in question, and the like. And often, as suggested in Chapter 15 (this volume), the expert's opinion represents an hypothesis that can be empirically tested using standard social science research methods.

The testing of hypotheses is not necessarily limited to the expert's opinions, by the way. When one has access to depositions and reports of opposing expert witnesses, those materials may reveal opposing opinions that challenge one's own. In the rare case that those opinions are empirically supported, one should examine the methods carefully and look for methodological flaws and rival explanations. And when one's opposing expert has not tested a testable opinion, one can sometimes try to refute the opinion by testing it oneself.

Obviously, perhaps, empirical testing and other especially creative approaches to the research should not be pursued without approval of the hiring attorney. In some cases, the hiring attorney may have strategic reasons for rejecting the approach, and in others he or she may like the idea but be unable to budget the additional costs. I am reminded here of a lawsuit involving an accident with a certain type of inflatable tube ridden while towed behind a motorboat. A defense expert hired to give an opinion praising the thoroughness of the safety instructions decided to go ride the tube himself for additional insight and evidence that the tube was safe if used as instructed. But his attorney dropped him as an expert, fearing that the opposing attorney could find one or more details of the instructions that the expert would have to admit to having not complied with, thus damaging his claim that the instructions were easy to follow.

Finally, during the course of performing the research, not only is the "good news" to be reported back to the attorney, but the "bad news" as well (Hamilton, 2009). This not only puts the relative strength of the favored opinion into its proper perspective, but also serves to preview points that may be raised by the opposing attorney or an opposing expert.

THE REPORT

Usually but not always, an expert-witness or litigation consulting job will require a written report. Certain length and format requirements will vary from state to state, and other format preferences will vary from attorney to attorney. It is probably wise for the novice to ask the attorney for a model report from an earlier case to use as a guide. Many of the usual standards of good report writing familiar to academics still apply—logical organization; clarification via good analogies and examples; avoidance of jargon, technical terms, and acronyms; early preview, then presentation, then concluding summary of main points; and so forth. There are a few simple additional admonitions, however.

Most important, perhaps, is to stay within one's specific area of expertise, stick to the specific question(s) for which an opinion has been solicited, and make one's points clearly, simply, and succinctly. Although an academic audience may reward breadth and depth in research reports, readers of expert-witness reports want neither breadth nor depth to exceed what is absolutely necessary to present clear support for the opinion(s). This is not to say that technical or detailed information should be avoided, but rather that superfluous information should be avoided. When technical information needs to be presented, it is important to recognize that the report is destined for attorneys and judges who are intelligent but nonacademic readers. Such concepts as the function of statistical tests, interpretation of alpha levels, assumptions of standard theories, and the like, should be explained if they are necessary to clarify the opinion.

Similarly, it is worth noting that legal and academic standards of evidence are not necessarily the same. For example, opinion without empirical support in the social science sense often is acceptable, even preferred, in court. And when empirical support is offered, the .05 threshold common to academia is more strict than what is often acceptable as evidence to support a court case. The attorney should advise on these matters, of course.

As suggested earlier, the report should avoid advocating for the attorney or the client, and avoid opinions and inferences on what constitutes a just outcome of the case. Rather, the opinions and discoveries should be presented objectively. Similarly, although one should present the opinions as confidently as is justified by the evidence, it is important to not overstate that confidence. Modifiers such as "absolutely," "definitely," "certainly," and so forth should be avoided unless completely justified. Along the same lines, if the attorney has asked that the report critique an opposing expert's report or deposition, disagreements should be presented respectfully. Using terms like "insane," "juvenile," "foolish," and so on are likely to make the report writer look more juvenile and foolish than the object of the comments (Hamilton, 2009).

Finally, it is advisable to clearly label all versions of the report as "Draft" until it has been approved and finalized (Wiesen, 2007). It can be awkward if the opposing attorney interrogates about changes made to what is ostensibly a final report. Indeed, some attorneys may prefer that preliminary versions be read over the phone, but that is rare in this writer's experience.

Usually an appendix should list all documents and evidence examined, including superfluous documents that were provided by the attorney but did not play a role in formulating the opinion(s). Those that did indeed inform the opinion(s) should be cited by page and paragraph numbers or other specific identifiers if there is any chance that they may be needed in court or in deposition as examples, exhibits, or visual aids.

DEPOSITION AND TRIAL

Most cases will require a deposition as the penultimate step before trial. The deposition is requested by the opposing attorney and usually consists of a 2- to 3-hour round of questions directed by him or her to the expert witness. Usually only the expert, the hiring attorney, the opposing attorney, and a court stenographer are present. The deposition will probably be audiotaped and may be videotaped. The opposing attorney's goal is to discover the nature of the expert's opinions and support—both strengths and weaknesses. Obviously, there will be an effort to find vulnerabilities in the expert's opinions that might be exploited in court if the case goes to trial. But there almost certainly will be an effort to find vulnerabilities in the expert's credibility, as well, and perhaps vulnerabilities in style and personal disposition also. Because the deposition goes on record and parts may be read during trial, testimony during a deposition is critical, with little or no room for error. Very often, civil and criminal cases are settled before going to trial. But if not, then the expert's deposition can be critical in court. With only a few exceptions, the advice for the expert witness is the same for depositions and for trials.

Typically, the opposing attorney will begin by challenging the expert's credibility and qualifications. At the most, the challenge may be whether the expert witness is even qualified to testify in court. At the least, the challenge will be that the expert is not as qualified as he or she should be. The best defense here is a vita that establishes the expert's qualifications and expertise—usually the same vita submitted at the outset of one's involvement in the case. There are differences of opinion as to the appropriate thoroughness of the vita. My approach has been to provide a complete vita, especially at the outset when the hiring attorney and client are deciding which experts to retain (i.e., all education, employment, publications, papers, courses taught, etc.). Others advocate a scaled-down vita—a simple and precise list including only the training, publications, and so forth, germane to formulating the opinions solicited in a given case (Daly, 1996). A compromise, of course, would be a complete vita with the most relevant entries highlighted. In any case, an impressive vita will be the best insurance against oral grilling aimed at challenging the expert's general credibility.

Once the credibility issue has been exhausted, the interrogation by the opposing attorney in deposition or in court tends to take the form of a contest, with the expert presenting his or her opinions and the attorney trying to challenge, dismiss, and trivialize the opinions and their support. The attorney's style during this testimony is likely to include periods that are pleasantly cordial, sincerely so or disarmingly so, periods that are emotionally neutral and matter-of-fact, and periods that are at least ostensibly hostile and antagonistic. Unlike questioning by, say, graduate students in a class, the *a priori* assumption behind the opposing attorney's questions is that the expert's opinions are flawed and can be shown to be flawed. There are cautions for the expert witness during this sometimes trying experience regarding language, style, and specificity.

Language

Word choice during court testimony can be crucial. The expert witness needs to be accurate, precise, and unambiguous. Although many have made fun of Bill Clinton's famous attempt to seek clarification on the meaning of the word "is" before answering a question during trial, that degree of precision represents a level of language and word-choice vigilance that often is appropriate for legal testimony. The witness should be alert to any ambiguities in the attorneys' (either attorney's) questions and should feel free to insist on clarification before answering. Likewise, the witness should feel free to take advantage of the freedoms offered by an ambiguous question by answering in the form, "If what you mean by that is X, then my answer is . . . , but if what you mean is Y, then my answer is. . . ." In any case, better to disambiguate the question before answering it, lest you be in the awkward position later of explaining that you didn't mean what you said earlier because you were interpreting the question differently then than now.

In addition to monitoring the ambiguity within the attorneys' questions, it is especially crucial, of course to monitor for, and minimize or eliminate, ambiguity within one's own answers. In court, the opposing attorney can embarrass and fluster the expert witness, or weaken the expert's case, by intentionally or unintentionally assigning a different legitimate meaning to an answer than the one the expert intended. And in depositions, the attorney may elect to ignore an ambiguity for the time being, saving it instead as a card to play in court. In short, the expert needs to say precisely what he or she means to say, with minimal ambiguity.

Another language-related admonition is to realize that, depending on the case and one's area of expertise, certain ordinary words may have different meanings in a legal context than in a lay or academic context. "Negligent," "fault," "rights," "responsible," are but a few examples. Often, one discovers these differences in the course of discussing the case with the attorney, but sometimes these misuses do not show up until deposition or court, and some of those times they will be challenged by the opposing attorney. It is perfectly acceptable (at least in my experience) for the expert witness to simply acknowledge humbly that he or she was using the term in the lay sense (or academic sense) and was unaware of the legal sense. But it is of course preferable to avoid these ostensible blunders, and often this can be done by asking the hiring attorney for a "heads up" in advance of the deposition or trial.

A final matter regarding testimony language is that of the appropriate intelligence level for which to address one's responses. During deposition the audience is the opposing attorney, so responses should be appropriate to an intelligent, well-educated adult who is familiar with the case and can easily understand well-explained but unfamiliar concepts. The primary audience in court is the jury, however, and opinions differ as to the appropriate level of language for that group. This writer favors the advice to use language and speech appropriate to a college freshman or sophomore audience, whereas others advise the witness to talk at a level appropriate to "an intelligent 16-year-old" (Kolczynski, 1997).

Style

A second area of caution in the contest between opposing attorney and expert witness is that of style and ethos. The most highly credentialed expert with the most supportable of opinions can still damage the hiring attorney's case by coming off as an unlikable person. It is important that the witness appear competent but humble, be at least reasonably articulate, and maintain his or her composure in the face of blunt challenges. Within the context of the assigned opinions, the witness should be confident but not arrogant. Outside the area of expertise it is usually better to be humbly ignorant than to be defensive. It is fairly obvious that there can be consequences when undesirable character traits are displayed in the courtroom with the jury present. But even in depositions it is important to maintain high ethos, as weaknesses can become targets for the attorney to try to exploit in court.

There usually is at least one episode during a deposition or trial where the opposing attorney will try to throw the expert off balance—"get their goat," so to speak. I have heard comments such as: "Now communication is not really a science, is it?" "So you do this because you get paid, right?" "You've never actually taken any courses in law, have you?" "So your area is sort of like psychology without being a real psychologist?" Sometimes these are such blatant attempts merely to rile that they are easy to laugh off. Other times they seem at first like serious queries that require a serious answer. In either case, the advice to the expert witness is, "don't let 'em get your goat," that is, to put ego aside, eschew defensiveness, maintain composure, and in a straightforward way answer in the abstract without taking the challenge personally.

A variation on this theme is for the opposing attorney to repeatedly ask the same question(s) again and again. This often is an intentional tactic designed to trip up the witness (Babitsky & Mangraviti, 2007). The idea is to fool the witness into thinking that the earlier answer was insufficient and thus manipulate the witness into either giving a different answer this time or getting flustered and losing his or her composure from the frustration of repeating the same answer. The best response to multiple instances of the same question is to simply answer it again. Rather than demonstrating annoyance via comments like "For the umpteenth time . . . ," "How many times do I have to tell you . . . ," "Like I said the last jillion times you asked me that . . . ," just stay composed and respectfully stand your ground.

This applies throughout the deposition or trial. Even when the opposing attorney is not trying to goad the witness, but merely trying to interrogate and find weaknesses, the expert witness should not approach the experience as being in a battle with the attorney, lest unprofessional remarks or nuances leak into the responses. It is much better to leave the ego out of it and simply answer the questions—even the annoying ones—as someone who has studied certain specific issues on a specific case and has an informed opinion with which the interrogator certainly will not acknowledge agreement, but with which objective listeners should agree.

The novice expert witness is likely to become at least slightly unnerved also by interruptions that occur when either attorney objects to the other's questions when the witness is trying to answer. Typically, one attorney objects, the other calls the objection unfounded, and a minor skirmish ensues. Sometimes the witness will not understand the reason for the objection, sometimes he or she will understand the objection and welcome it, sometimes he or she will understand and not welcome it. In any case, advice for the witness is to never begin or finish an answer that has been interrupted by an objection, but rather simply sit back and let the attorneys hash it out, answering when the objection has been resolved and the questioning resumes (Faller, 2008).

Specificity

In addition to language and style, the expert witness is advised to take care with specificity, that is, to stay within the parameters of the case, the solicited opinions, one's expertise, and the question being asked. This includes the earlier advice to be appropriately liberal with acknowledging when one does not know the answer to a question, has not been asked for an opinion on a question, has not studied an issue, or does not have the expertise to provide an informed answer to a question. As an expert witness, you do the *opposing* attorney a favor when you claim to know more than you do, only to be shown wrong (or even merely disagreed with) by an opposing witness with demonstrable expertise of the kind you were feigning. Furthermore, it helps to keep the questions and testimony "on track" when the expert witness refuses to be baited into venturing beyond what he or she has specifically studied for the particular case.

As another example of specificity, witnesses often are admonished to answer only what is asked (Daly, 1996), resisting the temptation to use a question as a jumping-off point to address questions one wishes to be asked. Although this may be an advisable strategy during media interviews, job interviews, and the like, in court one would be at risk for providing the opposing attorney with an exploitable tangent. Similarly, expert witnesses are well advised to answer only questions, that is, to avoid responding to statements made by the attorneys, instead waiting for questions and responding with answers (Faller, 2008). Similarly, specificity is advised even for hypothetical questions. That is, the witness should insist that details be provided for hypothetical questions, so that there can be agreement on the variables and conditions assumed to be operating (Kolczynski, 1997). Finally, it is difficult to be as specific as is needed in deposition or trial if one only relies on memory. The expert witness is advised to have all potentially helpful reports and documents available. It may or may not be impressive for a witness to testify without reference to notes and exhibits, but unless one has been blessed with a simple case or an incredible memory, memory alone can undermine specificity.

CONCLUSION

Clearly, some expert witnesses, especially in their first couple of cases, will find depositions and trials to be intimidating. At least a little anxiety is to be expected; sometimes more. The advice in this regard is similar to what often is advised for public speaking anxiety (e.g., Motley, 1977): Realize that observers detect very little or none of a speaker's anxiety, remember that you are prepared to explain and support certain opinions, and realize that you are not required to venture beyond what you have prepared.

Intimidating or not, expert-witness experiences are virtually always extremely enjoyable and satisfying. They provide an exciting opportunity to apply one's expertise to questions that truly matter to specific individuals, and they allow the academician to experience different standards and ways of thinking. Should you decide to venture into litigation consulting for the first time, the information in this chapter should help you get started and should provide an idea of what to expect. There are many other sources of advice for expert-witness consulting, of course, some of which may be helpful as well. Above all, however, do take advantage of the hiring attorney's willingness to explain what is needed and what can be expected at any phase of the process. As suggested earlier, his or her advice and instructions supersede that found anywhere else.

REFERENCES

Babitsky, S., & Mangraviti, J.J. (2007). *Depositions: The comprehensive guide for expert witnesses.* Falmouth, MA: SEAK Publishing.

Daly, T.T. (1996). Pretrial preparations can improve a physician's value as an expert witness. *Canadian Medical Association Journal, 154*, 573–575.

Faller, R. (2008). *Expert witness preparation for deposition and trial.* Clearwater, FL: Expert Communications.

Hamilton, R. (2009, May 30). Are you sabotaging your practice? *Expert News*, pp. 1–5.

Kolczynski, P.J. (1977). *How to be a successful expert witness.* Los Angeles: Aviation Law.

Motley, M.T. (1997). *Overcoming your fear of public speaking.* New York: Houghton Mifflin.

Wiesen, J.P. (2007). *Tips on writing an expert witness report.* St. Louis, MO: International Personnel Management Association Assessment Council.

About the Editor

Michael T. Motley (PhD, Pennsylvania State University, 1970) is Professor Emeritus with the Department of Communication at the University of California at Davis, where he teaches in the areas of interpersonal communication and quantitative research methods. Before UC Davis, he held full-time teaching positions at Pennsylvania State University, California State University at Fresno, California State University at Los Angeles, and Ohio State University. In addition to *Forensic Communication*, he has authored *Orientations to Language and Communication, Overcoming Your Fear of Public Speaking: A Proven Method, Improving Communication* (with S. Osborn), and *Studies in Applied Interpersonal Communication* (Editor). He has published scores of articles in the major journals of the communication discipline, as well as in *Scientific American, Psychology Today,* and major journals in the fields of psychology, speech pathology, language, and psycholinguistics. He also has written about a dozen book chapters and well over 100 research papers. Most of his earlier work was in the areas of public speaking anxiety and language cognition. Most of his later work has been in interpersonal communication. Five of his publications have received best-article awards from professional associations, and 13 of his convention papers have received special recognition. For the quantity of his collective work, he has been recognized as among the "Top 1%" of Communication Scholars of the 1970s, 1980s, and 1990s. He has held several division-level offices in national and regional professional associations and served for 3 years as the National Communication Association's representative to the American Association for the Advancement of Science. He also is active as a consultant and expert witness in court cases involving the interpretation of warning labels, instructions, and other documents.

About the Authors

Franklin J. Boster (PhD, Michigan State University, 1978) is professor of communication at Michigan State University. He has an adjunct appointment in the College of Law at Michigan State University where he is a fellow of the Trial Practice Institute. He has published numerous articles and chapters, his research interests focusing on social influence processes and group dynamics. He has received awards for his teaching, including the B. Aubrey Fisher Mentorship Award from the International Communication Association in 2005; awards for his research, including the Charles H. Woolbert Award from the National Communication Association in 1989; and he also received the Distinguished Faculty Award from Michigan State University in 2003.

Ann Burnett (PhD, University of Utah, 1986) is professor of communication at North Dakota State University, where she is the director of Women and Gender Studies. Her main area of research is in jury decision making, studying the role of argument in mediated and actual trials, the effect of nonverbal communication on jurors, rhetorical power as evidenced in *US v. Leonard Peltier,* and jury decision making in the O.J. Simpson criminal trial. In her trial consulting business, she specializes in running jury focus groups and mock trials, preparing witnesses for trial, creating and analyzing jury questionnaires, and conducting post-trial interviews.

Mark A. deTurck (PhD, Michigan State University, 1984) is a trial consultant at R&D Strategic Solutions in Atlanta. He is a former professor of communication at Cornell University and has authored numerous research articles and chapters on jury research, social cognition, attitude change, and deception detection. He has consulted on hundreds of civil and criminal cases throughout the country for leading law firms and Fortune 500 companies, as well as the federal and state governments. His consulting includes jury selection and research, strategic analysis, and witness preparation.

Shannon S. Dyer (MS Cornell University, 1992) is associate professor of communication studies at Ottawa University. Her primary areas of interest include interpersonal influence, persuasion in public speaking, visual communication, and legal communication. She is a member of the American Society of Trial Consultants.

Raymond J. Hsieh (PhD, State University of New York at Buffalo, 2004) is associate professor in criminal justice at California University of Pennsylvania. His research and teaching focuses on online security and privacy policy, cognitive analysis and comparison by multidimensional scaling and perceptual mapping, computer forensics, digital image authentication system and forensic video analysis, and cyber security and privacy. In addition to scholarly essays and book chapters, he is author of *Cognitive Mapping & Comparison—an Example of Online Legal Polices*. Besides his several forensic certifications, he was certificated as Computer Forensics Examiner. He has chaired several IEEE international intelligence and security conferences, and has edited several peer reviewed journals

Charles Wesley Kim Jr. (JD, Columbia University, 1982) is counsel to Yelman & Associates, a San Diego law firm handling family law, guardianships, adoptions, harassment, stalking, domestic violence, business law, and regulatory matters. He has worked in the area of threat assessment for more than two decades through the San Diego Stalking Strike Force, Citizens' Review Board on Police Practices, Regional Community Policing Institute, Police Department Use of Force Task Force, Association of Threat Assessment Professionals, InfraGard Members Alliance, Joint Critical Infrastructure Partnership, and New York Police Department Auxiliary Force. He serves on San Diego's Managed Competition Independent Review Board and County Assessment Appeals Board, has been a judge *pro tem* of the California court and adjunct professor of Law at California Western, Thomas Jefferson and University of San Diego Schools of Law, and served on the California Judicial Council's Commission for Impartial Courts. He is an International Law Enforcement Auditors Association Certified Law Enforcement Auditor and member of the International Network to Promote the Rule of Law, National Center for State Courts consultant database, and Center for Complex Operations. He has presented nationally and locally on threat assessment to judges, attorneys, mental health professionals, and law enforcement. In addition to advocating for stalking victims, he himself is currently a stalking victim.

Nadia Lepastourel (PhD, University of Rennes, 2007) is associate professor of social psychology at the University of Le Havre (France) and a member of the CIRTAI laboratory (UMR Idees 6266). Her research broadly focuses on intergroup relations and she is especially interested in communication processes and language, discrimination and prejudice, and media effects.

Daniel Linz received his PhD in psychology from the University of Wisconsin-Madison. He is a professor in the Department of Communication and the past chair of the Law and Society Program at the University of California Santa Barbara. His research involves empirically testing the social psychological assumptions made by the law and legal actors in the area of the First Amendment and freedom of speech. His research spans the topics of media violence, pornography, other sex-oriented entertainment, pretrial publicity, news and race, censorship, and on line privacy. His work on pornography and its effects on human behavior and on the negative secondary effects of adult businesses has been relied on extensively by legislatures and courts nationwide.

Dan Mangis (PhD, University of Texas at Austin, 2005) is a nonpracticing attorney and former adjunct assistant professor of communication at the University of Maryland-College Park. His scholarship focuses on legal communication and judicial rhetoric. He often collaborates with his wife, Susan Szmania. He currently works as a diplomat at the U.S. Embassy in Baghdad, Iraq.

Gerald R. McMenamin (Doctorado, El Colegio de México) is Professor Emeritus of Linguistics at California State University, Fresno, where he has been since 1980. His research specialties include Spanish linguistics, clinical linguistics, language variation, and forensic linguistics. He is the author of several books and articles on language acquisition, linguistic variation, and forensic linguistics. He consults in forensic linguistics, frequently testifying as an expert witness in English- and Spanish-language cases of questioned authorship and questioned meaning.

Patricia E. Paola (MA, Duquesne University, 2010) focuses on early childhood and adolescent internet security and methods that will aid family communication and safety. Her studies within the prestigious Cyril H. Wecht Institute of Forensic Science and Law and Duquesne University provided solid research into the dynamics of computer forensics and computer crimes. Ms. Paola examined much of this research in her master's thesis.

Merrie Jo Pitera (PhD, University of Kansas, 1996) is CEO of Litigation Insights, a national trial consulting, graphics and presentation technology firm. She has expertise in cases concerning employment, commercial, intellectual property, environmental, and products liability litigation. In addition to conducting jury research, she specializes in preparing witnesses for deposition, trial, and congressional testimony. She has published a number of articles on various topics, including juror hindsight bias and Daubert and junk science. She has been honored as one of the "25 Women Who Mean Business" by the *Kansas City Business Journal* and recently presented a seminar to members of the Lloyds of London Syndicates on how to be an effective witness when preparing for deposition testimony.

Brian H. Spitzberg (PhD, University of Southern California, 1981) is Senate Distinguished Professor in the School of Communication at San Diego State University. His areas of research include interpersonal communication competence, conflict, jealousy, infidelity, intimate violence, sexual coercion, and stalking. He is author, co-author, and co-editor of several scholarly books on communication competence and the dark side, including with William Cupach, the co-author of *The Dark Side of Relationship Pursuit: From Attraction to Obsession and Stalking.* He also serves as an active member of the San Diego District Attorney's Stalking Case Assessment Team and is an active member of the Association of Threat Assessment Professionals.

Susan J. Szmania (PhD, University of Texas at Austin, 2004) is an independent scholar and former assistant professor of communication at the University of Wisconsin-Milwaukee. She is a trained and experienced victim–offender mediator for crimes of severe violence. Her research on restorative justice practice and victim impact statements has been published in both legal journals and scholarly communication publications. She often collaborates with her husband, Dan Mangis. She currently works as a political analyst at the U.S. Embassy in Stockholm, Sweden.

Benoît Testé (PhD, University of Rennes, 1999) is associate professor of social psychology at the University of Rennes 2 (France) and a member of the CRPCC laboratory (LAUREPS, EA 1285). His research interests are in the fields of ideology, social norms, communication, and social judgments.

Debra L. Worthington (PhD, University of Kansas, 1994) is associate professor in the Department of Communication and Journalism at Auburn University. She has served on the board of the American Society of Trial Consultants and chaired the Division on Communication and Law of the National Communication Association. Her research reflects her interest in the psychosocial factors that affect persuasion and social influence processes, particularly as related to juror decision making. She has published in a variety of communication and psychology journals, and her research has been recognized with Top Paper awards from divisions of the Southern Communication Association, the National Communication Association, and the Eastern Communication Association. Other research awards include the Burton Award for Legal Achievement and the Ralph G. Nichols Award.

Author Index

Subject Index

CPSIA information can be obtained at www.ICGtesting.com
Printed in the USA
BVOW071049310512

291446BV00002B/5/P

9 781612 890814